# THE ESSENTIAL
# WOK
# COOKBOOK

# THE ESSENTIAL
# WOK
# COOKBOOK

whitecap

This edition published in Canada by Whitecap Books.

Whitecap Books
351 Lynn Avenue
North Vancouver, BC
V7J 2C4
Canada
Phone: 1-888-870-3442

First published by Murdoch Books® a division of Murdoch Magazines Pty Ltd.

Editor: Zoë Harpham  Editorial Director: Diana Hill
Designer: Wing Ping Tong  Design Concept: Marylouise Brammer
Food Editor: Kathleen Gandy  Food Director: Jane Lawson
Stylist (cover and special features): Mary Harris
Photographer (cover and special features): Ian Hofstetter
Food Preparation (cover and special features): Ross Dobson
Home Economists: Alison Adams, Ross Dobson, Shauna Stockwell, Angela Tregonning
Picture Librarian: Genevieve Huard  Indexer: Russell Brooks

Chief Executive: Juliet Rogers
Publisher: Kay Scarlett
Production Manager: Kylie Kirkwood

ISBN 1-55285-439-6

PRINTED IN CHINA by Toppan Printing Co. (HK) Ltd.

First printed 2002

OUR STAR RATING: When we test recipes, we rate them for ease of preparation.
The following cookery ratings are used in this book:
☆ A single star indicates a recipe that is simple and generally quick to make—perfect for beginners.
☆☆ Two stars indicate the need for just a little more care, or perhaps a little more time.
☆☆☆ Three stars indicate special dishes that need more investment in time,
care and patience—but the results are worth it. Even beginners can make these
dishes as long as the recipe is followed carefully.

IMPORTANT: Those who might be at risk from the effects of salmonella food poisoning
(the elderly, pregnant women, young children and those suffering from immune deficiency
diseases) should consult their family doctor with any concerns about eating raw eggs.

# WOK

In this book, we explore the versatile wok. The great all-rounder, this one piece of equipment functions as a pot, a pan, a steamer and a deep-fryer. For the beginner, it can seem daunting—how can one wok do so much? Once you've read this book, you will understand. Each chapter explores a different way of using your wok, whether it be to make soups, curries or stir-fries, or to use it as a deep-fryer or steamer. The chapters begin with introductory pages that fully explain just how a wok can be a steamer one minute and a fryer the next. You might want to start by mastering one technique before moving onto the next, or you might want to jump straight in and try everything at once. Whichever way you use it, you'll soon be exploring delicious recipes from all over Asia, all linked by one thing—the wok.

# CONTENTS

# SPECIAL FEATURES

# WOK COOKING

Invented centuries ago, woks remain the quintessential Asian kitchen tool. And, as the popularity of Asian cuisine has increased worldwide, the wok has moved far beyond its traditional home to kitchens around the world.

## TO PREPARE A WOK

New carbon steel woks have a thin oily lacquer to prevent them from rusting.

Once you have boiled water and bicarbonate of soda in the wok, scrub the coating off with a scourer.

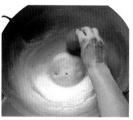

To season the wok, put it over high heat. Dip paper towels in oil and wipe over the inner surface.

A wok will blacken as you season it and get darker as you use it. In time, it will develop a non-stick coating.

Woks work on the principle of bringing food very close to the heat source. Designed in times when fuel supplies were scarce, the basic design has remained unchanged for centuries as both the shape and material of woks allow them to evenly absorb heat, and to retain and transmit it quickly across the entire surface area.

The wok offers a quick, healthy way of cooking. While preparation and organisation are involved, this is usually offset by the short cooking time—stir-fries are an obvious example. In terms of health benefits, the wok's wide surface area means that less oil needs to be used to cook food. Also, the fast cooking of stir-fries and many steamed dishes, in particular, retains the nutrient values of the ingredients to a larger extent than many other cooking methods.

### TYPES OF WOKS

While all woks are based on the same basic design there are some variations, including size. For general domestic cooking, a 30–35 cm (12–14 inch) diameter wok is the most versatile size, as it is easier to cook small batches of food in a large wok than vice versa.

Some woks have two small handles on either side and some have only one long handle. Two-handled woks are more stable, which is valuable when steaming or deep-frying, whereas one-handled woks are better for stir-frying, as the handle can be held in one hand and the charn in the other to create the constant movement required when stir-frying.

Woks are available with either a round or flat bottom. Round-bottom woks are best suited to cooking on a gas stove, as the flames can be regulated to reach up and hit the exterior of the wok. A wok stand can be used to ensure that the wok remains stable on the stove. Flat-bottomed woks are a better option if cooking on an electric stove, as this ensures the surface is in constant contact with the heat source.

### CHOOSING THE RIGHT MATERIAL

Originally, woks were made from cast iron, and some cooks still prefer to use these, as cast iron retains heat well. However, cast iron woks are very heavy so they are not suitable for everyone.

Today, there are many other choices of material. The most common material in Asian countries is lightweight carbon steel. A good heat conductor, it promotes good searing and flavour, especially when used on a gas stove. There is also a wide variety of other materials available. One popular choice is stainless steel; however, it is not a good heat conductor unless sandwiched between another metal that conducts heat well, such as aluminium. And, with the growth of health-consciousness, non-stick woks have become popular. They are easy to clean and require minimal oil. However, many manufacturers of non-stick kitchen tools advise against using their products over high heat, whereas high heat is essential for successful stir-frying. There are newer anodised non-stick woks on the market that may be able to withstand high temperatures, but check with the manufacturer. Another option is the electric wok, which is convenient, but some models don't reach the high temperatures needed for successful wok cooking—choose the highest wattage possible.

### SEASONING YOUR WOK

New carbon steel woks must be cleaned and seasoned before use to eliminate the coating that is placed on these woks to prevent them from rusting before being bought. This procedure is not necessary for stainless steel, cast-iron or non-stick woks.

To initially season a carbon steel wok, place it on the stove top, fill it with cold water and add 2 tablespoons bicarbonate of soda. Bring the water to the boil and boil rapidly for 15 minutes. Drain, then scrub off the coating with a scourer, repeating the process if there is any coating remaining. Rinse and dry the wok thoroughly. Have a small bowl of peanut or vegetable oil and paper towels ready. Place the wok over high heat, then scrunch up a handful of paper towels in the oil and wipe over the entire inner surface of the wok—you may wish to use some long-handled tongs. Repeat until the paper towels come away clean from the wok. Reduce the heat to low and leave for 15 minutes so the wok can absorb the oil. Repeat the oiling process just prior to using your wok for the first time.

The coating builds up over time and provides a non-stick effect. In fact, carbon steel woks turn a brownish-black colour through continued use, which is not only normal, it is also highly desirable. This filmy layer of residue cooks onto the wok with the high heat and imparts the distinctive and characteristic somewhat smoky wok aroma. For many, the flavour of the wok's aroma defines an authentic stir-fry.

## CARE AND MAINTENANCE

Cast-iron, stainless steel or non-stick woks should be treated as you would any other utensils made from these materials. To clean a carbon steel wok, first allow it to cool, then wash it with hot water, using a soft brush or cloth. Ensure that it is dried thoroughly before storing. Many Asian cooks place the clean wok over low heat for 1–2 minutes to make sure it is completely dry. To keep carbon steel woks in top condition, they should be wiped or brushed inside with a thin layer of oil before being stored.

A properly seasoned carbon steel wok should rarely, if ever, be scoured with an abrasive material like steel wool. The outside, however, may occasionally need to be scrubbed. Avoid using detergents unless absolutely necessary, as they damage the seasoning. If you do burn something in the wok, you may need to use detergent and even a piece of fine steel wool to clean your wok. It will then need re-seasoning.

## ACCESSORIES FOR WOK COOKING

The tools in the adjacent picture are useful for cooking with a wok, but you may not need them all.

● The one essential tool if you do a lot of stir-frying is a 'cham' or wok turner—a spade-like scoop that is ideal for the continuous, fast scooping and turning required when stir-frying.

● A wok lid is necessary for making some soups, curries and casseroles, which need to be covered to prevent evaporation during cooking, as well as to cover steamed foods if a lidded bamboo steamer is not being used. Not all woks come with lids, so check before you buy.

● For deep-frying in a wok, a mesh ladle is useful for lifting and draining the fried food. They are available in many different sizes. A pair of long wooden chopsticks is also good for turning deep-fried food over to brown and crisp evenly.

● Bamboo steamers are useful for a whole range of foods, from dumplings to whole fish, and can go straight from the wok to the table. It is best to line them with baking paper or banana leaves to stop pieces of food from falling into the wok.

● Cleavers can prove indispensable when chopping up lots of ingredients for a stir-fry.

● The thin rolling pin is perfect for making dumplings, but you can use a regular one.

# BASIC ASIAN PANTRY

## BAMBOO SHOOTS
The edible young shoots of certain varieties of bamboo, picked soon after they appear above the ground. Fresh bamboo shoots are not easy to find, and must be peeled and partially cooked before use—boil for 5 minutes to remove the bitter taste. Canned and bottled bamboo shoots are commonly available in good supermarkets and in Asian food stores.

## BEAN SAUCES & PASTES
A seasoning made from fermented and salted yellow or black soy beans, bean pastes have been used by the Chinese to flavour food for thousands of years. Bean pastes appear in many guises on the supermarket shelf and the labels vary enormously, making it difficult to distinguish between the varieties. The differences between black bean sauce, brown bean sauce and yellow bean sauce (see below) are small enough to allow substitution without adversely affecting a recipe.

**Black bean sauce** is made from puréed fermented black soy beans, flavoured with soy sauce, sugar, salt and spices. Some varieties also contain chillies, ginger or garlic.

**Brown bean sauce** or paste (right in photograph) is sometimes called ground bean sauce, bean sauce, brown bean paste or yellow bean sauce. Despite sometimes being labelled yellow bean sauce, it is different to the Southeast Asian yellow bean sauce—it is browner, thicker and richer. Made from ground or crushed yellow soy beans that have been salted and fermented, it has a sweet and salty flavour and has a long shelf life. While it is commonly sold as a smooth purée, some brands include whole soy beans, giving the sauce more texture.

**Yellow bean sauce** is sometimes called fermented yellow soy bean paste. Not to be confused with the Chinese variety of the same name (see brown bean sauce, above), the Southeast Asian version is also made from salted and fermented yellow soy beans, but it has a runnier consistency and paler colour. In Malaysia it is called taucheo and in Thailand, tao jiew—they are interchangeable. In our recipes, yellow bean sauce refers to one of these sauces rather than to the Chinese one.

**Chilli bean paste** (toban jiang) (left in photograph) is sometimes called red bean chilli paste, hot bean paste or chilli bean sauce. Originating in China's Sichuan province, chilli bean paste is similar to brown bean sauce, but is hotter due to the addition of chillies. Often it is made with fermented ground broad beans rather than soy beans.

## BESAN
Besan (chickpea flour) is a pale yellow flour made from ground chickpeas and used most commonly in Indian cuisine, giving a unique texture and flavour. Often used as a thickener in sauces and batters.

## BLACK BEANS
Black beans are fermented and heavily salted black soy beans. Rinse them before use. Available canned (above left) or in packets (above right), the canned version is often saltier, so drain and rinse thoroughly before use. Vacuum-packed black beans need to be rehydrated in a little hot water and rinsed before using. Once opened, store in an airtight container in the refrigerator.

## BLACK FUNGUS
Available dried and fresh; in its dried form, it is black and hard—soak in warm water until soft. Any hard woody bits of stem should be removed.

## CANDLENUTS
These are large cream-coloured nuts similar to macadamias in shape. They cannot be eaten raw as the oil is toxic unless cooked. Candlenuts are often roasted, then ground and used to thicken and enrich curries and sauces. You can substitute macadamias if you can't obtain them.

## CARDAMOM
Available as pods (above left), seeds (above right) or ground. The pods, each up to 1.5 cm (⁵/8 inch) long, are tightly packed with brown or black seeds. Use to flavour Indian food. The fragrant seeds have a sweet, spicy flavour. Lightly bruise the pods before using.

## CHILLI FLAKES
Made by crushing dried red chillies, usually with the seeds.

## CHILLI PASTE AND JAM
Chilli paste and jam are both available in Asian food stores. They are generally made with

tomato, onion, chilli, oil, tamarind, garlic, sugar, salt, spices and vinegar. For vegetarian cooking, check the label to ensure the brand you buy does not contain shrimp paste. For our purposes, they are interchangeable.

## CHILLI POWDER
Made by finely grinding dried red chillies, chilli powder can vary in heat from mild to fiery. Chilli flakes can be substituted, but not Mexican chilli powder, which is mixed with cumin and has a quite different flavour.

## CHINESE BARBECUED PORK
(char siu) A pork fillet that has been marinated in a mixture of soy sauce, five-spice powder and sugar, then barbecued over charcoal. Available from Chinese barbecue shops.

## CHINESE RICE WINE
A fermented rice wine with a rich, sweetish taste, similar to dry sherry. It is amber-coloured and is made from glutinous rice in Shaosing in southern China.

## COCONUT CREAM AND MILK
These are both extracted from the flesh of fresh coconuts. The cream (above, back) is pressed out first and is thicker than the milk. The milk (above, front) is extracted after the cream has been pressed out and is thinner and has a lower fat content than the cream. The quality and consistency of the commercial products vary enormously from brand to brand. Coconut cream is often sold in separate cans to the milk, but all coconut milk, if left to sit long enough, will separate and the remaining cream will rise to the top.

## CRISP FRIED SHALLOTS
Commonly used as a garnish in Southeast Asia, crisp fried shallots are thin slices of small red Asian shallots that are cut lengthways and deep-fried until light brown. They are available from Asian food stores in packets or tubs. Store them in the freezer to prevent the oil from going rancid.

## CUMIN
These small, pale brown, aromatic seeds (above left) have a warm, earthy flavour. In its ground form, cumin is an essential component of spice mixes. Black cumin (above right) is smaller and darker than common cumin and is sweeter in taste.

## DASHI GRANULES
Made from dried kelp (kombu) and dried fish (bonito), dashi is available as granules or as powder. Dissolve in hot water to make a Japanese stock, dashi.

## DRIED SHRIMP
Small sun-dried prawns that are available whole or shredded, but they are usually ground before use. Some are more salty than others—if they are too salty, soak and rinse before use.

## FISH SAUCE
A salty sauce with a strong fishy smell. Small fish are packed

into wooden barrels, seasoned with salt and fermented for several months. The brown liquid run-off is fish sauce.

## FIVE-SPICE POWDER
This fragrant, ground spice blend is used extensively in Chinese cooking. It contains cloves, star anise, Sichuan peppercorns, fennel and cinnamon. Use it sparingly, as it can overpower more subtle flavours.

## GARAM MASALA
Garam masala is a mixture of ground spices that usually includes cinnamon, black pepper, coriander, cumin, cardamom, cloves and mace or nutmeg; however, it can sometimes be made with mostly hot spices or with just the more fragrant spices. Commercially made mixtures are available, but garam masala is best freshly made (see page 75 for a recipe). Unlike other spice mixtures, it is often added near the end of the cooking time.

## HOISIN SAUCE
Hoisin sauce is a thick, sweet-spicy Chinese sauce made from soy beans, garlic, sugar and spices. It is used both in cooking and as a dipping sauce. Once opened, store hoisin sauce in the refrigerator.

## KECAP MANIS
A thick, dark, sweet soy sauce used in Indonesian and Malaysian cooking, taking the place of the more common seasoning, fish sauce, that is used throughout most of Southeast Asia. If it is not available, simply stir a little soft brown sugar into regular soy sauce until it dissolves.

## MIRIN
A sweet spirit-based rice liquid used predominantly in Japanese cooking in basting sauces and marinades, but also good in salad dressings and stir-fries.

## MISO PASTE
A paste made from fermented soy beans used as a staple in Japanese soups, sauces and marinades. Generally, the lighter the paste, the milder the flavour. It varies in colour from white, yellow, light brown to brown and red.

## MUSTARD SEEDS
Black, brown, yellow and white mustard seeds are a

common ingredient in many curries. Mustard seeds are fried before grinding to release essential oils and increase their flavour. Black and brown mustard seeds are the smallest and hottest, whereas yellow and white mustard seeds are larger and have a milder flavour.

### NORI SHEETS
A marine algae found on the surface of the sea off Japan, China and Korea. It is formed into paper-like sheets, compressed and then dried. Its colour ranges from green to purple. It is used in Japan to wrap around rice and various fillings to make sushi.

### OYSTER SAUCE
Commonly used in Cantonese cooking, oyster sauce is also used in Thai dishes that have a Chinese influence. It is a rich, thick, salty sauce made from dried oysters, and it is used for both flavour and colour. Readily available in supermarkets,

once opened it should be stored in the refrigerator. Vegetarian oyster sauce has a similar taste and is made using mushrooms as its flavour base instead of oysters.

### PALM SUGAR
A dark, unrefined sugar from the sap of sugar palm trees. The sap is collected from the trees, boiled until it turns into a thick syrup, then poured into moulds where it dries to form dense, heavy cakes. It is widely used in Southeast Asia, not only in sweet dishes but to balance the flavours in savoury dishes. Shave the sugar off the cake with a sharp knife. Buy it in blocks or in jars from Asian shops. Thai palm sugar (shown) is lighter in colour, softer and more refined than the Indonesian or Malay versions.

### PICKLED GINGER
Pickled ginger is a feature of Japanese cuisine. It has a very sharp taste. There is a variety of pickled gingers on the

market, either in brine or sweet vinegars. It is often used as an accompaniment to sushi and sashimi. It acts as a palate cleanser.

### RICE FLOUR
Sold in fine, medium or coarse grades for different uses—as a binder and thickener, to make noodles, sweets and pastries, and as a coating for frying and roasting. Glutinous rice flour is ground from glutinous or sticky rice and is used primarily in sweets.

### SAKE
An alcoholic liquid made by fermenting cooked, ground rice mash. It has a dry, sherry-like taste and is used as a cooking liquid and, in its more refined form, as a drink. Available both clear and amber in colour.

### SAMBAL OELEK
A hot paste made from fresh red chillies, chopped and mixed with sugar, salt and vinegar or tamarind. It is used like a relish or served as a side dish. It can also be used as a substitute for fresh chillies in most recipes. If covered, it will keep in the refrigerator for months. See page 87 for a recipe to make your own.

### SESAME OIL
Asian sesame oil is an aromatic oil made from roasted sesame seeds. It is best bought in small quantities as it loses its aroma quickly. Sometimes it is added to other oils for stir-frying, but generally it is sprinkled on or added to food at the end of cooking as a seasoning. Use sparingly as it has a very strong, rich flavour.

### SESAME PASTE
Made from toasted ground sesame seeds. Available in jars from Asian grocers. Substitute smooth peanut butter.

### SHIITAKE MUSHROOMS (DRIED)
These distinctly flavoured dried mushrooms must be soaked in boiling water for 20 minutes before use. They are also available fresh.

### SHRIMP PASTE/SAUCE
A pungent mixture made from fermented prawns. It can be pink, soft and with a liquidy consistency (available in jars) or dried and sold in dark, hard bricks. Cover in plastic wrap and store in an airtight container in the fridge. Usually fried or roasted before use.

### SICHUAN PEPPERCORNS
A Chinese spice made from the red berries of the prickly ash tree and sold whole or ground. The flavour is woody and it has a strong, hot, numbing aftertaste. Often the powder is dry-fried to bring out the flavours.

### SOY SAUCE
Soy sauce is extracted from fermented and salted soy beans. Chinese cuisine distinguishes between light and dark soy sauce, as they have different flavours and uses. Where a recipe does not specify which soy sauce to use, it generally requires light soy sauce, as this is the type most commonly sold as generic soy sauce. If possible, use a Japanese brand of soy sauce with Japanese recipes, and a Chinese brand for Chinese recipes.

**Dark soy sauce** (back in photograph) is aged longer than its light counterpart and has a heavier consistency. It is mainly used in braises and stews, and is integral to the Chinese 'red' cooking technique as it imparts its deep colour to the food. It is also used as a dipping sauce, as it is less salty than light soy sauce. **Light soy sauce** (front in photograph), while lighter in colour with a thinner consistency, is actually saltier than dark soy sauce, and is made from the first pressing of the soy beans. It is mainly used in cooking, especially in dishes featuring pale food, such as fish or poultry, where a pale colour is desired. **Mushroom soy sauce** is dark soy sauce that has been infused with dried straw mushrooms. **Japanese soy sauce** (shoyu) is a much lighter and sweeter form than the Chinese version.

### STAR ANISE
A star-shaped Chinese fruit made up of eight segments. They are sun-dried until hard and brown, and they have a pronounced aniseed aroma and sweet aniseed flavour. Use them whole to infuse stocks, soups and sauces, then remove before serving. Star anise is one of the five ingredients that make up five-spice powder.

### STRAW MUSHROOMS
These small, unopened, button-shaped mushrooms are very high in protein. While available fresh in southern Asia, in other areas of the world they are most commonly found canned—drain and rinse them well before using. Very popular in Chinese cuisine.

### TAMARI
A naturally fermented, thick, dark Japanese soy sauce with a stronger flavour than regular Japanese soy sauce (shoyu). Although true tamari is wheat-free, there are many lesser brands that have misapplied the name. Check the label on the bottle to be sure. It is often sold in health-food stores.

## TAMARIND

A large, brown, bean-like pod with a fruity, tart flavour. It is available as a dried shelled fruit, a block of compressed pulp (usually containing seeds), a purée or a concentrate. It is often added to cooking in the form of tamarind water. It adds a sweet–sour flavour.

## TOFU

Tofu products are made from yellow soy beans that have been soaked, ground, combined with water and then cooked for a short time, until they solidify into a mass.

**Firm tofu** (above, back) is rather soft, but will hold its shape during cooking. Suitable for stir-frying, pan-frying, marinating and baking.

**Silken firm tofu** (above left) is slightly firmer than silken tofu, and holds its shape a little better. It is suitable for soups.

**Fried tofu puffs** (above right) are cubes of tofu with an aerated texture that have

been deep-fried. Use for stir-fries, curries and soups.

**Silken tofu** has a smooth, silky texture and, when blended, is similar to cream. It doesn't stir-fry well due to its delicate texture, but it is often added to soups in cubes.

**Tempeh** is similar to tofu, but it differs in that it is fermented (like miso and soy sauce). It is made by adding a culture to the cooked soy beans and then compressing the mixture into firm blocks. As tempeh is quite bland, it is often available marinated in a mixture of spices.

## VINEGAR

**Chinese black vinegar** (above, back) is usually made from glutinous rice but sometimes wheat, millet or sorghum. It is darkly coloured with a robust depth of flavour. It is mostly used in northern Chinese cuisine—in sauces, noodles and braised dishes, and is sometimes served as a dipping sauce. It can be purchased from Asian grocers and large supermarket chains. One of the best-quality black rice vinegars comes from Zhejiang in China, and is labelled 'Chinkiang vinegar'.

**Rice vinegar** (above, front) is made from vinegar and a natural rice extract. It is used in dressings and marinades. Rice vinegar is the type most commonly used

vinegar in our recipes and is the most commonly available.

**Japanese rice vinegar** is sweeter and not as pungent as regular vinegar.

**Seasoned rice vinegar** has sugar and salt added, but is only used in sushi rice.

## WAKAME

(curly seaweed) A type of curly-leafed brown algae found in coastal waters, with a soft texture and mild vegetable taste. The whole leaf is blanched and sold fresh in Japan or dried and exported. Wakame is used in soups, salads or as a vegetable after being boiled for about 10 minutes.

## WASABI PASTE

Wasabi paste is a pungent paste made from the knobbly green root of the Japanese wasabi plant. It is often referred to as 'Japanese horseradish' because of its flavour, but it is not related to horseradish. Wasabi paste is served as a condiment with

sushi, sashimi and noodles. It is very hot—use sparingly.

## WATER CHESTNUTS

Small, rounded, crisp vegetables, usually sold canned (if fresh, they need peeling). They give a crunchy texture to many Asian dishes. Any unused water chestnuts will keep fresh for 4 days if immersed in water in the fridge; change the water daily.

## WRAPPERS

**Gow gee wrappers** (above, on top) are round pieces of dough made from wheat flour and water. Usually used in steamed dishes.

**Won ton wrappers** (above, in middle) are thin squares of a wheat flour and egg dough.

**Rice paper wrappers** (above, on base) are paper-thin, brittle rounds made from rice flour, salt and water. Available dry in sealed packets and will keep indefinitely in this state. Soak briefly in warm water before using.

# NOODLES AND RICE

### CELLOPHANE NOODLES
(bean thread vermicelli, mung bean vermicelli or glass noodles) Made from mung bean and tapioca starch. Deep-fry from the packet or soak in boiling water for 3–4 minutes, then rinse and drain.

### DRIED RICE NOODLES
**Dried rice vermicelli** (above left) is used in stir-fries and soups or deep-fried. Deep-fry from the packet until crispy, or soak in boiling water for 6–7 minutes.

**Dried rice stick noodles** (above right) are broader and thicker than rice vermicelli. Soak in warm water for 15–20 minutes. Drain and add to stir-fries. For soups, soak in hot water for 5 minutes.

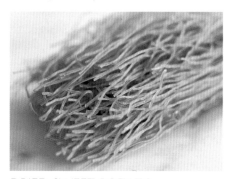

### DRIED SWEET POTATO STARCH NOODLES
(dang myan) Made from sweet potato starch, they have a very chewy texture.

Often labelled Korean vermicelli, check the ingredients for 'sweet potato starch' to make sure you are buying the right thing. Before use, soak in boiling water for 10 minutes, or until softened, or cook in boiling water for 3 minutes, then drain and rinse.

### EGG NOODLES
Made from wheat flour and eggs, these noodles are available fresh and dried in a variety of widths. The thin round variety are used in soups, stir-fries and for deep-frying, while the flatter, wider noodles are used mainly in soups. Fresh egg noodles can be stored in the fridge for 1 week. Cook in boiling water for 1 minute, then drain and rinse. Dried noodles will keep indefinitely. Cook for 3 minutes until tender, then rinse and drain. If using in soups, add straight to the wok.

### FRESH RICE NOODLES
Made from a thin dough of rice flour, these are available uncut as fresh rice sheet noodles or pre-cut into different widths. Use the sheets within a few days as they shouldn't be stored in the fridge—they will go hard and be difficult to separate. Before use, cover them with boiling water and gently separate. Drain and rinse.

### HOKKIEN NOODLES
Thick, fresh egg noodles that have been cooked and lightly oiled before packaging. Most often found vacuum-packed. Use in stir-fries, soups or salads. Cover with boiling water for 1 minute to separate before draining and rinsing.

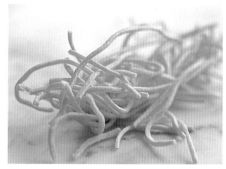

### PANCIT CANTON
(Chinese e-fu noodles) Referred to as 'birthday' or 'long-life' noodles, the longer the noodle, the longer the eater's life, so don't cut them. These round cakes of pre-boiled, deep-fried noodles are delicate and break easily. Boil them for 2–3 minutes, then drain.

### RAMEN NOODLES
These Japanese wheat flour noodles are bound together with egg. Available fresh, dried and in instant form. They need to be boiled before use—2 minutes for fresh

noodles, 4 minutes for dried, and for instant, just add boiling stock.

## SHANGHAI NOODLES
These thick, round noodles are very similar to Hokkien noodles, but have not been cooked or oiled. They are sold loosely packaged and dusted with flour. Cook the noodles in boiling water for 4–5 minutes, then drain and rinse.

## SOBA NOODLES
Made from plain buckwheat or buckwheat and wheat flour. Available fresh and dried. Cook the noodles in a large saucepan of boiling water and stir to separate. Return to the boil, adding 1 cup (250 ml/8 fl oz) cold water, and repeat this step three times, as it comes to the boil. Drain and rinse under cold water until cold.

**Chasoba** are soba noodles with the addition of green tea powder.

## SOMEN NOODLES
These fine, white Japanese noodles are made from wheat flour and are most

commonly eaten cold or sometimes with a little broth. They need to be cooked in boiling water for 2 minutes before use, then rinsed in cold water and drained.

## UDON NOODLES
These white Japanese noodles are made from wheat flour and are sold in a variety of widths, both fresh and dried. Boil for 1–2 minutes before use. They are most often eaten in soups but may also be served in braised dishes.

## WHEAT NOODLES
Available fresh or dried, these egg-free noodles are extremely versatile and need to be cooked in boiling water (2 minutes for fresh, 4 minutes for dried), then rinsed in cold water. Fresh noodles will keep refrigerated for up to 1 week. They come in varying thicknesses.

## BASMATI RICE
This is an aromatic, long, narrow-grained rice. The grains remain firm and separate when cooked. Basmati rice is commonly

used as an accompaniment to Indian dishes, such as curries.

## JASMINE RICE
A long-grain, fragrant, white rice used throughout Southeast Asia. Usually steamed or cooked using the absorption method and served as an accompaniment (see page 163).

## LONG-GRAIN RICE
As the name suggests, this is a long, white, all-purpose grain, processed to remove any husk or bran. It is mainly used in savoury dishes.

## SHORT-GRAIN RICE
Roundish, short grains, processed in the same way as long-grain rice. In Asia, short-grain rice is prized for its sticky properties and is often used to make sticky rice. Medium-grain is essentially the same, but with a slightly longer grain.

# FRESH ASIAN PRODUCE

## BOK CHOY
(Chinese chard, Chinese white cabbage or pak choy) A member of the cabbage family with a slightly mustardy taste. It has fleshy white stems and dark green leaves. Separate the leaves and wash well before use. Use both the leaf and stem in soups and stir-fries, steam and serve with oyster sauce, or fry in oil. A smaller variety is called Shanghai or baby bok choy—use it in the same way.

## CHILLIES
**Bird's eye chillies** are very hot chillies. Between 1 and 3 cm (1/2–1 1/4 inches) long, they are available fresh, dried or pickled in brine.

**Small red chillies** are approximately 5 cm (2 inches) long and are also very hot.

**Medium chillies** are 10–15 cm (4–6 inches) long and are reasonably hot.

**Large chillies** are 15–20 cm (6–8 inches) long, and are thicker, sweeter and milder than medium chillies.

## CHOY SUM
(Chinese flowering cabbage) Choy sum is slimmer than bok choy and has smooth green leaves and pale green stems with clusters of tiny yellow flowers on the tips of the inner shoots. The leaves and flowers cook quickly and have a light, sweet mustard flavour; the stems are crunchy and juicy.

## CORIANDER
(cilantro) Coriander is an aromatic, green, leafy herb used as a flavouring and a garnish. The whole fresh plant is used—roots, stems and leaves. The seeds can also be roasted and are often ground to a powder.

## CURRY LEAVES
Small, pointed leaves with a spicy, toasty curry flavour. Used widely in southern Indian and Malay cooking.

## DAIKON RADISH
A large white radish used in Japan. It is grated or thinly sliced for a garnish, or pickled. It is also cooked in soups and stews and eaten as a side dish.

## GAI LARN
(Chinese broccoli) is a green vegetable with thick, green stalks, slightly leathery leaves and white flowers. It can be steamed whole, or the leaves and stems can be cut up and added to soups and stir-fries. Young, thinner stalks are crisp and mild; thicker stalks need to be peeled and halved.

## GALANGAL
A rhizome with brown skin and cream-coloured flesh. It is related to ginger but has a distinct flavour and perfume. Available fresh, as fresh slices in brine, dried slices in packets, and powdered.

## GARLIC CHIVES
Also known as Chinese chives, these thick, flat, garlic-scented chives are stronger in flavour than the slender variety used in Western cooking. The flowerbud is edible.

GINGER
Look for firm, unwrinkled roots and store in a plastic bag in the fridge. The brown skin is usually peeled before use.

KAFFIR LIMES AND LEAVES
A knobbly, dark-skinned lime with shiny, dark green leaves with a pungent perfume. Available fresh or dried, each leaf is shaped in a figure of eight—in our recipes, half of the eight represents one leaf.

LEMON GRASS
Lemon grass is an aromatic herb, best used fresh. Trim the base, remove the tough

outer layers and finely chop the inner white layers. The whole stem can also be used in dishes such as curry, but remove before serving.

MUSHROOMS
**Oyster mushrooms** (above, back) are a fan or oyster-shell shaped mushroom, pale creamy grey or brown in colour with a slightly peppery flavour that becomes milder when cooked.
**Shiitake mushrooms** (above, middle) grow on rotting wood. Available fresh or dried—the dried variety must be soaked before use and their stems discarded.
**Enoki mushrooms** (above, front) are tiny white Japanese mushrooms on long, thin stalks growing in clumps. Need little cooking.

RED ASIAN SHALLOTS
Small, red onions that grow in bulbs and are sold in segments that look like large cloves of garlic. They have a very concentrated flavour.

SLENDER EGGPLANT
(Japanese eggplant/Japanese aubergine) A cigar-shaped long, thin, purple eggplant.

SNAKE BEANS
(longbean, cowpea or yard-long bean) A long, green, stringless bean. Look for firm, deep green beans. Use as soon as possible after purchase.

THAI BASIL
(holy basil) A member of the basil family with smaller and darker leaves than regular basil and a stronger aniseed and clove flavour and aroma. The stems and younger leaves have a purplish colour.

VIETNAMESE MINT
This has narrow, pointed leaves with distinctive dark markings that vary from leaf to leaf. Its flavour resembles coriander, but is slightly sharper.

WATER SPINACH
A leafy Asian vegetable with long, dark green, pointed leaves and paler, hollow stems. It needs very little cooking.

WOM BOK
(Chinese cabbage, napa cabbage or celery cabbage) Shaped like a cos lettuce with tightly packed leaves. It has a delicate flavour.

# SOUPS

The ultimate in comfort food, soups are as good for the soul as they are for the body. In Asia, people have understood for centuries that soups should be enjoyed throughout the day, not relegated to a starter. You might balk at the idea of eating a noodle soup for breakfast, but that is exactly what the Vietnamese do. In Thailand, market stallholders who sell laksas or custom-made soups do a brisk trade throughout the day to satisfy the hunger pangs of workers in nearby buildings. The Cantonese value soups for their healing properties, making them as needed to assuage various ailments or to remove toxins from the body. Whatever the time of day, there is a perfect soup to enjoy.

# MAKING SOUPS Asian soups can

be hearty meal-in-a-bowl fare, palate-cleansing, or simply soothing comfort food, and

all are easy to make in your trusty wok if you follow a few easy steps.

Many Asian soups are substantial enough to eat as a meal in themselves, such as noodle-laden laksas (pages 24–25) or the classic Vietnamese beef pho (page 40). Other soups are so intensely flavoured that they are best served as one of the dishes in a multi-course meal. Lighter, broth-style soups are also popular, and in many Asian cultures these are eaten during or after a main meal to flavour and soften the rice and act as the meal-time beverage.

There is also a strong regional tradition of soups being eaten for medicinal purposes. Chinese cuisine, for example, has an entire school of cooking based on Taoist concepts of yin and yang, or balance between opposing qualities. Foods are attributed with being either warming, cooling or neutral and are prescribed as tonics.

## QUICK-COOKING SOUPS

Many Asian soups use a spice paste to provide the underlying flavour. The spices are fried in a little oil, then liquid and other ingredients are added to make the soup. Woks are perfect for these types of soups because they provide the perfect vessel for frying spices and are so close to the heat source that the flavours of the seasoning ingredients can develop rapidly. Strongly flavoured ingredients, such as fish sauce, shrimp paste, lime, tamarind juice and chilli, are often added to such soups as they impart their flavour immediately. One example is Hot and sour prawn soup (page 32).

## BROTH-BASED SOUPS

Woks are also good for cooking quickly compiled soups—that is, soups that are based on a good stock with fast-cooking ingredients added to them. Examples of these include noodle soups, such as Ramen noodle soup with barbecued pork and greens (page 47), those with dumplings, like Chinese combination short soup (page 30), and those with thinly sliced ingredients that only need to be just cooked through; for instance, Eight treasure soup (page 31). The nature of the ingredients means that slow simmering isn't needed.

## SLOW-COOKED SOUPS

Not all Asian soups are cooked quickly. There is also a tradition of slow-cooked soups, which includes Sichuan beef noodle soup (page 43) and Chinese hot and sour noodle soup (page 46). These soups are often flavoured with spices such as star anise and cinnamon, as well as dried ingredients including citrus peel, Chinese or shiitake mushrooms and black fungus. When using a wok to cook these soups, pay attention to the liquid levels because liquid can evaporate too quickly and will need to be replenished. It is also important to cover them with a lid (where this is specified in the recipe) otherwise the evaporation created by the wok's large surface area will concentrate the flavours and result in a very strong-tasting, thick soup.

Because woks have such excellent heat conductivity, it is important to cook long-simmered soups on as low a heat as is possible, and to follow instructions for using a lid. Additional water or stock may need to be added if the liquid evaporates too rapidly.

## THE RIGHT WOK

When choosing a wok for soups, it is a good idea to pick a non-stick or stainless steel wok for soups that include a lot of tamarind or lime juice, as the acidity level of these ingredients can strip the seasoning layer off carbon steel woks. These woks are also best for clear or slow-cooked soups, as the long cooking time of such soups can also result in the stripping off of the seasoning layer, which will discolour the soup. When cooking soups, carbon steel woks are best suited to quickly cooked or compiled soups, or those started by frying off a spice paste.

## SOUPS WITH NOODLES

When cooking noodle soups, soak or cook the noodles before adding them to the soup, otherwise the starches released will make the soup cloudy. Another approach is to place the noodles in the serving bowls before ladling the soup over the top.

## THE IMPORTANCE OF STOCK

As with all soups, it is important to start with a good-quality stock. If time doesn't permit you to make your own, there is a range of good commercially available stocks. In addition to the tetra packs found in most supermarkets, many Asian grocery stores sell good stock in cans (it is very salty, so it might need to be diluted if you are using a lot). Some butchers and fish retailers also sell stock made on the premises, so check with your local outlets.

While different stock bases are used in the various regional Asian cuisines, the most useful stock for Asian cooking is a basic chicken stock. Suitable flavours can be added to the stock for soups from different countries to give them their distinctive regional character. The soups in this chapter include the appropriate seasonings as an integral part of the recipe. Some soups specify to use a home-made stock, but others will work just as well with a good-quality bought stock.

## REGIONAL VARIATIONS IN STOCKS

Although chicken stock is the most widely used stock in Chinese cuisine, pork or vegetarian stock can also be used. Fish stock is not at all common in Chinese cuisine. Typical seasonings used in Chinese soups include soy sauce, rice wine, ginger and spring onion.

In Southeast Asian cuisines, chicken stock is also the most widely used soup base; however, fish and prawn stocks are used for seafood soups. Various aromatics are added, such as galangal, kaffir lime leaves, coriander and fish sauce.

In Japan, dashi is the most common stock. Dashi is made from a form of seaweed called kombu and dried bonito fish. For convenience, dashi stock can be made with bought dashi granules. It is easy to regulate the strength of the stock by adjusting the amount of granules used. Various miso pastes can be added to dashi stock to make the ubiquitous miso soup that accompanies many Japanese meals.

*SECRETS TO MAKING SOUPS*

*The flavour of soups is improved by using home-made stock. If possible, make your stock a day ahead and store it in the fridge. This will improve the flavours and allow any fat to easily be skimmed off.*

*Many soups start with a spice paste, which is fried off quickly to release a lot of flavour.*

*Once the soup is simmering, check the liquid levels regularly. Because of the large surface area of a wok, sometimes too much evaporation can occur, and you need to top up the soups with more stock or water.*

---

### BASIC CHICKEN STOCK

1.5 kg (3 lb) chicken bones
3 cloves garlic, sliced
2 × 1 cm (1/2 inch) slices fresh ginger
4 spring onions, white part only, bruised

Wash the chicken bones and place them in a large saucepan or stockpot. Add 3.5 litres (112 fl oz) water and bring to a simmer but do not boil. Simmer for 30 minutes, removing any scum that rises to the surface. Add the garlic, ginger and the spring onion and simmer gently, partially covered, for 3 hours. Strain through a fine sieve and cool. Cover and refrigerate overnight. Remove the fat from the top of the stock once it has solidified. Makes 2 litres (64 fl oz).

# PRAWN LAKSA
(Laksa lemak)

Preparation time: 30 minutes
Total cooking time: 35 minutes
Serves 4–6

☆ ☆

**LAKSA**
There are several versions of the popular noodle soup, laksa. The best known is the laksa lemak, a dish of rice noodles and prawn or chicken in a broth enriched with coconut milk, as featured on this page. Another type is the thin, fragrant sour Penang laksa which is a fish soup based on a broth flavoured with tamarind instead of coconut milk (see recipe page 25). Finally, there is the lesser known Johore laksa which combines puréed fish with noodles and coconut milk. Each version has its faithful adherents.

1¹/₂ tablespoons coriander seeds
1 tablespoon cumin seeds
1 teaspoon ground turmeric
1 onion, roughly chopped
2 teaspoons roughly chopped fresh ginger
3 cloves garlic
3 stems lemon grass, white part only, sliced
6 candlenuts or macadamias, roughly chopped
4–6 small fresh red chillies, roughly chopped
2–3 teaspoons shrimp paste
1 litre (32 fl oz) good-quality chicken stock
¹/₄ cup (60 ml/2 fl oz) vegetable oil
3 cups (750 ml/24 fl oz) coconut milk
4 fresh kaffir lime leaves
2¹/₂ tablespoons lime juice
2 tablespoons fish sauce
2 tablespoons grated palm sugar
750 g (1¹/₂ lb) raw medium prawns, peeled and deveined, with tails intact
250 g (8 oz) dried rice vermicelli

1 cup (90 g/3 oz) bean sprouts, tailed
4 fried tofu puffs, cut into julienne strips
3 tablespoons roughly chopped fresh Vietnamese mint
²/₃ cup (20 g/³/₄ oz) fresh coriander leaves
lime wedges, to serve

1 Dry-fry the coriander seeds in a small frying pan over medium heat for 1–2 minutes, or until fragrant, tossing constantly. Grind finely. Repeat the process with the cumin seeds.
2 Place the ground coriander and cumin, turmeric, onion, ginger, garlic, lemon grass, candlenuts, chilli and shrimp paste in a food processor or blender. Add about ¹/₂ cup (125 ml/4 fl oz) of the stock and blend to a fine paste.
3 Heat a wok over low heat, add the oil and swirl. Cook the paste for 3–5 minutes, stirring constantly. Pour in the remaining stock and bring to the boil, then reduce the heat and simmer for 15 minutes, or until reduced slightly.
4 Add the coconut milk, lime leaves, lime juice, fish sauce and sugar and simmer for 5 minutes. Add the prawns and simmer for 2 minutes, or until pink and cooked. Do not boil or cover.
5 Meanwhile, soak the vermicelli in boiling water for 6–7 minutes, or until soft. Drain and divide among serving bowls along with most of the sprouts. Ladle on the hot soup, then top with the tofu, mint, coriander and the remaining sprouts. Serve with lime wedges.

*RIGHT: Prawn laksa*

# PENANG FISH LAKSA
(Assam laksa)

Preparation time: 20 minutes +
  20 minutes soaking
Total cooking time: 40 minutes
Serves 4

☆ ☆

1 whole snapper (750 g/1 ½ lb), scaled
  and cleaned

3 cups (750 ml/24 fl oz) good-quality
  chicken stock

6 fresh Vietnamese mint stalks

4 dried red chillies

2 x 3 cm (³/₄ x 1 ¹/₄ inch) piece fresh
  galangal, finely chopped

4 red Asian shallots, finely chopped

2 stems lemon grass, white part only,
  finely chopped

1 teaspoon ground turmeric

1 teaspoon shrimp paste

4 tablespoons tamarind purée

1 tablespoon sugar

500 g (1 lb) fresh round rice noodles

1 small Lebanese cucumber, seeded and
  cut into strips

¹/₂ cup (10 g/¹/₄ oz) fresh Vietnamese mint

1 large fresh green chilli, sliced

1 Trim the fins and tail off the fish with kitchen scissors. Make several deep cuts through the thickest part of the fish on both sides.
2 Pour the stock and 3 cups (750 ml/24 fl oz) water into a non-stick wok. Add the mint stalks and bring to the boil over high heat. Place the fish in the wok and simmer for 10 minutes, or until cooked. The fish should remain submerged during cooking; add more water if necessary. Remove the fish and allow to cool.
3 Soak the chillies in 1 cup (250 ml/8 fl oz) boiling water for 20 minutes. Drain and chop. To make the laksa paste, place the chilli, galangal, shallots, lemon grass, turmeric and shrimp paste in a food processor or blender and blend to a smooth paste, adding a little water if needed.
4 Flake the flesh off the fish and remove all the bones, reserving both. Add the bones and tamarind to the stock in the wok and bring to the boil. Simmer for 10 minutes, then strain and return the liquid to a clean wok—make sure no bones slip through. Stir the laksa paste into the liquid and simmer over medium heat for 10 minutes. Stir in the sugar, add the fish flesh and simmer for 1–2 minutes, or until the fish is heated through.
5 Place the noodles in a heatproof bowl, cover with boiling water, then gently separate. Drain immediately and refresh under cold water. Divide the noodles among four bowls. Ladle on the fish pieces and broth, then sprinkle with cucumber, mint and chilli and serve.

SHRIMP PASTE
There are two types of shrimp paste. The most common type in Malaysia and Indonesia is a compressed block made from partially fermented shrimps that have been dried and ground. The Chinese version is softer and more sauce-like and is sold in jars rather than blocks. In both cases, the paste should be used very sparingly as it can easily overpower other elements in the dish.

*ABOVE: Penang fish laksa*

25

LEMON GRASS

If you are using lemon grass to impart flavour to a soup or broth, there is no need to remove the green part—simply bruise the stem and add it to the broth to infuse its delicious lemony flavour, then remove the stem before serving. However, if you are adding chopped lemon grass to a curry paste or other dish, it is necessary to remove the fibrous green part of the stem and finely chop only the tender, white parts. The greener parts of the lemon grass do not break down at all during cooking and remain fibrous and tough, giving an unpleasant sensation in the mouth. A simple tip is to peel the lemon grass until you reach the first layer of purple—all of the lemon grass below this layer is tender enough to be used.

*ABOVE: Spicy Vietnamese beef and pork noodle soup*

## SPICY VIETNAMESE BEEF AND PORK NOODLE SOUP
(Bun bo Hué)

Preparation time: 20 minutes +
    30 minutes freezing
Total cooking time: 40 minutes
Serves 4

☆ ☆

300 g (10 oz) beef fillet steak
1/4 cup (60 ml/2 fl oz) vegetable oil
300 g (10 oz) pork leg fillet, cut into
    3 cm (1 1/4 inch) cubes
1 large onion, cut into thin wedges
2 litres (64 fl oz) good-quality beef stock
2 stems lemon grass
2 tablespoons fish sauce
1 teaspoon ground dried shrimp
1 teaspoon sugar
2 large fresh red chillies, sliced
400 g (13 oz) fresh round rice noodles
2 cups (180 g/6 oz) bean sprouts, tailed
1/2 cup (10 g/1/4 oz) fresh mint
1/2 cup (15 g/1/2 oz) fresh coriander leaves
thinly sliced fresh chilli, to serve (optional)
lemon wedges, to serve

1 Place the beef in the freezer for 20–30 minutes, or until partially frozen, then cut into paper-thin slices across the grain. Set aside.

2 Heat a wok until hot, add 1 tablespoon of the oil and swirl to coat the side of the wok. Stir-fry the pork in batches for 2–3 minutes, or until browned. Remove from the wok. Add another tablespoon of oil and stir-fry the onion for 2–3 minutes, or until softened. Pour in the stock and 2 cups (500 ml/16 fl oz) water. Bruise one of the lemon grass stems and add it to the wok. Return the pork to the wok and bring the liquid to the boil, then reduce the heat and simmer for 15 minutes, or until the pork is tender, periodically skimming off any scum that rises to the surface. Meanwhile, thinly slice the white part of the remaining lemon grass stem.

3 Remove the whole lemon grass stem from the broth and stir in the fish sauce, dried shrimp and sugar and keep at a simmer.

4 Heat the remaining oil in a small frying pan over medium heat and cook the sliced lemon grass and chilli for 2–3 minutes, or until fragrant. Stir into the broth. Just before serving, bring the broth to the boil over medium–high heat.

5 Place the rice noodles in a large heatproof bowl, cover with boiling water and gently separate the noodles. Drain immediately and rinse. Divide the noodles among four warm serving bowls. Top with the bean sprouts and cover with the boiling broth. Add the beef to the soup—the heat of the soup will cook it. Sprinkle with the mint and coriander, and fresh chilli, if desired. Serve immediately with some wedges of lemon.

# CHICKEN NOODLE SOUP

Preparation time: 10 minutes
Total cooking time: 10 minutes
Serves 4

85 g (3 oz) fresh egg noodles
1.5 litres (48 fl oz) good-quality chicken stock
2 tablespoons soy sauce
1 tablespoon mirin
3 x 3 cm (1¼ x 1¼ inch) piece fresh ginger,
   cut into julienne strips
2 chicken breast fillets, thinly sliced
1 kg (2 lb) baby bok choy, stalks trimmed,
   leaves separated
fresh coriander leaves, to garnish
sweet chilli sauce, to serve (optional)

1 Cook the noodles in a saucepan of boiling water for 1 minute, then drain and rinse.
2 Pour the stock into a wok, heat to simmering point, then add the soy sauce, mirin, ginger, chicken and noodles. Cook for 5 minutes, or until the chicken is tender and the noodles are warmed through. Remove any scum that rises to the surface.
3 Add the bok choy and cook for a further 2 minutes, or until the bok choy has wilted. Serve in deep bowls and garnish with coriander. Serve with sweet chilli sauce, if desired.

# THAI CHICKEN AND GALANGAL SOUP
(Tom kha kai)

Preparation time: 20 minutes
Total cooking time: 20 minutes
Serves 4

2 x 5 cm (¾ x 2 inch) piece fresh galangal,
   cut into thin slices
2 cups (500 ml/16 fl oz) coconut milk
1 cup (250 ml/8 fl oz) good-quality chicken
   stock
4 fresh kaffir lime leaves, torn
1 tablespoon finely chopped fresh coriander
   roots, well rinsed
500 g (1 lb) chicken breast fillets, cut into
   thin strips

1–2 teaspoons finely chopped fresh red chillies
2 tablespoons fish sauce
1½ tablespoons lime juice
3 teaspoons grated palm sugar
4 tablespoons fresh coriander leaves

1 Place the galangal, coconut milk, stock, lime leaves and coriander root in a wok. Bring to the boil, reduce the heat and simmer for 10 minutes, stirring occasionally.
2 Add the chicken and chilli and simmer for 8 minutes, or until the chicken is cooked through.
3 Stir in the fish sauce, lime juice and palm sugar and cook for 1 minute. Stir in the coriander leaves. Serve immediately, garnished with extra coriander, if desired.

*BELOW: Thai chicken and galangal soup*

## JAPANESE VEGETABLE RAMEN NOODLE SOUP

Preparation time: 15 minutes
Total cooking time: 15 minutes
Serves 6

250 g (8 oz) fresh ramen noodles
1 tablespoon vegetable oil
1 tablespoon finely chopped fresh ginger
2 cloves garlic, crushed
150 g (5 oz) oyster mushrooms, halved
1 small zucchini (courgette), thinly sliced
1 leek, halved lengthways and thinly sliced
100 g (3¹/₂ oz) snow peas (mangetout), halved on the diagonal
100 g (3¹/₂ oz) fried tofu puffs, cut into julienne strips
¹/₃ cup (80 g/2³/₄ oz) white miso paste
¹/₃ cup (80 ml/2³/₄ fl oz) light soy sauce
¹/₄ cup (60 ml/2 fl oz) mirin

1 cup (90 g/3 oz) bean sprouts, tailed
¹/₂ teaspoon sesame oil
4 spring onions, thinly sliced
100 g (3¹/₂ oz) enoki mushrooms

1 Bring a large saucepan of lightly salted water to the boil. Add the noodles and cook, stirring to prevent them sticking together, for 2 minutes, or until just tender. Drain, rinse under cold running water, then drain again.
2 Heat a wok over medium heat, add the vegetable oil and swirl to coat. Add the ginger and garlic and stir-fry for 30 seconds, then add the oyster mushrooms, zucchini, leek, snow peas and sliced tofu puffs and stir-fry for 4 minutes. Pour in 1.5 litres (48 fl oz) water and bring to the boil, then reduce the heat and simmer. Stir in the miso paste, soy sauce and mirin until heated through, but don't let it boil. Just before serving, stir in the bean sprouts and sesame oil.
3 Place the noodles in the bottom of six serving bowls, then pour the broth over the top. Sprinkle with the sliced spring onion and enoki mushrooms.

NOODLE SLURPING
Children in the West are taught from an early age not to slurp their food. However, in Japan, slurping is encouraged! It is considered socially acceptable to make a loud slurping noise when eating noodles. This has a dual purpose—it shows appreciation of a good meal, but also makes it possible to eat steaming hot noodles by sucking in cool air with the food. Another difference between Western and Japanese etiquette is that the Japanese pick up all the solid morsels in the soup with chopsticks and eat them before holding the bowl near their chin and drinking the liquid.

RIGHT: Japanese vegetable ramen noodle soup

# COCONUT PRAWN SOUP

Preparation time: 20 minutes +
    20 minutes soaking
Total cooking time: 45 minutes
Serves 4

## CURRY PASTE

6 long dried red chillies
2 teaspoons coriander seeds
I teaspoon cumin seeds
I teaspoon ground turmeric
1/2 teaspoon paprika
1/2 teaspoon black peppercorns
4 red Asian shallots, chopped
4 cloves garlic, roughly chopped
I tablespoon sliced fresh ginger
4 fresh coriander roots, well rinsed
2 tablespoons chopped fresh coriander stems
I teaspoon grated lime rind
2 stems lemon grass, white part only, sliced
    (reserve the stems for the stock)
2 fresh kaffir lime leaves, thinly shredded
I teaspoon shrimp paste
2 tablespoons vegetable oil

## STOCK

700 g (I lb 7 oz) raw medium prawns
4 red Asian shallots, chopped
I clove garlic
reserved grassy ends of lemon grass stems
6 black peppercorns

2 tablespoons vegetable oil
800 ml (26 fl oz) coconut milk
1/4 cup (60 ml/2 fl oz) fish sauce
fresh coriander leaves, to garnish
thinly sliced lime rind, to garnish

I To make the curry paste, soak the chillies in boiling water for 20 minutes, then drain. Toss the spices and peppercorns in a dry frying pan over medium heat for 1 minute, or until fragrant. Grind to a powder, then transfer to a food processor and add the remaining paste ingredients and 1 teaspoon salt. Process until smooth, adding a little water, if necessary.
2 Peel and devein the prawns, leaving the tails intact. Cover with plastic wrap and refrigerate. Reserve the heads and shells.

3 To make the stock, dry-fry the prawn heads and shells in a wok over high heat for 5 minutes, or until orange. Add the remaining stock ingredients and 1.5 litres (48 fl oz) water and bring to the boil. Reduce the heat, simmer for 15–20 minutes, then strain into a bowl.
4 Heat a clean, dry wok over medium heat, add the oil and swirl to coat the side. Add 3 tablespoons of the curry paste and stir constantly over medium heat for 1–2 minutes, or until fragrant. Stir in the stock and coconut milk and bring to the boil, then reduce the heat and simmer for 10 minutes. Add the prawns and cook, stirring, for 2 minutes, or until they are cooked. Stir in the fish sauce and garnish with coriander leaves and lime rind.
NOTE: Freeze the leftover curry paste in an airtight container.

*ABOVE: Coconut prawn soup*

reserving the soaking liquid. Discard the woody stalks and thinly slice the caps.

**2** Bring 2 litres (64 fl oz) water to the boil in a large saucepan and cook the noodles for 1–2 minutes, or until tender. Drain immediately and rinse under cold water. Set aside.

**3** Pour the stock and 1 litre (32 fl oz) water into a wok and bring to the boil, then reduce the heat and simmer. Add the chicken and cook for 2–3 minutes, or until almost cooked through.

**4** Add the mushrooms and cook for 1 minute. Add the bok choy halves and simmer for a further minute, or until beginning to wilt, then add the miso paste, dashi granules, wakame and reserved mushroom liquid. Stir to dissolve the dashi and miso paste. Do not allow to boil.

**5** Gently stir in the tofu. Distribute the noodles among the serving bowls, then ladle the hot soup over them. Sprinkle with the spring onion.

## CHINESE COMBINATION SHORT SOUP

Preparation time: 20 minutes +
  2 hours refrigeration
Total cooking time: 2 hours 20 minutes
Serves 4–6

☆☆

STOCK

1.5 kg (3 lb) whole chicken
1/4 cup (60 ml/2 fl oz) Chinese rice wine
1/2 star anise
8 spring onions, chopped
2 leafy celery tops
1/2 teaspoon white peppercorns
4 cloves garlic, bruised
2 x 10 cm (3/4 x 4 inch) piece fresh ginger, thinly sliced

24 won tons
12 raw medium prawns, peeled and deveined
200 g (6 1/2 oz) Chinese barbecued pork, thinly sliced
1/3 cup (60 g/2 oz) Chinese straw mushrooms
70 g (2 1/4 oz) sliced bamboo shoots
500 g (1 lb) baby bok choy, thinly sliced
2 spring onions, cut into 3 cm (1 1/4 inch) lengths
2 1/2 tablespoons light soy sauce
1 tablespoon oyster sauce
1/2 teaspoon sesame oil

## JAPANESE UDON MISO SOUP WITH CHICKEN

Preparation time: 15 minutes +
  20 minutes soaking
Total cooking time: 15 minutes
Serves 4–6

☆

8 dried shiitake mushrooms
400 g (13 oz) fresh udon noodles
1 litre (32 fl oz) good-quality chicken stock
600 g (1 1/4 lb) chicken breast fillets, cut into 1.5 cm (5/8 inch) thick strips
300 g (10 oz) baby bok choy, halved lengthways
1/4 cup (60 g/2 oz) white miso paste
2 teaspoons dashi granules
1 tablespoon wakame flakes or other seaweed
150 g (5 oz) silken firm tofu, cut into 1 cm (1/2 inch) cubes
3 spring onions, sliced on the diagonal

*ABOVE: Japanese udon miso soup with chicken*

**1** Soak the mushrooms in 1 cup (250 ml/8 fl oz) boiling water for 20 minutes. Squeeze dry,

1 Put all the stock ingredients in a stockpot and cover with 4 litres (128 fl oz) water. Bring to the boil over high heat and skim off any scum that forms on the surface. Reduce the heat and simmer for 2 hours. Cool slightly, then remove the chicken and strain the stock into a bowl. Cover and refrigerate the meat and stock separately until chilled. Skim off the fat from the top of the stock.
2 Pour 2 litres (64 fl oz) of the stock into a large wok and bring to the boil. Meanwhile, remove one breast from the chicken, then discard the skin and thinly slice the flesh.
3 Add the won tons to the boiling stock and cook for 2–3 minutes, or until they have risen to the surface and are cooked. Remove with a slotted spoon and divide among serving bowls. Reduce the stock to a simmer, add the prawns, pork, mushrooms and bamboo shoots and cook for 30 seconds, or until the prawns are just curled, then add the bok choy, spring onion, chicken and the combined soy sauce, oyster sauce and sesame oil and cook for 2 minutes, or until the prawns are completely cooked. Ladle the soup over the won tons and serve.

## EIGHT TREASURE SOUP

Preparation time: 15 minutes
  + 20 minutes soaking
Total cooking time: 1 hour
Serves 4–6

☆ ☆

4 dried shiitake mushrooms
1 tablespoon vegetable oil
1 teaspoon sesame oil
2 teaspoons finely chopped fresh ginger
1 tablespoon finely chopped spring onion
60 g (2 oz) Chinese bacon or ham, cut into
  thin strips (see Note)
1 litre (32 fl oz) good-quality chicken stock
1 tablespoon soy sauce
1 tablespoon rice wine
250 g (8 oz) chicken breast fillet
1 carrot, cut into 1 cm (1/2 inch) slices
12 small raw prawns, peeled and deveined
200 g (61/2 oz) firm tofu, cut into 2 cm
  (3/4 inch) cubes
50 g (13/4 oz) sliced bamboo shoots
100 g (31/2 oz) English spinach, chopped
2 spring onions, thinly sliced on the diagonal,
  extra

1 Soak the mushrooms in 1/2 cup (125 ml/ 4 fl oz) boiling water for 20 minutes. Squeeze dry, reserving the soaking liquid. Discard the woody stalks and cut the caps into quarters.
2 Heat a wok over high heat. Add the oils and swirl to coat the side of the wok, then add the ginger, spring onion and bacon. Cook for about 10 seconds before adding the stock, soy sauce, rice wine, mushroom liquid and 1/2 teaspoon salt. Bring to the boil, then add the chicken. Reduce the heat to low, cover with a lid and poach the chicken for 40 minutes. Remove the chicken from the stock and, when cool enough to handle, shred the meat.
3 Return the stock to the boil, add the carrot and cook for 5 minutes. Add the prawns, tofu, bamboo shoots, spinach and chicken meat to the wok and cook over low heat for a further 5 minutes. Serve with the extra spring onion.
NOTE: Chinese bacon has a dryish flesh with a strong flavour very much like prosciutto. You can substitute prosciutto.

*BELOW: Eight treasure soup*

THAI CUISINE

Thai cuisine is characterised by four main flavour elements—hot (spicy), sour, sweet and salty. These elements are often represented by chillies, lime juice, palm sugar and fish sauce, respectively. Aromatic herbs such as fresh coriander, lime leaves and lemon grass combine with these elements to create a complex yet subtle cuisine. People new to Thai cuisine often pick up spiciness as the predominant characteristic but not all Thai food is spicy. However, tolerance to chillies is an acquired ability and, like Thai children, those without an existing tolerance should be allowed to develop their tolerance over time.

*ABOVE: Hot and sour prawn soup*

## HOT AND SOUR PRAWN SOUP
(Tom yam kung)

Preparation time: 20 minutes
Total cooking time: 40 minutes
Serves 4

☆ ☆

1 kg (2 lb) raw medium prawns
1 tablespoon vegetable oil
2 tablespoons tom yam paste
2 stems lemon grass, white part only, bruised
4 fresh kaffir lime leaves
3 small fresh red chillies, thinly sliced
80–100 ml (2³/4–3¹/2 fl oz) fish sauce
80–100 ml (2³/4–3¹/2 fl oz) lime juice
2 teaspoons grated palm sugar
4 spring onions, thinly sliced on the diagonal
4 tablespoons fresh coriander leaves

1 Peel and devein the prawns, leaving the tails intact. Reserve the shells and heads. Cover the prawns and refrigerate.
2 Heat a wok over medium heat, add the oil and swirl to coat. Cook the prawn shells and heads for 8–10 minutes, or until they turn orange.
3 Add the tom yam paste and ¹/4 cup (60 ml/ 2 fl oz) water and cook for 1 minute, or until fragrant. Add 2.2 litres (70 fl oz) water, bring to

the boil, then reduce the heat and simmer for 20 minutes. Strain into a bowl. Return the stock to the wok.
4 Add the prawns, lemon grass, lime leaves and chilli and simmer for 4–5 minutes, or until the prawns are cooked. Stir in the fish sauce, lime juice, sugar, spring onion and coriander. Discard the lemon grass and serve immediately.

## VIETNAMESE FISH AND NOODLE SOUP

Preparation time: 30 minutes
Total cooking time: 20 minutes
Serves 4

☆ ☆

1 teaspoon shrimp paste
150 g (5 oz) cellophane noodles
2 tablespoons peanut oil
6 cloves garlic, finely chopped
1 small onion, thinly sliced
2 large fresh red chillies, chopped
2 stems lemon grass, white part only, thinly sliced
1.25 litres (40 fl oz) home-made chicken stock (see page 23) or 1 litre (32 fl oz) purchased stock diluted with 1 cup (250 ml/8 fl oz) water
¹/4 cup (60 ml/2 fl oz) fish sauce

1 tablespoon rice vinegar

4 ripe tomatoes, peeled, seeded and chopped

500 g (1 lb) firm white fish fillets (blue-eye or
  swordfish), cut into 3 cm (1¼ inch) pieces

½ cup (10 g/¼ oz) fresh Vietnamese mint,
  torn, plus extra to garnish

½ cup (15 g/½ oz) fresh coriander leaves,
  torn, plus extra to garnish

1 cup (90 g/3 oz) bean sprouts, tailed

2 large fresh red chillies, sliced, extra

lemon wedges, to serve

1 Wrap the shrimp paste in foil and place it under a hot grill for 1 minute.
2 Soak the noodles in boiling water for 3–4 minutes. Rinse under cold water, drain and cut into 15 cm (6 inch) lengths.
3 Heat a wok over medium heat, add the oil and swirl. Add the garlic and cook for 1 minute, or until golden, then add the onion, chilli, lemon grass and shrimp paste and cook, stirring, for a further 1 minute. Pour in the stock, fish sauce, vinegar and tomato, then bring to the boil. Reduce the heat and simmer for 10 minutes. Add the fish pieces and simmer gently for 3 minutes, or until cooked. Stir in the herbs.
4 Divide the noodles and bean sprouts among four bowls and ladle on the soup. Top with the extra chilli, mint and coriander. Serve with lemon wedges.

## CURRIED CHICKEN NOODLE SOUP

Preparation time: 15 minutes
Total cooking time: 50 minutes
Serves 4

☆

175 g (6 oz) dried thin egg noodles

¼ cup (60 ml/2 fl oz) peanut oil

2 x 250 g (8 oz) chicken breast fillets

1 onion, sliced

1 small fresh red chilli, seeded and finely chopped

1 tablespoon finely chopped fresh ginger

2 tablespoons Indian curry powder

3 cups (750 ml/24 fl oz) good-quality chicken stock

800 ml (26 fl oz) coconut milk

300 g (10 oz) baby bok choy, cut into long strips

4 tablespoons torn fresh basil

1 Cook the egg noodles in a large saucepan of boiling water for 3 minutes. Drain and rinse.
2 Heat a wok over medium heat, add 1 tablespoon oil and swirl to coat. Add the chicken and cook on each side for 5 minutes, or until cooked. Remove the chicken and keep warm. Clean the wok.
3 Return the wok to the heat, add the rest of the oil and swirl to coat. Add the onion and cook over low heat for 4–6 minutes, or until soft but not brown. Add the chilli, ginger and curry powder and cook for a further 1–2 minutes. Pour in the stock and bring to the boil. Reduce the heat and simmer for 10 minutes. Thinly slice the chicken on the diagonal.
4 Add the coconut milk to the wok and simmer for 8 minutes, then add the bok choy and cook for 3 minutes. Stir in the basil just before serving.
5 To serve, divide the noodles among four deep serving bowls. Top with slices of chicken and ladle in the soup. Serve immediately.

*BELOW: Curried chicken noodle soup*

# INDONESIAN SPICY CHICKEN SOUP

(Soto ayam)

Preparation time: 30 minutes +
 overnight refrigeration
Total cooking time: 2 hours 15 minutes
Serves 6

☆ ☆

2 teaspoons coriander seeds
2 tablespoons vegetable oil
1.4 kg (2 lb 13 oz) whole chicken,
 jointed into 8 pieces
4 cloves garlic
1 onion, chopped
2 teaspoons julienned fresh ginger
1 dried red chilli, halved
2 stems lemon grass, white part only,
 roughly chopped
50 g (1³/4 oz) coriander roots and
 stems, well rinsed, roughly chopped
2 teaspoons ground turmeric
1 teaspoon galangal powder

1 teaspoon sugar
1 litre (32 fl oz) good-quality chicken stock
2 tablespoons lemon juice
120 g (4 oz) cellophane noodles
1¹/2 tablespoons fish sauce
1 cup (90 g/3 oz) bean sprouts, tailed
3 tablespoons chopped fresh coriander leaves
4 spring onions, thinly sliced on the diagonal
¹/4 cup (20 g/³/4 oz) crisp fried onions
1 tablespoon sambal oelek

1 Toss the coriander seeds in a small, dry frying pan over medium heat for 1 minute, or until fragrant. Cool, then finely grind.
2 Heat a wok to very hot, add 2 teaspoons of the oil and swirl to coat. Add the chicken pieces and cook in batches for 3–4 minutes, or until browned all over. Remove from the wok.
3 Heat the remaining oil in the same wok, then add the garlic, onion, ginger and chilli and stir-fry for 5 minutes, or until softened. Add the lemon grass, coriander root and stem, turmeric, galangal, sugar and ground coriander and cook for 5 minutes. Return the chicken to the wok and pour in the stock, lemon juice and 2 cups

## SOTO AYAM

There are as many versions of soto ayam as there are nonyas in Indonesia, but it is essentially a fragrant chicken broth with cellophane noodles. Soto ayam is usually eaten as a snack or as part of a meal served with rice and other accompaniments. The side dishes served with soto ayam range from a simple bowl of rice and sambal oelek to more elaborate garnishes such as crisp fried potatoes, shredded cabbage and hard-boiled eggs. Traditionally, a small amount of each side dish is placed in the bottom of the soup bowl and the hot broth is then ladled over the top. Rice is then served on a separate plate and the broth is spooned over it as it is eaten.

RIGHT: Indonesian spicy chicken soup

(500 ml/16 fl oz) water to cover the chicken.

**4** Cover the wok with a lid and simmer for 20 minutes, skimming the surface periodically to remove any fat and scum that rises to the surface. Remove only the chicken breast pieces, then cover the wok and simmer (still skimming the surface occasionally) for 20 minutes before removing the rest of the chicken pieces. Cover and refrigerate the chicken until needed. Return the lid to the wok and simmer the broth over low heat for a further 1 hour.

**5** Strain the broth through a fine sieve, and allow to cool to room temperature before covering with plastic wrap and refrigerating overnight.

**6** Soak the cellophane noodles in boiling water for 3–4 minutes, then drain and rinse.

**7** Remove any fat from the top of the cold broth. Remove the flesh from the chicken and shred with a fork. Place the broth and chicken flesh in the wok, and place over medium heat. Bring to the boil, then stir in the fish sauce, bean sprouts, coriander leaves and noodles. Season well, then ladle into large bowls. Sprinkle with spring onion and crisp fried onion, and then serve with sambal oelek.

## SCALLOPS WITH SOBA NOODLES AND DASHI BROTH

Preparation time: 10 minutes
Total cooking time: 15 minutes
Serves 4

☆ ☆

250 g (8 oz) dried soba noodles

1/4 cup (60 ml/2 fl oz) mirin

1/4 cup (60 ml/2 fl oz) light soy sauce

2 teaspoons rice vinegar

1 teaspoon dashi granules

2 spring onions, sliced on the diagonal

1 teaspoon finely chopped fresh ginger

24 large scallops (without roe)

5 fresh black fungus, chopped (see Note)

1 sheet nori, shredded

**1** Add the noodles to a large saucepan of boiling water and stir to separate. Return to the boil, adding 1 cup (250 ml/8 fl oz) cold water and repeat this step 3 times, as it comes to the boil. Drain and rinse under cold water.

**2** Place the mirin, soy sauce, vinegar, dashi and

3 1/2 cups (875 ml/28 fl oz) water in a non-stick wok. Bring to the boil, then reduce the heat and simmer for 3–4 minutes. Add the spring onion and ginger and keep at a gentle simmer.

**3** Heat a chargrill pan or hot plate until very hot and sear the scallops in batches for 30 seconds each side. Remove from the pan.

**4** Divide the noodles and black fungus among four deep serving bowls. Pour 3/4 cup (185 ml/ 6 fl oz) broth into each bowl and top with 6 scallops each. Garnish with the shredded nori and serve immediately.

NOTE: If fresh black fungus is not available, use dried and soak it in warm water for 20 minutes.

*ABOVE: Scallops with soba noodles and dashi broth*

1 Put the fish in a food processor and process until smooth. Combine the rice flour and $1/3$ cup (80 ml/$2^3/4$ fl oz) water in a small bowl until smooth, then add to the fish and process for 5 seconds. Using 2 teaspoons of mixture at a time, shape into balls with wet hands.

2 Cook the noodles in a large saucepan of boiling water for 2 minutes, or until tender. Drain and set aside.

3 Pour 2 litres (64 fl oz) water into a non-stick wok and bring to the boil. Reduce the heat to low, add the dashi granules and stir until dissolved. Increase the heat to high and bring to the boil, then add the soy sauce, mirin and some salt to taste. Add the fish balls, reduce the heat to medium and simmer for 3 minutes, or until they rise to the surface and are cooked through. Add the wom bok, increase the heat to high and return to the boil. Stir in the noodles and cook for 1 minute, or until warmed through.

4 To serve, divide the noodles and fish balls among the serving bowls, then ladle on the liquid. Sprinkle with the spring onion and cucumber.

## CHINESE LAMB, GARLIC CHIVE AND CELLOPHANE NOODLE SOUP

Preparation time: 10 minutes +
   3 hours marinating
Total cooking time: 20 minutes
Serves 4

☆

2 tablespoons light soy sauce
1 tablespoon oyster sauce
1 tablespoon Chinese rice wine
1 teaspoon sugar
$1^1/4$ teaspoons sesame oil
3 slices fresh ginger plus 1 tablespoon finely
   chopped ginger
250 g (8 oz) lamb fillet
100 g ($3^1/2$ oz) cellophane noodles
1 tablespoon vegetable oil
3 spring onions, 2 finely chopped and 1 thinly
   sliced on the diagonal
1 cup (125 g/4 oz) chopped garlic chives
1 litre (32 fl oz) good-quality chicken stock

1 Combine the soy sauce, oyster sauce, rice wine, sugar, $1/4$ teaspoon of the sesame oil and the ginger slices in a bowl. Add the lamb and

## FISH BALL AND NOODLE SOUP

Preparation time: 15 minutes
Total cooking time: 15 minutes
Serves 4–6

☆

500 g (1 lb) soft white fish fillets (e.g. ling
   or perch), skin and bones removed
2 tablespoons rice flour
200 g ($6^1/2$ oz) dried somen noodles
$2^1/2$ teaspoons dashi granules
2 tablespoons light soy sauce
1 tablespoon mirin
200 g ($6^1/2$ oz) wom bok (Chinese cabbage),
   shredded
2 spring onions, thinly sliced on the diagonal
$1/2$ Lebanese cucumber, peeled, seeded and
   thinly cut into 5 cm (2 inch) strips

*ABOVE: Fish ball and noodle soup*

marinate for 3 hours, turning occasionally. Remove the lamb and ginger from the marinade with tongs.

**2** Soak the noodles in boiling water for 3–4 minutes, then rinse and drain.

**3** Heat a wok over high heat, add the vegetable oil and the remaining sesame oil and swirl to coat the side of the wok. Add the chopped ginger, chopped spring onion and garlic chives and cook for 30 seconds, stirring constantly. Slowly pour in the stock, then bring to the boil. Add the lamb and ginger slices, reduce the heat to low, cover with a lid and poach the lamb for 10 minutes.

**4** Remove the lamb from the wok. Bring the soup to the boil over medium–high heat. Meanwhile, thinly slice the lamb. Return the sliced lamb to the wok and add the noodles at the same time, stirring well until mixed together. Serve hot with the sliced spring onion scattered over the top.

**2** Heat a wok over medium–high heat, add the oil and swirl to coat. Add the spring onion, garlic and ginger and stir-fry for 30 seconds before adding the stock, corn kernels, creamed corn, soy sauce, rice wine and 1 cup (250 ml/ 8 fl oz) water. Stir until the soup comes to the boil, then reduce the heat and simmer for 10 minutes. Add the chicken meat.

**3** Stir the cornflour, sesame oil and 1 tablespoon water together in a small bowl until smooth. Add a little of the hot stock, stir together, then pour this mixture into the soup. Bring to simmering point, stirring constantly for 3–4 minutes, or until slightly thickened. Season to taste. Garnish with the chopped reserved spring onion greens.

NOTE: This isn't an authentic Chinese recipe. It was invented by homesick Chinese Americans.

*BELOW: Chinese chicken and corn soup*

## CHINESE CHICKEN AND CORN SOUP

Preparation time: 10 minutes
Total cooking time: 15 minutes
Serves 4

3 cups (750 ml/24 fl oz) good-quality chicken
    stock
2 x 200 g (6¹/₂ oz) chicken breast fillets
3–4 corn cobs
1 tablespoon vegetable oil
4 spring onions, thinly sliced, greens chopped
    and reserved for garnish
1 clove garlic, crushed
2 teaspoons grated fresh ginger
310 g (10 oz) can creamed corn
2 tablespoons light soy sauce
1 tablespoon Chinese rice wine
1 tablespoon cornflour
2 teaspoons sesame oil

**1** Bring the stock to simmering point in a small saucepan. Add the chicken and remove the pan from the heat. Cover the pan and leave the chicken to cool in the liquid. Remove the chicken with a slotted spoon, then finely shred the meat using your fingers. Cut the corn kernels from the cobs—you should get about 2 cups (400 g/13 oz).

## PORK AND BUTTERED CORN RAMEN NOODLE SOUP

Preparation time: 15 minutes
Total cooking time: 30 minutes
Serves 4

200 g (6¹/₂ oz) Chinese barbecued pork fillet, in one piece
2 small fresh corn cobs
200 g (6¹/₂ oz) dried ramen noodles
2 teaspoons peanut oil
1 teaspoon grated fresh ginger
1.5 litres (48 fl oz) good-quality chicken stock
2 tablespoons mirin
2 spring onions, sliced on the diagonal
20 g (³/₄ oz) unsalted butter
1 spring onion, extra, sliced on the diagonal

1 Cut the pork into thin slices and slice down the sides of the corn cobs with a sharp knife to release the kernels.

2 Cook the ramen noodles in a large saucepan of boiling water for 4 minutes, or until tender. Drain, rinse in cold water, then drain again.
3 Heat a wok over high heat, add the oil and swirl to coat the side of the wok. Stir-fry the ginger for 1–2 minutes, then pour in the stock, mirin and 2 cups (500 ml/16 fl oz) water. Bring to the boil, then reduce the heat and simmer for 6–8 minutes.
4 Add the pork to the broth and cook for 5 minutes, then add the corn kernels and spring onion and cook for a further 4–5 minutes, or until the kernels are tender.
5 Separate the noodles by running them under hot water, then divide among four deep bowls, shaping them into mounds. Ladle over the liquid and top with the pork and corn. Place 1 teaspoon butter on top of each mound and garnish with the extra spring onion. Serve immediately.

## THAI PUMPKIN AND COCONUT SOUP

Preparation time: 20 minutes
Total cooking time: 30 minutes
Serves 4

¹/₂ teaspoon shrimp paste
2 long fresh red chillies, chopped
¹/₄ teaspoon white peppercorns
2 tablespoons chilli paste
2 cloves garlic
3 teaspoons vegetable oil
5 spring onions, sliced on the diagonal
¹/₂ cup (125 ml/4 fl oz) coconut cream
2 cups (500 ml/16 fl oz) good-quality chicken stock
2 stems lemon grass, white part only, bruised
3¹/₂ cups (875 ml/28 fl oz) coconut milk
750 g (1¹/₂ lb) jap pumpkin, cut into 2 cm (³/₄ inch) cubes
250 g (8 oz) peeled small raw prawns, deveined
1 tablespoon fish sauce
4 tablespoons small fresh Thai basil leaves

1 Wrap the shrimp paste in foil and put under a hot grill for 1 minute. Unwrap the foil and put the shrimp paste in a food processor with the chilli, peppercorns, chilli paste, garlic and a pinch of salt, and process until smooth.

*BELOW: Pork and buttered corn ramen noodle soup*

**2** Heat a wok over high heat, add the oil and swirl to coat. Cook the spring onion for 1–2 minutes, or until lightly golden, then remove from the wok. Add the coconut cream and bring to the boil over high heat, then simmer for 10 minutes, or until the oil starts to separate from the cream—this is called cracking.
**3** Stir in the processed paste and simmer over medium heat for 1–2 minutes, or until fragrant. Add the stock, lemon grass, coconut milk, pumpkin and cooked spring onion, cover with a lid and simmer for 8–10 minutes, or until the pumpkin is tender. Remove the lid, add the prawns and cook for a further 2–3 minutes, or until cooked through. Stir in the fish sauce and basil and serve.

## THAI RICE NOODLE SOUP WITH DUCK

Preparation time: 40 minutes
Total cooking time: 25 minutes
Serves 4–6

1 whole Chinese roast duck (see Note)
4 fresh coriander roots and stems, well rinsed
50 g (1 3/4 oz) fresh galangal, sliced
4 spring onions, sliced on the diagonal into
    3 cm (1 1/4 inch) lengths
400 g (13 oz) Chinese broccoli, cut into
    5 cm (2 inch) lengths
2 cloves garlic, crushed
1/4 cup (60 ml/2 fl oz) fish sauce
1 tablespoon hoisin sauce
2 teaspoons grated palm sugar
1/2 teaspoon ground white pepper
500 g (1 lb) fresh rice noodles
crisp fried garlic, to garnish (optional)
fresh coriander leaves, to garnish (optional)

**1** To make the stock, cut off the duck's head with a sharp knife and discard. Remove the skin and fat from the duck, leaving the neck intact. Carefully remove the flesh from the bones and set aside. Cut any visible fat from the carcass along with the parson's nose, then discard. Break the carcass into large pieces, then put in a large stockpot with 2 litres (64 fl oz) water.
**2** Bruise the coriander roots and stems with the back of a knife. Add to the pot with the galangal and bring to the boil. Skim off any scum from the surface. Boil over medium heat for

10 minutes. Strain the stock through a fine sieve—discard the carcass and return the stock to a large clean wok.
**3** Slice the duck flesh into strips. Add to the stock with the spring onion, Chinese broccoli, garlic, fish sauce, hoisin sauce, palm sugar and white pepper. Gently bring to the boil.
**4** Put the noodles in a heatproof bowl, cover with boiling water and gently separate. Drain well and refresh under cold water. Divide the noodles and soup evenly among the serving bowls. If desired, garnish with the garlic flakes and coriander leaves. Serve immediately.
NOTE: Whole Chinese roast duck is available from Chinese barbecue shops.

*ABOVE: Thai rice noodle soup with duck*

PHO
Noodle soups are a way of life in Vietnam and pho (pronounced fur) is the most well known of these soups. Vietnamese people eat pho at any time of the day—breakfast, lunch or dinner. The aromatic accompaniment of fresh herbs gives the pho a fragrance that typifies Vietnamese cuisine, while the extra seasonings on the side allow each diner to create a tailor-made pho. The soup is originally from the North but is now a classic throughout Vietnam.

*ABOVE: Beef pho*

# BEEF PHO
(Pho bo)

Preparation time: 15 minutes +
  15 minutes soaking
Total cooking time: 35 minutes
Serves 4

☆ ☆

2 litres (64 fl oz) good-quality beef stock
1 star anise
1 x 4 cm (1/2 x 1 1/2 inch) piece fresh ginger, sliced
2 pigs' trotters (ask your butcher to cut in half)
1/2 onion, studded with 2 cloves
2 stems lemon grass, bruised
2 cloves garlic, crushed
1/4 teaspoon ground white pepper
1 tablespoon fish sauce, plus extra to serve
200 g (6 1/2 oz) fresh thin round rice noodles
300 g (10 oz) beef fillet, partially frozen, thinly sliced
1 cup (90 g/3 oz) bean sprouts, tailed
2 spring onions, thinly sliced on the diagonal

1/2 cup (25 g/3/4 oz) chopped fresh coriander leaves, plus extra to serve
4 tablespoons chopped fresh Vietnamese mint, plus extra to serve
1 fresh red chilli, thinly sliced, plus extra to serve
2 limes, cut into quarters

1 Put the beef stock, star anise, ginger, pigs' trotters, onion, lemon grass, garlic and white pepper in a wok and bring to the boil. Reduce the heat to very low and simmer, covered, for 30 minutes. Strain, return to the wok and stir in the fish sauce.
2 Meanwhile, put the noodles in a heatproof bowl, cover with boiling water and gently separate. Drain well, then refresh under cold running water.
3 Divide the noodles among four deep soup bowls, then top with beef strips, bean sprouts, spring onion, coriander, mint and chilli. Ladle on the broth.
4 Place the extra chilli, mint, coriander, lime quarters and fish sauce in small bowls on a platter, serve with the soup and allow your guests to help themselves.

# CLEAR CHINESE PORK BALL AND NOODLE SOUP

Preparation time: 20 minutes +
  1 hour refrigeration
Total cooking time: 30 minutes
Serves 4–6

☆ ☆

1 tablespoon peanut oil

2 teaspoons sesame oil

4 cloves garlic, crushed

2 teaspoons grated fresh ginger

150 g (5 oz) wom bok (Chinese cabbage),
  shredded

300 g (10 oz) pork mince

1 egg white

1 1/2 tablespoons cornflour

1/4 teaspoon ground white pepper

1/3 cup (80 ml/2 3/4 fl oz) light soy sauce

2 tablespoons Chinese rice wine

6 spring onions, thinly sliced

1/2 cup (15 g/1/2 oz) fresh coriander leaves,
  finely chopped

1.5 litres (48 fl oz) home-made chicken stock
  (see page 23) or 1.25 litres (40 fl oz)
  purchased stock diluted with 1 cup
  (250 ml/8 fl oz) water (see Note)

3 teaspoons grated fresh ginger, extra

200 g (6 1/2 oz) fresh thin egg noodles

finely chopped fresh red chilli, to garnish
  (optional)

1 Heat a wok over high heat, add the peanut oil and 1 teaspoon of the sesame oil, then swirl to coat the side of the wok. Add the garlic, ginger and wom bok and stir-fry for 1 minute, or until the garlic begins to brown. As soon as this happens, remove the wok from the heat and allow to cool.

2 Transfer the cooled wom bok mixture to a large bowl and add the mince, egg white, cornflour, white pepper, 2 tablespoons of the soy sauce, 1 tablespoon of the rice wine, half the spring onion and 3 tablespoons of the coriander. Mix thoroughly, then cover with plastic wrap and refrigerate for 1 hour. Shape 1 tablespoon of the mixture into a ball using wet hands. Repeat with the remaining mixture.

3 Clean and dry the wok, then pour in the stock. Bring the stock to the boil, then reduce the heat and simmer for 1–2 minutes. Add the extra ginger, remaining soy sauce and rice wine and cook, covered, for 5 minutes before adding the pork balls. Cook, uncovered, for a further 8–10 minutes, or until the balls rise to the top and are cooked through.

4 Meanwhile, cook the noodles in a large saucepan of boiling water for 1 minute, or until they separate. Drain, then rinse well. Divide the noodles among serving bowls, then ladle on the soup. Sprinkle with the remaining spring onion and coriander, then add a couple of drops of the remaining sesame oil. Serve with chilli and extra soy sauce, if desired.

NOTE: Because many purchased stocks are very salty, when used in large quantities, they need to be diluted with water. Home-made stocks tend to be less salty, so they do not require dilution.

*ABOVE: Clear Chinese
pork ball and noodle soup*

## SHANGHAI CHICKEN AND NOODLE SOUP

Preparation time: 10 minutes
Total cooking time: 35 minutes
Serves 4–6

2.5 litres (80 fl oz) home-made chicken
    stock (see page 23) or 2 litres (64 fl oz)
    purchased stock diluted with 2 cups
    (500 ml/16 fl oz) water
1 star anise
4 x 5 mm (¼ inch) slices fresh ginger
600 g (1¼ lb) chicken breast fillets
375 g (12 oz) Shanghai noodles
200 g (6½ oz) fresh asparagus, cut into
    3 cm (1¼ inch) pieces
1 tablespoon julienned fresh ginger
1½ tablespoons light soy sauce, plus extra
    to serve
1 tablespoon Chinese rice wine
½ teaspoon sugar
4 spring onions, thinly sliced on the diagonal
50 g (1¼ oz) watercress tips (optional)
¼ teaspoon sesame oil, to drizzle

1 Pour the stock into a non-stick wok and bring to the boil. Reduce to medium–low, add the star anise, ginger slices and chicken and poach the chicken for 15–20 minutes, or until cooked through. Remove the chicken with a slotted spoon and cool. Leave the stock in the wok.
2 Meanwhile, bring 2 litres (64 fl oz) water to the boil in a large saucepan and cook the noodles for 3 minutes. Drain and refresh under cold water.
3 Cut the chicken across the breast into 5 mm (¼ inch) slices. Return the stock to the boil and add the asparagus, julienned ginger, soy sauce, rice wine, sugar and ½ teaspoon salt. Reduce the heat, add the noodles and simmer for 2 minutes. Return the chicken to the wok and cook for 1 minute, or until heated through.
4 Remove the noodles from the liquid with tongs and evenly divide among serving bowls. Divide the chicken, asparagus, spring onion and watercress (if using) among the bowls, then ladle the broth on top. Drizzle with sesame oil and serve with extra soy sauce, if desired.

## THAI SWEET AND SOUR CHICKEN SOUP

Preparation time: 20 minutes +
    20 minutes soaking
Total cooking time: 20 minutes
Serves 4–6

6 large dried red chillies
4 red Asian shallots, chopped
4 cloves garlic, chopped
2 tablespoons finely chopped fresh galangal
2 teaspoons chopped fresh turmeric
2 stems lemon grass, white part only, finely
    chopped
½ teaspoon grated lime rind
1 teaspoon shrimp paste
1 litre (32 fl oz) good-quality chicken stock
6 fresh kaffir lime leaves
2 tablespoons tamarind purée
2 tablespoons fish sauce
¼ cup (45 g/1½ oz) grated palm sugar
450 g (14 oz) chicken breast fillets, thinly sliced
200 g (6½ oz) fresh asparagus, cut into thirds
100 g (3½ oz) fresh baby corn, cut in half
    lengthways
200 g (6½ oz) fresh pineapple, cut into
    2 cm (¾ inch) cubes

*BELOW: Shanghai chicken and noodle soup*

1 Soak the chillies in 1 cup (250 ml/8 fl oz) boiling water for 20 minutes, then drain and chop. Put the chilli, shallots, garlic, galangal, turmeric, lemon grass, lime rind and shrimp paste in a food processor or blender and blend to a smooth paste, adding a little water if necessary to form a smooth paste.

2 Pour the stock and 1 cup (250 ml/8 fl oz) water into a non-stick wok, add the lime leaves and bring to the boil over high heat. Stir in the blended chilli paste and simmer for 5 minutes. Add the tamarind, fish sauce, palm sugar, chicken (using your hands to separate the chicken slices), asparagus and baby corn and stir to prevent the chicken clumping. Simmer for 10 minutes, or until the chicken is cooked and the vegetables are tender. Stir in the pineapple.

3 Serve in warmed, deep soup bowls as part of a banquet.

NOTE: Use a non-stick or stainless steel wok for this recipe as the tamarind purée reacts with a regular wok and will taint the whole dish.

## SICHUAN BEEF NOODLE SOUP

Preparation time: 10 minutes
Total cooking time: 3 hours
Serves 4

☆☆

1.5 litres (48 fl oz) good-quality beef stock

1 tablespoon peanut oil

400 g (13 oz) piece chuck steak

1/2 cinnamon stick

2 star anise

1 1/2 teaspoons Sichuan peppercorns, crushed

1 tablespoon julienned fresh ginger

2 tablespoons dark soy sauce

1 tablespoon Chinese rice wine

1 tablespoon brown bean sauce

3 x 5 cm (1 1/4 x 2 inch) piece dried mandarin peel (see Note)

125 g (4 oz) fresh thin egg noodles

3 spring onions, thinly sliced on the diagonal

1 Pour the beef stock and 2 litres (64 fl oz) water into a stockpot and simmer over low heat; keep warm until needed.

2 Heat a wok over high heat, add the oil and swirl to coat. Add the steak and sear it for 2–3 minutes on each side. Add the cinnamon stick, star anise, peppercorns, ginger, soy sauce,

rice wine, bean sauce and mandarin peel. Pour in the hot broth, then cover and bring to simmering point over medium heat. Reduce the heat to low and simmer, covered, for 2–2 1/2 hours, or until the steak is tender—you should be able to shred it; if not, return to the simmer until tender.

3 Remove the steak and discard the mandarin peel. Meanwhile, cook the noodles in a large saucepan of boiling water for 1 minute to separate them. Drain. Just before serving, add the noodles to the broth and let them stand for 1–2 minutes, or until heated through. Shred the steak into bite-sized pieces and divide evenly among four large serving bowls. Ladle on the broth and noodles, sprinkle with spring onion and serve.

NOTE: Dried citrus peel is one of the most important Chinese flavourings and the dried peel of mandarins, tangerines and oranges is sold at many Asian food stores.

*ABOVE: Sichuan beef noodle soup*

1 Discard any broken mussels, or open ones that don't close when tapped on the bench. Rinse them well.

2 Heat a wok over medium heat, add the oil and swirl to coat the side of the wok. Cook the spring onion and garlic for 1 minute, or until softened. Add the stock, galangal, lemon grass, chilli, lime leaves and 3 cups (750 ml/24 fl oz) water and rapidly simmer for 15 minutes.

3 Add the mussels, cover with a lid, bring to the boil over high heat and cook for 7–8 minutes, or until the mussels open, tossing occasionally. Discard any unopened mussels.

4 Stir in half the coriander, then divide the broth and mussels among four large serving bowls. Sprinkle with the remaining coriander, then serve immediately.

NOTES: Because many purchased stocks are very salty, either use home-made stock (see page 23 for chicken stock) or use 2 cups (500 ml/16 fl oz) bought stock and dilute it with 1 cup (250 ml/8 fl oz) water.

Place a large empty bowl in the centre of the table for the empty mussel shells.

## CAMBODIAN SOUR CHICKEN SOUP

Preparation time: 20 minutes
Total cooking time: 40 minutes
Serves 4

☆☆

800 g (1 lb 10 oz) chicken quarters (leg and thigh), skin removed, cut into 5 cm (2 inch) pieces on the bone
1 tablespoon tamarind pulp, soaked in 1/4 cup (60 ml/2 fl oz) boiling water
1/4 cup (60 ml/2 fl oz) fish sauce
1/2 teaspoon sugar
200 g (6 1/2 oz) fresh pineapple, cut into 2 cm (3/4 inch) cubes
2 small ripe tomatoes, cut into wedges
3 spring onions, cut into 3 cm (1 1/4 inch) lengths
1 teaspoon vegetable oil
4 cloves garlic, finely chopped
2 tablespoons chopped fresh coriander leaves
3 tablespoons chopped fresh basil
1 fresh red chilli, thinly sliced on the diagonal
2 tablespoons lime juice
1 cup (90 g/3 oz) bean sprouts, tailed

## THAI LEMON GRASS BROTH WITH MUSSELS

Preparation time: 20 minutes
Total cooking time: 25 minutes
Serves 4

☆

1.5 kg (3 lb) black mussels, scrubbed and debearded
1 tablespoon vegetable oil
5 spring onions, thinly sliced on the diagonal
2 cloves garlic, crushed
3 cups (750 ml/24 fl oz) good-quality chicken or fish stock (see Notes)
2 1/2 tablespoons sliced fresh galangal or ginger
4 stems lemon grass, white part only, bruised
2 long fresh red chillies, halved lengthways
6 fresh kaffir lime leaves, crushed
2 tablespoons roughly chopped fresh coriander leaves

*ABOVE: Thai lemon grass broth with mussels*

1 Pour 1.25 litres (40 fl oz) water into a non-stick wok, then bring to the boil over medium heat. Add the chicken pieces and cook, periodically skimming any scum that forms on the surface, for 30 minutes, or until the stock is clear. Remove the chicken from the wok with a slotted spoon, then take the meat off the bones and discard any fat and bones. Cool the meat slightly, then shred the chicken meat, keeping the stock simmering while you do this.

2 Strain the tamarind liquid to remove the seeds, then add the strained liquid to the stock. Return the shredded chicken meat to the wok, add the fish sauce, sugar, pineapple, tomato and spring onion and season to taste with salt, then cook for 1–2 minutes over medium heat, or until the chicken, tomato and pineapple are heated through.

3 Heat the oil in a small frying pan over medium heat and add the garlic. Cook for 2 minutes, or until golden. Remove the garlic with a slotted spoon and add it to the soup. Remove the wok from the heat and stir in the coriander, basil, chilli and lime juice. To serve, place the bean sprouts in the bottom of four bowls and ladle the soup over the top. Serve immediately.

## CRAB AND CORN EGGFLOWER NOODLE BROTH

Preparation time: 15 minutes
Total cooking time: 15 minutes
Serves 4

75 g (2¹/2 oz) dried thin egg noodles
1 tablespoon peanut oil
1 teaspoon finely chopped fresh ginger
3 spring onions, thinly sliced, white and
   green parts separated
1.5 litres (48 fl oz) good-quality chicken stock
¹/3 cup (80 ml/2³/4 fl oz) mirin
250 g (8 oz) fresh baby corn, sliced on
   the diagonal into 1 cm (¹/2 inch) slices
175 g (6 oz) fresh crab meat
1 tablespoon cornflour mixed with
   1 tablespoon water
2 eggs, lightly beaten
2 teaspoons lime juice
1 tablespoon soy sauce
3 tablespoons torn fresh coriander leaves

1 Cook the noodles in a large saucepan of boiling salted water for 3 minutes, or until just tender. Drain, then rinse under cold water.

2 Heat a non-stick wok over high heat, add the oil and swirl to coat the side of the wok. Add the ginger and white part of the spring onion and cook over medium heat for 1–2 minutes. Add the stock, mirin and corn and bring to the boil, then simmer for 3 minutes. Stir in the noodles, crab meat and cornflour mixture. Return to a simmer, stirring constantly until it thickens. Reduce the heat and pour in the egg in a thin stream, stirring constantly—do not boil. Gently stir in the lime juice, soy sauce and half the coriander.

3 Divide the noodles among four bowls and ladle on the soup. Top with the green part of the spring onion and coriander leaves.

*ABOVE: Crab and corn eggflower noodle broth*

# CHINESE HOT AND SOUR NOODLE SOUP

Preparation time: 45 minutes +
  overnight refrigeration + 10 minutes standing
Total cooking time: 4 hours
Serves 6

☆ ☆

STOCK

1.5 kg (3 lb) chicken bones, washed

2 x 1 cm (1/2 inch) slices fresh ginger

4 spring onions, white part only, bruised

200 g (6 1/2 oz) fresh Shanghai noodles

200 g (6 1/2 oz) chicken breast fillet, cut into
  very thin strips

2 tablespoons garlic and red chilli paste

1/4 cup (60 ml/2 fl oz) light soy sauce

3/4 teaspoon ground white pepper

4 fresh shiitake mushrooms, stems removed,
  caps thinly sliced

100 g (3 1/2 oz) enoki mushrooms, trimmed
  and separated

115 g (4 oz) fresh baby corn, cut into quarters
  lengthways

1/4 cup (60 ml/2 fl oz) Chinese black vinegar

65 g (2 1/4 oz) black fungus, roughly chopped

200 g (6 1/2 oz) firm tofu, cut into 2.5 cm
  (1 inch) cubes

3 eggs, lightly beaten

1/4 cup (30 g/1 oz) cornflour

1 teaspoon sesame oil

spring onions, thinly sliced on the diagonal
  in long strips, to garnish

1 To make the stock, put the chicken bones and 3.5 litres (112 fl oz) water in a large saucepan and bring to a simmer, but do not boil. Cook for 30 minutes, removing any scum that rises to the surface. Add the ginger and spring onion and simmer gently, partially covered, for 3 hours. Strain through a fine sieve and allow to cool. Cover and refrigerate overnight. Remove the layer of fat from the surface.

2 Cook the noodles in a large saucepan of boiling water for 4–5 minutes, then drain and rinse.

3 To make the soup, pour 2 litres (64 fl oz) of the stock into a non-stick wok, bring to the boil over high heat, then reduce the heat to medium, add the chicken, garlic and chilli paste, soy sauce and white pepper and stir well. Simmer, covered, for 10 minutes, or until the chicken is cooked. Add the mushrooms, corn, vinegar, black fungus and tofu, season with salt, return the lid to the wok and simmer gently for 5 minutes—do not stir.

4 Mix the cornflour with 1/4 cup (60 ml/2 fl oz) water. Add to the soup with the noodles, return to a simmer, then pour the eggs in a very thin stream over the surface. Turn off the heat and stand for 10 minutes before gently stirring in the sesame oil. Divide among the serving bowls and garnish with the spring onion strips.

HOT AND SOUR SOUPS
Traditionally, Chinese hot and sour soups don't contain chilli—the heat comes from a very liberal use of ground white pepper. Chinese cooks prefer white pepper to black pepper as it has not only heat but also flavour. In order to get a good flavour from white pepper it must be freshly ground. The perfect hot and sour soup should be one which satisfies the age-old Taoist principles of yin and yang (female/male; cold/hot; water/fire), in its marriage and balance of opposite flavours and textures. One of the principal concerns of Taoism is the effect of nutrition on the body, and the life-giving attributes of various foods.

*RIGHT: Chinese hot and sour noodle soup*

CHINESE BARBECUED
PORK
Char siu, or barbecued
pork, is a Cantonese
speciality that can be
seen hanging in Chinese
restaurants. Char siu means
'suspended over fire' and
is traditionally dyed red.
Generally in China, char siu
is bought from take-aways
as most homes do not
have an oven. The pork
marinade may include
hoisin sauce, oyster sauce,
bean sauce and fermented
bean curd.

## RAMEN NOODLE SOUP WITH BARBECUED PORK AND GREENS

Preparation time: 15 minutes + 20 minutes soaking
Total cooking time: 10 minutes
Serves 4

15 g (1/2 oz) dried shiitake mushrooms
350 g (11 oz) Chinese broccoli, trimmed and
    cut into 4 cm (1 1/2 inch) lengths
375 g (12 oz) fresh ramen noodles
1.5 litres (48 fl oz) home-made chicken stock
    (see page 23) or 1.25 litres (40 fl oz) purchased
    stock diluted with 1 cup (250 ml/8 fl oz) water
1/4 cup (60 ml/2 fl oz) soy sauce
1 teaspoon sugar
200 g (6 1/2 oz) Chinese barbecued pork,
    thinly sliced
chilli flakes (optional)

1 Soak the mushrooms in 1/2 cup (125 ml/
4 fl oz) boiling water for 20 minutes. Squeeze
the mushrooms dry, reserving the liquid. Discard
the stalks, then thinly slice the caps.
2 Blanch the Chinese broccoli in a large
saucepan of boiling salted water for 3 minutes,
or until tender but firm to the bite. Drain, then
refresh in cold water.
3 Cook the noodles in a large saucepan of
boiling water for 2 minutes, or until just tender.
Drain, rinse under cold water, then drain again.
4 Pour the stock and 2 cups (500 ml/16 fl oz)
water into a non-stick wok and bring to the
boil. Add the sliced mushrooms and reserved
mushroom liquid, soy sauce and sugar. Simmer
for 2 minutes, then add the broccoli.
5 Divide the noodles among bowls. Ladle on the
hot stock and vegetables. Top with the pork and
chilli flakes, if desired.
NOTE: If using a commercially made stock, it is
wise to dilute it because it is often much saltier than
home-made stocks. In general, for every 1.5 litres
(48 fl oz) stock, add 1 cup (250 ml/8 fl oz) water.

*ABOVE: Ramen noodle
soup with barbecued pork
and greens*

COCONUT AND
LEMON GRASS SOUP
WITH PRAWN
WON TONS

Seal the won tons by
gathering the wrapper
around the filling to make
a pouch.

## COCONUT AND
## LEMON GRASS SOUP
## WITH PRAWN WON TONS

Preparation time: 30 minutes +
  overnight refrigeration
Total cooking time: 1 hour 10 minutes
Serves 4

☆ ☆

STOCK
1.5 kg (3 lb) chicken bones, washed
1 onion, roughly chopped
1 cup (125 g/4 oz) roughly chopped celery

WON TONS
325 g (11 oz) raw small prawns, peeled and
  deveined, finely chopped
2 tablespoons finely chopped fresh coriander
  leaves
1 tablespoon shredded fresh Thai basil
2 tablespoons finely chopped celery
2 spring onions, finely chopped
12 won ton wrappers
1 egg, lightly beaten

BROTH
2 tablespoons tom yam paste
3 stems lemon grass, white part only,
  thinly sliced
6 fresh kaffir lime leaves
2 small fresh red chillies, finely chopped
200 ml (6$^{1}$/2 fl oz) coconut milk
1 tablespoon grated palm sugar
1 tablespoon lime juice
1 tablespoon fish sauce
fresh coriander leaves, to garnish

1 To make the stock, put the chicken bones,
onion, celery and 3 litres (96 fl oz) water in a
large saucepan and bring slowly to a simmer
over medium heat. Skim off any scum that rises
to the surface. Reduce the heat and simmer for
1 hour, skimming the surface when necessary.
Strain the stock through a fine sieve and allow
to cool. Cover with plastic wrap and refrigerate
overnight. Remove the layer of fat from the
surface once it has solidified.
2 To make the won tons, combine the prawn
meat, coriander, basil, celery and spring onion.
Lay the won ton wrappers out on a clean work
surface. Place a heaped teaspoon of prawn

*ABOVE: Coconut and
lemon grass soup with
prawn won tons*

mixture in the centre of each wrapper. Brush the edge of each wrapper with a little of the beaten egg. Lift the sides up tightly and pinch around the filling to form a pouch. Repeat with the remaining wrappers and filling to make 20 won tons in total. Cover and refrigerate.

**3** Heat a wok over medium heat, add the tom yam paste and cook for 10 seconds, or until fragrant. Gradually whisk in 1 litre (32 fl oz) of the chicken stock until combined, then bring to the boil over high heat. Reduce the heat to medium, then add the lemon grass, lime leaves, chilli and coconut milk and simmer for 5 minutes. Stir in the sugar, lime juice and fish sauce. Gently add the won tons and simmer for 2 minutes, or until cooked through. Remove the won tons with a slotted spoon and place five in each serving bowl. Ladle the broth into the bowls and garnish with fresh coriander leaves. NOTE: Freeze the remaining stock.

## FIVE-SPICE DUCK AND SOMEN NOODLE SOUP

Preparation time: 10 minutes
Total cooking time: 30 minutes
Serves 4

☆ ☆

4 duck breasts, skin on
1 teaspoon five-spice powder
1 teaspoon peanut oil
200 g (6½ oz) dried somen noodles

STAR ANISE BROTH
2 litres (64 fl oz) good-quality chicken stock
3 star anise
5 spring onions, chopped
3 tablespoons chopped fresh coriander leaves

**1** Preheat the oven to moderately hot 200°C (400°F/Gas 6). Trim the duck breast of excess fat, then lightly sprinkle both sides with the five-spice powder.

**2** Heat a wok over high heat, add the oil and swirl to coat the side of the wok. Add the duck breasts, skin-side down, and cook over medium heat for 2–3 minutes, or until browned and crisp. Turn and cook the other side for 3 minutes. Transfer to a baking tray and roast, skin-side-up, for a further 8 minutes for medium–rare, or until cooked to your liking.

**3** Meanwhile, put the chicken stock and star anise in a clean non-stick wok. Bring to the boil,

then reduce the heat and simmer, covered, for 5 minutes. Add the spring onion and coriander and simmer for a further 5 minutes.

**4** Cook the noodles in a saucepan of boiling water for 2 minutes, or until tender. Drain and divide among four large bowls. Ladle the broth on the noodles and top each bowl with one sliced duck breast.

## QUICK MISO SOUP

Soak 5 g (¼ oz) dried wakame in water for 10 minutes, or until tender. Drain. Dissolve 2½ teaspoons instant dashi powder in 1.5 litres (48 fl oz) boiling water. Put ½ cup (125 ml/4 fl oz) shiro miso in a wok and stir in ⅓ cup (80 ml/2¾ fl oz) of the dashi stock until smooth. Add the rest of the dashi stock and stir well. Drain 300 g (10 oz) silken tofu, cut into 1.5 cm (⅝ inch) cubes and add to the stock with the wakame. Simmer until hot. Serves 4.

*BELOW: Five-spice duck and somen noodle soup*

## CHINESE LONG AND SHORT NOODLE SOUP

Preparation time: 30 minutes
Total cooking time: 15 minutes
Serves 6

☆ ☆

300 g (10 oz) pork mince

4 spring onions, sliced

3 cloves garlic, roughly chopped

2 teaspoons grated fresh ginger

2 teaspoons cornflour

110 ml (3 1/2 fl oz) light soy sauce

1/4 cup (60 ml/2 fl oz) Chinese rice wine

30 won ton wrappers

3 litres (96 fl oz) home-made chicken stock (see page 23) or 2.25 litres (70 fl oz) purchased stock diluted with 3 cups (750 ml/24 fl oz) water

20 g (3/4 oz) fresh ginger, thinly sliced

200 g (6 1/2 oz) dried flat egg noodles

2 spring onions, extra, sliced on the diagonal

1 teaspoon sesame oil

*BELOW: Chinese long and short noodle soup*

1 Put the mince, spring onion, garlic, ginger, cornflour, 1 1/2 tablespoons of the soy sauce and 1 tablespoon of the rice wine in a food processor and process until well combined.

2 Place 2 teaspoons of the mixture in the centre of a won ton wrapper and lightly brush the edges with water. Lift the sides up tightly and pinch around the filling to form a pouch. Repeat with the remaining filling and wrappers.

3 Pour the chicken stock into a large wok, add the ginger and bring to a simmer over medium–high heat. Stir in the remaining soy sauce and wine.

4 Meanwhile, bring a large saucepan of water to the boil. Reduce the heat, add the won tons and simmer for 1 minute, or until they float to the surface and are cooked through. Remove the won tons with a slotted spoon and set aside. Return the water to the boil, add the egg noodles and cook for 3 minutes, or until just tender. Drain and rinse.

5 Remove the ginger slices from the broth, then add the won tons and simmer for 2 minutes, or until they float to the top and are heated through. Add the noodles to the soup to reheat.

6 Divide the soup and won tons among six large serving bowls, sprinkle with extra spring onion and drizzle each with sesame oil to taste.

## SUKIYAKI SOUP

Preparation time: 20 minutes +
  20 minutes soaking
Total cooking time: 15 minutes
Serves 4–6

☆

10 g (1/4 oz) dried shiitake mushrooms

100 g (3 1/2 oz) dried rice vermicelli

2 teaspoons vegetable oil

1 leek, halved lengthways and sliced

1.5 litres (48 fl oz) good-quality chicken stock

1 teaspoon dashi granules dissolved in 2 cups (500 ml/16 fl oz) boiling water

1/2 cup (125 ml/4 fl oz) soy sauce

2 tablespoons mirin

1 1/2 tablespoons sugar

100 g (3 1/2 oz) wom bok (Chinese cabbage), shredded

300 g (10 oz) silken firm tofu, cut into 2 cm (3/4 inch) cubes

400 g (13 oz) rump steak, thinly sliced

4 spring onions, sliced on the diagonal

1 Soak the shiitake mushrooms in ½ cup (125 ml/4 fl oz) boiling water for 20 minutes. Squeeze dry, reserving the soaking liquid. Discard the stalks and slice the caps. Meanwhile, soak the noodles in boiling water for 6–7 minutes, or until soft. Drain.

2 Heat a non-stick wok over medium heat, add the oil and swirl to coat. Add the leek and cook for 1–2 minutes, or until softened. Add the chicken stock, dashi broth, soy sauce, mirin, sugar and mushrooms and their soaking liquid. Bring to the boil, then reduce the heat and simmer for 5 minutes.

3 Add the wom bok and simmer for a further 5 minutes. Next, add the tofu and beef, and simmer for 2 minutes, or until the beef is cooked but still tender. Divide the noodles among the serving bowls and ladle on the soup. Serve garnished with the spring onion.

## VIETNAMESE COMBINATION SEAFOOD SOUP
(Canh chua)

Preparation time: 30 minutes
Total cooking time: 30 minutes
Serves 4

☆☆

1 tablespoon vegetable oil
1 stem lemon grass, white part only, finely chopped
1 fresh red chilli, finely chopped
2 cloves garlic, finely chopped
2 litres (64 fl oz) home-made fish or chicken stock (see page 23) or 1.5 litres (48 fl oz) purchased stock diluted with 2 cups (500 ml/16 fl oz) water
1 tablespoon tamarind purée
1 tablespoon fish sauce
400 g (13 oz) black mussels, scrubbed and debearded
500 g (1 lb) raw medium prawns, peeled and deveined, with tails intact
500 g (1 lb) firm white fish fillets (e.g. ling, blue eye or snapper), cut into 2.5 cm (1 inch) pieces
1 ripe tomato, cut into thin wedges
3 tablespoons fresh coriander leaves
1 tablespoon fresh Vietnamese mint
1 cup (90 g/3 oz) bean sprouts, tailed

1 Heat a non-stick wok over high heat, add the oil and swirl to coat the side of the wok. Add the lemon grass, chilli and garlic, then cook for 2 minutes, or until softened and fragrant. Add the stock, tamarind and fish sauce, bring to the boil, then reduce the heat to low and simmer for 15 minutes.

2 Discard any broken mussels or those that don't close when tapped on the bench. Increase the heat to medium–high, add the mussels, cover with a lid and cook for 2–3 minutes, tossing occasionally. Remove the lid and add the prawns, fish pieces and tomato wedges. Cook for a further 3 minutes, or until the seafood is completely cooked. Discard any unopened mussels. Stir in the coriander leaves and mint.

3 Divide the bean sprouts among four soup bowls, ladle in the soup and serve immediately.
NOTE: It is important to use a non-stick or stainless steel wok for this recipe as the tamarind purée will strip the seasoning layer from a regular wok.

*BELOW: Vietnamese combination seafood soup*

# CURRIES AND ASIAN ONE-POTS

Mention the word curry, and most people will immediately think of India. While the curry did first appear in India, like many other cooking styles it has transformed as it has travelled across cultures. The Vietnamese have their own version that combines Indian spices, French finesse and local ingredients. And in Malaysia, fish head curry demonstrates the delicate fusion of Indian and Chinese cuisine. Whatever the origin of the dish, the only essential accompaniment needed to set off a curry is a generous bowl of steamed rice.

# COOKING CURRIES AND ONE-POTS

The secret to curries is to fry up a great spice paste, then allow time for the flavours to develop.

## WHAT IS A CURRY?

The English word curry is derived from the Tamil word *kari*, meaning a 'spiced sauce'. Not confined to Indian cuisine, curries have spread to Southeast Asia. Today, curries are usually started with a spice powder or paste that is fried to release its aromas before the addition of the remaining ingredients.

There are two main types of curries, defined by the amount and consistency of the sauce. Curries with lots of sauce are classified as 'wet', whereas those with a thick, sticky sauce are regarded as 'dry'.

## COOKING CURRIES IN A WOK

Although most people associate woks with stir-frying, they are versatile enough to be used for curries (both Indian and Southeast Asian) and Asian one-pots.

India has developed a similar invention to the wok, called a 'karahi' or 'kadhai'. The same shape as a wok, karahis are two-handled and traditionally made from cast iron, which retains heat and prevents food from sticking during slower cooking, making them ideal for cooking the region's many curries. Baltistan, the home of Balti-style cooking in the far north of Pakistan, has a version of the karahi, called a 'balti'. Here the term balti refers to both the cuisine and the utensil, which is the region's primary piece of cooking equipment. Baltis also double as serving vessels, as the food is generally transferred from stovetop to table.

Woks are good for the initial spice-frying stage of cooking curries, while their large surface area is excellent for the rapid evaporation and concentration of flavour of dry curries. Beef rendang (page 78) is a classic example of a dry curry, as the liquid evaporates during cooking, leaving behind a deliciously rich coating, with enough oil to fry the meat and seal in its flavours. This process, called 'tempering', is suited to wok cooking, although care needs to be taken to ensure that the food doesn't burn or stick to the bottom of the wok.

## SOUTHEAST ASIAN CURRIES

Southeast Asian style curries are also often cooked in woks. Many are much quicker to cook than other curries; for example Thai red pork curry with baby corn (page 74) is ready to eat in 35 minutes. For these quick-cooking curries, the meat is often sliced in slender strips rather than cut into large cubes; this minimises the cooking time as they only need to be cooked long enough to just cook through and allow the sauce flavours time to develop.

## COOKING ASIAN ONE-POTS IN A WOK

When using a wok for slowly cooked braises and saucy dishes, the temperature and liquid levels should be closely monitored so that the sauce doesn't evaporate too quickly and start to stick before the meat or poultry becomes tender. This is relevant when cooking some of the Asian one-pots in this chapter; for example, Chicken braised

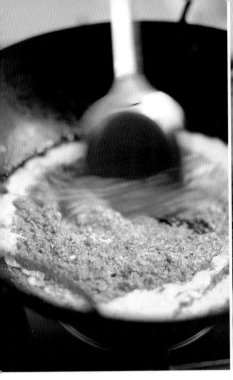

with ginger and star anise (page 78) and North Vietnamese braised pork leg (page 66). Our recipes specify whether a lid needs to be used, and at what stage it can be removed if the sauce needs to reduce and thicken, so it is important to follow these instructions during cooking.

## COCONUT MILK AND CREAM

Coconut milk and cream are very important in many curries, adding thickness and creaminess. Some recipes will ask for coconut milk and some will specify coconut cream, and some will use both. Both coconut milk and cream come from pressing the flesh of the coconut—the cream is the first pressing and the milk comes from subsequent pressings.

The thickness of the commercially available product varies enormously, depending on how much water was added to the coconut flesh and how many times the flesh was pressed. To confuse matters further, some brands don't distinguish between the milk and the cream. But in all cases, the thicker, creamier substance will float to the top.

When using the milk or cream, don't shake the can unless the recipe asks you to, because many recipes require the thicker substance from the top of the can to be added at a different stage than the thinner liquid on the bottom.

## COCONUT MILK IN CURRIES

Coconut milk is treated very differently from recipe to recipe and region to region. For instance, in India, there is no distinction between the cream and the milk. The difference becomes more important in Thai cuisine, where the thick layer of cream is often brought to the boil and 'cracked'—this refers to the process of heating the coconut cream to the point where it splits and a layer of oil separates. Curry pastes are often added to this oil to fry off and become fragrant, before the other ingredients are added.

In contrast, the spices for dishes from other countries, such as Malaysia, are often fried in oil first. The ingredients are then simmered in the thinner coconut milk, while the thick cream is stirred in at the final cooking stage to enrich and add a creamy consistency.

In Asian cuisines, it is considered preferable not to cover any dish containing thick coconut cream while it cooks—otherwise the coconut cream can curdle, affecting the dish's appearance so the sauce looks split. This can also leave an excessively oily slick on the surface.

## HINTS AND TIPS

● When using tamarind to make a slowly cooked dish, it is best to use either a stainless steel or non-stick wok. The acidity in tamarind reacts badly with carbon steel woks and can strip off their much-desired seasoning layer if left in contact with the wok for long periods. Food can also be tainted.
● Spices are an essential item in curries and contribute immeasurably to their

*SECRETS OF MAKING A CURRY*
*Most curries start with a spice paste as the basis of the flavour. In many cases, you can use one of the commercially made curry pastes now available. However, it's not hard to make your own and the flavour is unsurpassable.*

*A mortar and pestle is a good way to crush the spices, but a small food processor or spice blender will work just as well.*

*The treatment of coconut milk in curries varies enormously, but often it is brought to the boil and 'cracked'—heated until a layer of oil separates— before the spice paste is added.*

flavour. Because spices lose their potency quickly, they are best purchased in small amounts. Leftovers should be stored in airtight containers in a cool, dark place to prevent them going stale or rancid.
● Traditionally, authentic curries are made from scratch, including the toasting and grinding of whole spices. Toasting brings out the depth of flavour of spices.
● As with many slow-cooked dishes, the flavour of curries and Asian one-pots is enhanced by leaving them to mature, covered in the refrigerator, for up to 3 days. They can be frozen for up to 1 month. Seafood dishes are an exception to this, and should be eaten on the day they are made, and should not be frozen.
● There are thousands of curry pastes, and in most cases they can be interchanged or substituted with ready-made ones.

# THAI CURRY PASTES

Curry pastes are great to make in advance and store. They are surprisingly easy to make and they are a great flavour starter for soups and curries, and will also spice up other dishes.

Curry pastes will keep in an airtight container for 2 weeks in the fridge or 2 months in the freezer. To ensure that your container is clean, preheat the oven to very slow 120°C (250°F/Gas ½). Thoroughly wash a glass jar and its lid in hot, soapy water (or preferably a dishwasher) and rinse well with hot water. Put the jar in the oven for 20 minutes, or until completely dried—don't dry it with a tea towel or germs can be transferred to the jar.

### THAI RED CURRY PASTE
Preheat the oven to moderate 180°C (350°F/Gas 4). Put 15 large dried red chillies in a heatproof bowl, cover with boiling water and soak for 20 minutes. Drain, then remove the seeds and roughly chop the flesh.

Meanwhile, place 2 teaspoons shrimp paste (wrapped in foil), 2 teaspoons coriander seeds and 1 teaspoon each of white peppercorns and cumin seeds in a roasting tin and bake for 5–10 minutes, or until aromatic. Remove the foil.

Transfer the shrimp paste to a food processor or mortar and pestle with the chopped chilli, then add 5 chopped red Asian shallots, 10 chopped cloves garlic, 2 thinly sliced stems lemon grass (white part only), 1 tablespoon chopped fresh galangal, 2 tablespoons chopped fresh coriander root and 1 teaspoon finely grated kaffir lime rind. Process or grind until it forms a smooth paste. Makes 1 cup.

### THAI GREEN CURRY PASTE
Preheat the oven to moderate 180°C (350°F/Gas 4). Place 2 tablespoons coriander seeds, 2 teaspoons shrimp paste (wrapped in foil) and 1 teaspoon each of white peppercorns and cumin seeds in a roasting tin and bake for 5–10 minutes, or until aromatic. Remove the foil from the shrimp paste.

Transfer to a food processor or mortar and pestle and add 1 teaspoon sea salt, 4 finely chopped stems lemon grass (white part only), 2 teaspoons each of chopped fresh galangal and finely shredded fresh kaffir lime leaves, 1 tablespoon chopped fresh coriander root, 5 chopped red Asian shallots, 10 chopped cloves garlic and 16 seeded and chopped large green chillies. Process or grind until it forms a smooth paste. Makes 1 cup.

## CHU CHEE CURRY PASTE
Preheat the oven to moderate 180°C (350°F/Gas 4). Put 10 large dried red chillies in a heatproof bowl, cover with boiling water and soak for 20 minutes. Drain, then remove the seeds and roughly chop the flesh.

Meanwhile, put 1 teaspoon coriander seeds, 1 tablespoon shrimp paste (wrapped in foil) and 1 tablespoon white peppercorns in a roasting tin and bake for 5 minutes, or until aromatic. Remove the foil from the shrimp paste.

Transfer the toasted spices to a food processor or mortar and pestle with the chopped chilli and add 10 finely shredded fresh kaffir lime leaves, 10 chopped red Asian shallots, 2 teaspoons finely grated kaffir lime rind, 1 tablespoon chopped fresh coriander stem and root, 1 finely chopped stem lemon grass (white part only), 3 tablespoons chopped fresh galangal, 1 tablespoon chopped Krachai (see Note) and 6 chopped cloves garlic. Process or grind to a smooth paste. You may need to add a little lemon juice if the paste is too thick. Makes 1/2 cup.
NOTE: Krachai (bottled lesser galangal) is available from Asian grocery stores. It is an optional ingredient—you can omit it without detrimentally affecting the recipe.

## THAI YELLOW CURRY PASTE
Put 8 small fresh green chillies, 5 roughly chopped red Asian shallots, 1 chopped stem lemon grass (white part only), 2 chopped cloves garlic, 2 tablespoons finely chopped fresh galangal, 1 tablespoon each of lime juice and finely chopped fresh coriander stem and root, 1 teaspoon each of ground coriander and cumin and 1/2 teaspoon each of ground turmeric and black peppercorns in a food processor or mortar and pestle. Process or grind to a smooth paste. Makes 1/2 cup.

*FROM LEFT: Thai red curry paste, Thai green curry paste, Chu chee curry paste, Thai yellow curry paste.*

57

# ASSORTED CURRY PASTES

### BALTI CURRY PASTE

One at a time, dry-fry 4 tablespoons coriander seeds, 2 tablespoons cumin seeds, 2 crumbled cinnamon sticks, 2 teaspoons each of fennel seeds, black mustard seeds and cardamom seeds, 1 teaspoon fenugreek seeds and 6 whole cloves in a small frying pan over medium heat for 2–3 minutes, or until each spice starts to become aromatic.

Transfer the spices to a food processor or mortar and pestle, allow to cool and process or grind to a fine powder. Add

20 fresh curry leaves, 4 fresh bay leaves, 1 tablespoon ground turmeric, 2 crushed cloves garlic, 1 tablespoon grated fresh ginger, 1 1/2 teaspoons chilli powder and 3/4 cup (185 ml/6 fl oz) malt vinegar, and mix together well.

Heat 1/2 cup (125 ml/4 fl oz) vegetable oil in the frying pan, add the paste and cook, stirring, for 5 minutes. Add 1/4 cup (60 ml/2 fl oz) malt vinegar and mix well. Makes 1 cup.

### MADRAS CURRY PASTE

Dry-fry 2 1/2 tablespoons coriander seeds and 1 tablespoon cumin seeds separately in a frying pan for 30 seconds–1 minute, or until aromatic, being careful not to burn them. Cool, then grind the seeds in a food processor or mortar and pestle.

Transfer to a small bowl and add 2 crushed cloves garlic, 2 teaspoons grated fresh ginger, 1 teaspoon each of brown mustard seeds, chilli powder, ground turmeric and salt, and 1/2 teaspoon cracked black peppercorns.

Mix together well. Add 3–4 tablespoons white vinegar and mix to a smooth paste. Makes 1/2 cup.

## VINDALOO CURRY PASTE
Put 2 tablespoons grated fresh ginger, 4 chopped cloves garlic, 4 chopped fresh red chillies, 1 tablespoon each of ground coriander and cumin seeds, 2 teaspoons each of ground turmeric and ground cardamom, 1 teaspoon ground cinnamon, 4 whole cloves, 6 peppercorns and 1/2 cup (125 ml/4 fl oz) cider vinegar in a food processor and process for 20 seconds, or until well combined and smooth. Makes 1/2 cup.

## MUSAMAN CURRY PASTE
Preheat the oven to moderate 180°C (350°F/Gas 4). Put 10 dried red chillies in a heatproof bowl and cover with boiling water. Soak for 20 minutes.

Drain, remove the seeds and roughly chop the flesh.

Meanwhile, put 5 chopped red Asian shallots, 1 finely chopped stem lemon grass (white part only), 1 tablespoon chopped fresh galangal, 10 chopped cloves garlic, 3 cardamom pods, 1 tablespoon coriander seeds, 1 teaspoon cumin seeds, 1 teaspoon shrimp paste (wrapped in foil) and 1/4 teaspoon black peppercorns in a roasting tin and bake for 5 minutes, or until aromatic. Remove the foil from the shrimp paste.

Transfer the roasted ingredients to a food processor or mortar and pestle, then add the chopped chilli, 1/2 teaspoon ground nutmeg and 1/4 teaspoon each of ground cinnamon and ground cloves. Process or grind to a smooth paste. If the mixture is too dry, add a little white vinegar. Makes 1/2 cup.

## JUNGLE CURRY PASTE
Soak 12 large dried red chillies in boiling water for 20 minutes. Drain and chop.

Meanwhile, wrap 1 tablespoon shrimp paste in foil and heat under a hot grill for 1 minute, or until aromatic. Remove the foil from the shrimp paste.

Transfer the shrimp paste to a food processor, add the chopped chilli, 4 red Asian shallots, 4 sliced cloves garlic, 1 sliced stem lemon grass (white part only), 2 chopped small coriander roots, 1 tablespoon each of finely chopped fresh galangal and finely chopped fresh ginger and 1 teaspoon each of ground white pepper and salt, then blend until a smooth paste forms—add a little water, if necessary. Makes 1/2 cup.

*FROM LEFT: Balti curry paste, Madras curry paste, Vindaloo curry paste, Musaman curry paste, Jungle curry paste.*

**1** Scoop the thick coconut cream from the top of the can—you should have about 1/2 cup (125 ml/ 4 fl oz). Put this thick cream in a wok and bring to the boil, then simmer for 10 minutes, or until the oil starts to separate from the cream. Add the curry paste and simmer, stirring regularly, for 5 minutes, or until fragrant.

**2** Add the meat and cook, stirring, for 3–5 minutes, or until it changes colour. Stir in the fish sauce, palm sugar, lime leaves, coconut milk and remaining coconut cream, and simmer for 1 hour, or until the meat is tender and the sauce slightly thickened.

**3** Add the eggplant and cook for 10 minutes, or until tender. If the sauce is too thick, add a little water. Stir in half the basil, garnish with the remainder and serve with rice.

## RED COOKED PORK BELLY

Preparation time: 10 minutes + 20 minutes soaking
Total cooking time: 2 hours 10 minutes
Serves 6

☆

6 dried shiitake mushrooms
2 teaspoons peanut oil
1 kg (2 lb) piece pork belly
2 cups (500 ml/16 fl oz) good-quality chicken
   stock
1/4 cup (60 ml/2 fl oz) dark soy sauce
1/4 cup (60 ml/2 fl oz) Chinese rice wine
4 cloves garlic, bruised
5 x 5 cm (2 x 2 inch) piece fresh ginger, sliced
1 piece dried mandarin or tangerine peel
2 teaspoons Sichuan peppercorns
2 star anise
1 cinnamon stick
1 1/2 tablespoons Chinese rock sugar (see Note)

**1** Cover the mushrooms in 1 cup (250 ml/8 fl oz) boiling water and soak for 20 minutes, or until soft. Squeeze dry, reserving the liquid.

**2** Heat a large wok over high heat, add the oil and swirl to coat. Add the pork, skin-side-down, and cook for 5 minutes, or until well browned, then turn over and cook for a further 6 minutes, or until sealed.

**3** Add the stock, soy sauce, rice wine, garlic, ginger, citrus peel, spices, reserved mushroom soaking liquid and 2 cups (500 ml/16 fl oz) water. Bring to the boil, then reduce the heat to low and simmer, covered, for 1 1/4 hours.

## THAI RED BEEF CURRY WITH THAI EGGPLANT
(AUBERGINE)

Preparation time: 40 minutes
Total cooking time: 1 hour 30 minutes
Serves 4

☆ ☆

270 ml (9 fl oz) can coconut cream
   (do not shake the can)
2 tablespoons Thai red curry paste
   (see page 56)
500 g (1 lb) round or topside steak,
   cut into strips
2 tablespoons fish sauce
1 tablespoon grated palm sugar
5 fresh kaffir lime leaves
2 cups (500 ml/16 fl oz) coconut milk
8 Thai eggplants (aubergines), halved
2 tablespoons finely shredded fresh Thai basil

*ABOVE: Thai red beef curry*
*with Thai eggplant*

4 Add the sugar and mushrooms to the wok and cook for a further 45 minutes, or until the pork is very tender. Remove the pork from the stock and cut into slices about 1 cm (1/2 inch) thick. Strain the liquid into a bowl, then return the strained liquid to the wok. Bring to the boil and continue boiling until reduced to about 3/4 cup (185 ml/6 fl oz).

5 Place the pork on a platter with the mushrooms and spoon on some of the cooking liquid. Serve with steamed rice as part of a banquet.

NOTE: Chinese rock sugar is the crystallised form of saturated sugar liquor. It is named for its irregular rock-shaped pieces. It imparts a rich flavour, especially to braised or 'red cooked' foods as well as sweets, glazing them with a translucent sheen. Available in the Asian section of large supermarkets, or in Asian grocery stores.

## BUTTER CHICKEN
(Murgh makhani)

Preparation time: 10 minutes
Total cooking time: 35 minutes
Serves 4–6

☆ ☆

2 tablespoons peanut oil
1 kg (2 lb) chicken thigh fillets, quartered
60 g (2 oz) butter or ghee
2 teaspoons garam masala
2 teaspoons sweet paprika
2 teaspoons ground coriander
1 tablespoon finely chopped fresh ginger
1/4 teaspoon chilli powder
1 cinnamon stick
6 cardamom pods, bruised
350 g (11 oz) puréed tomatoes
1 tablespoon sugar
1/4 cup (60 g/2 oz) plain yoghurt
1/2 cup (125 ml/4 fl oz) cream
1 tablespoon lemon juice

1 Heat a wok to very hot, add 1 tablespoon oil and swirl to coat. Add half the chicken and stir-fry for about 4 minutes, or until nicely browned. Remove from the wok. Add a little extra oil, if needed, and brown the remaining chicken thigh fillets. Remove from the wok.

2 Reduce the heat to medium, add the butter and stir until melted. Add the garam masala, paprika, coriander, ginger, chilli powder, cinnamon stick and cardamom pods, and stir-fry for 1 minute, or until the spices are fragrant. Return the chicken pieces to the wok and mix them in until they are coated in the spices.

3 Add the puréed tomatoes and sugar to the wok and simmer, stirring, for 15 minutes, or until the chicken is tender and the sauce is thick.

4 Stir in the yoghurt, cream and lemon juice and simmer for 5 minutes, or until the sauce has thickened slightly. Serve with poppadoms.

BUTTER CHICKEN
Butter chicken is such a popular meal in Indian restaurants outside India that many people believe it was created to make Indian food more accessible to Western palates. In fact, Butter chicken hails from the Punjab region in northwest India. This region of India has a culinary heritage influenced by many past invaders, including Persians, Afghans, Greeks and Mongols, which has resulted in a rich and diverse cuisine. The Punjabis have a reputation as being the greatest food lovers in India and no doubt the spread of Punjabi food somewhat accounts for the popularity of Indian food outside India—Tandoori chicken being another favourite. Butter chicken, or 'Murgh makhani' is a staple dish of roadside eateries, or 'dhabas', all over the Punjab.

*LEFT: Butter chicken*

1 Put the tamarind pulp and ½ cup (125 ml/ 4 fl oz) boiling water in a bowl and set aside to cool. Mash the pulp with your fingertips to dissolve the pulp, then strain and reserve the liquid—discard the pulp.

2 Heat a non-stick wok over high heat, add the oil and swirl to coat. Add the beef in batches and cook over high heat for 5 minutes each batch, or until browned all over. Reduce the heat, add the coconut milk and cardamom pods, and simmer for 1 hour, or until the beef is tender. Remove the beef from the wok, then strain the cooking liquid into a bowl.

3 Heat the coconut cream in the wok and stir in the curry paste. Cook for 10 minutes, or until the oil starts to separate from the cream.

4 Add the fish sauce, onions, potatoes, beef mixture, palm sugar, peanuts, tamarind water and the reserved cooking liquid. Simmer for 25–30 minutes, or until thickened and the meat is tender.

NOTES: It is important that the pickling onions and baby potatoes are small and similar in size (about 25–30 g (¾–1 oz) each), to ensure that they cook evenly.

It is important to use a non-stick or stainless steel wok as the tamarind purée will react with the metal in a regular wok and badly taint the dish.

## THAI MUSAMAN BEEF CURRY
(Gaeng Musaman nuer)

Preparation time: 30 minutes + cooling
Total cooking time: 2 hours
Serves 4

☆ ☆

1 tablespoon tamarind pulp

2 tablespoons vegetable oil

750 g (1½ lb) lean stewing beef, cubed

2 cups (500 ml/16 fl oz) coconut milk

4 cardamom pods, bruised

2 cups (500 ml/16 fl oz) coconut cream

2 tablespoons Musaman curry paste
  (see page 59)

2 tablespoons fish sauce

8 pickling onions (see Notes)

8 baby potatoes (see Notes)

2 tablespoons grated palm sugar

½ cup (80 g/2¾ oz) unsalted peanuts, roasted
  and ground

*ABOVE: Thai Musaman beef curry*

## INDIAN EGGPLANT
(AUBERGINE) **PICKLE**
(Brinjal achar)

Cut 1 kg (2 lb) slender eggplants (aubergines) in half lengthways, then sprinkle with salt and leave for 30 minutes. Meanwhile, put 6 cloves garlic, 1 tablespoon roughly chopped fresh ginger, 1 tablespoon garam masala, 1 teaspoon ground turmeric, 1 teaspoon chilli powder and 1 tablespoon vegetable oil in a food processor or blender, and process to a paste. Rinse the salt off the eggplant and pat dry with paper towels. Heat ⅓ cup (80 ml/2¾ fl oz) vegetable oil in a large frying pan, add the eggplant and cook for 5 minutes, or until golden brown. Add the spice paste and cook, stirring, for 2 minutes. Stir in 1⅔ cups (410 ml/13 fl oz) vegetable oil and cook for 10–15 minutes, stirring occasionally. Spoon into clean, warm jars and seal. Store in the fridge for up to 5 days. Serve with Indian curries. Makes 2 cups (serves 24).

TAM/
Becau
tamar
is ver
do no
steel
tamar
when
are lo
strip
seaso
metal
and le
black

RIGH

# SALTY MALAYSIAN CHICKEN CURRY
(Ayam kapitan)

Preparation time: 35 minutes
Total cooking time: 1 hour 20 minutes
Serves 4–6

1 1/2 teaspoons dried shrimp

6–8 fresh red chillies, seeded and finely chopped

4 cloves garlic, finely chopped

3 stems lemon grass, white part only, finely chopped

2 teaspoons ground turmeric

10 candlenuts

1/3 cup (80 ml/2 3/4 fl oz) vegetable oil

2 large onions, chopped

1 cup (250 ml/8 fl oz) coconut milk

1.5 kg (3 lb) chicken, cut into 8 pieces

1/2 cup (125 ml/4 fl oz) coconut cream

2 tablespoons lime juice

1 Put the shrimp in a frying pan and dry-fry over low heat, shaking the pan regularly, for 3 minutes, or until dark orange and aromatic. Transfer to a food processor and finely grind.
2 Put the chilli, garlic, lemon grass, turmeric, candlenuts and 2 tablespoons of the oil in a food processor and process in short bursts until very finely chopped, regularly scraping down the side of the bowl with a rubber spatula.
3 Heat a wok over high heat, add the remaining oil and swirl. Add the onion and 1/4 teaspoon salt, and cook, stirring regularly, over low heat for 8 minutes, or until golden. Add the processed spice mixture and ground shrimp, and stir for 5 minutes, or until the mixture is cooked thoroughly. If it begins to stick to the bottom of the wok, add 2 tablespoons coconut milk.
4 Add the chicken to the wok and cook, stirring, for 5 minutes, or until beginning to brown. Stir in the remaining coconut milk and 1 1/2 cups (375 ml/12 fl oz) water, and bring to the boil. Reduce the heat to very low and simmer, covered, for 45 minutes. Remove the lid and skim off any excess oil with a spoon. Simmer, uncovered, for 25 minutes, or until the chicken is cooked and the sauce has thickened slightly. Skim off any excess oil. Add the coconut cream and bring the mixture back to the boil, stirring constantly, until combined. Stir in the lime juice, then serve with rice.

NONYA COOKING
Incorporating the saltiness of dried shrimps with the heat of chillies and fragrance of lemon grass, Ayam kapitan is a classic example of Malaysia's tradition of Nonya cooking. Nonya cooking developed from combining Chinese and Malaysian ingredients and cooking techniques when Malaysia was settled by Chinese immigrants from the 15th century onwards. The subsequent marriage between Chinese immigrants and the native Malaysian population led to the creation of a distinct cuisine referred to as Nonya cooking. Nonya is the label for the Malaysian wives of Chinese men (the husbands were called 'Baba'). Chillies, shrimp paste, coconut milk and aromatic herbs and spices are combined with Chinese staples such as pork and noodles.

*LEFT: Salty Malaysian chicken curry*

THE ESSENTIAL WOK COOKBOOK

## NORTH VIETNAMESE BRAISED PORK LEG

Preparation time: 30 minutes + 2 hours marinating
Total cooking time: 1 hour 45 minutes
Serves 4–6

☆☆

1 1/2 tablespoons vegetable oil
1 kg (2 lb) boned pork leg in one piece, skin and fat intact (1.3 kg/2 lb 10 oz with bone in)
1 teaspoon shrimp paste
5 cloves garlic, crushed
3 large red Asian shallots, finely chopped
3 teaspoons ground galangal
1 teaspoon ground turmeric
2 teaspoons sugar
2 tablespoons fish sauce
700 ml (23 fl oz) home-made chicken stock (see page 23) or 2 cups (500 ml/16 fl oz) purchased stock diluted with 200 ml (6 1/2 fl oz) water
2 tablespoons Chinese black vinegar
1 teaspoon cornflour
3 spring onions, thinly sliced on the diagonal

1 Heat a wok to very hot, add 2 teaspoons of the oil and swirl to coat. Put the pork in the wok, skin-side-down, and cook for 2 minutes until well browned. Turn and cook the other side for a further 2 minutes, or until browned. Remove and set aside to cool. Cut the pork into 3 cm (1 1/4 inch) cubes.
2 Preheat the grill to high, wrap the shrimp paste in foil, and put under the hot grill for 5 minutes. Cool, remove the foil, then put the paste in a large bowl with the garlic, shallots, galangal, turmeric, sugar and fish sauce and mix well. Add the pork to the bowl and coat it in the marinade. Cover and refrigerate for 1–2 hours.
3 Heat the wok until hot, add the remaining oil, and swirl to coat. Add the pork and stir-fry in batches for 1–2 minutes, or until browned. Pour in the stock and vinegar, and simmer, covered, over low heat for 1 1/2 hours, or until very tender. Skim the surface constantly to remove any fat and scum that floats to the surface.
4 Dissolve the cornflour in 1 teaspoon water. Remove the pork from the liquid with a slotted spoon and set aside. Bring the remaining stock to a simmer and skim the surface. Mix in the cornflour paste. Simmer for 2 minutes, or until thickened, then return the pork to the wok and add the spring onion. Season and serve.

VIETNAM
Divided geographically and culturally into three main regions, the small Southeast Asian nation of Vietnam has been influenced by many cultures, principally China, which colonised it for over 1,000 years. The cuisine of northern Vietnam more closely resembles that of China than the other regions (due to their shared border). The cuisine in central Vietnam is the spiciest due to the introduction of chillies by the Portuguese. It is also considered Vietnam's most refined cuisine, as it centres around the ancient royal capital Hué, and is influenced by the court cuisine that was developed for local royalty. Southern Vietnamese cuisine centres on Saigon (Ho Chi Minh City) and is characterised by French and Indian influences. Vietnam is the only Southeast Asian country to widely retain the Chinese practice of eating with chopsticks.

*RIGHT: North Vietnamese braised pork leg*

66

Scrub the mussels clean
with a stiff brush.

Pull out the hairy beards
from the mussels.

# MUSSELS WITH BLACK BEANS AND CORIANDER

Preparation time: 20 minutes
Total cooking time: 10 minutes
Serves 4

 ☆ ☆

1.5 kg (3 lb) black mussels
1 tablespoon peanut oil
2 tablespoons black beans, rinsed and mashed
2 cloves garlic, finely chopped
1 teaspoon finely chopped fresh ginger
2 long fresh red chillies, seeded and finely
  chopped
1 teaspoon finely chopped fresh coriander
  leaves
1 tablespoon finely chopped fresh coriander
  root
1/4 cup (60 ml/2 fl oz) Chinese rice wine
2 tablespoons lime juice
2 teaspoons sugar
1/2 cup (15 g/1/2 oz) fresh coriander leaves,
  roughly chopped, extra

1 Scrub the mussels with a stiff brush and pull out the hairy beards. Discard any broken mussels, or open ones that don't close when tapped on the bench. Rinse well.

2 Heat a wok until very hot, add the oil and swirl to coat. Add the black beans, garlic, ginger, chilli, chopped coriander leaves and coriander root, and cook over low heat for 2–3 minutes, or until fragrant.

3 Pour in the rice wine and increase the heat to high. Add half the mussels in a single layer and cover with a tight-fitting lid. Cook for 2–3 minutes, or until the mussels have just opened. Discard any that do not open. Remove from the wok, and repeat with the remaining mussels.

4 Transfer the mussels to a serving dish, leaving the cooking liquid in the wok. Add the lime juice, sugar and extra coriander leaves to the wok and cook for 30 seconds. Pour the sauce over the mussels and serve with rice.

*ABOVE: Mussels with black beans and coriander*

GOSHT KORMA
While the word 'korma' is derived from the Turkish word 'qawurmah', which comes from the verb 'to fry', it is now most widely associated with a Moghul Indian dish consisting of a main ingredient which is braised or stewed in liquid. Kormas are generally characterised by the addition of ingredients such as cream or yoghurt, or nuts such as almonds, which enrich the flavour and texture of the dish.

# SPICY INDIAN LAMB STEW
(Gosht korma)

Preparation time: 30 minutes + 1 hour marinating
Total cooking time: 2 hours
Serves 4–6

2 kg (4 lb) leg of lamb, boned, trimmed
    and cut into 3 cm (1¼ inch) cubes
1 onion, chopped
2 teaspoons grated fresh ginger
3 cloves garlic
2 teaspoons ground coriander
2 teaspoons ground cumin
¾–1 teaspoon ground cardamom
large pinch of cayenne pepper
2 tablespoons ghee or vegetable oil
1 onion, extra, sliced
1 tablespoon tomato paste (tomato purée)
½ cup (125 g/4 oz) plain yoghurt
1 cinnamon stick
½ cup (125 ml/4 fl oz) thick (double) cream
½ cup (50 g/1¾ oz) ground almonds
toasted slivered almonds, to garnish

1 Put the lamb in a bowl. Grind the onion, ginger, garlic, coriander, cumin, cardamom, cayenne pepper and ½ teaspoon salt into a smooth paste in a food processor. Coat the lamb in the spice mix and marinate for 1 hour.
2 Heat the ghee in a wok over medium heat, add the extra onion and cook, stirring, over low heat for 5–7 minutes, or until the onion is soft. Add the lamb and cook, stirring constantly, for 8–10 minutes, or until the lamb changes colour.
3 Stir in the tomato paste, yoghurt, cinnamon stick and 3 cups (750 ml/24 fl oz) water. Reduce the heat and simmer, covered, stirring occasionally, for 1¼ hours, or until the meat is tender. If it becomes too dry, pour in ½ cup (125 ml/4 fl oz) water. Add the cream and almonds and cook for 10–15 minutes. Season and garnish with slivered almonds. Serve with rice.

# PUMPKIN CURRY

Preparation time: 20 minutes
Total cooking time: 30 minutes
Serves 4

2 tablespoons sesame seeds
1 tablespoon peanut oil
1 onion, finely chopped
3 cloves garlic, crushed
2 teaspoons finely chopped fresh ginger
1 teaspoon ground coriander
2 teaspoons ground cumin
2 teaspoons finely chopped fresh red chilli

RIGHT: Spicy Indian
lamb stew

800 g (1 lb 10 oz) pumpkin, cut into 2 cm
  (³/4 inch) cubes
1 cup (250 ml/8 fl oz) coconut cream
1 cup (250 ml/8 fl oz) vegetable stock
2 tablespoons fresh coriander leaves

1 Heat a wok to hot. Stir-fry the sesame seeds for
1–2 minutes, or until toasted. Remove. Swirl the
oil in the wok. Stir-fry the onion for 3 minutes,
or until soft. Add the garlic, ginger, spices and
chilli, and cook for 1 minute, or until fragrant.
2 Add the pumpkin, stir-fry for 1 minute, then
pour in the coconut cream and stock and bring
to the boil. Reduce the heat and simmer, loosely
covered, for 10 minutes. Uncover and simmer
for 5–10 minutes, or until the pumpkin is tender
and the liquid is thickened. Season with salt and
scatter with the sesame seeds and coriander.

# THAI GREEN CHICKEN CURRY
(Gaeng khiao wang gai)

Preparation time: 15 minutes
Total cooking time: 30 minutes
Serves 4

## CURRY PASTE
1 tablespoon shrimp paste
1 teaspoon coriander seeds, toasted
¹/2 teaspoon cumin seeds, toasted
¹/4 teaspoon white peppercorns
5 fresh coriander roots
3 tablespoons chopped fresh galangal
10 long fresh green chillies, chopped
1 stem lemon grass, white part only, chopped
6 red Asian shallots
3 cloves garlic
1 teaspoon grated kaffir lime or lime rind
2 tablespoons peanut oil

1 cup (250 ml/8 fl oz) coconut cream
500 g (1 lb) chicken thigh fillets, thinly sliced
125 g (4 oz) snake beans, sliced
2 cups (500 ml/16 fl oz) coconut milk
150 g (5 oz) broccoli, cut into small florets
1 tablespoon grated palm sugar
2–3 tablespoons fish sauce
5 tablespoons fresh coriander leaves, plus
  extra, to garnish

1 To make the curry paste, preheat the grill to
high, wrap the shrimp paste in foil, and put
under the hot grill for 5 minutes. Cool, remove
the foil, then put in a food processor.
2 Put the coriander seeds, cumin seeds and
peppercorns in a mortar and pestle and grind
into a fine powder. Transfer to the food
processor with ¹/4 teaspoon salt and the
remaining paste ingredients. Blend until smooth.
3 Put the coconut cream in a wok over
high heat, bring to the boil, then simmer for
10 minutes, or until the oil starts to separate
from the cream.
4 Reduce the heat to medium. Stir in half
the curry paste and cook for 2–3 minutes, or
until fragrant. Add the chicken and cook for
3–4 minutes. Stir in the beans, coconut milk and
broccoli. Bring to the boil, then reduce the heat
and simmer for 4–5 minutes, or until cooked.
Stir in the sugar, fish sauce and coriander leaves.
Garnish with coriander and serve with rice.
NOTE: Store the remainder of the curry paste
in an airtight container in the fridge for up to
2 weeks.

*ABOVE: Thai green
chicken curry*

Stir in the pork and shallots. Add the fish sauce, kecap manis, pepper and 1 cup (250 ml/8 fl oz) warm water. Stir until all the sugar has melted.
**3** Cover and cook for 10 minutes, stirring occasionally, then cook, uncovered, stirring often, for 20–30 minutes, or until the sauce is sticky and the meat is cooked. Garnish with coriander and serve with rice.

## MALAYSIAN FISH HEAD CURRY

Preparation time: 20 minutes
Total cooking time: 40 minutes
Serves 6

CURRY PASTE

4 cloves garlic, chopped

4 red Asian shallots, chopped

I stem lemon grass, white part only, finely chopped

2 x 3 cm (3/4 x 1 1/4 inch) piece fresh galangal, finely chopped

2 large fresh red chillies, chopped

400 ml (13 fl oz) can coconut cream (do not shake)

10 fresh curry leaves

2 tablespoons Malaysian seafood curry powder

1/2 teaspoon ground turmeric

2 cups (500 ml/16 fl oz) good-quality fish stock

2 tablespoons tamarind purée

2 tablespoons fish sauce

I tablespoon sugar

200 g (6 1/2 oz) slender eggplants (aubergines), cut into 1 cm (1/2 inch) slices

150 g (5 oz) okra, cut into 1 cm (1/2 inch) slices

4 x 200 g (6 1/2 oz) fish heads (ask your fishmonger to clean and scale them)

2 ripe tomatoes, cut into eighths

2 large fresh green chillies, cut into 1 cm (1/2 inch) slices

**1** To make the curry paste, put the ingredients in a food processor or blender and blend to a smooth paste, adding a little water if needed.
**2** Lift the thick cream off the top of the coconut cream. Put the cream in a non-stick wok and bring to the boil, then simmer for 10 minutes, or until the oil starts to separate from the cream. Add the curry paste and stir-fry for 5 minutes,

## THAI SWEET PORK
(Moo wan)

Preparation time: 10 minutes
Total cooking time: 50 minutes
Serves 4–6

850 g (1 lb 12 oz) pork spareribs

1/2 cup (125 g/4 oz) grated palm sugar

4 red Asian shallots, sliced

I tablespoon fish sauce

I tablespoon kecap manis

1/2 teaspoon ground white pepper

fresh coriander leaves, to garnish

**1** Remove the bone and outer rind from the ribs. Cut into 1 cm (1/2 inch) slices.
**2** Put the sugar in a wok with 2 tablespoons water and stir over low heat until the sugar has dissolved. Increase the heat and boil, without stirring, for 5 minutes, or until the sugar turns evenly golden.

*ABOVE: Thai sweet pork*

or until fragrant. Add the curry leaves, curry powder and turmeric and cook for 1 minute. **3** Stir in the stock, tamarind purée, fish sauce, sugar and remaining coconut cream and bring to the boil for 1 minute. Add the eggplant and okra, reduce the heat and simmer for 15 minutes. Add the fish heads and cook for a further 5 minutes, turning to cook evenly. Stir in the tomato and green chilli until heated through and the vegetables are tender and the fish eyes opaque. Season with salt and pepper, then serve with rice.

## SICHUAN CHICKEN

Preparation time: 10 minutes
Total cooking time: 25 minutes
Serves 4

☆

1/4 teaspoon five-spice powder
750 g (1 1/2 lb) chicken thigh fillets, halved
2 tablespoons peanut oil
1 tablespoon julienned fresh ginger

1 teaspoon chilli bean paste
1 teaspoon Sichuan peppercorns, crushed
2 tablespoons light soy sauce
1 tablespoon Chinese rice wine
600 g (1 1/4 lb) baby bok choy, leaves separated

**1** Rub the five-spice powder over the chicken pieces. Heat a wok to very hot, add half the oil and swirl to coat the side of the wok. Add the chicken and cook for 2 minutes on each side, or until nicely browned. Remove from the wok.
**2** Reduce the heat to medium. Add the ginger and cook for 30 seconds. Add the chilli bean paste and crushed peppercorns. Return the chicken to the wok, then add the soy sauce, Chinese rice wine and 1/2 cup (125 ml/4 fl oz) water and simmer for 15–20 minutes, or until the chicken is cooked through.
**3** Meanwhile, heat the remaining oil in a saucepan. Add the bok choy and toss gently and constantly for 1 minute, or until the leaves wilt and the stems are tender. Serve with the chicken and steamed rice.

SICHUAN AROMATICS
Sichuan, in China, is considered to be the land of aromatics, where pungent, hot spices, such as hot chilli peppers and Sichuan peppers, are relished. Nearly all the dishes are flavoured with fermented bean paste and sesame oil or sesame purée, which give rise to some often very colourful names such as 'strange flavoured' or 'familiar taste'. The fiery nature of Sichuan cooking suits the climate, helping to cool the body in the hot humid summers and warm the soul during the bitterly cold winters.

*LEFT: Sichuan chicken*

# FLAVOURED RICE

### INDONESIAN COCONUT RICE
(Nasi lemak)
Wash 1½ cups (300 g/10 oz) medium-grain rice in a sieve until the water runs clear. Set aside for 30 minutes.

Put the rice, 1 cup (250 ml/8 fl oz) water, 1 cup (250 ml/8 fl oz) coconut milk and 1 pandanus leaf, tied in a knot, in a large saucepan. Bring to the boil, cover, reduce the heat to very low and simmer for 12 minutes. Remove from the heat and set aside for 10 minutes. Take out the pandanus leaf. Fluff the rice with a fork and serve garnished with spring onion, if desired. An excellent accompaniment to both Indonesian and Malaysian dishes. Serves 4.

### INDIAN SPICED GHEE RICE
Wash 1½ cups (300 g/10 oz) basmati rice in a sieve until the water runs clear. Set aside for 30 minutes.

Heat 25 g (¾ oz) ghee or clarified butter in a large saucepan. Add 4 bruised cardamom pods, 1 cinnamon stick, 3 dried curry leaves, 1 chopped clove garlic, 2 teaspoons grated fresh ginger and 1 teaspoon cumin seeds and stir-fry until fragrant. Add the rice, stirring to coat well, then pour in 2 cups (500 ml/16 fl oz) water. Bring to the boil, cover, reduce the heat to very low and simmer for 12 minutes. Remove from the heat and set aside for 10 minutes, covered. Remove the lid, stir in 2 tablespoons sultanas, and an extra teaspoon of ghee, then serve with curries. Serves 4.

### SAFFRON RICE
Wash 1½ cups (300 g/10 oz) long-grain rice in a sieve until the water runs clear, then set aside for 30 minutes.

Meanwhile, put ¼ teaspoon saffron threads in a small bowl, cover with 2 tablespoons hot water and stand for 2–3 minutes.

Thinly slice 1 onion. Heat 1 tablespoon olive oil in a large saucepan, add the onion and sauté for 7–8 minutes over medium heat, or until golden brown. Remove the onion from the pan and keep warm.

Add the rice to the saucepan, and stir to coat with the remaining oil. Add 1 cup (250 ml/8 fl oz) chicken stock and 1 cup (250 ml/8 fl oz) water, bring to the boil then add the saffron threads and the soaking water. Simmer for 2–3 minutes before covering with a tight-fitting lid. Reduce the heat to very low and cook for 10 minutes. Remove from the heat and set aside, covered, for 10 minutes, before stirring in the onion. Serve immediately. An excellent accompaniment to curries. Serves 4.

## LEMON GRASS AND LIME RICE

Wash 2 cups (400 g/13 oz) long-grain rice in a sieve until the water runs clear, then set aside for 30 minutes.

Put in a saucepan with 1 cup (250 ml/8 fl oz) water, 2 cups (500 ml/16 fl oz) coconut cream, 1 bruised lemon grass stem, 2 fresh kaffir lime leaves and 1 teaspoon salt. Bring to the boil over high heat, stir well, then reduce the heat to very low. Cover with a tight-fitting lid and cook for 15 minutes. Remove from the heat and leave to stand, covered, for 5 minutes. Lightly stir the rice with a fork to incorporate any coconut cream that has not been absorbed. Remove the lemon grass and lime leaves. Great with stir-fries. Serves 4–6.

## GINGER AND SPRING ONION RICE

Wash 1¼ cups (250 g/8 oz) jasmine rice in a sieve until the water runs clear, then set aside for 30 minutes.

Transfer the rice to a large saucepan. Add 1¾ cups (440 ml/14 fl oz) water and bring to the boil. Reduce the heat to very low and cook, covered, for 10 minutes. Remove the pan from the heat and stand, covered, for 10 minutes.

Heat 1 tablespoon vegetable oil in a small saucepan over medium–low heat. When the oil is warm but not smoking, remove the pan from the heat and add 2 teaspoons grated fresh ginger and 3 finely chopped spring onions. Season with ¼ teaspoon salt, stirring quickly to combine, taking care not to brown. Stir this mixture through the rice and add 1 tablespoon soy sauce. Great with stir-fries. Serves 4.

*FROM LEFT: Indonesian coconut rice, Indian spiced ghee rice, Saffron rice, Lemon grass and lime rice, Ginger and spring onion rice.*

I small carrot, quartered lengthways and
  thinly sliced on the diagonal
150 g (5 oz) snake beans, cut into 2 cm
  ($^3/_4$ inch) lengths
50 g (1$^3/_4$ oz) sliced bamboo shoots
fresh Thai basil, to garnish

1 Heat a wok over medium heat, add the oil
and swirl to coat the side of the wok. Add
the garlic and curry paste and cook, stirring,
for 5 minutes.
2 Add the fish sauce, ground candlenuts, fish
stock, whisky, kaffir lime leaves, prawns, carrot,
beans and bamboo shoots. Bring to the boil,
then reduce the heat and simmer for 5 minutes,
or until cooked. Garnish with the basil, then serve.

## THAI RED PORK CURRY WITH BABY CORN

Preparation time: 10 minutes
Total cooking time: 25 minutes
Serves 4

400 ml (13 fl oz) can coconut cream
  (do not shake)
1$^1/_2$ tablespoons Thai red curry paste
  (see page 56)
500 g (1 lb) pork loin, trimmed of excess fat
  and sinew, cut into 2 cm ($^3/_4$ inch) cubes
2 tablespoons fish sauce
I tablespoon grated palm sugar
4 fresh kaffir lime leaves, halved lengthways
115 g (4 oz) fresh baby corn, cut in half on the
  diagonal
I cup (30 g/1 oz) loosely packed fresh Thai basil
thinly sliced fresh red chilli, to garnish

1 Open the can of coconut cream and lift off
the thick cream from the top. Put the cream
in a wok and bring to the boil, then simmer for
10 minutes, or until the oil starts to separate from
the cream. Add the curry paste and mix well.
Simmer for 2–3 minutes, or until fragrant,
stirring frequently.
2 Add the pork cubes and cook, stirring, for
2–3 minutes, or until it changes colour. Stir in the
fish sauce, sugar, lime leaves, corn and remaining
coconut cream. Simmer for 4–5 minutes, or until
the pork is cooked and tender. Stir in the basil,
garnish with chilli, then serve.

## JUNGLE CURRY PRAWNS

Preparation time: 20 minutes
Total cooking time: 10 minutes
Serves 6

☆ ☆

I tablespoon peanut oil
I clove garlic, crushed
$^1/_4$ cup (60 g/2 oz) jungle curry paste
  (see page 59)
I tablespoon fish sauce
$^1/_4$ cup (30 g/1 oz) ground candlenuts
300 ml (9$^1/_2$ fl oz) fish stock
I tablespoon whisky
3 fresh kaffir lime leaves, torn
600 g (1$^1/_4$ lb) raw medium prawns, peeled
  and deveined, with tails intact

*ABOVE: Jungle curry prawns*

# MUSSELS MASALA

Preparation time: 40 minutes
Total cooking time: 20 minutes
Serves 6

☆ ☆

CURRY PASTE

I teaspoon grated fresh ginger

I stem lemon grass, white part only, finely
chopped

3 cloves garlic, crushed

3 fresh green chillies, finely chopped

2 teaspoons garam masala

I teaspoon ground cumin

2 tablespoons chopped fresh coriander stems

I tablespoon tomato paste (tomato purée)

1/3 cup (80 ml/2³/4 fl oz) lemon juice

I tablespoon vegetable oil

1.5 kg (3 lb) black mussels

I tablespoon ghee

I large red onion, sliced

4 tablespoons chopped fresh coriander leaves

1 To make the curry paste, put the ginger,
lemon grass, garlic, chilli, garam masala, cumin,
coriander stems and tomato paste in a food
processor or blender, and grind until smooth.
With the motor running, gradually pour in
the lemon juice and oil until the mixture forms
a smooth paste.

2 Thoroughly scrub the mussels with a stiff
brush to remove any grit or weed from the shell.
Pull out the hairy beards. Discard any broken
mussels or open ones that don't close when
tapped lightly on the bench. Rinse well under
cold running water.

3 Heat the ghee in a wok. Add the onion and
cook for 5 minutes, or until it has softened. Stir
in the curry paste and cook for 2 minutes, or
until fragrant. Add 2¹/2 cups (625 ml/20 fl oz)
water, bring to the boil, then reduce the heat
and simmer. Add the mussels and cook for
5 minutes, or until they open. Remove the
mussels from the wok as soon as they open,
transfer to a plate and keep warm. Discard any
mussels that do not open.

4 Continue to boil the liquid for 5 minutes, or
until it has reduced and thickened slightly. Stir
in the coriander.

5 Place the mussels in a serving bowl, then pour
the sauce over them and serve with steamed rice
to soak up the juices.

## GARAM MASALA

Dry-fry separately 8 cardamom pods,
4 x 6 cm (2½ inch) cinnamon sticks that
have been broken up, 4 tablespoons
coriander seeds, 2 tablespoons cumin seeds,
1½ tablespoons whole black peppercorns
and 1 teaspoon cloves until each becomes
fragrant, setting each aside to cool. Peel the
cardamom, keeping the seeds and
discarding the pods. Put all the spices into
an electric blender and blend until it forms
a fine powder. Add ¹/2 teaspoon grated
nutmeg. Store in a sterilised glass jar for up
to 3 months. Makes 1 cup.

*BELOW: Mussels masala*

then reduce the heat to very low and cook, covered, for 40–50 minutes, or until the meat is almost cooked through. Drain, reserving the sauce. Wipe the wok clean.

**2** Heat the ghee in the clean wok over medium heat. Add the onion and cook for 5–7 minutes, or until it is soft and golden brown. Add the garlic and garam masala and cook for a further 2–3 minutes. Increase the heat, add the remaining curry paste and return the lamb to the wok. Cook for 5 minutes, or until the meat has browned. Slowly add the reserved sauce and simmer over low heat, stirring occasionally, for 15 minutes.

**3** Add the chopped coriander leaves and 1 cup (250 ml/8 fl oz) water and simmer for 15 minutes, or until the meat is tender and the sauce has thickened slightly. Season to taste with salt and freshly ground black pepper. Garnish with the extra coriander leaves and serve with poppadoms and steamed rice.

## NONYA LIME CHICKEN

Preparation time: 20 minutes
Total cooking time: 25 minutes
Serves 4–6

☆

CURRY PASTE
2/3 cup (75 g/2 1/2 oz) red Asian shallots
4 cloves garlic
2 stems lemon grass, white part only, chopped
2 teaspoons finely chopped fresh galangal
1 teaspoon ground turmeric
2 tablespoons sambal oelek
1 tablespoon shrimp paste

1/4 cup (60 ml/2 fl oz) vegetable oil
1 kg (2 lb) chicken thigh fillets, cut into 3 cm (1 1/4 inch) cubes
400 ml (13 fl oz) coconut milk
1 teaspoon finely grated lime rind
1/2 cup (125 ml/4 fl oz) lime juice
6 fresh kaffir lime leaves, finely shredded
2 tablespoons tamarind purée
lime wedges, to garnish
fresh kaffir lime leaves, extra, to garnish

**1** Combine the curry paste ingredients in a blender and blend until smooth.

**2** Heat a non-stick wok until very hot, add the

## BALTI LAMB

Preparation time: 15 minutes
Total cooking time: 1 hour 25 minutes
Serves 4

☆ ☆

1 kg (2 lb) lamb leg steaks, cut into 3 cm (1 1/4 inch) cubes
5 tablespoons Balti curry paste (see page 58)
2 tablespoons ghee or vegetable oil
1 large onion, finely chopped
3 cloves garlic, crushed
1 tablespoon garam masala
2 tablespoons chopped fresh coriander leaves
fresh coriander leaves, extra, to garnish

**1** Put the lamb, 1 tablespoon of the curry paste and 1 litre (32 fl oz) boiling water in a wok and mix together. Bring to the boil over high heat,

*ABOVE: Balti lamb*

oil and swirl. Add the curry paste and stir-fry for 1–2 minutes, or until fragrant. Add the chicken and stir-fry for 5 minutes, or until browned.
**3** Add the coconut milk, lime rind and juice, lime leaves and tamarind purée. Reduce the heat and simmer for 15 minutes, or until the chicken is cooked and the sauce has reduced and thickened slightly. Season well with salt. Garnish with lime wedges and lime leaves, and serve with steamed rice.

## YELLOW VEGETABLE CURRY

Preparation time: 20 minutes +
  20 minutes soaking
Total cooking time: 20 minutes
Serves 4

YELLOW CURRY PASTE
8 small dried red chillies
1 teaspoon black peppercorns
2 teaspoons coriander seeds
2 teaspoons cumin seeds
1 teaspoon ground turmeric
1¹/₂ tablespoons chopped fresh galangal
5 cloves garlic, chopped
1 teaspoon grated fresh ginger
5 red Asian shallots, chopped
2 stems lemon grass, white part only, chopped
1 teaspoon shrimp paste
1 teaspoon finely chopped lime rind

2 tablespoons peanut oil
2 cups (500 ml/16 fl oz) coconut cream
¹/₂ cup (125 ml/4 fl oz) vegetable stock
150 g (5 oz) snake beans, cut into 3 cm
  (1¹/₂ inch) lengths
150 g (5 oz) fresh baby corn
1 slender eggplant (aubergine), cut into 1 cm
  (¹/₂ inch) slices
100 g (3¹/₂ oz) cauliflower, cut into small florets
2 small zucchini (courgettes), cut into 1 cm
  (¹/₂ inch) slices
1 small red pepper (capsicum), cut into 1 cm
  (¹/₂ inch) slices
1¹/₂ tablespoons fish sauce
1 teaspoon grated palm sugar
chopped fresh red chilli, to garnish
fresh coriander leaves, to garnish

**1** To make the curry paste, soak the chillies in boiling water for 20 minutes. Drain and chop. Heat a frying pan, add the peppercorns, coriander seeds, cumin seeds and turmeric and dry-fry over medium heat for 3 minutes. Transfer to a mortar and pestle or food processor and finely grind.
**2** Put the ground spices, chilli, galangal, garlic, ginger, shallots, lemon grass and shrimp paste in a mortar and pestle and pound until smooth. Stir in the lime rind.
**3** Heat a wok over medium heat, add the oil and swirl to coat. Add 2 tablespoons of the curry paste and cook for 1 minute. Add 1 cup (250 ml/ 8 fl oz) of the coconut cream. Bring to the boil, then simmer for 10 minutes, or until thick and the oil starts to separate from the cream.
**4** Add the stock, vegetables and remaining coconut cream and cook for 5 minutes, or until the vegetables are tender. Stir in the fish sauce and sugar. Garnish with chilli and coriander.
NOTE: You could use the yellow curry paste on page 57 instead.

*ABOVE: Yellow vegetable curry*

Add the ginger and garlic and cook over low heat for 1–2 minutes, or until lightly golden. Add the chicken, increase the heat to medium and cook for 3 minutes, or until browned all over.
**3** Add the remaining ingredients, reduce the heat and simmer, covered, for 20 minutes, or until the chicken is tender. Serve with rice.

## INDONESIAN DRY BEEF CURRY
(Beef rendang)

Preparation time: 20 minutes
Total cooking time: 2 hours 30 minutes
Serves 6

2 teaspoons coriander seeds
1/2 teaspoon fennel seeds
2 teaspoons cumin seeds
2 onions, roughly chopped
2 cloves garlic, crushed
800 ml (26 fl oz) coconut milk
1/4 teaspoon ground cloves
1.5 kg (3 lb) chuck steak, cut into 2.5 cm (1 inch) cubes
4–6 small fresh red chillies, chopped
1 tablespoon lemon juice
1 stem lemon grass, white part only, bruised, cut lengthways
2 teaspoons grated palm sugar

**1** Toss the coriander, fennel and cumin seeds separately in a dry frying pan for 30 seconds– 1 minute, or until fragrant, taking care not to burn them. Grind the seeds in a spice grinder or mortar and pestle.
**2** Put the onion and garlic in a food processor, and process until it forms a smooth paste—you may need to add a little water.
**3** Pour half the coconut milk into a non-stick wok and bring to the boil, then reduce the heat and simmer, stirring occasionally, for 10 minutes, or until the milk has reduced by half and the oil starts to separate from the cream.
**4** Add the cloves and ground coriander, fennel and cumin to the wok, and stir for 1 minute. Add the meat and cook for 2 minutes, or until it browns, then add the onion mixture, chilli, lemon juice, lemon grass, sugar, 1 teaspoon salt and the remaining coconut milk. Cook, covered, over medium heat for 2 hours, or until

## CHICKEN BRAISED WITH GINGER AND STAR ANISE

Preparation time: 10 minutes
Total cooking time: 30 minutes
Serves 4

1 teaspoon Sichuan peppercorns
2 tablespoons peanut oil
2 x 3 cm (3/4 x 1 1/4 inch) piece fresh ginger, cut into julienne strips
2 cloves garlic, chopped
1 kg (2 lb) chicken thigh fillets, cut in half
1/3 cup (80 ml/2 3/4 fl oz) Chinese rice wine
1 tablespoon honey
1/4 cup (60 ml/2 fl oz) light soy sauce
1 star anise

**1** Heat a wok over medium heat, add the peppercorns and cook, stirring often, for 2–4 minutes, or until fragrant. Remove and lightly crush with the back of a knife.
**2** Reheat the wok, add the oil and swirl to coat.

*ABOVE: Chicken braised with ginger and star anise*

78

the liquid has reduced and the mixture has thickened, stirring frequently to prevent it sticking to the bottom of the wok.

**5** Uncover and cook for 8–10 minutes, or until the oil from the coconut milk begins to separate from the cream, but be careful that the curry does not burn. Serve with lime wedges.

## INDIAN LAMB IN SPICES AND YOGHURT
(Rogan josh)

Preparation time: 25 minutes
Total cooking time: 2 hours
Serves 4–6

1 tablespoon ghee or vegetable oil
2 onions, chopped
1/2 cup (125 g/4 oz) plain yoghurt
1 teaspoon chilli powder
1 tablespoon ground coriander
2 teaspoons ground cumin
1 teaspoon ground cardamom
1/2 teaspoon ground cloves
1 teaspoon ground turmeric

3 cloves garlic, crushed
1 tablespoon grated fresh ginger
400 g (13 oz) can chopped tomatoes
1 kg (2 lb) boned leg of lamb, trimmed and
    cut into 2.5 cm (1 inch) cubes
1/4 cup (30 g/1 oz) slivered almonds
1 teaspoon garam masala
chopped fresh coriander leaves, to garnish

**1** Heat the ghee or oil in a wok over medium heat, add the onion and cook, stirring, for 5 minutes, or until it has softened. Stir in the yoghurt, chilli powder, coriander, cumin, cardamom, cloves, turmeric, garlic and ginger. Add the tomato and 1 teaspoon salt, then simmer for a further 5 minutes.

**2** Add the lamb and stir until coated. Cover and cook over low heat, stirring occasionally, for 1 1/2–1 3/4 hours, or until the lamb is tender. Add 1/2 cup (125 ml/4 fl oz) water to the wok if the lamb is sticking.

**3** Meanwhile, toast the almonds in a dry frying pan over medium heat for 3–4 minutes, shaking gently, until golden. Remove from the pan at once—if left in the pan, they will continue to cook.

**4** Add the garam masala to the curry and mix through. Sprinkle the slivered almonds and coriander leaves over the top, then serve.

YOGHURT
In India, yoghurt and other milk products are an important source of protein, especially in vegetarian diets. Yoghurt is served with nearly every meal either as raita, lassi (a smooth, sweet drink), stirred into sauces for thickness and flavour, or mixed with spices and used as a marinade. Yoghurt in India and Sri Lanka is made mostly from buffalos' milk, which is much higher in butterfat than yoghurt made from cows' milk.

*LEFT: Indian lamb in spices and yoghurt*

1 Heat a wok until very hot, add the peanut oil and swirl to coat the side. Stir-fry the beef in four batches for 1–2 minutes each batch, or until browned all over. Remove from the wok.
2 Add the ginger and garlic to the wok and stir-fry for a few seconds. Add the stock, rice wine, hoisin sauce, cassia bark, tangerine peel, star anise, Sichuan peppercorns, sugar, daikon and 3½ cups (875 ml/28 fl oz) water, then return the beef to the wok.
3 Bring to the boil, skimming any scum that forms on the surface, then reduce to a simmer and cook, stirring occasionally for 1½ hours, or until the beef is tender and the sauce has thickened slightly. Add the spring onion and the bamboo shoots 5 minutes before the end of the cooking time. Stir in a few drops of sesame oil and garnish with extra spring onion, if desired. Serve with rice.
NOTE: You can remove the star anise, cassia bark and tangerine peel before serving or leave them in the serving dish for presentation.

## CHICKEN AND EGGPLANT
(AUBERGINE) **RED CURRY**

Preparation time: 15 minutes + standing
Total cooking time: 35 minutes
Serves 4

☆

500 g (1 lb) eggplant (aubergine), cut into
    2 cm (³/4 inch) cubes
¹/4 cup (60 ml/2 fl oz) peanut oil
500 g (1 lb) chicken breast fillets, cut into
    2 cm (³/4 inch) cubes
4 spring onions, chopped
2¹/2 tablespoons red curry paste
1 cup (250 ml/8 fl oz) coconut cream
¹/2 cup (125 ml/4 fl oz) chicken stock
4 fresh kaffir lime leaves, shredded
3 teaspoons grated palm sugar
2 tablespoons fish sauce
2 tablespoons fresh Vietnamese mint

1 Lay out the eggplant in a shallow bowl and sprinkle with salt. Leave for 30 minutes, then rinse and drain thoroughly.
2 Heat a wok until very hot, add 1 tablespoon peanut oil and swirl. Add half the chicken and stir-fry for 4 minutes, or until browned. Remove. Add another tablespoon oil and the rest of the chicken, and stir-fry. Remove. Heat

## HOISIN BEEF STEW

Preparation time: 15 minutes
Total cooking time: 1 hour 45 minutes
Serves 6

☆

1¹/2 tablespoons peanut oil
1 kg (2 lb) stewing beef (e.g. chuck), cut into
    3 cm (1¹/4 inch) cubes
1 tablespoon finely chopped fresh ginger
1 tablespoon finely chopped garlic
1 litre (32 fl oz) good-quality beef stock
¹/3 cup (80 ml/2³/4 fl oz) Chinese rice wine
¹/3 cup (80 ml/2³/4 fl oz) hoisin sauce
1 x 5 cm (¹/2 x 2 inch) piece cassia bark
1 piece dried tangerine peel
1 star anise
1 teaspoon Sichuan peppercorns, lightly crushed
2 teaspoons brown sugar
300 g (10 oz) daikon, cut into 3 cm (1¹/4 inch)
    chunks
3 spring onions, cut into 3 cm (1¹/4 inch)
    lengths, plus extra, to garnish (optional)
50 g (1³/4 oz) sliced bamboo shoots
a few drops sesame oil (optional)

*ABOVE: Hoisin beef stew*

the remaining oil, add the eggplant and spring onion, and stir-fry for 3–4 minutes.

**3** Return the chicken to the wok and add the curry paste. Cook, stirring, over high heat for 1 minute, or until fragrant. Add the coconut cream, stock, lime leaves, palm sugar and fish sauce, and bring to the boil. Reduce the heat and simmer for 15–20 minutes, or until the eggplant and chicken are tender and cooked.

**4** Season with salt and scatter the Vietnamese mint over the top. Serve with steamed rice.

## MALAYSIAN FISH CURRY

Preparation time: 25 minutes
Total cooking time: 25 minutes
Serves 4

☆☆

2 x 4 cm (³/₄ x 1¹/₂ inch) piece fresh ginger
3–6 fresh red chillies
1 onion, chopped
4 cloves garlic, chopped
3 stems lemon grass, white part only, sliced
2 teaspoons shrimp paste
¹/₄ cup (60 ml/2 fl oz) vegetable oil
1 tablespoon fish curry powder (see Notes)
1 cup (250 ml/8 fl oz) coconut milk
1 tablespoon tamarind purée

1 tablespoon kecap manis
500 g (1 lb) firm white skinless fish fillets,
   cut into cubes (e.g. ling, flake or hake)
2 ripe tomatoes, chopped
1 tablespoon lemon juice
crisp fried onion, to sprinkle

**1** Slice the ginger and process in a small food processor with the chillies, onion, garlic, lemon grass and shrimp paste until roughly chopped. Add 2 tablespoons of the oil and process until a paste forms, regularly scraping the side of the bowl with a spatula.

**2** Heat a non-stick wok over high heat, add the remaining oil and swirl to coat, then add the paste. Cook for 3–4 minutes over low heat, stirring constantly, until fragrant. Add the curry powder and stir for 2 minutes. Add the coconut milk, tamarind, kecap manis and 1 cup (250 ml/ 8 fl oz) water. Bring to the boil, stirring occasionally, then reduce the heat and simmer for 10 minutes.

**3** Add the fish, tomato and lemon juice. Season, then simmer for 5 minutes, or until the fish is just cooked (it will flake easily). Serve with rice. Sprinkle with crisp fried onion.

NOTES: Fish curry powder blend is available from speciality stores.

Use a non-stick or stainless steel wok as the tamarind purée will react with the metal in a regular wok and taint the dish.

FISH CURRY POWDER
Fish curry powder is a blend of coriander, cumin, fennel seeds, turmeric, peppercorns and chillies and is perfect for use in fish curries because the proportion of spices is different, creating a lighter style curry powder that suits the delicate flavours of fish. Specific curry powders such as this one are usually only found in Asian food stores. Avoid curry powders that are sold in cardboard packaging as the cardboard tends to absorb the oils and aromas of the spices. Instead, look for spices sold in sealed plastic or glass containers.

# PANANG BEEF

Preparation time: 30 minutes +
   20 minutes soaking
Total cooking time: 1 hour
Serves 4–6

CURRY PASTE
8–10 large dried red chillies
6 red Asian shallots, chopped
6 cloves garlic, chopped
1 teaspoon ground coriander
1 tablespoon ground cumin
1 teaspoon white pepper
2 stems lemon grass, white part only,
   bruised, sliced
1 tablespoon chopped fresh galangal
6 fresh coriander roots
2 teaspoons shrimp paste
2 tablespoons roasted peanuts

400 ml (13 fl oz) can coconut cream (do
   not shake)
1 kg (2 lb) round or blade steak, cut into
   1 cm (1/2 inch) slices
400 ml (13 fl oz) can coconut milk
1/3 cup (90 g/3 oz) crunchy peanut butter
4 fresh kaffir lime leaves
1/4 cup (60 ml/2 fl oz) lime juice
2 1/2 tablespoons fish sauce
3–4 tablespoons grated palm sugar
chopped roasted peanuts, to garnish
fresh Thai basil, to garnish

1 To make the curry paste, put the chillies in
a bowl and cover with boiling water. Soak
them for 20 minutes, or until softened. Remove
the seeds and roughly chop the flesh. Put the
chopped chillies in a food processor along with
the shallots, garlic, ground coriander, ground
cumin, white pepper, lemon grass, galangal,
coriander roots, shrimp paste and roasted peanuts
and process until a smooth paste forms—you
might need to add a little water if the paste is
too thick.
2 Open the can of coconut cream and scoop
off the really thick cream from the top. Put this
thick cream in a wok and cook over medium
heat for 10 minutes, or until the oil starts to
separate from the cream. Stir in 8 tablespoons
of the curry paste and cook, stirring often, for
5–8 minutes, or until fragrant.
3 Add the beef, coconut milk, peanut butter,
lime leaves and the remaining coconut cream
to the wok and cook for 8 minutes, or until the
beef just starts to change colour. Reduce the
heat to low and simmer for 30 minutes, or until
the beef is tender, stirring every few minutes to
prevent it from catching on the bottom.
4 Stir in the lime juice, fish sauce and sugar until
they are mixed into the curry. Serve in bowls,
garnished with the roasted peanuts and basil.
NOTE: Panang curry and Musaman curry are the
two Thai curries with the most similarities to
Indian curries. The similarity is due to the
inclusion of many of the same dried spices that
are used to make Indian curries. The heavier
spice flavours of these two curries are traceable
to Muslim origins in the south of Thailand. It is
these same spices that make them more suitable
to be made with red meats, such as beef or lamb,
than poultry or seafood.

*BELOW: Panang beef*

## LION'S HEAD MEATBALLS

Preparation time: 20 minutes +
   20 minutes soaking
Total cooking time: 45 minutes
Serves 4

☆ ☆

6 dried shiitake mushrooms

100 g (3 1/2 oz) cellophane noodles

600 g (1 1/4 lb) pork mince

1 egg white

4 cloves garlic, finely chopped

2 tablespoons finely grated fresh ginger

1 tablespoon cornflour

1 1/2 tablespoons Chinese rice wine

6 spring onions, thinly sliced

2 tablespoons peanut oil

2 litres (64 fl oz) home-made chicken stock
   (see page 23) or 1.5 litres (48 fl oz) purchased
   stock diluted with 2 cups (500 ml/16 fl oz)
   water

1/4 cup (60 ml/2 fl oz) light soy sauce

1 teaspoon sugar

400 g (13 oz) bok choy, cut in half lengthways
   and leaves separated

 Soak the mushrooms in 1 cup (250 ml/8 fl oz) boiling water for 20 minutes. Squeeze dry, reserving the soaking liquid. Discard the stems and thinly slice the caps. Meanwhile, put the noodles in a heatproof bowl, cover with boiling water and soak for 4–5 minutes, or until soft. Drain and rinse.

**2** Put the mince, egg white, garlic, ginger, cornflour, rice wine, two-thirds of the spring onion, and a pinch of salt in a food processor. Using the pulse button, process until smooth and well combined. Divide the mixture into eight portions and shape into large balls using wet hands.

**3** Heat a wok over high heat, add the peanut oil and swirl to coat. Cook the meatballs in batches for 2 minutes on each side, or until golden but not cooked through. Drain.

**4** Clean and dry the wok, then pour the stock into the wok and bring to the boil. Add the meatballs, soy sauce, sugar and mushrooms with the soaking liquid, then cover and cook over low heat for 20–25 minutes, or until the meatballs are cooked through.

**5** Add the bok choy and noodles, cover and cook for 5 minutes, or until the noodles are heated through. Sprinkle with the remaining spring onion, then serve.

LION'S HEAD
MEATBALLS
This eastern Chinese speciality is traditionally made with wom bok (Chinese cabbage), but can also be made with bok choy. It gained its name from the large meatballs, which are said to resemble a lion's head, with the leaves representing the mane. Legend has it that the dish was invented by a woman especially for her aged father-in-law, who had lost all his teeth and could only eat soft food. It is a rather wet-braised dish, but is eaten as a meal with noodles (as in the adjacent recipe) or with rice, rather than being eaten as a soup.

*ABOVE: Lion's head meatballs*

PORK VINDALOO
This famous Indian dish hails from Goa in Southern India. Its Portuguese origins are still evident today, especially in its most common form using pork. It is based on a Portuguese pork stew flavoured with vinegar (vinho) and garlic (alhos), hence the correct spelling 'vindalho'. The addition of vinegar was not only intended to add to the dish's flavour but also its shelf-life, as it acted as a preservative, which meant that a big batch could be eaten over a number of days.

*ABOVE: Pork vindaloo*

## PORK VINDALOO
(Shikar vindaloo)

Preparation time: 20 minutes
Total cooking time: 1 hour 45 minutes
Serves 4

1 kg (2 lb) pork fillets
1/4 cup (60 ml/2 fl oz) vegetable oil
2 onions, finely chopped
4 cloves garlic, finely chopped
1 tablespoon finely chopped fresh ginger
1 tablespoon garam masala
2 teaspoons brown mustard seeds
4 tablespoons vindaloo curry paste (see page 58)
1 tablespoon white vinegar

1 Trim the pork of any excess fat and sinew and cut into bite-sized pieces.
2 Heat a wok over medium heat, add the oil and swirl to coat the side of the wok. Add the meat in small batches and cook for 5–7 minutes, or until browned. Remove from the wok.
3 Add the onion, garlic, ginger, garam masala and mustard seeds to the wok, and cook, stirring, for 5 minutes, or until the onion is soft. Add the vindaloo paste and cook for 2 minutes.
4 Return all the meat to the wok, add 3 cups (750 ml/24 fl oz) water and bring to the boil. Reduce the heat and simmer, covered, for 1 1/2 hours, or until the meat is tender. Stir in the vinegar 15 minutes before serving and season to taste with salt. Serve with rice and poppadoms.

## INDONESIAN PUMPKIN AND SPINACH CURRY

Preparation time: 20 minutes
Total cooking time: 25 minutes
Serves 4

CURRY PASTE
3 candlenuts
1 tablespoon raw peanuts
2 red Asian shallots
2 cloves garlic
2–3 teaspoons sambal oelek
1/4 teaspoon ground turmeric
1 teaspoon grated fresh galangal

2 tablespoons vegetable oil
1 onion, finely chopped
600 g (1 1/4 lb) butternut pumpkin, cut into 2 cm (3/4 inch) cubes
1 cup (250 ml/8 fl oz) vegetable stock
350 g (11 oz) English spinach, roughly chopped
400 ml (13 fl oz) can coconut cream
1/4 teaspoon sugar

1 To make the curry paste, combine all the ingredients in a food processor or blender and process to a smooth paste.

2 Heat a wok over high heat, add the oil and swirl. Add the curry paste and cook, stirring, over low heat for 3–5 minutes, or until fragrant. Add the onion and cook for 5 minutes.

3 Add the pumpkin and half the stock and cook, covered, for 10 minutes, or until the pumpkin is almost cooked through. Pour in more stock, if required. Add the spinach, coconut cream and sugar, and season with salt. Bring to the boil, stirring constantly, then reduce the heat and simmer for 3–5 minutes, or until the spinach is cooked and the sauce has thickened slightly.

## CURRY MEE NOODLES

Preparation time: 30 minutes + 20 minutes soaking
Total cooking time: 30 minutes
Serves 4

☆ ☆

2 large dried red chillies

1 teaspoon shrimp paste

400 g (13 oz) fresh Hokkien noodles

1 onion, chopped

4 cloves garlic, chopped

4 stems lemon grass, white part only, thinly
    sliced

1 teaspoon grated fresh ginger

2 cups (500 ml/16 fl oz) coconut cream

1/4 cup (60 g/2 oz) Malaysian curry powder

400 g (13 oz) chicken thigh fillets, thinly sliced

120 g (4 oz) green beans, trimmed and cut into
    5 cm (2 inch) lengths

3 cups (750 ml/24 fl oz) chicken stock

10 fried tofu puffs, halved on the diagonal

2 tablespoons fish sauce

2 teaspoons sugar

180 g (6 oz) bean sprouts, tailed

2 hard-boiled eggs, quartered

2 tablespoons crisp fried shallots

lime wedges, to serve

1 Soak the chillies in boiling water for 20 minutes. Drain, then chop. Wrap the shrimp paste in foil and put under a hot grill for 1–2 minutes. Unwrap the shrimp paste.

2 Put the noodles in a bowl, cover with boiling water and soak for 1 minute to separate. Rinse under cold water, drain and set aside.

3 Put the onion, garlic, lemon grass, ginger, shrimp paste and chilli in a food processor or blender and blend to a rough paste, adding a little water if necessary.

4 Put 1 cup (250 ml/8 fl oz) of the coconut cream in a wok and bring to the boil, then simmer for 10 minutes, or until the oil starts to separate from the cream. Stir in the paste and curry powder and cook for 5 minutes, or until fragrant.

5 Add the chicken and beans and cook for 3–4 minutes, or until the chicken is almost cooked. Add the stock, tofu, fish sauce, sugar and the remaining coconut cream. Simmer, covered, over low heat for 10 minutes, or until the chicken is cooked.

6 Divide the noodles and bean sprouts among four bowls, then ladle the curry over the top. Garnish with the egg quarters and crisp fried shallots. Serve with the lime wedges.

*BELOW: Curry mee noodles*

# ACCOMPANIMENTS

The right accompaniment can make the meal. Whether it be a raita with curry to cool down the palate or sambal oelek to add spice to a meal, these side dishes have an important place.

The accompaniments on this page (except the raita) can be made ahead of time and stored in a jar. To clean the jars, preheat the oven to very slow 120°C (250°F/Gas ½). Thoroughly wash the jars and lids in hot, soapy water (or preferably in a dishwasher) and rinse well with hot water. Put the jars in the oven for 20 minutes, or until they are fully dried and you are ready to use them. Do not dry the jars or the lids with a tea towel.

## CUCUMBER RAITA

Put 2 peeled, seeded and finely chopped Lebanese cucumbers and 1 cup (250 g/ 8 oz) plain yoghurt in a bowl, and mix together well.

Dry-fry 1 teaspoon ground cumin and 1 teaspoon mustard seeds in a small frying pan over medium heat for 1 minute, or until fragrant and lightly browned, then add to the yoghurt mixture. Stir in ½ teaspoon grated fresh ginger, season to taste with salt and freshly ground black pepper, and mix together well. Garnish with paprika. Refrigerate in an airtight container for up to 3 days. Serve chilled. Makes 1⅓ cups. Serve with curry puffs or samosas.

## SWEET MANGO CHUTNEY

Cut the cheeks from the rounded side of 3 large green mangoes and use a large spoon to scoop out the flesh. Cut the remaining flesh from around the sides of the seed and chop all the flesh into large slices. Sprinkle with salt.

Put ½ teaspoon garam masala and 1½ cups (375 g/12 oz) sugar in a bowl and mix together well. Transfer to a large saucepan with 1 cup (250 ml/8 fl oz) white vinegar. Bring to the boil, then reduce the heat and simmer for 5 minutes. Add the mango slices, 2 seeded and finely chopped small fresh red chillies, 1 tablespoon finely grated fresh ginger and ½ cup (95 g/3 oz) finely

chopped dates, and simmer for 1 hour, or until the mango is tender. Stir often during cooking to prevent the chutney from sticking and burning on the bottom, especially towards the end of the cooking time. Spoon immediately into very clean, warm jars and seal. Turn the jars upside-down for 2 minutes, then invert and leave to cool. Store for up to 6 months. Makes 3 cups. Serve with curries.

## HOT CHILLI PASTE
(Sambal oelek)
Remove the stems from 200 g (6½ oz) small fresh red chillies and discard them. Roughly chop the chillies, wearing gloves to protect your hands, then put in a saucepan with ½ cup (125 ml/4 fl oz) water and bring to the boil. Reduce the heat and simmer, covered, for 15 minutes.

Pour the chilli and the soaking liquid into a food processor or blender and add 1 teaspoon sugar, 1 tablespoon vinegar, 1 tablespoon vegetable oil and 1 teaspoon salt. Process the mixture until it is finely chopped. Pour immediately into a clean, warm jar and carefully seal. Leave to cool. Label and date. Store in the refrigerator for up to 1 month. Makes 1 cup. Serve with seafood.

## SWEET CHILLI JAM
Soak 3 tablespoons dried shrimp in hot water for 5 minutes, drain well, then dry and roughly chop.

Heat 2 cups (500 ml/16 fl oz) vegetable oil in a small saucepan over medium heat and add 2 cups (220 g/7 oz) sliced red Asian shallots, 1 cup (110 g/ 7 oz) thinly sliced garlic and cook for 10 minutes, stirring constantly, until the shallots and garlic turn golden. Add the shrimp and 4–5 long, seeded and finely chopped fresh red chillies and cook for 5 minutes, stirring constantly. Remove from the heat. Drain, reserving the oil.

Transfer the fried mixture to a food processor and blend gradually, adding ¼ cup (60 ml/2 fl oz) of the reserved cooking oil to form a paste. Transfer the mixture to a saucepan over medium heat and, when it begins to simmer, add ½ cup (90 g/3 oz) grated light palm sugar, 3 tablespoons tamarind purée and 2 tablespoons fish sauce. Cook the mixture for 5 minutes, stirring frequently, until it thickens. Allow to cool before serving. Store in a clean jar in the fridge for up to 6 months. Makes about 3 cups. Serve with Thai food or finger food (for example, spring rolls or money bags).

*FROM LEFT: Cucumber raita, Sweet mango chutney, Hot chilli paste, Sweet chilli jam.*

1 Put the onion, sambal oelek, ginger, lemon grass, coriander, cardamom and tomato paste in a food processor, and process to a smooth paste.
2 Heat a wok over medium heat, add the oil and swirl to coat. Add the paste and cook, stirring, over medium heat for 4 minutes, or until fragrant.
3 Stir in the fish sauce, coconut milk and 1 cup (250 ml/8 fl oz) water. Bring to the boil and boil for 5 minutes, then reduce the heat and simmer for a further 5 minutes, or until the sauce has reduced and thickened slightly.
4 Add the fish balls and lime juice and cook for 2 minutes. Do not overcook or the fish balls will be tough and rubbery. Stir in the coriander and garnish with extra coriander. Serve with rice.
NOTE: Fish balls are available from the refrigerated section of large supermarkets.

## INDONESIAN CHICKEN IN COCONUT MILK
(Opar ayam)

Preparation time: 20 minutes + cooling
Total cooking time: 1 hour 10 minutes
Serves 6

☆ ☆

CURRY PASTE
2 teaspoons coriander seeds, dry-roasted and ground
1/2 teaspoon cumin seeds, dry-roasted and ground
1/2 teaspoon shrimp paste, dry-roasted
1 stem lemon grass, white part only, sliced
2 red onions, chopped
3 cloves garlic
1 tablespoon chopped fresh ginger
1 1/2 tablespoons chopped fresh galangal
2 teaspoons ground white pepper
1/4 teaspoon ground nutmeg
1/4 teaspoon ground cloves

2 x 270 ml (9 fl oz) cans coconut cream
1.5 kg (3 lb) chicken, cut into 8–10 pieces
4 x 400 ml (13 fl oz) cans coconut milk
2 tablespoons tamarind purée
1 tablespoon white vinegar
1 cinnamon stick

1 To make the curry paste, put all the paste ingredients in a blender and blend until a thick paste forms.

## FISH BALL CURRY

Preparation time: 20 minutes
Total cooking time: 20 minutes
Serves 6

☆

1 large onion, chopped
1 teaspoon sambal oelek
1 tablespoon finely chopped fresh ginger
1 stem lemon grass, white part only, finely chopped
3 tablespoons chopped fresh coriander roots
1/2 teaspoon ground cardamom
1 tablespoon tomato paste (tomato purée)
1 tablespoon vegetable oil
1 tablespoon fish sauce
2 cups (500 ml/16 fl oz) coconut milk
24 fish balls (if frozen, thawed) (see Note)
2 teaspoons lime juice
3 tablespoons chopped fresh coriander
fresh coriander, extra, to garnish

*ABOVE: Fish ball curry*

**2** Heat a large non-stick wok over medium heat, add the coconut cream and curry paste, and cook, stirring, for 20 minutes, or until thick and oily.
**3** Add the chicken and the remaining ingredients, and 1 teaspoon salt, and simmer gently for 50 minutes, or until the chicken is tender. Serve with rice and sauce.
NOTE: Store the remaining sauce in an airtight container in the refrigerator for up to 5 days and use as a base for soups or curry.

## CRAB CURRY

Preparation time: 25 minutes
Total cooking time: 20 minutes
Serves 6

4 raw large blue swimmer or mud crabs
1 tablespoon vegetable oil
1 large onion, finely chopped
2 cloves garlic, crushed
1 stem lemon grass, white part only, finely chopped
1 teaspoon sambal oelek

1 teaspoon ground cumin
1 teaspoon ground turmeric
1 teaspoon ground coriander
270 ml (9 fl oz) coconut cream
2 cups (500 ml/16 fl oz) chicken stock
1/3 cup (20 g/3/4 oz) firmly packed fresh Thai basil

**1** Pull back the apron and remove the top shell from the crabs. Remove the intestines and grey feathery gills. Cut each crab into four pieces. Use a cracker to crack the claws open; this will make the crabs easier to eat and will also allow the flavours of the curry to be absorbed into the crab meat.
**2** Heat a wok over medium heat, add the oil and swirl. Add the onion, garlic, lemon grass and sambal oelek and cook for 2–3 minutes.
**3** Add the cumin, turmeric, coriander and 1/2 teaspoon salt, and cook for 2 minutes, or until fragrant.
**4** Stir in the coconut cream and stock. Bring to the boil, then reduce the heat, add the crab pieces and cook, stirring occasionally, for 10 minutes, or until the liquid has reduced and thickened slightly and the crabs are cooked through. Stir in the basil, then serve with rice.

CRAB CURRY

Pull back the apron and remove the top shell from each crab.

Remove the intestines and grey feathery gills from the crabs.

*LEFT: Crab curry*

## YELLOW FISH CURRY

Preparation time: 10 minutes
Total cooking time: 15 minutes
Serves 4

150 ml (5 fl oz) vegetable stock
1 tablespoon Thai yellow curry paste
   (see page 57)
1 tablespoon tamarind purée
1 tablespoon grated palm sugar
1 1/2 tablespoons fish sauce
150 g (5 oz) green beans, trimmed and cut
   into 4 cm (1 1/2 inch) lengths
1 cup (140 g/4 1/2 oz) sliced bamboo shoots
400 ml (13 fl oz) coconut cream
400 g (13 oz) white fish fillets (e.g. ling,
   snapper), cut into cubes
1 tablespoon lime juice
lime wedges, to serve
fresh coriander leaves, to garnish

1 Pour the stock into a non-stick wok and bring to the boil. Add the curry paste and cook, stirring, for 3–4 minutes, or until fragrant. Stir in the combined tamarind purée, palm sugar and 1 tablespoon of the fish sauce. Add the beans and bamboo shoots, and cook over medium heat for 3–5 minutes, or until the beans are almost tender.
2 Add the coconut cream and bring to the boil, then reduce the heat, add the fish and simmer for 3–5 minutes, or until the fish is just cooked. Stir in the lime juice and remaining fish sauce. Garnish with the lime wedges and fresh coriander leaves. Serve with rice.

## AROMATIC SPICY BEEF STEW WITH ASIAN FLAVOURS

Preparation time: 15 minutes
Total cooking time: 2 hours 15 minutes
Serves 4–6

1/2 cup (125 ml/4 fl oz) vegetable oil
1.5 kg (3 lb) chuck steak, cut into 2.5 cm
   (1 inch) cubes
2 large onions, chopped
5 cloves garlic, chopped
1 x 5 cm (1/2 x 2 inch) piece fresh ginger, thinly
   sliced
10 red Asian shallots
2 stems lemon grass, white part only, bruised
1 litre (32 fl oz) beef stock
1/2 cup (125 g/4 oz) brown miso paste
1/2 teaspoon chilli powder
4 star anise
3 cm (1 1/4 inch) piece of cinnamon stick
1/2 teaspoon black peppercorns
1 tablespoon grated palm sugar

1 Heat a wok over high heat, add 1/4 cup (60 ml/2 fl oz) oil and swirl to coat the side of the wok. Reduce the heat to medium and cook the meat in batches for 5–10 minutes, or until browned, adding 2 teaspoons of oil between batches. Remove from the wok and drain on crumpled paper towels.
2 Clean the base of the wok with paper towels. Reheat the wok, add the remaining oil and swirl. Add the onion, garlic, ginger, shallots and lemon grass, then cook over medium heat for 5 minutes, or until the onion is soft and starting to brown. Remove the shallots from the wok.
3 Return the meat and any juices to the wok, then add the stock, miso paste, chilli powder,

*BELOW: Yellow fish curry*

star anise, cinnamon, peppercorns and sugar and bring to the boil. Reduce the heat to low and simmer, covered, for 1¼–1½ hours, or until the meat is tender.

**4** Remove the lid, return the shallots to the wok, then increase the heat to medium–high and cook for a further 15–20 minutes, or until the sauce has thickened a little. Discard the lemon grass, season to taste and serve with steamed jasmine rice.

## PRAWN AND COCONUT CURRY

Preparation time: 30 minutes
Total cooking time: 20 minutes
Serves 4

1 onion, chopped
2 cloves garlic, crushed
1 stem lemon grass, white part only, finely chopped
½ teaspoon sambal oelek
2 teaspoons garam masala
4 fresh kaffir lime leaves, finely shredded
3 tablespoons chopped fresh coriander stems
1 tablespoon peanut oil
1 cup (250 ml/8 fl oz) chicken stock
400 ml (13 fl oz) can coconut milk
1 kg (2 lb) raw medium prawns, peeled and deveined
1 tablespoon fish sauce
3 tablespoons fresh coriander leaves, to serve

**1** To make the curry paste, put the onion, garlic, lemon grass, sambal oelek, garam masala, kaffir lime leaves, chopped coriander stems and 2 tablespoons water in a food processor and process until a smooth paste forms.

**2** Heat a wok over medium heat, add the oil and swirl to coat. Add the curry paste and cook for 2–3 minutes, or until fragrant. Stir in the stock and coconut milk, bring to the boil, then reduce the heat and simmer for 10 minutes, or until slightly thickened.

**3** Add the prawns and cook for 3–5 minutes, or until cooked through. Stir in the fish sauce. Sprinkle with coriander and serve with rice.

NOTE: Instead of prawns, you can use bite-sized pieces of boneless ling or gemfish fillets. Cook for 3–5 minutes, or until cooked through.

*ABOVE: Prawn and coconut curry*

93

MILD VIETNAMESE
CHICKEN CURRY

Remove the skin and any
excess fat from the chicken.

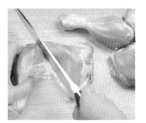

Cut each chicken quarter
into three even pieces.

# MILD VIETNAMESE
# CHICKEN CURRY

Preparation time: 30 minutes +
  overnight refrigeration
Total cooking time: 1 hour 10 minutes
Serves 6

☆ ☆

4 large chicken quarters (leg and thigh), skin
  and excess fat removed, cut into thirds
1 tablespoon good-quality curry powder
1 teaspoon caster sugar
1/3 cup (80 ml/2³/4 fl oz) vegetable oil
500 g (1 lb) orange sweet potato, peeled, cut
  into 3 cm (1¹/4 inch) cubes
1 large onion, cut into thin wedges
4 cloves garlic, chopped
1 stem lemon grass, white part only, finely
  chopped
2 bay leaves
1 large carrot, cut into 1 cm (¹/2 inch) pieces
  on the diagonal
400 ml (13 fl oz) coconut milk

1 Pat the chicken dry with paper towels. Put
the curry powder, sugar, ¹/2 teaspoon black
pepper and 2 teaspoons salt in a bowl, and mix
together well. Rub the curry mixture onto the
chicken pieces, then place the chicken on a
plate, cover with plastic wrap and refrigerate
overnight.
2 Heat a wok over high heat, add the oil and
swirl to coat. Add the sweet potato and cook
over medium heat for 3 minutes, or until lightly
golden. Remove with a slotted spoon.
3 Remove all but 2 tablespoons of the oil from
the wok. Add the onion and cook, stirring, for
5 minutes. Add the garlic, lemon grass and bay
leaves, and cook for 2 minutes.
4 Add the chicken and cook, stirring, over
medium heat for 5 minutes, or until well coated
in the mixture and starting to change colour.
Add 1 cup (250 ml/8 fl oz) water and simmer,
covered, over low heat for 20 minutes, stirring
once or twice.
5 Stir in the carrot, sweet potato and coconut
milk, and simmer, uncovered, stirring
occasionally, for 30 minutes, or until the chicken
is cooked and tender. Be careful not to break up
the sweet potato cubes. Serve with steamed rice
or dried rice noodle sticks.

*ABOVE: Mild Vietnamese
chicken curry*

# BALINESE SEAFOOD CURRY

Preparation time: 20 minutes +
  20 minutes marinating
Total cooking time: 20 minutes
Serves 6

CURRY PASTE

2 tomatoes

5 small fresh red chillies, seeded and chopped

5 cloves garlic, chopped

2 stems lemon grass, white part only, sliced

1 tablespoon coriander seeds, dry-roasted
  and ground

1 teaspoon shrimp powder, dry-roasted
  (see Notes)

1 tablespoon ground almonds

1/4 teaspoon ground nutmeg

1 teaspoon ground turmeric

3 tablespoons tamarind purée

1 tablespoon lime juice

250 g (8 oz) swordfish, cut into 3 cm (1 1/4 inch)
  cubes

400 g (13 oz) raw medium prawns

250 g (8 oz) calamari tubes

1/4 cup (60 ml/2 fl oz) vegetable oil

2 red onions, chopped

2 small fresh red chillies, seeded and sliced

1/2 cup (125 ml/4 fl oz) fish stock

shredded fresh Thai basil, to garnish

1 To make the curry paste, score a cross in the base of each tomato. Soak the tomatoes in boiling water for 30 seconds, then plunge into cold water and peel the skin away from the cross. Cut the tomatoes in half and scoop out the seeds with a teaspoon. Roughly chop the flesh, then put in a blender or food processor with the remaining paste ingredients. Blend until a thick paste forms.

2 Pour the lime juice into a bowl and season with salt and freshly ground black pepper. Add the fish, coat well and marinate for 20 minutes. Meanwhile, peel and devein the prawns, leaving the tails intact. Cut the calamari tubes into 1 cm (1/2 inch) rings.

3 Heat a non-stick wok over high heat, add the oil and swirl to coat the side of the wok. Add the onion, chilli and curry paste, and cook, stirring occasionally, over low heat for 10 minutes, or until fragrant.

4 Add the swordfish and prawns, and stir to coat in the curry paste mixture. Cook for 3 minutes, or until the prawns just turn pink, then add the calamari and cook for 1 minute.

5 Pour in the stock and bring to the boil, then reduce the heat and simmer for 2 minutes, or until the seafood is cooked and tender. Season to taste with salt and pepper. Garnish with the shredded fresh basil.

NOTES: If you can't find shrimp powder, put some dried shrimp in a mortar and pestle or small food processor and grind or process into a fine powder.

Use a non-stick or stainless steel wok to cook this recipe as the tamarind will react with the metal in a regular wok and badly taint the dish and strip off the seasoning layer.

*BELOW: Balinese seafood curry*

# THAI DUCK AND PINEAPPLE CURRY

Preparation time: 10 minutes
Total cooking time: 15 minutes
Serves 4–6

1 tablespoon peanut oil
8 spring onions, sliced on the diagonal into
    3 cm (1 1/4 inch) lengths
2 cloves garlic, crushed
2–4 tablespoons Thai red curry paste
    (see page 56)
750 g (1 1/2 lb) Chinese roast duck, chopped
400 ml (13 fl oz) coconut milk
450 g (14 oz) can pineapple pieces in syrup,
    drained
3 fresh kaffir lime leaves
3 tablespoons chopped fresh coriander
2 tablespoons chopped fresh mint

*BELOW: Thai duck and pineapple curry*

1 Heat a wok until very hot, add the oil and swirl. Add the spring onion, garlic and red curry paste, and stir-fry for 1 minute, or until fragrant.
2 Add the duck pieces, coconut milk, pineapple pieces, kaffir lime leaves, and half the fresh coriander and mint. Bring to the boil, then reduce the heat and simmer for 10 minutes, or until the duck is heated through and the sauce has thickened slightly. Stir in the remaining fresh coriander and mint, and serve with jasmine rice.

# THAI SOUR ORANGE FISH CURRY

Preparation time: 30 minutes +
    20 minutes soaking
Total cooking time: 20 minutes
Serves 4

6 large dried red chillies
4 red Asian shallots, finely chopped
1 1/2 tablespoons finely chopped fresh galangal
2 teaspoons finely chopped fresh turmeric
2 stems lemon grass, white part only, finely
    chopped
1 teaspoon shrimp paste
1 litre (32 fl oz) good-quality chicken stock
600 g (1 1/4 lb) oily fish fillets (e.g. mahi mahi,
    Spanish mackerel, kingfish), cut into 3 cm
    (1 1/4 inch) cubes
2 tablespoons tamarind purée
2 tablespoons fish sauce
2 tablespoons grated palm sugar
200 g (6 1/2 oz) snake beans, cut into 5 cm
    (2 inch) lengths
2 ripe tomatoes, cut into sixths
400 g (13 oz) water spinach, roughly chopped

1 Cover the chillies with 1 cup (250 ml/8 fl oz) boiling water and soak for 20 minutes. Drain and chop. To make the curry paste, put the chopped chillies, shallots, galangal, turmeric, lemon grass and shrimp paste in a food processor or blender and blend to a fine paste, adding a little water if needed.
2 Pour the stock into a non-stick wok over high heat and bring to the boil. Stir in the curry paste, return to the boil, then reduce the heat and simmer for 5 minutes. Add the fish, tamarind, fish sauce, sugar and beans. Stir and simmer for 5 minutes, or until the fish is cooked. Add the tomato and water spinach and simmer for 2 minutes. Season. Serve as part of a banquet.

## GREEN CURRY WITH SWEET POTATO AND EGGPLANT
### (AUBERGINE)

Preparation time: 15 minutes
Total cooking time: 25 minutes
Serves 4–6

☆ ☆

1 tablespoon vegetable oil

1 onion, chopped

1–2 tablespoons green curry paste (see Note)

1 eggplant (aubergine), quartered and sliced

1 1/2 cups (375 ml/12 fl oz) coconut milk

1 cup (250 ml/8 fl oz) vegetable stock

6 fresh kaffir lime leaves, plus, extra, to garnish (optional)

1 orange sweet potato, peeled, cut into cubes

2 teaspoons grated palm sugar

2 tablespoons lime juice

2 teaspoons lime rind

fresh coriander leaves, to garnish

 Heat the oil in a large wok. Add the onion and green curry paste and cook, stirring, over medium heat for 3 minutes. Add the eggplant and cook for a further 4–5 minutes, or until softened. Pour in the coconut milk and vegetable stock, bring to the boil, then reduce the heat and simmer for 5 minutes. Add the kaffir lime leaves and sweet potato and cook, stirring occasionally, for 10 minutes, or until the eggplant and sweet potato are very tender.

2 Mix in the sugar, lime juice and lime rind until well combined with the vegetables. Season to taste with salt. Garnish with some fresh coriander leaves and extra kaffir lime leaves if desired, and serve with steamed rice.

NOTE: To make this a completely vegetarian meal, make sure you read the label and choose a green curry paste without shrimp paste. Alternatively, make the Thai green curry paste on page 56.

## COCONUT AND LIME LASSI

Blend together 400 ml (13 fl oz) coconut milk, 3/4 cup (185 g/6 oz) plain yoghurt, 1/4 cup (60 ml/2 fl oz) lime juice, 1/4 cup (60 g/2 oz) caster sugar and 8–10 ice cubes in a blender until the mixture is well combined and the ice cubes are well crushed. Pour into tall glasses and serve immediately, garnished with slices of fresh lime. Makes 2 glasses.

NOTE: A great accompaniment to many wok meals, particularly Indian ones.

KAFFIR LIME LEAVES
The leaves of the kaffir lime tree are widely used in Thai and Southeast Asian cooking and give a unique aroma and tang to soups and curries. To chop fresh kaffir lime leaves, stack two or three leaves in a pile, roll into a tight bundle from the tip to the stem, then thinly slice. Discard the tough central stem. Whole leaves can be simmered in dishes but are not edible as they are tough and bitter. The juice and flesh of the kaffir lime are not used because they are bitter. Kaffir lime leaves can be found fresh, frozen or dried at Asian food stores; however, because of the racist connotations of the word 'kaffir', they are increasingly likely to be found as 'makrut' limes.

*ABOVE: Green curry with sweet potato and eggplant*

## SPICY PRAWNS
(Masala jheengari)

Preparation time: 30 minutes +
 15 minutes standing
Total cooking time: 55 minutes
Serves 4–6

1 kg (2 lb) raw medium prawns, peeled and
  deveined, with tails intact (reserve the
  shells and heads)
3/4 teaspoon ground turmeric
1/4 cup (60 ml/2 fl oz) vegetable oil
2 onions, finely chopped
4–6 cloves garlic, finely chopped
1–2 small fresh green chillies, seeded and
  chopped
2 teaspoons ground cumin
2 teaspoons ground coriander
1 teaspoon paprika
1/3 cup (90 g/3 oz) plain yoghurt
1/3 cup (80 ml/2¾ fl oz) thick (double) cream
4 tablespoons chopped fresh coriander leaves

1 Bring 1 litre (32 fl oz) water to the boil in a
large saucepan. Add the reserved prawn shells
and heads, reduce the heat and simmer for
2 minutes. Skim any scum that forms on the
surface during cooking with a skimmer or
slotted spoon. Drain, discard the shells and heads
and return the liquid to the pan. You will need
3 cups (750 ml/24 fl oz) liquid—make it up with
water, if necessary. Return the liquid to the boil,
then add the turmeric and prawns, and cook for
1 minute, or until the prawns just turn pink.
Remove the prawns.
2 Heat a wok over medium heat, add the oil and
swirl to coat. Add the onion and cook, stirring,
for 6 minutes, or until lightly golden brown.
Take care not to burn the onion. Add the garlic
and chilli, and cook for 2 minutes, then add the
cumin, coriander and paprika, and cook, stirring,
for 1–2 minutes, or until fragrant.
3 Gradually add the reserved stock, bring to
the boil and cook, stirring occasionally, for
35 minutes, or until the mixture has reduced by
half and thickened.
4 Remove from the heat and stir in the yoghurt.
Add the prawns and stir over low heat for
2–3 minutes, or until the prawns are warmed
through. Do not boil. Stir in the cream and
coriander leaves. Cover and leave to stand for
15 minutes to allow the flavours to infuse.
Reheat gently and serve with rice.
NOTE: This is a rich curry, so you don't need
much of it. Serve it as part of a banquet.

*ABOVE: Spicy prawns*

# INDONESIAN SOY-BRAISED BEEF
(Semur daging)

Preparation time: 20 minutes +
   15 minutes marinating
Total cooking time: 1 hour 40 minutes
Serves 4

800 g (1 lb 10 oz) chuck steak, trimmed and
   cut into 2 cm (3/4 inch) cubes
2 cloves garlic, crushed, plus 4 cloves, chopped
1 tablespoon grated fresh ginger
4 red Asian shallots, sliced
1/2 onion, chopped
1 tablespoon tamarind pulp, soaked in
   1/4 cup (60 ml/2 fl oz) hot water
1/4 cup (60 ml/2 fl oz) peanut oil
1/2 teaspoon ground cardamom
1/4 teaspoon ground cinnamon
1/2 teaspoon ground nutmeg
2 cloves
1/3 cup (80 g/2 3/4 oz) kecap manis
1 1/2 cups (375 ml/12 fl oz) beef stock
2 potatoes, cut into 2 cm (3/4 inch) chunks
1 tablespoon lime juice
lime wedges, to serve

1 Put the beef, crushed garlic and half the ginger in a non-metallic bowl and season with salt and freshly ground black pepper. Mix, cover with plastic wrap and refrigerate for 15 minutes.
2 To make the curry paste, put the red Asian shallots, onion, chopped garlic and remaining ginger in a small food processor and blend until a paste is formed.
3 Strain the tamarind liquid to remove the seeds and set aside.
4 Heat a non-stick wok over medium–high heat, add the oil and swirl to coat. Add the curry paste and cook for 3 minutes, or until fragrant. Add the beef and stir-fry for 3 minutes, or until browned and coated in the paste, taking care not to burn the paste.
5 Add a little extra oil if necessary, then add the cardamom, cinnamon, nutmeg, cloves and 1/2 teaspoon freshly ground black pepper. Cook for 1–2 minutes, or until fragrant, then add the kecap manis, stock, tamarind liquid and 1 1/2 cups (375 ml/12 fl oz) water. Cover and cook over low heat for 1 hour, then add the potato and continue to cook, uncovered, over low heat for 30 minutes, or until the meat is very tender and the potato is cooked. Remove the cloves. Stir in the lime juice, then serve with steamed rice and lime wedges.
NOTE: In Indonesia, the traditional garnish for this dish is a salad of sliced tomato and cucumber, accompanied by boiled egg and hot chilli sauce.

*BELOW: Indonesian soy-braised beef*

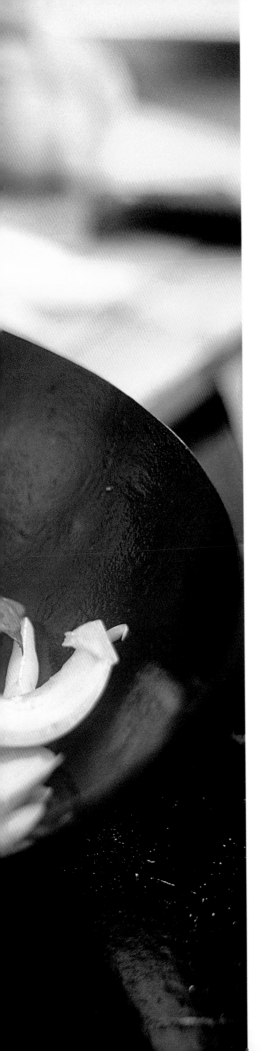

# STIR-FRIES

A flash of fire, a wisp of smoke, a toss of the wok and a blur of vegetables. Action and suspense accompany any stir-frying adventure. You'll need to be quick on your feet and ready with a rapid turn of the wrist to transform those colourful piles of carefully sliced and diced food into a smoking hot stir-fry. Stir-fries are the quintessential wok cooking experience, and they are arguably the most fun to prepare. The intense flavour of a well-cooked stir-fry satisfies—moist with just a hint of smokiness tantalising the taste buds. No second guesses are allowed—once you begin the stir-frying journey, there's no turning back.

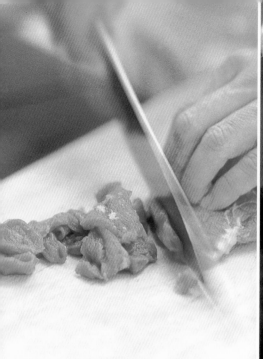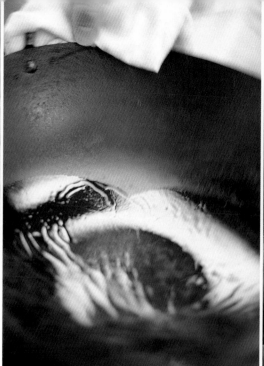

# HOW TO STIR-FRY

With a searing hot wok, a drizzle of oil and some fresh, colourful ingredients all

chopped up and ready to go, you're well on your way to the perfect stir-fry.

### WHAT IS STIR-FRYING?

Stir-frying involves the quick cooking of small pieces of food over high heat using minimal oil. The characteristic action of stir-frying is to toss the food constantly with a shovel-like utensil called a 'wok charn'. The aim of stir-frying is for food to retain its flavour, colour, texture and nutritive value.

The marriage of the wok to cooking style is at its most perfect in the stir-fry. The wide, conical shape of the wok continually tips food back into the centre where the heat is at its most intense, thus searing food and cooking it in a few minutes, while imparting a delicious smoky flavour.

The Chinese refer to the movement and rhythm associated with stir-frying as *wok hei*, which roughly translates as 'the breath of the wok'. It is hard to describe in English, but means that the food is at the perfect heat, is perfectly cooked and is ready to be eaten. It diminishes as the food cools, so stir-fries are best eaten piping hot from the wok.

### HEALTH BENEFITS

Stir-frying is regarded as a healthy cooking method, with good reason. The rapid cooking time preserves many of the food's nutrients, particularly in vegetables, with most of their colour and vitamins retained.

Because properly seasoned woks develop a non-stick coating, very little oil is needed when stir-frying, and what little oil is used does not have time to be absorbed by the rapidly moving food.

### STIR-FRYING PREPARATION

The key to successful stir-frying is to remember that once you begin, you must keep going. There is no time to interrupt cooking to chop an ingredient or mix together a sauce. All foods to be stir-fried should be prepared before you even heat the wok.

Stir-fry aficionados often set out all the ingredients in small bowls, placing them in the order that they will be added to the wok. This prevents food already in the wok from burning and ensures the quick and even cooking of all ingredients.

When preparing stir-fry ingredients, cut them into small, even pieces, so that they cook rapidly and evenly. The dish will also look more appealing and be easier to eat, which is particularly important if chopsticks are being used.

Meat or poultry fillets should be sliced into thin, uniform-sized slices across the grain. This helps to tenderise the meat by breaking up the fibres, thus allowing the meat to cook quickly and evenly so that it retains its juices and remains tender rather than becoming tough. Slicing is easier if the meat is frozen for 30 minutes beforehand. However, don't refreeze meat that has already been thawed or there is a risk of food poisoning.

Long vegetables, such as leafy vegetable stems, asparagus and green beans are also generally cut on the diagonal, as this increases their exposed surface area, thereby hastening the cooking time. If vegetables have been washed, they should be dried thoroughly so that they don't stew.

## THE GOOD OIL

Choosing the right oil is important to both the method and flavour of stir-fries. The oil should have a high burning point due to the intensity of the heat required for successful stir-frying. It should also complement but not interfere with the main flavours. Oils with a high smoking point, which can withstand the high bursts of heat without turning bitter, include peanut, sunflower, safflower, canola and vegetable oil. These oils also have a comparatively bland flavour that makes them suitable for stir-frying, unlike the robust taste of olive oil, for example.

## STEPS TO STIR-FRYING

The first step is to heat the wok over high heat before the oil is added. This enables the oil to be swirled around to coat the wok's entire surface before it has a chance to burn and taint the flavour of the food.

Any ginger or garlic will usually be added straight after the oil before the oil starts to smoke—this will prevent them from burning.

Add food that takes the longest to cook first, leaving the fastest-cooking additions, such as leafy green vegetables, bean sprouts or snow peas until last. Meat is often the first ingredient introduced to the wok. Only enough meat should be added that can fit in a single layer at one time. It should be left to cook briefly before starting to toss from the centre of the wok to the sides,

so that it seals and doesn't stick to the bottom of the wok and tear when turned.

After the meat has been cooked, it is usually set aside while other ingredients such as vegetables or noodles are cooked, again using the method of tossing from the centre of the wok to the sides.

The meat is then returned to the wok to be heated through and combined with the other ingredients, usually at the same time that any seasoning ingredients, such as soy sauce or fish sauce, are added.

However, for 'wetter' dishes (those that have more sauce), the method is slightly different with the seasoning ingredients (often with some stock) added to the wok first and then reduced to a glossy consistency before returning the meat or other vegetables to the wok to coat with sauce.

The final addition of the flavourings helps unify the dish, bringing all the flavours together. There is another important reason why flavourings are added towards the end of the cooking time: if salty seasonings, such as soy sauce, are added earlier, the salt can draw out the liquid of other ingredients and make them go soggy.

## HINTS AND TIPS

● If you are cooking meat that has been marinated, make sure that you drain the meat thoroughly before you cook it. It might be tempting to add the marinade for flavour, but if you add it too early, all you are doing is encouraging the meat to

*THE GOLDEN RULES OF STIR-FRYING*
*Because stir-frying is such a quick process, all ingredients need to be ready before you start to cook. Meat cooks best if it is sliced across the grain into thin strips. Other ingredients should be chopped in a manner that exposes maximum surface area.*

*Heat the empty wok over the hotplate, then add the oil and swirl it around to coat the side. Add the food in order of longest cooking time to shortest cooking time, cooking ingredients of a similar size and shape at the same time. Keep the food constantly moving, using a tossing action with a cham.*

*Meat is often cooked separately in small batches to prevent it from stewing.*

stew in its juices.
● When large quantities of meat, poultry or seafood are called for, cook it in batches to avoid stewing the food. Most recipes will specify if it needs to be cooked in batches, but some might not. When increasing a recipe to feed more people, keep in mind the batch rule.
● Combine the stir-fry sauce in advance— it saves hassle when you're in the middle of cooking.
● To maintain the heat of the wok, you may need to reheat the wok between batches. The aim is to ensure that the heat of the wok is intense enough to sear the food and seal in any juices and prevent stewing, even accounting for the temperature drop once the food is added.

marinate in the fridge for 20 minutes.

**2** Heat a wok over high heat, add the peanut oil and swirl around to coat the side of the wok. Add the meat in batches and cook each batch for 2–3 minutes, or until browned.

**3** Arrange the beef on a serving platter, sprinkle with the chopped peanuts and fresh coriander, and serve with steamed rice.

## GARLIC BEEF WITH RED PEPPER (CAPSICUM)

Preparation time: 5 minutes +
    15 minutes marinating
Total cooking time: 15 minutes
Serves 4

1 tablespoon Chinese rice wine
2 teaspoons light soy sauce
1 clove garlic, finely chopped
1/4 teaspoon ground white pepper
2 tablespoons vegetable oil
500 g (1 lb) lean beef fillet, thinly sliced
    across the grain
1 small red pepper (capsicum), cut into
    4 cm (1 1/2 inch) batons

GARLIC SAUCE
1 teaspoon cornflour
2 teaspoons vegetable oil
4 cloves garlic, finely chopped
4 spring onions, finely chopped (white and
    green parts separated)
200 ml (6 1/2 fl oz) hot chicken stock
2 teaspoons vegetarian oyster sauce
2 teaspoons chilli garlic sauce
1/2–1 teaspoon chilli oil

**1** Combine the rice wine, soy sauce, garlic, white pepper, 1 teaspoon of the oil and 1/4 teaspoon salt in a non-metallic bowl. Add the beef, cover and refrigerate for at least 15 minutes.

**2** Heat a wok over high heat, add 2 teaspoons of the oil and swirl to coat. Add the red pepper strips and stir-fry for 1–2 minutes, or until the pepper is cooked. Remove from the wok.

**3** Heat the remaining oil in the wok, add the beef in two batches and stir-fry for 2–3 minutes per batch, or until cooked through. Remove from the wok.

**4** To make the garlic sauce, blend the cornflour

## CHILLI BEEF

Preparation time: 10 minutes +
    20 minutes marinating
Total cooking time: 10 minutes
Serves 4

1/4 cup (60 ml/2 fl oz) kecap manis
2 1/2 teaspoons sambal oelek
2 cloves garlic, crushed
1/2 teaspoon ground coriander
1 tablespoon grated palm sugar
1 teaspoon sesame oil
400 g (13 oz) lean beef fillet, thinly sliced
    across the grain
1 tablespoon peanut oil
2 tablespoons chopped roasted peanuts
3 tablespoons chopped fresh coriander leaves

**1** Combine the kecap manis, sambal oelek, garlic, ground coriander, palm sugar, sesame oil and 2 tablespoons water in a large bowl. Add the beef and toss well. Cover with plastic wrap and

*ABOVE: Chilli beef*

with 1 tablespoon water and set aside. Add the oil to the wok and reduce the heat to low. Add the garlic and white part of the spring onions and cook for 30 seconds, or until fragrant. Pour in the stock and stir thoroughly. Increase the heat to high, bring the sauce to the boil and reduce slightly. Add the oyster sauce, chilli garlic sauce and chilli oil and stir together, before mixing in the cornflour paste. Cook for 1–2 minutes, or until the sauce thickens.
**5** Return the red pepper and meat to the wok, quickly stir to coat and heat through, then serve immediately, garnished with the finely chopped green spring onion tops.

# CHINESE BEEF AND ASPARAGUS WITH OYSTER SAUCE

Preparation time: 10 minutes +
  15 minutes marinating
Total cooking time: 10 minutes
Serves 4

1 tablespoon light soy sauce
1/2 teaspoon sesame oil
1 tablespoon Chinese rice wine
500 g (1 lb) lean beef fillet, thinly sliced
  across the grain

2 1/2 tablespoons vegetable oil
200 g (6 1/2 oz) fresh thin asparagus, cut into
  thirds on the diagonal
3 cloves garlic, crushed
2 teaspoons julienned fresh ginger
1/4 cup (60 ml/2 fl oz) chicken stock
2–3 tablespoons oyster sauce

**1** Combine the soy sauce, sesame oil and 2 teaspoons of the rice wine in a large non-metallic bowl. Add the beef, cover with plastic wrap and marinate in the fridge for at least 15 minutes.
**2** Heat a wok over high heat, add 1 tablespoon of the vegetable oil and swirl to coat the side of the wok. Add the asparagus and stir-fry for 1–2 minutes. Remove from the wok.
**3** Heat another tablespoon of oil in the wok over high heat, then add the beef in two batches, stir-frying each batch for 1–2 minutes, or until cooked through. Remove the meat from the wok and add to the asparagus.
**4** Add the remaining oil to wok, add the garlic and ginger before the oil becomes too hot and stir-fry for 1 minute, or until fragrant. Pour the stock, oyster sauce and remaining rice wine into the wok, bring to the boil and boil rapidly for 1–2 minutes, or until the sauce is slightly reduced. Return the beef and asparagus to the wok and stir-fry for a further minute, or until heated through and coated in the sauce. Serve immediately with steamed rice.

CHINESE ETIQUETTE
Chinese etiquette requires both hands to be held above the table during meals, with one hand holding the rice bowl and the other holding the chopsticks. The origins of this rule date back to the third century when a famous banquet disintegrated into a massacre when soldiers at the banquet, who had kept their daggers concealed under the table, turned upon their fellow diners.

*LEFT: Chinese beef and asparagus with oyster sauce*

## ASIAN PEPPERED BEEF

Preparation time: 10 minutes + 2 hours marinating
Total cooking time: 15 minutes
Serves 4

2 onions, thinly sliced

2 cloves garlic, finely chopped

2 teaspoons finely chopped fresh ginger

2 tablespoons Chinese rice wine

1 tablespoon soy sauce

1 tablespoon oyster sauce

2 teaspoons sugar

1 teaspoon sesame oil

1 teaspoon Sichuan peppercorns, crushed

1 tablespoon black peppercorns, crushed

600 g (1 1/4 lb) lean beef fillet, thinly sliced
   across the grain

2 spring onions, cut into 2.5 cm (3/4 inch) lengths

2 tablespoons vegetable oil

1 Combine the onion, garlic, ginger, rice wine, soy sauce, oyster sauce, sugar, sesame oil and peppercorns in a non-metallic bowl. Add the beef, cover and marinate in the refrigerator for at least 2 hours.
2 Drain the beef, discarding any excess liquid, then stir in the spring onion.

3 Heat a wok over high heat, add half the oil and swirl to coat. Add half the beef and stir-fry for 6 minutes, or until seared and cooked to your liking. Repeat with the remaining oil and beef. Serve with steamed rice.

## CHINESE BEEF AND BLACK BEAN SAUCE

Preparation time: 15 minutes
Total cooking time: 20 minutes
Serves 4–6

2 tablespoons rinsed and drained black
   beans, chopped

1 tablespoon dark soy sauce

1 tablespoon Chinese rice wine

1 clove garlic, finely chopped

1 teaspoon sugar

1/4 cup (60 ml/2 fl oz) peanut oil

1 onion, cut into wedges

500 g (1 lb) lean beef fillet, thinly sliced
   across the grain

1/2 teaspoon finely chopped fresh ginger

1 teaspoon cornflour, combined with
   1 tablespoon water

1 teaspoon sesame oil

*ABOVE: Asian peppered beef*

1 Put the beans, soy sauce, rice wine and 1/4 cup (60 ml/2 fl oz) water in a small bowl and mix. In a separate bowl, crush the garlic and sugar to a paste.
2 Heat a wok over high heat, add 1 teaspoon peanut oil and swirl to coat. Add the onion and stir-fry for 1–2 minutes. Remove from the wok. Add 1 tablespoon of the peanut oil and swirl, then stir-fry half the beef for 5–6 minutes, or until browned. Add to the onion. Repeat with the remaining beef.
3 Add the remaining peanut oil to the wok with the garlic paste and ginger, and stir-fry for 30 seconds, or until fragrant. Add the bean mixture, onion and beef. Bring to the boil, then reduce the heat and simmer, covered, for 2 minutes. Stir in the cornflour mixture, stirring until the sauce boils and thickens. Stir in the sesame oil, then serve with steamed rice.

## THAI BEEF SALAD

Preparation time: 20 minutes + cooling
Total cooking time: 5 minutes
Serves 6

☆

2 tablespoons peanut oil
500 g (1 lb) lean beef fillet, thinly sliced across the grain
2 cloves garlic, crushed
1 tablespoon grated palm sugar

3 tablespoons finely chopped fresh coriander roots and stems
1/3 cup (80 ml/2 3/4 fl oz) lime juice
2 tablespoons fish sauce
2 small fresh red chillies, seeded and thinly sliced
2 red Asian shallots, thinly sliced
2 telegraph cucumbers, sliced into thin ribbons
1 cup (20 g/3/4 oz) fresh mint leaves
1 cup (90 g/3 oz) bean sprouts, tailed
1/4 cup (40 g/1 1/4 oz) chopped roasted peanuts

1 Heat a wok over high heat, add 1 tablespoon of the oil and swirl to coat the side of the wok. Add half the beef and cook for 1–2 minutes, or until medium–rare. Remove from the wok and put on a plate. Repeat with the remaining oil and beef.
2 Put the garlic, palm sugar, coriander, lime juice, fish sauce, 1/4 teaspoon ground white pepper and 1/4 teaspoon salt in a bowl, and stir until all the sugar has dissolved. Add the chilli and shallots, and mix well.
3 Pour the sauce over the hot beef, mix together well, then allow the beef to cool to room temperature.
4 In a separate bowl, toss together the cucumber and mint leaves, and refrigerate until required.
5 Pile up a bed of the cucumber and mint on a serving platter, then top with the beef, bean sprouts and peanuts.

BEAN SPROUTS
Bean sprouts are the edible, crisp young shoots of soy beans and mung beans. Within 5–6 days of germination, the sprouts are ready to eat. Bean sprouts are an excellent source of vitamin C—the green shoots contain vitamin C that was not present in the seeds. The Chinese have been sprouting them for 3,000 years and recently the rest of the world has discovered the secret. It's not only their nutritional content that is valued; they are also appreciated for their crunchy texture, particularly when served with foods with contrasting textures. The best sprouts should be short, firm, clean and unbruised. Ideally, sprouts should be eaten on the day of purchase, but they can be stored in cold water in the refrigerator for 2–3 days, changing the water daily. Mung bean sprouts shouldn't be eaten raw because they can contain high levels of salmonella. Blanch them before eating, but to retain their crispness, don't overcook them.

*LEFT: Thai beef salad*

CHINESE RICE WINE
Known as Shao Xing, Shao Hsing and Shaosing. China's best-known rice wine is Shaosing from the Chekiang (Zhejiang) province in the northeast of the country, where it has been made for more than 2000 years from a mixture of glutinous rice, millet, yeast and local spring water. In China it is known as 'carved flower' after the pattern on the urns in which it is stored. It is also known as 'daughter's wine' because there is an old tradition of putting some away at the birth of a daughter to be drunk at her wedding.

*ABOVE: Thai stir-fried noodles with beef*

## THAI STIR-FRIED NOODLES WITH BEEF
(Phad si-iew)

Preparation time: 20 minutes
Total cooking time: 20 minutes
Serves 4–6

☆ ☆

500 g (1 lb) fresh rice sheet noodles, cut lengthways into 2 cm (3/4 inch) strips
2 tablespoons peanut oil
2 eggs, lightly beaten
500 g (1 lb) lean beef fillet, thinly sliced across the grain
1/4 cup (60 ml/2 fl oz) kecap manis
1 1/2 tablespoons soy sauce
1 1/2 tablespoons fish sauce
300 g (10 oz) gai larn (Chinese broccoli), cut into 5 cm (2 inch) lengths
1/4 teaspoon ground white pepper

1 Cover the noodles with boiling water and gently separate the strips. Drain.
2 Heat a wok over high heat, add 1 tablespoon oil and swirl to coat. Add the egg, swirl to coat and cook over medium heat for 1–2 minutes, or until set. Remove and slice.
3 Reheat the wok over high heat, add the remaining oil and cook the beef in batches for

3 minutes, or until browned. Remove.
4 Reduce the heat to medium, add the noodles and cook for 2 minutes. Combine the kecap manis, soy and fish sauces. Add to the wok with the gai larn and white pepper, then stir-fry for 2 minutes. Return the egg and beef to the wok and cook for 3 minutes.

## TANGERINE BEEF STIR-FRY

Preparation time: 20 minutes + 20 minutes soaking
Total cooking time: 15 minutes
Serves 4–6

☆ ☆

10 g (1/4 oz) dried tangerine or mandarin peel
750 g (1 1/2 lb) lean beef fillet, thinly sliced across the grain
1 tablespoon cornflour
1 teaspoon sesame oil
3 1/2 tablespoons light soy sauce
1/3 cup (80 ml/2 3/4 fl oz) tangerine or orange juice
1 1/2 tablespoons Chinese rice wine
2 teaspoons sugar
100 ml (3 1/2 fl oz) peanut oil
1 onion, thinly sliced
3 cloves garlic, finely chopped
1/2 teaspoon chilli flakes
1/2 teaspoon crushed Sichuan peppercorns
4 spring onions, cut into 3 cm (1 1/4 inch) lengths

1 Soak the peel in warm water for 20 minutes, then remove and thinly slice. Meanwhile, put the beef in a bowl with the cornflour, sesame oil and 2 tablespoons of the soy sauce. Mix well. Cover and marinate in the fridge for 20 minutes.

2 Combine the citrus juice, Chinese rice wine, sugar and remaining soy sauce in a small bowl and set aside until needed.

3 Heat a wok over high heat, add ¼ cup (60 ml/2 fl oz) of the peanut oil and swirl to coat. Add the beef and stir-fry in batches until crisp, adding more oil when necessary. Remove the beef from the wok and drain on crumpled paper towels.

4 Heat the remaining oil in the wok, add the onion and stir-fry for 1–2 minutes, or until golden, then add the garlic, chilli flakes, Sichuan pepper and tangerine peel and stir-fry for a further 30 seconds.

5 Add the citrus juice mixture and stir well, cooking over medium heat for 3–4 minutes, or until the sauce reduces slightly and thickens. Return the beef to the wok, stir to coat with the sauce and continue cooking for 1–2 minutes, or until the beef is thoroughly reheated. Sprinkle with the spring onion, then serve with rice.

## EASY BEEF STIR-FRY

Preparation time: 15 minutes
Total cooking time: 15 minutes
Serves 4

2 tablespoons oyster sauce

1 clove garlic, crushed

1 teaspoon grated fresh ginger

2 tablespoons light soy sauce

2 tablespoons rice wine

1 tablespoon honey

1 teaspoon sesame oil

2 teaspoons cornflour

2 tablespoons peanut oil

350 g (11 oz) lean beef fillet, thinly sliced across the grain

1 large onion, cut into thin wedges

1 large carrot, thinly sliced on the diagonal

1 red pepper (capsicum), cut into thin strips

100 g (3½ oz) snow peas (mangetout), sliced in half on the diagonal

150 g (5 oz) baby corn, sliced in half on the diagonal

200 g (6½ oz) straw mushrooms, drained

1 To make the stir-fry sauce, combine the oyster sauce with the garlic, ginger, soy sauce, rice wine, honey, sesame oil and 1 tablespoon water in a small, non-metallic bowl or jug. Mix the cornflour with 1 tablespoon water in a separate small bowl until a paste forms. Set aside both bowls until needed.

2 Heat a wok over high heat, add 1 tablespoon of the peanut oil and swirl around to coat the side of the wok. Add the meat in batches and cook for 2–3 minutes, or until nicely browned. Remove the meat from the wok.

3 Heat the remaining peanut oil in the wok, add the onion, carrot and red pepper and cook, stirring, for 2–3 minutes, or until the vegetables are just tender. Add the snow peas, corn and straw mushrooms, cook for a further minute, then return all the meat to the wok. Pour the stir-fry sauce into the wok, then the cornflour paste and cook, stirring, for 1 minute, or until the sauce thickens and all the ingredients are combined. Season to taste with salt and freshly ground black pepper. Serve with thin egg noodles or steamed rice.

*BELOW: Easy beef stir-fry*

## STIR-FRIED BEEF AND SNOW PEAS (MANGETOUT)

Preparation time: 10 minutes
Total cooking time: 10 minutes
Serves 4

2 tablespoons soy sauce
$1/2$ teaspoon grated fresh ginger
400 g (13 oz) lean beef fillet, thinly sliced
    across the grain
2 tablespoons peanut oil
200 g ($6^{1}/2$ oz) snow peas (mangetout),
    topped and tailed
1 small red pepper (capsicum), sliced
$1^{1}/2$ teaspoons cornflour
$1/2$ cup (125 ml/4 fl oz) beef stock
1 teaspoon soy sauce, extra
$1/4$ teaspoon sesame oil

1 Combine the soy sauce and ginger in a large non-metallic bowl, add the beef and toss well.
2 Heat a wok over high heat, add the oil and swirl to coat the side of the wok. Add the beef in two batches and stir-fry for 2 minutes each batch, or until the meat is golden. Return all the beef to the wok and add the snow peas and red pepper. Stir-fry for a further 2 minutes.
3 Dissolve the cornflour in the stock. Add to the wok with the remaining stock, extra soy sauce and the sesame oil. Stir until the sauce boils and thickens. Serve with steamed rice.

## KOREAN BEEF AND POTATO NOODLE STIR-FRY

Preparation time: 20 minutes +
    15 minutes marinating
Total cooking time: 15 minutes
Serves 4

$1/4$ cup (60 ml/2 fl oz) vegetable oil
$1/4$ cup (60 ml/2 fl oz) light soy sauce
250 g (8 oz) lean beef fillet, thinly sliced
    across the grain
150 g (5 oz) dried sweet potato starch
    noodles
$1/3$ cup (80 ml/$2^{3}/4$ fl oz) chicken stock
1 tablespoon dark soy sauce
1 tablespoon Chinese black vinegar
1 tablespoon cornflour
1 teaspoon sugar
1 teaspoon sesame oil
1 onion, sliced
4 cloves garlic, finely chopped
4 x 4 cm ($1^{1}/2$ x $1^{1}/2$ inch) piece fresh ginger,
    finely chopped
2 small fresh red chillies, seeded and chopped
1 small carrot, julienned
1 small red pepper (capsicum), julienned
200 g ($6^{1}/2$ oz) broccoli, cut into small florets
115 g (4 oz) fresh baby corn, cut in half
    lengthways
100 g ($3^{1}/2$ oz) snow peas (mangetout),
    julienned
300 g (10 oz) bok choy, cut into 10 cm
    (4 inch) lengths
$1^{2}/3$ cups (150 g/5 oz) bean sprouts, tailed
4 spring onions, thinly sliced

*BELOW: Stir-fried beef and snow peas*

1 Combine 1 teaspoon of the vegetable oil and 1 tablespoon of the light soy sauce in a large non-metallic bowl, add the beef, then cover and marinate in the fridge for at least 15 minutes.
2 Put the noodles in a large heatproof bowl, cover with boiling water and soak for 10 minutes, or until softened. Rinse and drain. Cut into half lengths with scissors, then toss in 1 teaspoon of the oil.
3 To make the stir-fry sauce, combine the stock, dark soy sauce, Chinese black vinegar, cornflour, sugar and the remaining light soy sauce in a bowl and stir until the sugar has dissolved.
4 Heat a large wok over high heat, add 1 tablespoon of the vegetable oil and swirl to coat. Stir-fry the beef for 2–3 minutes, or until well browned. Remove from the wok.
5 Add the remaining vegetable oil, sesame oil and onion to the wok and stir-fry for 2 minutes, or until the onion is soft and starting to brown. Add the garlic, ginger and chilli and stir-fry for 30 seconds before adding the carrot, red pepper, broccoli, corn and snow peas. Stir-fry for 2 minutes, or until the vegetables are almost cooked but still crunchy. Add the bok choy and bean sprouts, and stir-fry for a further 1 minute.
6 Place the noodles in the wok, stir in the stir-fry sauce and return the beef and any juices to the wok. Toss together for 2 minutes, or until the noodles, sauce, beef and vegetables are well combined. Sprinkle with spring onion and serve.

## CHINESE BEEF AND GAI LARN (CHINESE BROCCOLI) STIR-FRY

Preparation time: 10 minutes
Total cooking time: 15 minutes
Serves 4

☆

1 kg (2 lb) fresh rice sheet noodles
1/4 cup (60 ml/2 fl oz) peanut oil
500 g (1 lb) lean beef fillet, thinly sliced across the grain
1 onion, cut into wedges
4 cloves garlic, chopped
400 g (13 oz) gai larn (Chinese broccoli), cut into 3 cm (1 1/4 inch) lengths
1 tablespoon soy sauce
1/4 cup (60 ml/2 fl oz) kecap manis
1 small fresh red chilli, chopped
1/2 cup (125 ml/4 fl oz) beef stock

1 Cut the noodles lengthways into 2 cm (3/4 inch) wide strips, then cover with boiling water and gently separate the strips.
2 Heat a wok over medium heat, add 2 tablespoons of the peanut oil and swirl to coat the side of the wok. Add the noodles and stir-fry for 2 minutes. Remove from the wok.
3 Reheat the wok over high heat, add the remaining oil and swirl to coat. Add the beef in batches and cook for 3 minutes, or until browned. Remove from the wok. Add the onion and stir-fry for 1–2 minutes, then add the garlic and cook for a further 30 seconds.
4 Return all the beef to the wok and add the gai larn, soy sauce, kecap manis, chilli and beef stock, and cook over medium heat for 2–3 minutes. Divide the noodles among four serving plates and top with the beef mixture. Serve immediately.
NOTE: The noodles may break up during cooking but this will not affect the flavour of the dish.

*ABOVE: Chinese beef and gai larn stir-fry*

TERIYAKI

Traditionally, teriyaki refers to any food (usually beef, chicken or fish) that is glazed with a special, sweet marinade in the final stages of being grilled or pan-fried. *Teri* means gloss and *yaki* refers to grilling or pan-frying in Japanese, its country of origin. As teriyaki has spread around the world, it has earnt a looser definition, referring more to the trio of favoured Japanese ingredients that go to make up teriyaki sauce (mirin, sake and soy sauce), than the cooking method (see the adjacent recipe). Teriyaki sauce can be easily made at home, but it is also commercially available.

*ABOVE: Teriyaki beef and soy bean stir-fry*

# TERIYAKI BEEF AND SOY BEAN STIR-FRY

Preparation time: 15 minutes
Total cooking time: 20 minutes
Serves 4

☆

1 tablespoon mirin

2 tablespoons sake

2 tablespoons Japanese soy sauce

2 teaspoons sugar

400 g (13 oz) frozen soy beans (see Note)

1 tablespoon peanut oil

700 g (1 lb 7 oz) lean beef fillet, thinly sliced across the grain

6 spring onions, thinly sliced

2 cloves garlic, chopped

2 teaspoons finely chopped fresh ginger

50 g (1 3/4 oz) soy bean sprouts, tailed

1 red pepper (capsicum), thinly sliced

1 To make the stir-fry sauce, combine the mirin, sake, Japanese soy sauce and sugar in a small bowl or jug and set aside until it is needed.

2 Cook the soy beans in a saucepan of boiling water for 2 minutes. Drain.

3 Heat a large wok over high heat. Add 2 teaspoons of the peanut oil and swirl it around to coat the side of the wok. Cook the beef in three batches for 3–4 minutes per batch, or until well browned. Remove from the wok. Add the spring onion and stir-fry for 30 seconds, or until it has wilted.

4 Return the beef to the wok, add the garlic, ginger, soy beans, soy bean sprouts and pepper, and stir-fry for 2 minutes. Add the stir-fry sauce to the wok and stir-fry until heated through. Serve hot with steamed rice.

NOTE: Frozen soy beans are available in packets, either in their pods or shelled. They are available from Asian food stores. This recipe uses the shelled variety.

# LEMON GRASS BEEF

Preparation time: 15 minutes +
    10 minutes marinating
Total cooking time: 25 minutes
Serves 4

3 cloves garlic, finely chopped

1 tablespoon grated fresh ginger

4 stems lemon grass (white part only),
    finely chopped

2¹/₂ tablespoons vegetable oil

600 g (1 ¹/₄ lb) lean beef fillet, thinly sliced
    across the grain

1 tablespoon lime juice

1–2 tablespoons fish sauce

2 tablespoons kecap manis

1 large red onion, cut into small wedges

200 g (6¹/₂ oz) green beans, sliced on the
    diagonal into 5 cm (2 inch) lengths

1 Combine the garlic, ginger, lemon grass and 2 teaspoons of the oil in a large non-metallic bowl. Add the beef, toss well until it is coated in the marinade, then cover with plastic wrap and marinate in the fridge for at least 10 minutes.

2 To make the stir-fry sauce, combine the lime juice, fish sauce and kecap manis in a small bowl or jug and set aside until needed.

3 Heat a wok over high heat, add 1 tablespoon oil and swirl to coat the side of the wok. Stir-fry the beef in batches for 2–3 minutes, or until browned. Remove from the wok.

4 Reheat the wok over high heat, heat the remaining oil, then add the onion and stir-fry for 2 minutes. Add the beans and cook for another 2 minutes, then return the beef to the wok. Pour in the stir-fry sauce and cook until heated through. Serve with steamed rice.

## LEMON GRASS

Ensure your lemon grass is fresh—the end of the stem should not be too dry and should still have a strong lemony scent. If you have difficulty finding a steady supply of fresh lemon grass, it is a good idea to buy an extra couple of stems when you do find it and freeze it wrapped tightly in plastic wrap—lemon grass retains its fragrance quite well when frozen. If you can't find any fresh lemon grass at all, it is better to replace it with lemon juice or zest than to use dried lemon grass, which has very little taste or scent.

*LEFT: Lemon grass beef*

**YAKISOBA**

Despite the name, the Japanese stir-fried noodle dish, yakisoba, does not traditionally include soba noodles. It more usually includes the more hearty and rustic wheat noodles, ramen. However, any thick, fresh noodle can be used in this dish, including Hokkien and udon.

# YAKISOBA

Preparation time: 30 minutes +
  20 minutes soaking
Total cooking time: 10 minutes
Serves 4

☆☆

4 dried shiitake mushrooms
600 g (1 1/4 lb) Hokkien noodles
3 teaspoons finely chopped fresh ginger
2 large cloves garlic, finely chopped
300 g (10 oz) lean beef fillet, thinly sliced across
  the grain
6 rashers streaky bacon, cut into 3 cm
  (1 1/4 inch) pieces
2 tablespoons peanut oil
1/2 teaspoon sesame oil
6 thin spring onions, cut into 3 cm (1 1/4 inch)
  lengths
1 carrot, thinly sliced on the diagonal
1 small green pepper (capsicum), thinly sliced
220 g (7 oz) wom bok (Chinese cabbage),
  shredded
pickled ginger and shredded nori, to serve
  (optional)

SAUCE
1/4 cup (60 ml/2 fl oz) Japanese soy sauce
2 tablespoons Worcestershire sauce
1 1/2 tablespoons Japanese rice vinegar
1 tablespoon sake
1 tablespoon mirin
1 tablespoon tomato sauce
1 tablespoon oyster sauce
2 teaspoons soft brown sugar

1 Soak the mushrooms in boiling water for 20 minutes, or until soft. Squeeze dry, reserving 2 tablespoons of the soaking liquid. Discard the stalks and thinly slice the caps.
2 Put the noodles in a heatproof bowl, cover with boiling water and soak for 1 minute. Drain and separate.
3 Combine half the ginger and half the garlic in a small bowl, then add the beef. Set aside.
4 To make the sauce, combine all the ingredients in a bowl with the reserved mushroom liquid and the remaining ginger and garlic.
5 Heat a wok over medium–high heat, add the bacon and cook for 2–3 minutes, or until softened and just starting to brown. Transfer to a large bowl. Combine the peanut and sesame oils. Increase the wok to high heat, add a little of the oil mixture and stir-fry the beef very quickly for

*RIGHT: Yakisoba*

1 minute, or until it just changes colour all over. Add to the bacon.

6 Heat a little more of the oil mixture in the wok, add the spring onion, carrot and pepper and stir-fry for 1 minute. Add the wom bok and mushrooms and cook for another 30 seconds, or until the vegetables are just cooked but still tender, then add to the bowl with the bacon.

7 Heat the remaining oil in the wok, add the noodles and stir-fry for 1 minute, then return the bacon, beef and vegetables to the wok, pour on the sauce and stir-fry for 2–3 minutes, or until heated through (the sauce shouldn't be too runny, it should be almost completely absorbed but not dry). Divide the noodles among four deep bowls and top with pickled ginger and shredded nori, if desired.

## BEEF AND SPINACH STIR-FRY

Preparation time: 20 minutes + 2 hours marinating
Total cooking time: 15 minutes
Serves 4

☆

¼ cup (60 ml/2 fl oz) sweet chilli sauce
2 tablespoons soy sauce
1 clove garlic, crushed
2 teaspoons grated fresh ginger
1 tablespoon dry sherry
500 g (1 lb) lean beef fillet, thinly sliced across
   the grain
2 tablespoons vegetable oil
2 onions, cut into wedges
500 g (1 lb) English spinach leaves, shredded

1 Combine the sweet chilli sauce, soy sauce, garlic, ginger and sherry in a large non-metallic bowl. Add the beef, toss well until it is coated in the marinade, then cover with plastic wrap and refrigerate for at least 2 hours, or overnight if time permits.

2 Remove the meat from the marinade with tongs or a slotted spoon. Heat a wok over high heat, add 1 tablespoon of the oil and swirl it around to coat the side of the wok. Add the meat in batches and stir-fry over high heat for 2–3 minutes each batch, or until it is well browned, adding a little more oil when necessary. Remove from the wok.

3 Reheat the wok over high heat, add another tablespoon of the oil and stir-fry the onion wedges for 3–4 minutes, or until tender and lightly browned. Return all the meat to the wok and mix together.

4 Just before serving, toss the English spinach leaves through the beef mixture until the spinach is just wilted. Serve immediately with steamed jasmine rice.

ENGLISH SPINACH
Native to Iran, spinach is a green leafy plant with slender stems. The young leaves are used in salads; the older ones are cooked. It contains iron and vitamins A and C, but also oxalic acid, which is responsible for the slightly bitter taste and which acts as an inhibitor to the body's ability to absorb calcium and iron. This knowledge has somewhat diminished its 'Popeye' reputation.

ABOVE: Beef and spinach stir-fry

## CORIANDER BEEF

Preparation time: 15 minutes +
    1–2 hours marinating
Total cooking time: 15 minutes
Serves 4

4 cloves garlic, finely chopped
1 tablespoon finely chopped fresh ginger
1/2 cup (25 g/3/4 oz) chopped fresh coriander
    roots, stems and leaves
1/4 cup (60 ml/2 fl oz) vegetable oil
500 g (1 lb) lean beef fillet, thinly sliced across
    the grain
oil, extra, for cooking
2 red onions, thinly sliced
1/2 red pepper (capsicum), thinly sliced
1/2 green pepper (capsicum), thinly sliced
1 tablespoon lime juice
1/2 cup (25 g/3/4 oz) chopped fresh coriander
    leaves, extra

1 Combine the garlic, ginger, coriander and oil
in a large non-metallic bowl. Add the beef,
cover and refrigerate for 1–2 hours.
2 Heat a wok over high heat, add the meat in
three batches and stir-fry each batch over high
heat for 2–3 minutes, or until the meat is just

*ABOVE: Coriander beef*

cooked. Remove all the meat from the wok
and keep it in a warm place.
3 Heat 1 tablespoon oil in the wok, add the
onion and cook over medium–high heat for
3–4 minutes, or until slightly softened. Add
the red and green pepper, and cook, tossing
constantly, for 3–4 minutes, or until the pepper
is slightly softened.
4 Return all the meat to the wok with the
lime juice and extra coriander. Toss well, then
remove from the heat and season well with salt
and pepper. Serve immediately.

## BEEF AND SHIITAKE MUSHROOM STIR-FRY

Preparation time: 25 minutes +
    20 minutes soaking
Total cooking time: 15 minutes
Serves 4

6 dried shiitake mushrooms
oil, for cooking
4 cloves garlic, finely chopped
1 fresh red chilli, finely chopped
400 g (13 oz) lean beef fillet, thinly sliced
    across the grain
2 onions, very thinly sliced

4 spring onions, chopped

1/2 red pepper (capsicum), thinly sliced

1/2 cup (125 ml/4 fl oz) tomato passata

2 teaspoons soft brown sugar

2 tomatoes, diced

2 teaspoons sesame oil

2 tablespoons shredded fresh basil

1 Soak the dried mushrooms in a heatproof bowl of boiling water for 20 minutes. Squeeze dry. Discard the woody stalks and thinly slice the caps.

2 Combine 2 tablespoons of the oil with the garlic, chilli and some salt and freshly ground black pepper in a large non-metallic bowl. Add the beef and toss until well coated.

3 Heat a wok over high heat, add the beef in two batches and stir-fry each batch for 30 seconds, or until just browned. Reheat the wok in between each batch. Remove the meat from the wok.

4 Reheat the wok over high heat, add 2 tablespoons of the oil and stir-fry the onion, spring onion and pepper for 3 minutes, or until golden. Add the mushrooms, tomato passata and sugar. Bring to the boil, then reduce the heat and simmer for 3 minutes. Add the beef, tomato and oil, and season with salt and freshly ground black pepper. Bring to the boil, allowing the tomato to heat through. Stir in the shredded fresh basil, then serve immediately.

## CHILLI PLUM BEEF

Preparation time: 15 minutes
Total cooking time: 15 minutes
Serves 4

☆

2 tablespoons vegetable oil

600 g (1 1/4 lb) lean beef fillet, thinly sliced across the grain

1 large red onion, cut into wedges

1 red pepper (capsicum), thinly sliced

1 1/2 tablespoons chilli garlic sauce

1/2 cup (125 ml/4 fl oz) good-quality plum sauce

1 tablespoon light soy sauce

2 teaspoons rice vinegar

good pinch of finely ground white pepper

4 spring onions, sliced on the diagonal

1 Heat a wok over high heat, add 1 tablespoon of the oil and swirl to coat the side of the wok.

Stir-fry the beef in two batches for 2–3 minutes, each batch, or until browned and just cooked. Remove from the wok.

2 Heat the remaining oil in the wok, add the onion and stir-fry for 1 minute before adding the red pepper and continuing to stir-fry for 2–3 minutes, or until just tender. Add the chilli garlic sauce and stir for 1 minute, then return the meat to the wok and add the plum sauce, soy sauce, vinegar, white pepper and most of the spring onion.

3 Toss everything together for 1 minute, or until the meat is reheated. Sprinkle with the remaining spring onion, then serve with steamed rice or noodles.

*BELOW: Chilli plum beef*

Add the beef in two batches and stir-fry each batch for 1 minute, or until it starts to turn pink. Remove from the wok.

**2** Add an extra tablespoon of oil to the wok, if necessary, then stir-fry the bamboo shoots for 3 minutes, or until starting to brown. Add the garlic, fish sauce and 1/4 teaspoon salt and stir-fry for 2–3 minutes. Add the spring onion and stir-fry for a further 1 minute, or until starting to wilt. Return the beef to the wok, stir quickly and cook for 1 minute, or until heated through. Remove from the heat, toss in the sesame seeds and serve with rice.

## KOREAN BULGOGI-STYLE BEEF STIR-FRY

Preparation time: 10 minutes +
  2 hours marinating
Total cooking time: 10 minutes
Serves 4

2 cloves garlic, crushed

2 teaspoons grated fresh ginger

3 spring onions, finely chopped

1/3 cup (80 ml/2 3/4 fl oz) Japanese soy sauce

2 teaspoons sugar

1 1/2 tablespoons sesame seeds, toasted and ground

sesame oil, to drizzle

600 g (1 1/4 lb) lean beef fillet, thinly sliced across the grain

1–2 tablespoons vegetable or peanut oil

1 spring onion, thinly sliced on the diagonal

**1** To make the marinade, combine the garlic, ginger, spring onion, soy sauce, sugar, 1 tablespoon of the ground sesame seeds and a drizzle of sesame oil in a non-metallic bowl. Add the beef slices, season with freshly ground black pepper, cover with plastic wrap and marinate in the refrigerator for 2 hours or overnight, if time permits.

**2** Heat a wok over high heat, add the vegetable oil and swirl to coat the side of the wok. Remove the beef from the marinade with a slotted spoon or tongs and add to the wok in three batches. Stir-fry each batch for 2–3 minutes, or until well seared. To serve, sprinkle with the remaining ground sesame seeds and spring onion and drizzle with a little extra sesame oil, if desired.

## VIETNAMESE-STYLE BEEF AND BAMBOO SHOOTS

Preparation time: 10 minutes
Total cooking time: 10 minutes
Serves 4

1/4 cup (60 ml/2 fl oz) vegetable oil

400 g (13 oz) lean beef fillet, thinly sliced across the grain

227 g (7 oz) can sliced bamboo shoots, drained and rinsed

3 cloves garlic, crushed with 1/4 teaspoon salt

2 tablespoons fish sauce

8 spring onions, cut into 4 cm (1 1/2 inch) lengths on the diagonal

1/4 cup (40 g/1 1/4 oz) sesame seeds, lightly toasted

*ABOVE: Vietnamese-style beef and bamboo shoots*

**1** Heat a wok over high heat, add 2 tablespoons of the oil and swirl to coat the side of the wok.

# SHAKING BEEF

Preparation time: 10 minutes + 1 hour marinating
Total cooking time: 10 minutes
Serves 4

1¹/₂ tablespoons fish sauce

1¹/₂ tablespoons light soy sauce

1¹/₂ teaspoons caster sugar

6 cloves garlic, crushed

3 spring onions, white part only, finely
    chopped

¹/₄ cup (60 ml/2 fl oz) vegetable oil

750 g (1¹/₂ lb) lean beef fillet, cut into 2 cm
    (³/₄ inch) cubes

2 teaspoons rice vinegar

2 teaspoons lime juice

1 teaspoon light soy sauce, extra

100 g (3¹/₂ oz) mignonette lettuce or green oak
    lettuce leaves, washed, trimmed and dried

1 Combine the fish sauce, soy sauce, sugar, garlic, spring onion, 1 teaspoon of the oil, ³/₄ teaspoon freshly ground black pepper and ¹/₂ teaspoon salt in a large non-metallic bowl. Add the beef, cover with plastic wrap and marinate in the fridge for at least 1 hour, or overnight if time permits.

2 To make the dressing, combine the rice vinegar, lime juice, extra soy sauce, 3 teaspoons of the oil and 2 teaspoons water in a small non-metallic bowl or jug.

3 Place the lettuce leaves on a serving plate, then pour on the dressing.

4 Heat a wok over high heat, add 1 tablespoon of the oil and swirl to coat the side of the wok. Add half the beef in one layer, allowing it to sit without stirring for 1 minute, so that a brown crust forms on the bottom. Stir-fry the beef briefly, or use the handle to shake the wok vigorously, tossing the beef around in the heat, for 3–4 minutes for medium–rare, or until cooked to your liking. Remove the beef from the wok, then repeat with the remaining oil and beef.

5 Arrange the beef over the lettuce leaves and serve immediately with steamed rice.

NOTE: The name of this dish derives from the French term 'sauté', from which the technique of shaking the meat has been borrowed.

SPRING ONIONS
Spring onions (also known as scallions) are now available all year round, so the meaning of the name has lost some of its significance. Some spring onions are immature onions that have been harvested young, but some are a species of onion that never bulbs. The spring onion is one of the most widely used ingredients in Chinese cookery, and has been part of China's cuisine for centuries.

*LEFT: Shaking beef*

# CHINESE SIZZLING BEEF STIR-FRY

Preparation time: 15 minutes +
  1 hour marinating
Total cooking time: 15 minutes
Serves 4–6

1 tablespoon light soy sauce
1 tablespoon Chinese rice wine
1 1/2 tablespoons peanut oil
750 g (1 1/2 lb) lean beef fillet, thinly sliced
  across the grain
1 large onion, cut into wedges
4 spring onions, cut into 3 cm (1 1/4 inch)
  lengths
1 green pepper (capsicum), cut into bite-sized
  pieces
3 cloves garlic, crushed
1 tablespoon julienned fresh ginger
1 1/2 tablespoons sesame seeds, lightly toasted

SAUCE
2 tablespoons hoisin sauce
2 tablespoons tomato sauce
2 tablespoons light soy sauce
2 tablespoons Chinese rice wine
2 teaspoons sesame oil

1 Combine the soy sauce, rice wine, 2 teaspoons of the peanut oil and 1/4 teaspoon freshly ground black pepper in a large non-metallic bowl. Add the beef, toss together, then cover with plastic wrap and marinate in the refrigerator for at least 1 hour.
2 To make the stir-fry sauce, combine all the ingredients in a small bowl.
3 Heat a wok over high heat, add the remaining oil and swirl it around to coat the side of the wok. Stir-fry the beef in two batches for 2–3 minutes each batch, or until nicely browned. Remove from the wok.
4 Add the onion and spring onion to the wok and stir-fry for 2–3 minutes, or until golden brown, then add the green pepper and cook for a further minute. Add the garlic and ginger and stir-fry for a further 30 seconds. Return the beef to the wok, pour in the stir-fry sauce, and cook, stirring, for 2 minutes, or until the sauce reduces slightly and coats the beef and vegetables. Transfer to a serving bowl, sprinkle with the sesame seeds and serve.

# SPICY DRY-FRIED SHREDDED BEEF

Preparation time: 15 minutes +
  2 hours marinating
Total cooking time: 10 minutes
Serves 4

1 tablespoon light soy sauce
1/2 teaspoon sesame oil
1 tablespoon Chinese rice wine
400 g (13 oz) lean beef fillet, thinly sliced across
  the grain, then shredded
2–3 tablespoons peanut oil
2 cloves garlic, finely chopped
1 teaspoon grated fresh ginger
3 spring onions, finely chopped

SAUCE
1 1/2 tablespoons brown bean sauce
1 tablespoon chilli bean paste
1/2 teaspoon caster sugar
1/2 teaspoon chilli oil
1/4 teaspoon sea salt

1 Combine the soy sauce, sesame oil, 2 teaspoons of the rice wine and 1/2 teaspoon salt in a large non-metallic bowl. Add the beef, cover with plastic wrap and marinate in the fridge for at least 2 hours.
2 To make the stir-fry sauce, combine all the ingredients in a small non-metallic bowl or jug.
3 Heat a wok over high heat, add 1 tablespoon of the peanut oil and swirl to coat the side of the wok. Add the beef in two batches, using your hands to break up any clumps as you drop the beef into the wok. Stir-fry each batch for 1 minute, or until the beef is browned. Remove, place on crumpled paper towels and drain off any liquid from the meat.
4 Clean and dry the wok, then heat over high heat, add the remaining oil and swirl to coat. Add the garlic and ginger and stir-fry for 30 seconds, or until fragrant. Return the beef to the wok and cook for 2 minutes, or until it is very dry. Add the remaining rice wine and stir-fry for 30 seconds, or until all the wine is absorbed. Add the bean sauce mixture and stir well, until the beef is well coated. Remove from the heat, stir in the spring onion and serve.

CHINESE SIZZLING BEEF Chinese sizzling beef is an old Chinese restaurant speciality. It is usually served on a heated cast iron platter, which produces the customary 'sizzle' that gives the dish its name. Cast iron sizzle platters can be purchased from Asian speciality stores. To use, place the iron platter (without the wooden casing) in a preheated very hot (250°C/500°F/Gas 10) oven and heat for 10 minutes. Remove the iron platter from the oven and place it in its wooden casing. Take care when removing and adding food from the wok to the plate, as it will sizzle and spit.

*OPPOSITE PAGE, FROM TOP: Chinese sizzling beef stir-fry; Spicy dry-fried shredded beef*

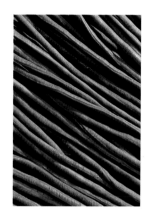

## STIR-FRIED BEEF WITH SNAKE BEANS AND BASIL

Preparation time: 10 minutes +
  2 hours marinating
Total cooking time: 10 minutes
Serves 4

3 fresh bird's eye chillies, seeded and
  finely chopped
3 cloves garlic, crushed
2 tablespoons fish sauce
1 teaspoon grated palm sugar
2 tablespoons peanut or vegetable oil
400 g (13 oz) lean beef fillet, thinly sliced
  across the grain
150 g (5 oz) snake beans, sliced into
  3 cm (1 1/4 inch) lengths
1 cup (30 g/1 oz) loosely packed fresh Thai basil
thinly sliced fresh bird's eye chilli, to garnish

1 Combine the chilli, garlic, fish sauce, palm
sugar and 1 tablespoon of the oil in a large
non-metallic bowl. Add the beef, toss well, then
cover and marinate in the fridge for 2 hours.
2 Heat a wok to hot, add 2 teaspoons of the oil
and swirl to coat. Stir-fry the beef in two batches
over high heat for 2 minutes each batch, or until
just browned. Remove from the wok.

3 Heat the remaining oil in the wok, then
add the snake beans and 1/4 cup (60 ml/2 fl oz)
water and cook over high heat for 3–4 minutes,
tossing regularly until tender. Return the beef
to the wok with the basil. Cook for a further
1–2 minutes, or until warmed through. Garnish
with chilli, then serve.

## STIR-FRIED BEEF AND CHILLI BEAN PASTE

Preparation time: 20 minutes
Total cooking time: 15 minutes
Serves 4–6

2 tablespoons light soy sauce
1 tablespoon Chinese rice wine
1 tablespoon oyster sauce
1 tablespoon chilli bean paste
2 teaspoons brown bean sauce
1–2 tablespoons peanut oil
600 g (1 1/4 lb) lean beef fillet, thinly sliced
  across the grain
1 onion, sliced into thin wedges
2 cloves garlic, crushed
1 fresh red chilli
120 g (4 oz) green beans, trimmed and
  halved if long

*RIGHT: Stir-fried beef with snake beans and basil*

1 To make the stir-fry sauce, combine the soy sauce, rice wine, oyster sauce, chilli bean paste and brown bean sauce in a small, non-metallic bowl or jug. Set aside until needed.

2 Heat a wok with a lid over high heat, add 1 tablespoon of the oil and swirl to coat the side of the wok. Stir-fry the beef in batches over high heat for 2 minutes each batch, or until browned. Remove from the wok.

3 Reheat the wok to hot, add the onion and stir-fry for 3–5 minutes, or until browned, then add the garlic and chilli and cook for a further minute. Toss in the beans, pour in the stir-fry sauce, then cover with a lid and cook for 3 minutes.

4 Remove the lid, return the beef to the wok and stir-fry for 1–2 minutes, or until the meat is coated with the sauce and heated through. Serve with steamed rice.

# GINGER BEEF STIR-FRY

Preparation time: 20 minutes +
   15 minutes marinating
Total cooking time: 15 minutes
Serves 4

1 clove garlic, crushed

1 teaspoon grated fresh ginger

1/4 cup (60 ml/2 fl oz) kecap manis

1/4 cup (60 ml/2 fl oz) Chinese rice wine

1 teaspoon sugar

pinch of five-spice powder

500 g (1 lb) lean beef fillet, thinly sliced across
   the grain

1/2 teaspoon cornflour

1/4 cup (60 ml/2 fl oz) peanut oil

1 red onion, sliced into thin wedges

1 1/2 tablespoons julienned fresh ginger

400 g (13 oz) gai larn (Chinese broccoli),
   cut into 6 cm (2 1/2 inch) lengths

1 Combine the garlic, grated ginger, kecap manis, rice wine, sugar and five-spice powder in a large non-metallic bowl. Add the beef, toss together, then cover and marinate in the fridge for at least 15 minutes.

2 Mix together the cornflour with 1 tablespoon water to form a paste.

3 Heat a wok over high heat, add 1 tablespoon of the oil and swirl to coat the side of the wok. Remove half the meat from the marinade with tongs or a slotted spoon, add to the wok and stir-fry for 2–3 minutes, or until browned and just cooked. Remove from the wok. Repeat with more oil and the rest of the beef, reserving the marinade.

4 Add the remaining oil to the wok and stir-fry the onion for 2–3 minutes, or until it starts to soften, then add the julienned ginger and stir-fry for another minute. Stir in the gai larn and cook for 2–3 minutes, or until wilted and tender.

5 Return the beef to the wok, along with the reserved marinade and any meat juices. Add the cornflour paste and stir until thoroughly combined. Continue to cook for 1–2 minutes, or until the sauce has thickened slightly and the meat is heated through. Serve with steamed rice or noodles.

*ABOVE: Ginger beef stir-fry*

Satay are short skewers
of beef, pork or chicken
marinated in coconut milk
and spices, then quickly
grilled over charcoal and
served with a spicy peanut
sauce. Satays are one of
a number of dishes often
prepared by street vendors
who find themselves a spot
near markets and popular
restaurants to tempt
passers-by. In some areas,
waiters from nearby
restaurants pass orders
from customers in the
restaurant to the street
vendor, then fetch the
finished satay and include
it on the restaurant bill. In
Malaysia, Thailand and
Indonesia, there is an entire
culinary sub-culture based
around street vendors.
While some tourists to
these countries have a
perception that the food
from street vendors is of
lesser quality than that
served in restaurants, in
many cases the opposite
is true and large crowds
form around the most
popular venues.

*ABOVE: Satay lamb*

## SATAY LAMB

Preparation time: 10 minutes
Total cooking time: 15 minutes
Serves 4

1/4 cup (60 ml/2 fl oz) peanut oil
750 g (1 1/2 lb) lamb loin fillets, thinly sliced
  across the grain
2 teaspoons ground cumin
1 teaspoon ground turmeric
1 red pepper (capsicum), sliced
1/4 cup (60 ml/2 fl oz) sweet chilli sauce
1/4 cup (60 g/2 oz) crunchy peanut butter
1 cup (250 ml/8 fl oz) coconut milk
2 teaspoons soft brown sugar
1–2 tablespoons lemon juice, to taste
4 tablespoons chopped fresh coriander leaves
1/4 cup (40 g/1 1/4 oz) unsalted peanuts, roasted,
  chopped, to serve

**1** Heat a wok over high heat, add 1 tablespoon
oil and swirl. Add half the lamb and stir-fry for
3 minutes, or until browned. Remove. Repeat
with 1 tablespoon oil and the remaining lamb.
**2** Reheat the wok, add the remaining oil and
cumin, turmeric and pepper, and stir-fry for
2 minutes, or until the pepper is tender.
**3** Return the lamb to the wok. Stir in the chilli

sauce, peanut butter, coconut milk and sugar.
Bring to the boil, then reduce the heat and
simmer for 5 minutes, or until the meat is tender
and the sauce has thickened slightly. Remove
from the heat and add the lemon juice. Stir in the
coriander and sprinkle with the peanuts. Serve.

## LAMB AND LETTUCE LEAF PARCELS

Preparation time: 15 minutes +
  10 minutes marinating
Total cooking time: 10 minutes
Serves 4

2 teaspoons light soy sauce
2 teaspoons Chinese rice wine
300 g (10 oz) lean lamb mince
8 baby cos leaves
2 tablespoons vegetable oil
2 cloves garlic, crushed
2 red Asian shallots, finely chopped
1 fresh bird's eye chilli, finely chopped
120 g (4 oz) water chestnuts, finely diced
5 fresh baby corn, finely diced
1 tablespoon vegetarian oyster sauce
1 tablespoon kecap manis
2–3 tablespoons chicken stock

pinch of white pepper

1 cup (90 g/3 oz) bean sprouts, tailed

2 tablespoons fresh mint, finely shredded

1 tablespoon fresh coriander leaves, chopped

crisp fried shallots, to garnish

1 Combine the light soy sauce and 1 teaspoon of the rice wine in a large non-metallic bowl. Add the lamb, toss together, then marinate for at least 10 minutes.

2 Meanwhile, wash and dry the baby cos leaves, then place on a serving plate.

3 Heat a wok over high heat, add 1 tablespoon of the oil and swirl to coat. When the oil is hot, add the garlic, Asian shallots and chilli and stir-fry for 30 seconds, or until fragrant. Add the water chestnuts and corn and continue to stir-fry for an extra minute, then remove everything from the wok.

4 Wipe the wok clean, heat over high heat, then add the remaining oil and swirl to coat. When the oil is smoking, add the lamb, toss briskly to break up any clumps, then stir-fry for 4–5 minutes, or until cooked through. Add the oyster sauce, kecap manis, stock and remaining rice wine, season with white pepper and stir thoroughly. Return the water chestnut mixture to the wok with the bean sprouts and mix together thoroughly. Remove from the heat, then stir in the mint.

5 Spoon equal portions of the lamb mixture onto each of the cos leaves, garnish with coriander and crisp fried shallots, then serve.

# LAMB AND MINT STIR-FRY

Preparation time: 10 minutes
Total cooking time: 15 minutes
Serves 4

1/4 cup (60 ml/2 fl oz) lime juice

2 tablespoons sweet chilli sauce

2 tablespoons fish sauce

2 tablespoons vegetable oil

750 g (1 1/2 lb) lamb loin fillets, thinly sliced across the grain

2 cloves garlic, finely chopped

1 small red onion, cut into wedges

1 fresh bird's eye chilli, finely chopped

1/2 cup (10 g/1/4 oz) fresh mint

1 To make the stir-fry sauce, combine the lime juice, chilli sauce and fish sauce in a small non-metallic bowl.

2 Heat a wok over high heat, add 1 tablespoon of the oil and swirl it around to coat the side of the wok. Add the lamb in batches and cook for 2 minutes each batch, or until browned. Remove from the wok.

3 Heat the remaining oil in the wok, add the garlic and onion and stir-fry for 1 minute, then add the chilli and cook for 30 seconds. Return the lamb to the wok, pour in the stir-fry sauce and cook for 2 minutes over high heat. Stir in the mint, then serve with steamed jasmine rice.

*LEFT: Lamb and mint stir-fry*

## WARM LAMB SALAD

Preparation time: 15 minutes +
  3 hours refrigeration
Total cooking time: 15 minutes
Serves 4–6

2 tablespoons Thai red curry paste (see page 56)
3 tablespoons chopped fresh coriander leaves
1 tablespoon finely grated fresh ginger
3–4 tablespoons peanut oil
750 g (1 1/2 lb) lamb loin fillets, thinly sliced
  across the grain
200 g (6 1/2 oz) snow peas (mangetout)
600 g (1 1/4 lb) fresh thick rice noodles
1 red pepper (capsicum), thinly sliced
1 Lebanese cucumber, thinly sliced
6 spring onions, thinly sliced

MINT DRESSING
1 1/2 tablespoons peanut oil
1/4 cup (60 ml/2 fl oz) lime juice

2 tablespoons soft brown sugar
3 teaspoons fish sauce
3 teaspoons soy sauce
4 tablespoons chopped fresh mint leaves
1 clove garlic, crushed

1 Combine the curry paste, coriander, ginger and 2 tablespoons oil in a non-metallic bowl. Add the lamb and coat well. Cover with plastic wrap and marinate in the refrigerator for 2–3 hours.
2 Steam or boil the snow peas until just tender, then refresh under cold water. Drain.
3 Cover the noodles with boiling water. Drain immediately and gently separate the noodles with your fingers.
4 To make the mint dressing, put all the ingredients in a screw-top jar and shake well.
5 Heat a wok over high heat, add 1 tablespoon of the oil and swirl to coat the side of the wok. Add half the lamb and stir-fry for 5 minutes, or until tender. Repeat with the remaining lamb, using more oil if needed.
6 Place the lamb, snow peas, noodles, pepper, cucumber and spring onion in a large bowl, drizzle with the dressing and toss to combine.

## STIR-FRIED LAMB AND LEEK

Preparation time: 10 minutes +
  1 hour marinating
Total cooking time: 10 minutes
Serves 4

2 cloves garlic, crushed
2 1/2 teaspoons dark soy sauce
2 teaspoons Chinese rice wine
2 teaspoons sesame oil
1 1/2 teaspoons rice vinegar
1 1/2 teaspoons cornflour
1 1/2 teaspoons sugar
350 g (11 oz) lamb loin fillets, thinly sliced
  across the grain
4 young, small leeks
1/4 cup (60 ml/2 fl oz) peanut oil
1 tablespoon finely chopped fresh ginger
1 tablespoon Chinese rice wine

1 Combine the garlic, soy sauce, rice wine, sesame oil, rice vinegar, cornflour, sugar and 1/4 teaspoon salt in a large non-metallic bowl.

*BELOW: Warm lamb salad*

Add the lamb and toss together. Cover with plastic wrap and marinate in the refrigerator for at least 1 hour.

**2** Cut the leeks in half lengthways, then into 2 cm (³/4 inch) lengths. Wash, being careful not to break the pieces up too much. Drain well.

**3** Heat a wok over high heat, add 1¹/2 tablespoons of the peanut oil and swirl to coat. Add the leek and ¹/4 teaspoon salt and stir-fry for 1–2 minutes, or until the leek is tender but still firm to the bite. Remove the leek from the wok and clean the wok with paper towels.

**4** Heat the remaining oil in the wok over high heat, then add the ginger and cook for 30 seconds. Add the lamb and the marinade, spreading it around the wok in a thin layer and cook for 1 minute without stirring. Toss the lamb, then cook for 30 seconds. Pour in the rice wine and return the leek to the wok. Toss until warmed through, then serve immediately with noodles or rice.

## LAMB WITH HOKKIEN NOODLES AND SOUR SAUCE

Preparation time: 25 minutes
Total cooking time: 15 minutes
Serves 4–6

450 g (14 oz) Hokkien noodles

¹/2 cup (125 ml/4 fl oz) chicken stock

15 g (¹/2 oz) palm sugar, grated

1 tablespoon lime juice

2 tablespoons vegetable oil

375 g (12 oz) lamb loin fillets, thinly sliced across the grain

75 g (2¹/2 oz) red Asian shallots, thinly sliced

3 cloves garlic, crushed

2 teaspoons finely chopped fresh ginger

1 small fresh red chilli, seeded and finely chopped

1¹/2 tablespoons Thai red curry paste (see page 56)

125 g (4 oz) snow peas (mangetout), trimmed and cut in half on the diagonal

1 small carrot, julienned

small whole fresh basil leaves, to garnish

**1** Cover the noodles with boiling water and soak for 1 minute. Drain well.

**2** To make the stir-fry sauce, combine the stock,

palm sugar and lime juice in a small non-metallic bowl or jug and stir until the sugar has dissolved. Set aside until needed.

**3** Heat a wok over high heat, add 1 tablespoon of the oil and swirl to coat the side of the wok. Stir-fry the lamb in batches over high heat for 2–3 minutes each batch, or until it just starts to brown. Remove from the wok.

**4** Heat the remaining oil in the wok, then add the shallots, garlic, ginger and chilli and stir-fry for 1–2 minutes. Stir in the curry paste and cook for 1 minute. Add the snow peas and carrot and return the lamb to the wok. Cook, tossing often, for 1–2 minutes, or until thoroughly combined.

**5** Pour in the stir-fry sauce, toss together well and cook for 2–3 minutes. Add the noodles and cook for 1 minute, or until heated through. Divide among serving bowls and garnish with the basil.

*ABOVE: Lamb with Hokkien noodles and sour sauce*

175 g (6 oz) baby English spinach leaves
5 spring onions, thinly sliced on the diagonal
1/3 cup (50 g/1 3/4 oz) unsalted peanuts, crushed
3 tablespoons chopped fresh coriander leaves
ground white pepper, to taste

1 Soak the mushrooms in boiling water for 20 minutes, or until soft. Squeeze dry, discard the stalks and thinly slice the caps. Meanwhile, soak the noodles in boiling water for 3–4 minutes, or until they are soft. Drain, then cut into 8 cm (3 inch) lengths with scissors.
2 Combine the soy sauce, sugar, 1 tablespoon sesame oil and half the garlic in a large non-metallic bowl. Add the lamb and toss well. Cover and marinate in the fridge for 1 hour.
3 Heat a large wok over high heat, add 1 tablespoon of the peanut oil and 1 teaspoon of the sesame oil and swirl to coat. Stir-fry the lamb in two batches (adding another teaspoon sesame oil and tablespoon peanut oil with each batch) for about 2 minutes, or until browned. Remove from the wok.
4 Wipe the wok clean, then return to high heat. Add the remaining peanut oil and swirl to coat. Stir-fry the chilli and remaining garlic for 30 seconds. Add the carrot and zucchini and cook for 2 minutes. Add the spinach, spring onion and mushrooms and cook for 1 minute. Return the lamb and any juices to the wok and stir-fry for 1–2 minutes, or until heated through. Add the noodles with half the crushed peanuts and coriander, season with white pepper and toss together until well combined. Garnish with the remaining peanuts and fresh coriander.

## OYSTER SAUCE LAMB STIR-FRY

Preparation time: 10 minutes
Total cooking time: 10 minutes
Serves 4

 ☆

1 tablespoon vegetable oil
750 g (1 1/2 lb) lamb loin fillets, thinly sliced
  across the grain
4 cloves garlic, finely chopped
2 small fresh red chillies, thinly sliced
1/3 cup (80 ml/2 3/4 fl oz) oyster sauce
2 1/2 tablespoons fish sauce
1 1/2 teaspoons sugar
1/2 cup (25 g/3/4 oz) chopped fresh mint
3 tablespoons whole fresh mint leaves

## CELLOPHANE NOODLES WITH LAMB AND PEANUTS

Preparation time: 20 minutes +
  20 minutes soaking + 1 hour marinating
Total cooking time: 15 minutes
Serves 4

 ☆

6 dried shiitake mushrooms
100 g (3 1/2 oz) cellophane noodles
1/4 cup (60 ml/2 fl oz) soy sauce
2 teaspoons sugar
1 1/2 tablespoons sesame oil
5 cloves garlic, finely chopped
300 g (10 oz) lamb loin fillets, thinly sliced
  across the grain
1/4 cup (60 ml/2 fl oz) peanut oil
2 small fresh red chillies, finely chopped
1 large carrot, julienned
2 small zucchini (courgettes), julienned

*ABOVE: Cellophane noodles
with lamb and peanuts*

1 Heat a wok over high heat, add the oil and swirl to coat. Add the lamb and garlic in batches and stir-fry for 1–2 minutes each batch, or until the lamb is almost cooked. Return to the wok. Stir in the chilli, oyster sauce, fish sauce, sugar and the chopped mint leaves, and cook for another 1–2 minutes.

2 Remove from the heat, fold in the whole mint leaves and serve immediately with rice.

## SPRING ONION LAMB

Preparation time: 10 minutes +
    10 minutes marinating
Total cooking time: 10 minutes
Serves 4

1 tablespoon Chinese rice wine

1/4 cup (60 ml/2 fl oz) soy sauce

1/2 teaspoon white pepper

600 g (1 1/4 lb) lean lamb loin fillets, thinly sliced
    across the grain

1 tablespoon Chinese black vinegar

1 teaspoon sesame oil

2 tablespoons vegetable oil

750 g (1 1/2 lb) choy sum, cut into 10 cm
    (4 inch) lengths

3 cloves garlic, crushed

6 spring onions, cut into 10 cm (4 inch) lengths

1 Combine the rice wine, 1 tablespoon of the soy sauce, the white pepper and 1/2 teaspoon salt in a large non-metallic bowl. Add the lamb and toss together well. Cover with plastic wrap, and marinate in the refrigerator for at least 10 minutes.

2 To make the stir-fry sauce, combine the black vinegar, sesame oil and 1 tablespoon of the soy sauce in a small, non-metallic bowl or jug. Set aside until needed.

3 Heat a wok over high heat, add 2 teaspoons of the oil and swirl to coat the side of the wok. Add the choy sum, stir-fry briefly, then add 1 clove of the crushed garlic and the remaining soy sauce. Cook for 3 minutes, or until cooked, but still crisp. Take the wok off the heat, then remove the greens from the wok and keep in a warm place.

4 Wipe the wok clean with paper towels, then reheat the wok over high heat. Add 1 tablespoon of the oil and swirl it around to coat the side of the wok. Add the lamb in two batches and stir-fry each batch over high heat for 1–2 minutes, or until nicely browned. Remove from the wok.

5 Add a little more oil to the wok, if necessary. Add the spring onion and remaining garlic and stir-fry for 1–2 minutes. Pour the stir-fry sauce into the wok and stir for 1 minute, or until combined. Return the lamb to the wok and continue to stir-fry for another minute, or until combined and heated through. Serve immediately with the greens.

### LAMB IN CHINA

Whereas cattle and pigs are indigenous to China, lamb was introduced during Mongol invasions. Lamb is very much the meat of survival in the north of China and it features in countless regional specialities. Beijing is considered the lamb capital of China, and in the city streets you can often smell the distinctive aroma of lamb cooking. However, in the south, lamb is very rare and the Cantonese, who are not fond of the taste or smell of lamb, are said to be able to distinguish 'mutton eaters' by their smell.

*LEFT: Spring onion lamb*

## GARLIC LAMB WITH WILTED MUSHROOMS AND NOODLES

Preparation time: 30 minutes
Total cooking time: 20 minutes
Serves 4

☆ ☆

8 red Asian shallots, very thinly sliced

4 cloves garlic, finely chopped

1 1/2 tablespoons vegetable oil

1 teaspoon soft brown sugar

1 teaspoon freshly ground black pepper

350 g (11 oz) lamb loin fillets, thinly sliced
   across the grain

300 g (10 oz) fresh egg noodles

oil, extra, for cooking

200 g (6 1/2 oz) button mushrooms, sliced

150 g (5 oz) small oyster mushrooms

2 tablespoons teriyaki sauce

75 g (2 1/2 oz) fresh garlic chives, cut into short
   pieces

1 Combine the shallots, garlic, oil, sugar,
1 teaspoon salt and the freshly ground black
pepper in a large non-metallic bowl. Add the
lamb and toss until well coated.

2 Cook the noodles in boiling water for
1 minute, or until separated. Drain and rinse.
3 Heat a wok over high heat, add 1 tablespoon
of the extra oil and swirl to coat. Stir-fry the lamb
in three batches, searing the meat and tossing
constantly until browned. Reheat the wok in
between each batch, adding a little more oil
when needed. Remove the meat from the wok.
4 Add the button mushrooms to the wok with
about 2 teaspoons of water, and stir-fry for
1 minute. Add the oyster mushrooms and teriyaki
sauce, and toss. Cover and steam for 10 seconds.
5 Return all the lamb and any juices to the wok
with the noodles and chives. Toss well to heat
through. Serve immediately.

## CHILLI BEAN LAMB

Preparation time: 15 minutes +
   30 minutes marinating
Total cooking time: 15 minutes
Serves 4

☆ ☆

2 cloves garlic, crushed

2 teaspoons finely grated fresh ginger

2 tablespoons chilli bean paste

600 g (1 1/4 lb) lamb loin fillets, thinly sliced
   across the grain

1/3 cup (80 ml/2 3/4 fl oz) chicken stock

1 tablespoon soy sauce

1 teaspoon sugar

1 teaspoon cornflour

1/4 cup (40 g/1 1/4 oz) raw unsalted peanuts

3 teaspoons vegetable oil

1 small onion, halved and thinly sliced

3 spring onions, thinly sliced on the diagonal

1 Combine the garlic, ginger and chilli bean
paste in a large non-metallic bowl. Add the lamb
and toss together. Cover with plastic wrap and
marinate in the refrigerator for 30 minutes.
2 To make the stir-fry sauce, mix together the
stock, soy sauce, sugar and cornflour in a small
non-metallic jug or bowl. Set aside until needed.
3 Roughly crush the peanuts in a mortar and
pestle. Heat a small frying pan over medium
heat, add 1 teaspoon of the oil, and cook the
peanuts until golden brown. Drain on crumpled
paper towels.
4 Heat a wok over high heat, add 1 teaspoon
of vegetable oil and swirl to coat the side of the
wok. Stir-fry the lamb in batches for 3 minutes,

*BELOW: Garlic lamb with wilted mushrooms and noodles*

or until browned. Remove from the wok. Add the remaining oil, then stir-fry the onion for 2 minutes. Return the lamb to the wok. Pour in the stir-fry sauce and add the spring onion. Toss together for 3 minutes, or until the sauce comes to the boil, and thickens enough to coat the lamb. Season to taste with salt and pepper, then serve immediately sprinkled with the crushed peanuts.

## SPICY LAMB AND EGGPLANT
(AUBERGINE) **STIR-FRY**

Preparation time: 15 minutes
Total cooking time: 20 minutes
Serves 4

2 tablespoons vegetable oil
1 onion, finely chopped
500 g (1 lb) eggplant (aubergine), peeled and
　cut into batons
600 g (1 1/4 lb) lamb loin fillets, thinly sliced
　across the grain
2 cloves garlic, finely chopped
1 small fresh red chilli, seeded and finely chopped
1 tablespoon ground cumin
1 tablespoon ground coriander
2 teaspoons ground turmeric
1 teaspoon ground cinnamon
1 cup (250 ml/8 fl oz) coconut cream
1 tablespoon chopped fresh mint
2 tablespoons chopped fresh parsley
lemon wedges, to serve

1 Heat a wok over high heat, add 2 teaspoons of the oil and swirl to coat the side of the wok. Stir-fry the onion until soft and golden. Remove from the wok.
2 Heat 1 tablespoon of the oil in the wok and cook the eggplant in two batches over high heat until golden and cooked. Drain on crumpled paper towels.
3 Reheat the wok, then add 2 teaspoons of the oil. Stir-fry the lamb in two batches over high heat for about 2 minutes each batch, or until browned and just cooked.
4 Return all the lamb to the wok with the onion and eggplant. Add the garlic, chilli and spices, and cook for 1 minute. Pour in the coconut cream and bring to the boil.
5 Stir in the fresh mint and parsley and season with salt and freshly ground black pepper. Serve with lemon wedges.

EGGPLANT (AUBERGINE)
A member of the nightshade family, eggplants are related to tomatoes and potatoes. Although generally considered as a vegetable, eggplants are actually classified as a fruit. When purchasing eggplant, choose smooth-skinned, firm fruit that feel heavy for their size.

*ABOVE: Spicy lamb and eggplant stir-fry*

1 Combine the garlic, ginger, Chinese rice wine, soy sauce, hoisin sauce and sesame oil in a large non-metallic bowl. Add the lamb and toss until well coated. Cover with plastic wrap and marinate in the refrigerator overnight, tossing occasionally.

2 Heat a wok over high heat, add 1 tablespoon of the peanut oil and swirl to coat the wok. Add the spring onion and stir-fry for 1 minute, or until lightly golden. Remove, reserving the oil in the wok.

3 Lift the lamb out of the marinade with tongs, reserving the marinade. Add the meat in four batches and stir-fry for 1–2 minutes per batch, or until browned but not completely cooked through, adding more oil and making sure the wok is very hot before cooking each batch. Return all the meat and any juices to the wok with the spring onion and stir-fry for 1 minute, or until meat is cooked through.

4 Remove the meat and spring onion from the wok with a slotted spoon and place in a serving bowl, retaining the liquid in the wok. Add any reserved marinade to the wok along with the chilli sauce and extra hoisin sauce, then boil for 3–4 minutes, or until the sauce thickens and becomes slightly syrupy. Spoon the sauce over the lamb, toss together well, then serve with steamed rice.

## CUMIN LAMB STIR-FRY

Preparation time: 15 minutes +
 10 minutes marinating
Total cooking time: 10 minutes
Serves 4

☆

1 tablespoon dark soy sauce
1 tablespoon Chinese rice wine
1 tablespoon light soy sauce
500 g (1 lb) lean lamb loin fillets, thinly sliced across the grain
1/3 cup (80 ml/2 3/4 fl oz) chicken or vegetable stock
2 teaspoons Chinese black vinegar
2 teaspoons chilli garlic sauce
2 tablespoons vegetable oil
1 red onion, cut into small wedges
1 teaspoon cumin seeds, lightly crushed
1 clove garlic, crushed
1 teaspoon fresh ginger, finely chopped
75 g (2 1/2 oz) garlic chives, trimmed and halved

## MONGOLIAN LAMB

Preparation time: 25 minutes +
 overnight marinating
Total cooking time: 15 minutes
Serves 4–6

☆ ☆

2 cloves garlic, crushed
2 teaspoons finely grated fresh ginger
1/4 cup (60 ml/2 fl oz) Chinese rice wine
1/4 cup (60 ml/2 fl oz) soy sauce
2 tablespoons hoisin sauce
1 teaspoon sesame oil
1 kg (2 lb) lamb loin fillets, thinly sliced across the grain
1/3 cup (80 ml/2 3/4 fl oz) peanut oil
6 spring onions, cut into 3 cm (1 1/4 inch) lengths
2 teaspoons chilli sauce
1 1/2 tablespoons hoisin sauce, extra

*ABOVE: Mongolian lamb*

1 Combine the dark soy sauce, Chinese rice wine and 2 teaspoons of the light soy sauce in a large non-metallic bowl. Add the lamb and toss well. Cover with plastic wrap and marinate in the refrigerator for at least 10 minutes.
2 To make the stir-fry sauce, combine the stock, black vinegar, chilli garlic sauce and remaining light soy sauce in a small non-metallic jug.
3 Heat a wok over high heat, add 1 tablespoon of the oil and swirl to coat. Add the lamb in two batches and stir-fry for 1–2 minutes, or until browned. Remove from the wok.
4 Heat the remaining oil in the wok, add the onion wedges and stir-fry for 2 minutes. Add the cumin, garlic, ginger and garlic chives and cook for 30 seconds, or until fragrant. Pour in the stir-fry sauce, and bring to the boil until thickened slightly and combined with the other ingredients. Return the lamb to the wok, quickly stir to coat with the sauce then serve with steamed rice and Asian greens.

## GREEN TEA NOODLE SALAD WITH LAMB AND TOMATO

Preparation time: 20 minutes +
  2 hours marinating
Total cooking time: 20 minutes
Serves 4

☆

1 teaspoon hot mustard
2 tablespoons vegetable oil
1/4 cup (60 ml/2 fl oz) balsamic vinegar
400 g (13 oz) lamb loin fillets, thinly sliced
  across the grain
250 g (8 oz) chasoba noodles (see Note)
1/4 cup (60 ml/2 fl oz) light soy sauce
2 tablespoons mirin
1–2 teaspoons sesame oil
1/2 teaspoon sugar
2 Lebanese cucumbers, cut in half lengthways
  and thinly sliced on the diagonal
2 large tomatoes, cut into 1 cm (1/2 inch) cubes
1/2 cup (15 g/1/2 oz) fresh coriander leaves
2 spring onions, thinly sliced on the diagonal
1 tablespoon sesame seeds, lightly toasted

1 Combine the mustard, 1 tablespoon of the oil, 1 tablespoon of the vinegar and 1/2 teaspoon pepper in a large non-metallic bowl. Add the lamb and toss. Cover, then refrigerate for 2 hours.

2 Add the noodles to a large saucepan of boiling water and stir to separate. Return to the boil, adding 1 cup (250 ml/8 fl oz) cold water and repeat this step three times, as it comes to the boil. Drain and rinse under cold water. Place in a large bowl.
3 Combine the soy sauce, mirin, sesame oil, sugar, the remaining balsamic vinegar and 1/2 teaspoon salt and stir until the sugar dissolves. Toss half of the dressing through the noodles.
4 Place the cucumber, tomato and 1/2 teaspoon salt in a bowl and toss well. Add to the noodles with the coriander and spring onion and toss well.
5 Heat a wok over high heat, add the remaining oil and swirl to coat. Drain the lamb, then, using tongs or a slotted spoon, add the lamb to the wok in two batches, and stir-fry each batch for 2–3 minutes, or until the lamb is seared and cooked to your liking. Divide the noodle salad among serving plates, then top with the lamb. Drizzle with as much of the dressing as you like. Sprinkle with the sesame seeds and serve.
NOTE: Chasoba noodles are soba noodles that have had green tea powder added to them.

*BELOW: Green tea noodle salad with lamb and tomato*

THE ESSENTIAL WOK COOKBOOK

## PHAD THAI

Preparation time: 30 minutes + 20 minutes soaking
Total cooking time: 10 minutes
Serves 4–6

☆☆

250 g (8 oz) dried rice stick noodles

1 small fresh red chilli, chopped

2 cloves garlic, chopped

2 spring onions, sliced

1 tablespoon tamarind purée, mixed
   with 1 tablespoon water

1½ tablespoons sugar

2 tablespoons fish sauce

2 tablespoons lime juice

2 tablespoons vegetable oil

2 eggs, beaten

150 g (5 oz) pork fillet, thinly sliced

*BELOW: Phad Thai*

8 raw large prawns, peeled and deveined,
   with tails intact

100 g (3½ oz) fried tofu puffs, julienned

1 cup (90 g/3 oz) bean sprouts, tailed

¼ cup (40 g/1¼ oz) chopped roasted peanuts

3 tablespoons fresh coriander leaves

1 lime, cut into wedges

1 Soak the noodles in warm water for
15–20 minutes, or until tender. Drain.
2 Pound together the chilli, garlic and spring
onion in a mortar and pestle. Gradually blend
in the tamarind mixture, sugar, fish sauce and
lime juice.
3 Heat a wok over high heat, add 1 tablespoon
of the oil and swirl to coat. Add the egg, swirl
to coat and cook for 1–2 minutes, or until set
and cooked. Remove and shred.
4 Heat the remaining oil, stir in the chilli
mixture, and stir-fry for 30 seconds. Add the
pork and stir-fry for 2 minutes, or until
tender. Add the prawns and stir-fry for a further
1 minute.
5 Stir in the noodles, egg, tofu and half the bean
sprouts, and toss to heat through.
6 Serve immediately, topped with the peanuts,
coriander, lime and remaining bean sprouts.
NOTE: Use a non-stick or stainless steel wok to
cook this dish as the tamarind purée will react
with the metal in a regular wok and badly taint
the dish.

## CHINESE BARBECUED PORK WITH GAI LARN
(CHINESE BROCCOLI)

Preparation time: 10 minutes
Total cooking time: 10 minutes
Serves 4

☆

¼ cup (60 ml/2 fl oz) chicken or vegetable
   stock

¼ cup (60 ml/2 fl oz) oyster sauce

1 tablespoon kecap manis

1.6 kg (3¼ lb) gai larn (Chinese broccoli), cut
   into 5 cm (2 inch) lengths

1 tablespoon peanut oil

2 cm (¾ inch) piece fresh ginger, julienned

2 cloves garlic, crushed

500 g (1 lb) Chinese barbecued pork, thinly
   sliced

Use a pair of scissors to trim the lettuce leaves into neat cups.

1 To make the stir-fry sauce, combine the stock, oyster sauce and kecap manis in a small bowl.
2 Put the gai larn in a steamer over a saucepan or wok of simmering water and cook for 5 minutes, or until just tender but still crisp.
3 Heat a wok over high heat, add the oil and swirl to coat. Add the ginger and garlic, and stir-fry for 30 seconds, or until fragrant. Add the gai larn and pork, and toss to coat. Pour in the stir-fry sauce and toss together until heated through. Serve with rice or noodles.

## SAN CHOY BAU

Preparation time: 25 minutes
Total cooking time: 10 minutes
Makes 12 small or 4 large

1/4 cup (60 ml/2 fl oz) oyster sauce
2 teaspoons soy sauce
1/4 cup (60 ml/2 fl oz) sherry
1 teaspoon sugar
1 1/2 tablespoons vegetable oil
1/4 teaspoon sesame oil
3 cloves garlic, crushed

3 teaspoons grated fresh ginger
6 spring onions, sliced on the diagonal
500 g (1 lb) pork mince
100 g (3 1/2 oz) bamboo shoots, finely chopped
100 g (3 1/2 oz) water chestnuts, drained and finely chopped
1 tablespoon pine nuts, toasted
12 small or 4 large whole lettuce leaves (e.g. iceberg), trimmed
oyster sauce, to serve (optional)

1 To make the stir-fry sauce, combine the oyster and soy sauces, sherry and sugar in a small bowl or jug and stir until the sugar dissolves.
2 Heat a wok over high heat, add the vegetable and sesame oils and swirl to coat. Add the garlic, ginger and half the spring onion and stir-fry for 1 minute. Add the mince and cook for 3–4 minutes, or until just cooked, breaking up any lumps.
3 Add the bamboo shoots, water chestnuts and remaining spring onion, then pour in the stir-fry sauce. Cook for 2–3 minutes, or until the liquid thickens a little. Stir in the pine nuts.
4 Divide among the lettuce cups to make either 12 small portions or four very large ones. Drizzle with oyster sauce, if desired, then serve.

*ABOVE: San choy bau*

## MA POR TOFU

Preparation time: 15 minutes +
    10 minutes marinating
Total cooking time: 15 minutes
Serves 4

3 teaspoons cornflour
1 teaspoon oyster sauce
1 clove garlic, finely chopped
1 tablespoon soy sauce
250 g (8 oz) pork mince
1 tablespoon vegetable oil
3 teaspoons chilli bean paste
3 teaspoons preserved bean curd
750 g (1 1/2 lb) firm tofu, drained, cubed
2 spring onions, sliced
3 teaspoons oyster sauce, extra
1 1/2 teaspoons sugar

1 Combine the cornflour, oyster sauce, garlic and 2 teaspoons soy sauce in a large bowl. Add the mince, then marinate for 10 minutes.
2 Heat a wok over high heat, add the oil and swirl. Add the mince and stir-fry for 5 minutes, or until browned. Add the chilli paste and bean curd, and cook for 2 minutes, or until fragrant. Add the remaining ingredients and stir for 3–5 minutes, or until heated through.

## SESAME PORK

Preparation time: 10 minutes
Total cooking time: 20 minutes
Serves 4

2 tablespoons hoisin sauce
2 tablespoons teriyaki sauce
2 teaspoons cornflour
1/4 cup (60 ml) peanut oil
600 g (1 1/4 lb) pork loin fillet, thinly sliced
    across the grain
2 teaspoons sesame oil
8 spring onions, sliced on the diagonal
2 cloves garlic, crushed
2 teaspoons finely grated fresh ginger
2 carrots, julienned
200 g (6 1/2 oz) snake beans, sliced
2 tablespoons sesame seeds, toasted

1 To make the stir-fry sauce, combine the hoisin and teriyaki sauces, cornflour and 1 tablespoon water in a small bowl. Set aside until needed.
2 Heat a wok to hot, add 1 tablespoon peanut oil and swirl. Add half the pork and stir-fry for 3 minutes, or until browned. Remove. Repeat.
3 Heat the remaining peanut oil and the sesame oil in the wok. Add the spring onion, garlic and ginger, and stir-fry for 1 minute.
4 Add the carrot and beans, and stir-fry for 3 minutes, or until almost cooked. Return the pork to the wok, add the stir-fry sauce and stir until the sauce thickens and everything is combined, the meat is tender and the vegetables are just cooked. Toss in the sesame seeds, then serve with steamed rice.

## CAMBODIAN MINCED PORK WITH EGGPLANT (AUBERGINE)

Preparation time: 10 minutes + 30 minutes
    marinating
Total cooking time: 50 minutes
Serves 4

1 large eggplant (aubergine), pierced
2 cloves garlic, crushed
1 red chilli, seeded and finely chopped
1 tablespoon light soy sauce
2 teaspoons fish sauce
1/2 teaspoon chilli powder
250 g (8 oz) pork mince
1 tablespoon vegetable oil
1/2 cup (125 ml/4 fl oz) chicken stock
1 tablespoon lime juice
2 teaspoons sugar
250 g (8 oz) raw prawn meat, finely chopped
thinly sliced spring onions, to garnish

1 Preheat the oven to hot 220°C (425°F/Gas 7). Place the eggplant on a baking tray and bake for 35–40 minutes, or until soft. Cool, peel the skin and cut lengthwise into 1 cm (1/2 inch) thick strips.
2 Combine the garlic, chilli, soy sauce, fish sauce and chilli powder in a bowl. Add the mince and mix well. Cover and refrigerate for 30 minutes.
3 Heat a wok over high heat, add the oil and swirl. Add the pork and stir-fry for 3 minutes, or until cooked. Add the stock, lime juice, sugar and eggplant and simmer for 5 minutes, then add the prawns and cook for 5 minutes. Transfer to a plate and garnish with the spring onion.

MA POR TOFU
This famous Sichuan dish was named after the woman who invented it. This woman was a restaurateur's wife whose face was reputedly scarred or pock-marked, Ma Por meaning 'pock-marked woman'. Despite this unfortunate association, it makes an excellent main course dish in a Chinese banquet.

*OPPOSITE PAGE, FROM TOP: Ma Por tofu; Sesame pork*

## PORK, PUMPKIN AND CASHEW STIR-FRY

Preparation time: 20 minutes
Total cooking time: 20 minutes
Serves 4

2–3 tablespoons vegetable oil
1/2 cup (80 g/2 3/4 oz) cashews
750 g (1 1/2 lb) pork loin fillet, thinly sliced
  across the grain
500 g (1 lb) pumpkin, cut into cubes
1 tablespoon grated fresh ginger
1/3 cup (80 ml/2 3/4 fl oz) chicken stock
1/4 cup (60 ml/2 fl oz) dry sherry
1 1/2 tablespoons soy sauce
1/2 teaspoon cornflour
500 g (1 lb) baby bok choy, chopped
1–2 tablespoons fresh coriander leaves

1 Heat a wok over high heat, add 1 tablespoon of the oil and swirl to coat. Stir-fry the cashews for 1–2 minutes, or until browned. Drain.
2 Reheat the wok, add a little extra oil and swirl to coat. Stir-fry the pork in batches for 5 minutes, or until lightly browned. Remove. Add 1 tablespoon oil and stir-fry the pumpkin and ginger for 3 minutes, or until lightly browned. Add the stock, sherry and soy sauce, and simmer

for 3 minutes, or until the pumpkin is tender.
3 Blend the cornflour with 1 teaspoon water, add to the wok and stir until the mixture boils and thickens. Return the pork and cashews to the wok, and add the bok choy and coriander. Stir until the bok choy has just wilted. Serve.

## THAI PORK WITH SNAKE BEANS

Preparation time: 25 minutes
Total cooking time: 15 minutes
Serves 4

1 1/2 tablespoons fish sauce
1 1/2 tablespoons oyster sauce
1 teaspoon sugar
2–3 tablespoons peanut oil
450 g (14 oz) pork loin fillet, thinly sliced
  across the grain
1 red onion, sliced into thin wedges
1 clove garlic, finely chopped
1–2 tablespoons chilli jam
300 g (10 oz) snake beans, cut into 4 cm
  (1 1/2 inch) lengths
3 tablespoons fresh Thai basil
2 tablespoons chopped fresh coriander leaves
1 small fresh red chilli, thinly sliced

*ABOVE: Pork, pumpkin and cashew stir-fry*

1 Combine the fish sauce, oyster sauce, sugar and 2 tablespoons water in a small bowl or jug.
2 Heat a wok over high heat, add 1 tablespoon of the oil and swirl to coat the side of the wok. Add the pork in two batches and stir-fry until just cooked through, adding more oil if necessary. Remove from the wok.
3 Add the remaining oil to the wok, then add the onion and cook for 2–3 minutes, or until just soft. Add the garlic, chilli jam and snake beans and stir-fry for 3 minutes, then return the pork and any juices to the wok. Stir in the sauce and stir-fry for 1–2 minutes, or until the meat is heated through. Toss in the basil and coriander. Serve immediately, garnished with chilli and accompanied with steamed rice.

## SHANGHAI PORK NOODLES

Preparation time: 25 minutes +
    30 minutes marinating
Total cooking time: 20 minutes
Serves 4

☆ ☆

¹/₂ teaspoon sesame oil

¹/₄ cup (60 ml/2 fl oz) soy sauce

2 tablespoons oyster sauce

250 g (8 oz) pork loin fillet, cut into julienne
    strips

2 tablespoons dried shrimp

8 dried shiitake mushrooms

1 teaspoon sugar

1 cup (250 ml/8 fl oz) chicken stock

300 g (10 oz) fresh Shanghai noodles

2 tablespoons peanut oil

1 clove garlic, thinly sliced

2 teaspoons grated fresh ginger

1 celery stick, julienned

1 leek, white part only, julienned

150 g (5 oz) wom bok (Chinese cabbage),
    shredded

50 g (1³/₄ oz) bamboo shoots, julienned

8 spring onions, thinly sliced

1 Combine the sesame oil and 1 tablespoon each of the soy sauce and oyster sauce in a large non-metallic bowl. Add the pork and toss in the marinade. Cover and marinate in the refrigerator for 30 minutes.
2 Meanwhile, place the dried shrimp in a bowl, cover with boiling water and soak for

20 minutes. Drain and finely chop. At the same time, soak the shiitake mushrooms in hot water for 20 minutes. Drain, discard the stalks and thinly slice the caps.
3 To make the stir-fry sauce, combine the sugar, chicken stock, remaining soy and oyster sauces and 1 teaspoon salt in a small non-metallic jug. Set aside until needed.
4 Cook the noodles in a large saucepan of boiling water for 4–5 minutes, or until tender. Drain and refresh under cold water. Toss with 1 teaspoon peanut oil.
5 Heat a wok over high heat, add 1 tablespoon of the peanut oil and swirl to coat. Add the pork and stir-fry for 1–2 minutes, or until the pork is no longer pink. Transfer to a plate. Heat the remaining peanut oil, add the garlic, ginger, celery, leek and wom bok and stir-fry for 1 minute, or until softened. Add the bamboo shoots, spring onion, mushrooms and shrimp and stir-fry for 1 minute. Add the noodles and the stir-fry sauce and toss together for 3–5 minutes, or until the noodles absorb the sauce. Return the pork to the wok, with any juices and toss through for 1–2 minutes, or until combined and heated through. Serve immediately.

*BELOW: Shanghai pork noodles*

# THAI PORK NOODLE SALAD
## (Yum woon sen)

Preparation time: 20 minutes
Total cooking time: 35 minutes
Serves 4–6

**BROTH**

I cup (250 ml/8 fl oz) chicken stock

3 coriander roots

2 fresh kaffir lime leaves

3 x 3 cm (1¼ x 1¼ inch) piece fresh ginger, sliced

30 g (1 oz) fresh black fungus

100 g (3½ oz) cellophane noodles or dried rice vermicelli

I small fresh red chilli, seeded and thinly sliced

2 red Asian shallots, thinly sliced

2 spring onions, thinly sliced

2 cloves garlic, crushed

I tablespoon vegetable oil

250 g (8 oz) pork mince

2½ tablespoons lime juice

2½ tablespoons fish sauce

1½ tablespoons grated palm sugar

¼ teaspoon ground white pepper

½ cup (15 g/½ oz) fresh coriander leaves, chopped

oakleaf or coral lettuce, torn or shredded

lime wedges, to garnish

fresh red chilli, extra, cut into strips, to garnish

fresh coriander leaves, extra, to garnish
  (optional)

I To make the broth, put the chicken stock, coriander roots, lime leaves, ginger and 1 cup (250 ml/8 fl oz) water in a wok. Simmer for 25 minutes, or until it has reduced to ¾ cup (185 ml/6 fl oz). Strain.

2 Discard the woody stems from the fungus, then thinly slice. Soak the noodles in boiling water for 3–4 minutes, or until pliable. Rinse, drain, then cut into 3 cm (1¼ inch) lengths. Combine the noodles, fungus, chilli, shallots, spring onion and garlic.

3 Heat a clean, dry wok over high heat, add the oil and swirl to coat. Add the pork mince and stir-fry, breaking up any lumps, for 1–2 minutes, or until the pork changes colour and is cooked. Add the broth and bring the mixture to the boil over high heat. Boil for 1 minute, then drain, and add the pork to the noodle mixture.

4 Combine the lime juice, fish sauce, palm sugar and white pepper, stirring until the sugar is dissolved. Add to the pork mixture with the coriander and mix well. Season to taste with salt.

5 Arrange the lettuce on a serving dish, spoon on the pork and noodle mixture and garnish with the lime, chilli and, if desired, fresh coriander leaves.

**YUM WOON SEN**
Literally meaning 'assembled' or 'mixed together', yums are a type of Thai salad that incorporate lightly cooked meat or seafood. Dressed with lime juice, fish sauce, sugar and chilli, they are an important feature of Thai cuisine, showcasing the Thai palate's emphasis on freshness and the balance between sour, salty, sweet and hot flavours.

*RIGHT: Thai pork noodle salad*

# PORK AND HOKKIEN NOODLE STIR-FRY

Preparation time: 15 minutes +
    10 minutes marinating
Total cooking time: 15 minutes
Serves 4

1/3 cup (80 ml/2 3/4 fl oz) soy sauce

1/4 cup (60 ml/2 fl oz) mirin

2 teaspoons grated fresh ginger

2 cloves garlic, crushed

1 1/2 tablespoons soft brown sugar

350 g (11 oz) pork loin fillet, thinly sliced
    across the grain

500 g (1 lb) Hokkien noodles

2 tablespoons peanut oil

1 onion, cut into thin wedges

1 red pepper (capsicum), cut into thin strips

2 carrots, thinly sliced on the diagonal

4 spring onions, thinly sliced on the diagonal

200 g (6 1/2 oz) fresh shiitake mushrooms, sliced

1 Combine the soy sauce, mirin, ginger, garlic and sugar in a large non-metallic bowl. Add the pork and toss to coat. Cover with plastic wrap and marinate in the refrigerator for at least 10 minutes.
2 Meanwhile, put the noodles in a heatproof bowl, cover with boiling water and soak for 1 minute to separate and soften. Drain well, then rinse under running water.
3 Heat a large wok over high heat, add 1 tablespoon of the oil and swirl it around to coat the side of the wok. Lift the pork out of the marinade with tongs or a slotted spoon, reserving the marinade. Stir-fry the pork in batches for 3 minutes each batch, or until nicely browned. Remove from the wok.
4 Reheat the wok over high heat, add the remaining oil and swirl to coat. Add the onion, pepper and carrot, and stir-fry for 2–3 minutes, or until just tender. Add the spring onion and shiitake mushrooms and cook for another 2 minutes. Return the pork to the wok along with the noodles and the reserved marinade. Toss together thoroughly until combined and heated through, then serve.

## FRIED CHILLI RELISH
(Sambal bajak)

Soak 25 g (3/4 oz) tamarind pulp in 1/4 cup (60 ml/2 fl oz) hot water for 10 minutes. Squeeze, then strain, reserving any liquid. Put 3–4 chopped small fresh red chillies, 100 g (3 1/2 oz) red Asian shallots, 2 cloves garlic, 7 candlenuts and 1/2 teaspoon grated fresh galangal in a food processor and grind to a paste. Heat 1/3 cup (80 ml/2 3/4 fl oz) vegetable oil in a wok or frying pan, add the paste and cook for 5 minutes, or until the oil starts to float. Add the tamarind liquid, 2 teaspoons kecap manis, 1 tablespoon sugar and salt to taste, and simmer over low heat, stirring often, for 5–10 minutes, or until the oil floats to the top again. Pour into a clean, warm jar and seal. Cool. Store in the fridge for up to 5 days. Makes 1/2 cup (serves 24).
NOTE: A sambal is a condiment used to accompany a meal in Southeast Asia.

*ABOVE: Pork and hokkien noodle stir-fry*

MU SHU PORK

Mix the flour and water mixture into a dough.

Having divided the dough into four even pieces, roll each piece into a sausage.

Flatten each piece of dough with the heel of your hand.

Roll the rounds of dough out as thinly as possible.

*OPPOSITE PAGE:*
*Mu shu pork*

# MU SHU PORK

Preparation time: 30 minutes +
  3 hours marinating + 30 minutes refrigeration
Total cooking time: 20 minutes
Serves 4

☆ ☆ ☆

2 cloves garlic, crushed
1 teaspoon finely grated fresh ginger
2¹/₂ tablespoons light soy sauce
1¹/₂ tablespoons Chinese rice wine
2 tablespoons hoisin sauce
2¹/₂ teaspoons cornflour
500 g (1 lb) pork loin fillet, sliced into julienne
  strips
20 g (³/₄ oz) dried black fungus
20 g (³/₄ oz) dried lily buds (see Notes)
2 tablespoons chicken stock
3 eggs
2 tablespoons vegetable oil
¹/₂ teaspoon sesame oil
2 cups (150 g/5 oz) finely shredded wom bok
  (Chinese cabbage)
¹/₄ cup (40 g/1¹/₄ oz) julienned bamboo shoots
5 spring onions, thinly sliced on the diagonal
white pepper, to taste
spring onion lengths, to garnish (optional)

PANCAKES
300 g (10 oz) plain flour
200 ml (6¹/₂ fl oz) boiling water
¹/₂ teaspoon vegetable oil
plain flour, for dusting

1 Combine the garlic, ginger, 1 tablespoon of the soy sauce, 1 tablespoon of the Chinese rice wine, 1 tablespoon of the hoisin sauce and 1 teaspoon of the cornflour in a large non-metallic bowl. Add the the pork, toss well, then cover with plastic wrap and marinate in the refrigerator for 3 hours.
2 To make the pancake dough, sift the flour into a large bowl and make a well in the centre. Slowly pour in the boiling water, stirring with a wooden spoon, then add the oil. Mix until a dough forms. Place the dough on a lightly floured workbench and knead for 5 minutes, or until smooth and elastic—be careful as the dough will be hot. Transfer the dough to a clean bowl, cover with plastic wrap, and refrigerate for 30 minutes.

3 Meanwhile, soak the black fungus and lily buds separately by covering with boiling water for 20 minutes. Drain, remove any hard ends from the lily buds, julienne the black fungus, and cut the lily buds into 1 cm (¹/₂ inch) pieces.
4 Combine the chicken stock and remaining soy sauce, rice wine, hoisin sauce and cornflour in a small jug. Whisk with a fork to dissolve the cornflour and form a paste.
5 Lightly whisk the eggs together with a fork. Heat a wok over high heat, add 1 teaspoon of vegetable oil and ¹/₄ teaspoon of the sesame oil, and add the eggs. Stir for about 30 seconds, or until scrambled. Remove from the wok.
6 Heat the same wok over high heat, add 2 teaspoons of the vegetable oil and the remaining sesame oil and swirl to coat. Stir-fry the pork in batches for 2 minutes, or until browned.
7 Add the remaining oil to the wok, then add the wom bok, bamboo shoots, spring onion, black fungus and lily buds and stir-fry for 3 minutes, or until the wom bok begins to wilt. Return the pork to the wok, add the sauce mixture and cook until it comes to the boil and begins to thicken. Stir in the reserved scrambled eggs and season with white pepper. Remove the wok from direct heat. Keep warm.
8 To make the pancakes, lightly flour a workbench, then divide the dough into four even pieces and roll each piece into a long sausage. Cut each sausage into four. Flatten each piece with your palm, then roll each piece out as thinly as possible to a pancake about 15 cm (6 inch) in diameter. The dough is quite elastic and you can roll the dough thin enough to almost see through it.
9 Heat a frying pan over medium heat. Dry-fry the pancakes on each side for about 30 seconds, or until some brown spots appear. Stack the cooked pancakes on a plate, covered with foil to keep warm while cooking the remaining pancakes. Wrap the filling in the pancakes, garnish with the spring onion lengths, if desired, then serve.
NOTES: Lily buds, also called golden needles, are the unopened flower buds of the tiger lily. Often used in Chinese cooking, they are soaked in water before use. Available in some Asian grocery stores.
If you are short on time, you can buy the pancakes ready-made from Asian supermarkets—store them in the freezer until required.

## THAI ETIQUETTE

Despite what many westerners think, Thais do not usually use chopsticks when eating (except for Chinese noodle dishes), and a request for chopsticks in a Thai restaurant in Thailand will result in a puzzled expression from the waiting staff. The reason for this is partly because Thais prefer to eat off a plate rather than a bowl, as the Chinese and Japanese do, and chopsticks aren't very useful for picking up rice from a plate. Originally, Thai food was eaten with the fingers, but today, the primary utensils used are forks and spoons. Knives are confined to the kitchen—food is chopped into bite-size pieces before ever leaving the kitchen, so there is no need for a knife on the table. Thai meals usually involve having several dishes placed in the centre of the table for people to help themselves. The fork is used to help manoeuvre food onto the spoon or to take a serve of food from communal dishes. It is considered good manners not to let the fork touch the mouth.

*ABOVE: Thai pork and mushroom stir-fry with pepper*

## THAI PORK AND MUSHROOM STIR-FRY WITH PEPPER
(Paht heht)

Preparation time: 20 minutes + 20 minutes soaking
Total cooking time: 5 minutes
Serves 4

15 g ($^1$/$_2$ oz) dried black fungus
1 tablespoon peanut oil
350 g (11 oz) pork loin fillet, thinly sliced across the grain
4 cloves garlic, thinly sliced
3 red Asian shallots, thinly sliced
1 carrot, thinly sliced on the diagonal
6 spring onions, cut into 2.5 cm (1 inch) lengths
2 tablespoons fish sauce
2 tablespoons oyster sauce
1 teaspoon ground white pepper

1 Soak the black fungus in a bowl of boiling water for 20 minutes. Rinse, then cut into slices.
2 Heat a wok over medium heat, add the oil and swirl to coat. Add the pork, garlic and shallots and stir-fry for 30 seconds. Add the carrot and spring onion and stir-fry for 2–3 minutes, or until the pork is cooked.
3 Add the fish and oyster sauces and ground white pepper and stir-fry for a further 1 minute. Serve hot with rice.

## JAPANESE PORK AND CABBAGE STIR-FRY

Preparation time: 15 minutes
Total cooking time: 10 minutes
Serves 4

$^1$/$_4$ teaspoon dashi granules
1 $^1$/$_2$ tablespoons vegetable oil
500 g (1 lb) pork loin fillet, very thinly sliced across the grain
4 spring onions, cut into 3 cm (1 $^1$/$_4$ inch) lengths
3 cups (225 g/7 oz) shredded wom bok (Chinese cabbage)
$^1$/$_4$ cup (60 ml/2 fl oz) soy sauce
2 teaspoons mirin
3 teaspoons very finely grated fresh ginger
2 cloves garlic, crushed
1–2 teaspoons sugar
black sesame seeds, to garnish (optional)

1 Dissolve the dashi in $^1$/$_2$ cup (125 ml/4 fl oz) hot water.
2 Heat a wok over high heat, then add 1 tablespoon of the oil and swirl to coat the side of the wok. Stir-fry the pork in three batches for 1 minute, or until it just changes colour, then remove from the wok.
3 Add the remaining oil to the wok and swirl to

coat, then add the spring onion and wom bok and stir-fry for 1 minute, or until softened slightly, then set aside with the pork.

4 Add the combined soy sauce, mirin, dashi broth, ginger, garlic and sugar to the wok, bring to the boil and cook for 1 minute. Return the pork and vegetables to the wok and stir-fry for 2–3 minutes, or until combined and the pork is just cooked through but still tender. Serve immediately with rice. If desired, garnish with black sesame seeds or thinly sliced spring onion.

## THAI PORK AND GINGER STIR-FRY
(Mao paht king)

Preparation time: 20 minutes
Total cooking time: 10 minutes
Serves 4

☆

2–3 tablespoons peanut oil

1 clove garlic, crushed

400 g (13 oz) pork loin fillet, thinly sliced across the grain

2 tablespoons julienned fresh ginger, plus extra, to garnish

3 red Asian shallots, thinly sliced

1 small red pepper (capsicum), cut into thin strips

4 spring onions, cut into 4 cm (1 1/2 inch) lengths

100 g (3 1/2 oz) snow peas (mangetout), cut in half on the diagonal

2 tablespoons soy sauce

2 tablespoons fish sauce

2 tablespoons grated palm sugar

2 tablespoons lime juice

2 tablespoons chopped fresh coriander leaves

1 Heat a wok over high heat. Add 1 tablespoon of the oil and swirl to coat the side of the wok. Add the garlic and cook for 30 seconds. Cook the pork in batches and stir-fry each batch for 1–2 minutes, or until lightly browned. Remove from the wok.

2 Heat the remaining oil in the wok, add the ginger and shallots and stir-fry for 1 minute, or until the shallots are tender. Add the pepper, spring onion and snow peas. Stir-fry for a further 1 minute, then return the pork to the wok.

3 Combine the soy sauce, fish sauce, palm sugar and lime juice, then add to the wok. Stir in the coriander and stir for 1 minute until combined and the pork is heated through. Garnish with ginger and serve with rice.

*LEFT: Thai pork and ginger stir-fry*

145

1 Cook the noodles in boiling water for 1 minute. Drain, rinse, then return to the saucepan. Stir in half the sesame oil.

2 Place the ginger, five-spice powder and rice flour in a bowl, season with salt and pepper, then mix well. Add the pork and toss to coat.

3 Heat a wok over high heat, add half the oil and swirl to coat. Add the pork in batches and stir-fry for 5 minutes, or until tender. Remove from the wok. Add the remaining oil, garlic, pepper, bok choy and spring onion, and stir-fry for 3 minutes, or until softened.

4 Return the pork to the wok and stir in the rice wine, hoisin sauce, soy sauce and the remaining sesame oil, and simmer for 2 minutes. Add the noodles and reheat gently before serving.

## PORK AND PICKLE STIR-FRY

Preparation time: 10 minutes +
  1 hour marinating
Total cooking time: 10 minutes
Serves 4

1/4 teaspoon sesame oil

1 teaspoon cornflour

5 teaspoons sugar

1 1/2 tablespoons light soy sauce

1 1/2 tablespoons Chinese rice wine

500 g (1 lb) pork loin fillet, sliced into julienne
  strips

2 tablespoons peanut oil

1 clove garlic, chopped

1 tablespoon thinly sliced fresh ginger

2 spring onions, finely chopped

1 teaspoon chilli paste

150 g (5 oz) pickled daikon, drained and rinsed

1 teaspoon rice vinegar

1 Combine the sesame oil, cornflour, 3 teaspoons of the sugar and 1 tablespoon each of the soy sauce and rice wine in a large non-metallic bowl. Add the pork, toss well, then cover and marinate in the fridge for at least 1 hour.

2 Heat a wok over high heat, add the peanut oil and swirl to coat the side of the wok. When the oil is hot, add half of the pork strips and stir-fry for 2 minutes. Remove with a slotted spoon and drain on paper towel. Repeat with the remaining pork.

3 Reheat the wok over high heat and add the garlic, ginger, spring onion and chilli paste.

## FIVE-SPICE PORK STIR-FRY

Preparation time: 20 minutes
Total cooking time: 20 minutes
Serves 4

☆ ☆

375 g (12 oz) fresh thin egg noodles

1 tablespoon sesame oil

3 teaspoons grated fresh ginger

1 1/2 teaspoons five-spice powder

2 teaspoons rice flour

500 g (1 lb) pork loin fillet, thinly sliced across
  the grain

2 tablespoons vegetable oil

2 cloves garlic, crushed

1 red pepper (capsicum), thinly sliced

300 g (10 oz) baby bok choy or wom bok
  (Chinese cabbage), chopped

6 spring onions, sliced on the diagonal

2 tablespoons Chinese rice wine

2 tablespoons hoisin sauce

1 tablespoon soy sauce

*ABOVE: Five-spice
pork stir-fry*

Cook for 30 seconds. Add the pickles to the wok and cook for 1 minute, then return the pork to the wok. Cook for 2 minutes, stirring constantly. Combine the vinegar with the remaining soy sauce, rice wine and sugar in a small bowl and add to the wok. Toss until combined, then serve with steamed rice.

## BARBECUED PORK AND BROCCOLI STIR-FRY

Preparation time: 25 minutes
Total cooking time: 10 minutes
Serves 4–6

1 tablespoon vegetable oil
1 large onion, thinly sliced
2 carrots, julienned
200 g (6¹/₂ oz) broccoli, cut into bite-sized
  florets
6 spring onions, sliced on the diagonal
1 tablespoon finely chopped fresh ginger
3 cloves garlic, finely chopped
400 g (13 oz) Chinese barbecued pork,
  thinly sliced
2 tablespoons soy sauce
2 tablespoons mirin
2 cups (180 g/6 oz) bean sprouts, tailed

1 Heat a wok over high heat, add the oil and swirl it around to coat the side of the wok. Reduce the heat to medium, add the onion and stir-fry for 3–4 minutes, or until slightly softened.
2 Add the carrot, broccoli, spring onion, ginger and garlic, and cook for 4–5 minutes, tossing constantly until thoroughly combined.
3 Increase the heat to high and add the pork. Toss constantly until the pork is well mixed with the vegetables and is heated through.
4 Pour in the soy sauce and mirin, and toss until the ingredients are well coated. The wok should be hot enough that the sauce reduces a little to form a glaze-like consistency. Toss in the bean sprouts, then season to taste with salt and freshly ground black pepper. Serve immediately with rice noodles, if desired.

*BELOW: Barbecued pork and broccoli stir-fry*

# VIETNAMESE CREPES WITH PRAWNS, PORK AND NOODLES

Preparation time: 45 minutes +
   4 hours resting
Total cooking time: 35 minutes
Serves 6

1 1/2 cups (265 g/8 oz) rice flour
1 teaspoon baking powder
1 1/2 teaspoons sugar
1/2 teaspoon ground turmeric
1 cup (250 ml/8 fl oz) coconut milk
3 teaspoons peanut oil
lime wedges, to serve

## DIPPING SAUCE

1 tablespoon fish sauce
2 tablespoons lime juice
1 tablespoon caster sugar
1 small fresh red chilli, thinly sliced

## SALAD

1 carrot, coarsely grated
120 g (4 oz) iceberg lettuce, shredded
1 Lebanese cucumber, julienned
100 g (3 1/2 oz) bean sprouts, tailed
1 cup (20 g/3/4 oz) fresh mint
1 cup (30 g/1 oz) fresh coriander leaves

## FILLING

75 g (2 1/2 oz) cellophane noodles, broken
1 tablespoon peanut oil
1 large onion, thinly sliced
6 cloves garlic, crushed
300 g (10 oz) lean pork loin fillet, finely
   chopped
150 g (5 oz) raw medium prawns, peeled,
   deveined and chopped
1 small red pepper (capsicum), thinly sliced
75 g (2 1/2 oz) button mushrooms, thinly sliced
1 tablespoon light soy sauce
1/4 teaspoon ground white pepper
4 spring onions, thinly sliced

1 To make the crepe batter, place the rice flour, baking powder, sugar, turmeric, coconut milk, 1/2 teaspoon salt and 1 cup (250 ml/8 fl oz) water in a blender and blend to a smooth batter. Cover and leave in a warm place for 2–4 hours.
2 Combine all of the dipping sauce ingredients in a small bowl.

## THE FRENCH INFLUENCE ON VIETNAMESE FOOD

Vietnamese food has had many influences, among them Chinese, Indian and Portuguese, but the French influence is arguably the greatest. This stems from 100 years of French control, beginning in the mid 1800s. Both cooking methods and food were influenced, particularly in the south. Being served French bread with a curry is considered quite normal and French-influenced pastries, such as brioche-like sweet breads are baked in patisseries in many Vietnamese cities.

*RIGHT: Vietnamese crepes with prawns, pork and noodles*

3 To make the salad, toss all the salad ingredients together in a large bowl.

4 To make the filling, soak the noodles in boiling water for 3–4 minutes, or until soft. Rinse and drain. Heat a wok over high heat, add the oil and swirl to coat. Add the onion and cook for 2 minutes, then add the garlic and cook for a further 30 seconds. Add the pork and cook for 2 minutes, or until browned. Stir in the prawns, red pepper and mushrooms and cook until the prawns change colour. Stir in the noodles, soy sauce, white pepper and spring onion until combined.

5 To make the crepes, whisk the batter until smooth. Heat 1/2 teaspoon of the oil in a 30 cm (12 inch) non-stick frying pan. Pour 1/3 cup (80 ml/2 3/4 fl oz) of the batter into the centre of the pan, and swirl to spread to the edges. Cook over medium heat for 1–2 minutes, or until golden and crispy. Turn and cook for another 1–2 minutes, or until golden and crispy. Repeat with the remaining batter.

6 To assemble, place a portion of the filling on half the crepe, folding the other side on top. Repeat with the remaining crepes and filling to make six in total. Serve with the dipping sauce, salad and lime wedges.

NOTE: The first crepe doesn't usually work; there is enough batter to allow for this.

## ANTS CLIMBING TREES

Preparation time: 15 minutes + 15 minutes
 marinating + 5 minutes soaking
Total cooking time: 15 minutes
Serves 4

1 teaspoon cornflour

1 1/2 tablespoons light soy sauce

2 tablespoons Chinese rice wine

1 teaspoon sesame oil

200 g (6 1/2 oz) pork mince

150 g (5 oz) cellophane noodles

2 tablespoons vegetable oil

4 spring onions, finely chopped

1 clove garlic, crushed

1 tablespoon finely chopped fresh ginger

2 teaspoons chilli bean sauce

3/4 cup (185 ml/6 fl oz) chicken stock

1/2 teaspoon sugar

2 spring onions, green part only, extra, thinly
 sliced on the diagonal

1 Combine the cornflour, 1 tablespoon each of the soy sauce and rice wine and 1/2 teaspoon of the sesame oil in a large non-metallic bowl. Add the mince and use a fork or your fingers to combine the ingredients and break up any lumps. Cover with plastic wrap and marinate in the fridge for 10–15 minutes.

2 Meanwhile, put the noodles in a heatproof bowl, cover with boiling water and soak for 3–4 minutes. Rinse and drain well.

3 Heat a wok over high heat, add the oil and swirl to coat the side of the wok. Cook the spring onion, garlic, ginger and chilli bean sauce for 10 seconds, then add the mince mixture and cook for 2 minutes, stirring to break up any lumps. Stir in the stock, sugar, 1/2 teaspoon salt and the remaining soy sauce, rice wine and sesame oil.

4 Add the noodles to the wok and toss to combine. Bring to a boil, then reduce the heat to low and simmer, stirring occasionally, for 7–8 minutes, or until the liquid is almost completely absorbed. Garnish with the extra spring onion and serve.

NOTE: This Chinese dish gets its name from the pork (ants) climbing the noodles (trees).

*ABOVE: Ants climbing trees*

## PORK AND BROWN BEAN SAUCE NOODLES

Preparation time: 10 minutes
Total cooking time: 15 minutes
Serves 4–6

☆☆

1/4 cup (60 ml/12 fl oz) brown bean sauce
2 tablespoons hoisin sauce
3/4 cup (185 ml/6 fl oz) chicken stock
1/2 teaspoon sugar
2 tablespoons peanut oil
3 cloves garlic, finely chopped
6 spring onions, sliced, white and green
   parts separated
650 g (1 lb 5 oz) pork mince
500 g (1 lb) fresh Shanghai noodles
1 telegraph cucumber, halved lengthways,
   seeded and sliced on the diagonal
1 cup (30 g/1 oz) fresh coriander leaves
1 cup (90 g/3 oz) bean sprouts, tailed
1 tablespoon lime juice

1 Combine the bean and hoisin sauces, stock and sugar and mix until smooth.
2 Heat a wok over high heat, add the oil and swirl. Add the garlic and spring onion (white part) and cook for 10–20 seconds. Add the pork and cook over high heat for 2–3 minutes, or

until it has browned. Add the bean mixture, reduce the heat and simmer for 7–8 minutes.
3 Cook the noodles in a large saucepan of boiling water for 4–5 minutes, or until tender. Drain and rinse, then divide among bowls. Toss together the cucumber, coriander, sprouts, lime juice and remaining spring onion. Spoon the sauce over the noodles and top with the salad.

## PORK FILLET IN BLACK BEAN SAUCE

Preparation time: 10 minutes + 1 hour marinating
Total cooking time: 15 minutes
Serves 4

☆

2 cloves garlic, crushed
2 teaspoons finely grated fresh ginger
2 tablespoons vegetable oil
600 g (1 1/4 lb) pork loin fillet, thinly sliced
   across the grain
2–3 tablespoons black beans, rinsed
1/4 cup (60 ml/2 fl oz) chicken stock
1 1/2 tablespoons soy sauce
1 1/2 teaspoons cornflour
1 teaspoon sugar
1/4 teaspoon sesame oil
1 small onion, thinly sliced
3 spring onions, thinly sliced on the diagonal

*ABOVE: Pork and brown bean sauce noodles*

1 Combine the garlic, ginger and 2 teaspoons of the vegetable oil in a large non-metallic bowl. Add the pork, cover and refrigerate for 1 hour.
2 Place the black beans in a small jug with the stock, soy sauce, cornflour and sugar. Mix well and mash the beans with a fork.
3 Heat a wok over high heat, add the sesame oil and 1 tablespoon of the vegetable oil and swirl. Stir-fry the meat in batches for 3 minutes, or until browned. Remove from the wok.
4 Add the remaining oil to the wok and stir-fry the onion for 2 minutes. Return the pork to the wok and add the black bean sauce and spring onion. Toss for 3 minutes, or until the sauce comes to the boil and thickens enough to coat the meat. Season. Serve as part of a banquet.

## CARAMEL PORK AND PUMPKIN STIR-FRY

Preparation time: 15 minutes
Total cooking time: 20 minutes
Serves 4

500 g (1 lb) pork fillet, thinly sliced across the grain
2 cloves garlic, crushed
2–3 tablespoons peanut oil

300 g (10 oz) butternut pumpkin, sliced into pieces about 2 x 4 cm (3/4 x 1 1/2 inch) and 5 mm (1/4 inch) thick
1/3 cup (60 g/2 oz) soft brown sugar
1/4 cup (60 ml/2 fl oz) fish sauce
1/4 cup (60 ml/2 fl oz) rice vinegar
2 tablespoons chopped fresh coriander leaves

1 Place the pork in a bowl, add the crushed garlic and about 2 teaspoons of the peanut oil, then season with salt and plenty of freshly ground pepper.
2 Heat a wok over high heat, add 1 tablespoon oil and swirl to coat the side of the wok. Stir-fry the pork in two batches for about 1 minute per batch, or until the meat changes colour. Transfer the meat to a plate.
3 Add the remaining oil to the wok and stir-fry the pumpkin for about 4 minutes, or until tender but not falling apart, then remove and add to the plate with the pork.
4 Put the sugar, fish sauce, rice vinegar and 1/2 cup (125 ml/4 fl oz) water in the wok, stir thoroughly, then bring to the boil and boil for about 10 minutes, or until syrupy. Return the pork and pumpkin to the wok and stir for 1 minute, or until well coated with the syrup and heated through. Stir in the coriander and serve immediately with steamed rice and some steamed Asian greens, if desired.

*BELOW: Caramel pork and pumpkin stir-fry*

## INDONESIAN-STYLE FRIED NOODLES
(Bahmi goreng)

Preparation time: 25 minutes
Total cooking time: 20 minutes
Serves 4

☆☆

400 g (13 oz) fresh flat egg noodles (5 mm/
    $^1/_4$ inch wide)
2 tomatoes
2 tablespoons peanut oil
4 red Asian shallots, thinly sliced
2 cloves garlic, chopped
1 small fresh red chilli, finely diced
100 g ($3^1/_2$ oz) pork loin fillet, thinly sliced
    across the grain

300 g (10 oz) chicken breast fillet, thinly sliced
200 g ($6^1/_2$ oz) small raw prawns, peeled and
    deveined, with tails intact
2 wom bok (Chinese cabbage) leaves, shredded
2 carrots, halved lengthways and thinly sliced
100 g ($3^1/_2$ oz) snake beans, cut into 3 cm
    ($1^1/_4$ inch) lengths
$^1/_4$ cup (60 ml/2 fl oz) kecap manis
1 tablespoon light soy sauce
4 spring onions, sliced on the diagonal
1 tablespoon crisp fried onion
fresh flat-leaf parsley, to garnish

1 Cook the noodles in a saucepan of boiling water for 1 minute, or until tender. Drain, then rinse under cold water.
2 Score a cross in the base of each tomato. Put the tomatoes in a bowl of boiling water for 30 seconds, then plunge into cold water and peel the skin away from the cross. Cut the tomatoes in half crossways, scoop out the seeds with a teaspoon, then chop the flesh.
3 Heat a wok over high heat, add the peanut oil and swirl to coat. Add the red Asian shallots and stir-fry for 1 minute. Add the garlic, chilli and pork and stir-fry for 2 minutes, then add the chicken and cook for a further 2 minutes. Add the prawns and stir-fry for a further 2 minutes, or until they are pink and cooked.
4 Stir in the wom bok, carrot and beans and cook for 3 minutes, then add the cooked noodles and stir-fry for another 4 minutes, or until everything is heated through.
5 Add the kecap manis, soy sauce, spring onion and tomato. Toss for 2 minutes. Season, then garnish with crisp fried onion and parsley. Serve.

## PEPPERED CHICKEN STIR-FRY

Preparation time: 10 minutes
Total cooking time: 10 minutes
Serves 4

☆

2 tablespoons oyster sauce
1 teaspoon soy sauce
1 teaspoon sugar
1 tablespoon vegetable oil
2 chicken breast fillets, cut into strips
$2^1/_2$ teaspoons seasoned peppercorns
1 onion, cut into wedges
1 red pepper (capsicum), cut into strips

*BELOW: Indonesian-style fried noodles*

1 To make the stir-fry sauce, put the oyster sauce, soy sauce and sugar in a small non-metallic bowl or jug. Stir until the sugar has dissolved.

2 Heat a wok over high heat, add the oil and swirl to coat the side of the wok. Add the chicken strips and stir-fry for 2–3 minutes, or until browned.

3 Throw in the peppercorns and stir-fry until fragrant. Add the onion and red pepper and stir-fry for 2 minutes, or until the vegetables have softened slightly. Reduce the heat to medium and pour in the stir-fry sauce. Toss together until everything is coated in the sauce. Serve hot with steamed rice or Asian noodles.

## TERIYAKI CHICKEN AND UDON NOODLES

Preparation time: 20 minutes +
  30 minutes marinating
Total cooking time: 20 minutes
Serves 4

1 clove garlic, crushed

1 1/2 teaspoons grated fresh ginger

1/3 cup (80 ml/2 3/4 fl oz) light soy sauce

1 tablespoon sake

1/4 cup (60 ml/2 fl oz) mirin

450 g (14 oz) chicken breast fillets, cut into
  2 cm (3/4 inch) cubes

400 g (13 oz) fresh udon noodles

2 tablespoons peanut oil

1 teaspoon sesame oil

1 onion, cut into thin wedges

2 teaspoons sugar

6 spring onions, thinly sliced on the diagonal

1 tablespoon sesame seeds, toasted

2 teaspoons black sesame seeds, toasted

1 Combine the garlic, ginger, soy sauce, sake and mirin in a large non-metallic bowl. Add the chicken and toss until well coated. Cover the bowl with plastic wrap and marinate in the refrigerator for 30 minutes.

2 Meanwhile, cook the noodles in a saucepan of boiling water for 1–2 minutes, or until tender. Drain thoroughly.

3 Drain the chicken, reserving the marinade. Combine the peanut and sesame oils. Heat a wok over high heat, add half the oil mixture and swirl to coat the side of the wok. Stir-fry the

chicken in batches for 2–3 minutes each batch, or until nicely browned. Remove from the heat. Heat the remaining oil in the wok over medium heat, then add the onion and stir-fry for 3–4 minutes, or until softened.

4 Meanwhile, pour the reserved marinade and the sugar into a small saucepan. Bring to the boil, then reduce the heat and simmer for 2 minutes, or until slightly syrupy, stirring occasionally. Remove the pan from the heat and keep in a warm place.

5 Return the chicken to the wok, along with the spring onion and udon noodles, tossing well to combine. Cook for 2 minutes before pouring in the reserved heated marinade. Stir thoroughly so that everything is coated in the mixture and heated through.

6 Divide the noodles among four serving bowls. Sprinkle with the black and white toasted sesame seeds and serve immediately.

*BELOW: Teriyaki chicken and udon noodles*

## CHICKEN WITH ALMONDS

A Chinese restaurant staple in Chinatowns across the globe, chicken with almonds is almost unheard of in China itself. The Chinese rarely use the 'true' almond; instead they generally use their own version of almond, called Chinese almond, which has a much stronger flavour. It is a near relation to the true almond, but is actually an apricot seed bred specially for its kernels. Chinese almonds available from markets have been blanched, but they should be roasted for 20 minutes in a moderately hot (200°C/400°F/Gas 6) oven before using.

*ABOVE: Tangy orange and ginger chicken*

## TANGY ORANGE AND GINGER CHICKEN

Preparation time: 15 minutes
Total cooking time: 20 minutes
Serves 4

☆

1/4 cup (60 ml/12 fl oz) vegetable oil
10 chicken thigh fillets, cut into small pieces
3 teaspoons grated fresh ginger
1 teaspoon grated orange rind
1/2 cup (125 ml/4 fl oz) chicken stock
2 teaspoons honey
1 bunch (550 g/1 lb 2 oz) bok choy, trimmed and halved
toasted sesame seeds, to garnish

1 Heat a wok over high heat, add the oil and swirl to coat the side of the wok. Add the chicken in batches and stir-fry each batch for 3–4 minutes, or until golden.
2 Return all the chicken to the wok, add the ginger and orange rind, and cook for 20 seconds, or until fragrant. Add the stock and the honey and stir to combine. Increase the heat and cook for 3–4 minutes, or until the sauce has thickened slightly. Add the bok choy and cook until slightly wilted. Season well, then sprinkle with toasted sesame seeds and serve with steamed rice.

## CHICKEN WITH ALMONDS AND ASPARAGUS

Preparation time: 15 minutes
Total cooking time: 15 minutes
Serves 4–6

☆

2 teaspoons cornflour
1/3 cup (80 ml/2 3/4 fl oz) chicken stock
1/4 teaspoon sesame oil
2 tablespoons oyster sauce
1 tablespoon soy sauce
3 cloves garlic, crushed
1 teaspoon very finely chopped fresh ginger
pinch ground white pepper
2 1/2 tablespoons peanut oil
1/3 cup (50 g/1 3/4 oz) blanched almonds
2 spring onions, cut into 3 cm (1 1/4 inch) lengths
500 g (1 lb) chicken thigh fillets, cut into 3 x 2 cm (1 1/4 x 3/4 inch) strips
1 small carrot, thinly sliced
155 g (5 oz) thin, fresh asparagus, trimmed and cut into 3 cm (1 1/4 inch) lengths
1/4 cup (60 g/2 oz) sliced bamboo shoots

1 To make the stir-fry sauce, put the cornflour and the chicken stock in a small bowl and mix

into a paste, then stir in the sesame oil, oyster sauce, soy sauce, garlic, ginger and white pepper. Set aside until needed.

**2** Heat a wok over high heat, add 2 teaspoons of the peanut oil and swirl to coat the side of the wok. Add the almonds and stir-fry for 1–2 minutes, or until golden—be careful not to burn them. Remove from the wok and drain on crumpled paper towels.

**3** Heat another teaspoon of the peanut oil in the wok and swirl to coat. Add the spring onion and stir-fry for 30 seconds, or until wilted. Remove from the wok.

**4** Heat another tablespoon of peanut oil in the wok over high heat, then stir-fry the chicken in two batches for 3 minutes per batch, or until the chicken is just cooked through. Set aside with the spring onion.

**5** Add the remaining peanut oil to the wok, then add the carrot and stir-fry for 1–2 minutes, or until just starting to brown. Toss in the asparagus and the bamboo shoots and stir-fry for a further 1 minute. Remove all the vegetables from the wok and set aside with the chicken and spring onion.

**6** Stir the stir-fry sauce briefly, then pour into the wok, stirring until the mixture thickens. Return the chicken and vegetables to the wok, and stir thoroughly for a couple of minutes until they are coated in the sauce and are heated through. Transfer to a serving dish and sprinkle with the almonds before serving immediately. Serve with steamed rice.

# CHICKEN STIR-FRY WITH SNOW PEA (MANGETOUT) SPROUTS

Preparation time: 15 minutes
Total cooking time: 15 minutes
Serves 4

2 tablespoons vegetable oil
1 onion, thinly sliced
3 kaffir lime leaves, shredded
3 chicken breast fillets, cut into 2 cm (³/4 inch) cubes
1 red pepper (capsicum), sliced
¹/4 cup (60 ml/2 fl oz) lime juice
100 ml (3¹/2 fl oz) soy sauce
100 g (3¹/2 oz) snow pea (mangetout) sprouts
2 tablespoons chopped fresh coriander leaves

**1** Heat a wok over medium heat, add the oil and swirl. Add the onion and lime leaves and stir-fry for 3–5 minutes, or until the onion begins to soften. Add the chicken and cook for 4 minutes, then add the pepper and stir-fry for 2–3 minutes.

**2** Stir in the lime juice and soy sauce and cook for 1–2 minutes, or until the sauce reduces slightly. Toss in the sprouts and coriander and cook until the sprouts have wilted slightly. Serve with steamed jasmine rice and extra coriander and chilli, if desired.

SNOW PEA SPROUTS
Snow pea sprouts are the peppery sprouts of the snow pea, which is itself a completely edible legume, hence the French name 'mangetout', which means 'eat it all'. Snow pea sprouts are an excellent addition to salads, and they add freshness and flavour to stir-fries. Because the shoots are usually the plants' growing tips, the flowers are removed to encourage more tips to grow, so they don't mature into full pods.

*LEFT: Chicken stir-fry with snow pea sprouts*

# STIR-FRIED DUCK WITH PLUM AND GINGER SAUCE

Preparation time: 10 minutes +
   3 hours marinating
Total cooking time: 10 minutes
Serves 4–6

1 tablespoon hoisin sauce

1/2 teaspoon sesame oil

1 teaspoon ground ginger

1 teaspoon five-spice powder

2 cloves garlic, crushed

3 teaspoons soy sauce

4 x 185 g (6 oz) skinless, boneless duck breasts,
   trimmed and thinly sliced across the grain

1/4 cup (60 ml/2 fl oz) chicken stock

1/4 cup (60 ml/2 fl oz) plum sauce

2 teaspoons orange juice

1/2 teaspoon cornflour

2 teaspoons vegetable oil

1 tablespoon julienned fresh ginger

5 spring onions, thinly sliced on the diagonal

1 Combine the hoisin sauce, sesame oil, ground ginger, five-spice powder, garlic and 2 teaspoons of the soy sauce in a large non-metallic bowl. Add the duck, cover with plastic wrap and marinate in the refrigerator for 3 hours.
2 To make the stir-fry sauce, combine the stock, plum sauce, orange juice and cornflour in a small jug or bowl. Whisk together with a fork.
3 Heat a wok over high heat, add 1 teaspoon of the vegetable oil and swirl to coat the side of the wok. Stir-fry the duck in batches for 30 seconds per batch, or until browned. Take care not to overcook the duck as it will turn tough and rubbery. Remove the duck from the wok.
4 Heat the remaining oil in the wok, then add the fresh ginger and most of the spring onion and stir-fry for 1 minute, or until softened and fragrant. Pour in the stir-fry sauce and bring to a simmer, stirring, for 1 minute, or until the sauce thickens. Return the duck meat to the wok and toss very briefly until mixed through. Season well, garnish with the remaining spring onion and serve immediately.

# KUNG PAO CHICKEN

Preparation time: 15 minutes +
   30 minutes marinating
Total cooking time: 15 minutes
Serves 4

1 egg white

2 teaspoons cornflour

1/2 teaspoon sesame oil

2 teaspoons Chinese rice wine

1 1/2 tablespoons soy sauce

600 g (1 1/4 lb) chicken thigh fillets, cut into
   2 cm (3/4 inch) cubes

1/4 cup (60 ml/2 fl oz) chicken stock

2 teaspoons Chinese black vinegar

1 teaspoon soft brown sugar

2 tablespoons vegetable oil

3 long dried red chillies, cut in half lengthways

3 cloves garlic, finely chopped

2 teaspoons finely grated fresh ginger

2 spring onions, thinly sliced on the diagonal

1/3 cup (50 g/1 3/4 oz) shelled unsalted raw
   peanuts, roughly crushed

1 Lightly whisk together the egg white, cornflour, sesame oil, Chinese rice wine and 2 teaspoons of the soy sauce in a large non-metallic bowl. Add the chicken and coat it in the marinade. Cover with plastic wrap and marinate in the fridge for 30 minutes.
2 To make the stir-fry sauce, combine the stock, vinegar, sugar and the remaining soy sauce in a small jug or bowl.
3 Heat a wok over high heat, add 1 tablespoon of the vegetable oil and swirl to coat the wok. Stir-fry the chicken in batches for 3 minutes, or until browned. Remove from the wok.
4 Heat the remaining oil in the wok, then add the chilli and cook for 15 seconds, or until it starts to change colour. Add the garlic, ginger, spring onion and peanuts, and stir-fry for 1 minute. Return the chicken to the wok, along with the stir-fry sauce, and stir-fry for 3 minutes, or until heated through and the sauce thickens slightly. Serve immediately.
NOTE: This dish is said to have been created for an important court official called Kung Pao (or Gong Bao) who was stationed in the Sichuan province of China. It is characterised by the flavours of the long, dried red chillies popular in Sichuan cuisine, and the crunchiness of peanuts. It can also be made with meat or prawns.

*OPPOSITE PAGE, FROM TOP: Stir-fried duck with plum and ginger sauce; Kung Pao chicken*

BASIL
Basil is often associated with the Mediterranean, but it has an important place in the cuisine of Southeast Asia, which is not surprising considering that it is native to India.

The leaves are prone to wilting quite quickly, so use them as soon as possible after purchase. If unavailable, substitute any variety of fresh basil. Basil should be torn, not chopped, and added to hot food at the last moment to preserve its flavour.

*ABOVE: Chicken with Thai basil*

## CHICKEN WITH THAI BASIL
(Gai paht bai graprao)

Preparation time: 15 minutes
Total cooking time: 15 minutes
Serves 4

1/4 cup (60 ml/12 fl oz) peanut oil
500 g (1 lb) chicken breast fillets, cut into thin strips
1 clove garlic, crushed
4 spring onions, thinly sliced
150 g (5 oz) snake beans, trimmed and cut into 5 cm (2 inch) lengths
2 small fresh red chillies, thinly sliced
3/4 cup (35 g/1 1/4 oz) tightly packed fresh Thai basil
2 tablespoons chopped fresh mint
1 tablespoon fish sauce
1 tablespoon oyster sauce
2 teaspoons lime juice
1 tablespoon grated palm sugar
fresh Thai basil, extra, to garnish

1 Heat a wok over high heat, add 1 tablespoon of the oil and swirl to coat. Cook the chicken in batches for 3–5 minutes each batch, or until lightly browned and almost cooked—add more oil if needed. Remove from the wok.
2 Heat the remaining oil. Add the garlic, onion, snake beans and chilli, and stir-fry for 1 minute, or until the onion is tender. Return the chicken to the wok.
3 Toss in the basil and mint, then add the combined fish sauce, oyster sauce, lime juice, palm sugar and 2 tablespoons water and cook for 1 minute. Garnish with the extra basil and serve with jasmine rice.

## CHICKEN AND ASPARAGUS STIR-FRY

Preparation time: 15 minutes
Total cooking time: 10 minutes
Serves 4

2 tablespoons vegetable oil
1 clove garlic, crushed
10 cm (4 inch) piece fresh ginger, thinly sliced
3 chicken breast fillets, sliced
4 spring onions, sliced
200 g (6 1/2 oz) fresh asparagus, cut into 1 cm (1/2 inch) diagonal pieces
2 tablespoons soy sauce
1/3 cup (40 g/1 1/4 oz) slivered almonds, roasted

1 Heat a wok over high heat, add the oil and swirl to coat the side of the wok. Add the garlic, ginger and chicken and stir-fry for 1–2 minutes, or until the chicken changes colour.

**2** Add the spring onion and asparagus and stir-fry for a further 2 minutes, or until the spring onion is soft.

**3** Stir in the soy sauce and 1/4 cup (60 ml/2 fl oz) water, cover and simmer for 2 minutes, or until the chicken is tender and the vegetables are slightly crisp. Sprinkle with the almonds and serve over steamed rice or Hokkien noodles.

## CHICKEN CHOW MEIN

Preparation time: 15 minutes +
  1 hour standing
Total cooking time: 40 minutes
Serves 4

250 g (8 oz) fresh thin egg noodles
2 teaspoons sesame oil
1/2 cup (125 ml/4 fl oz) peanut oil
1 tablespoon Chinese rice wine
1 1/2 tablespoons light soy sauce
3 teaspoons cornflour
400 g (13 oz) chicken breast fillets, cut into
  thin strips
1 clove garlic, crushed
1 tablespoon finely chopped fresh ginger
100 g (3 1/2 oz) sugar snap peas, trimmed
250 g (8 oz) wom bok (Chinese cabbage),
  finely shredded
4 spring onions, cut into 2 cm (3/4 inch) lengths
100 ml (3 1/2 fl oz) chicken stock
1 1/2 tablespoons oyster sauce
100 g (3 1/2 oz) bean sprouts, tailed
1 small fresh red chilli, seeded and julienned,
  to garnish (optional)

**1** Cook the noodles in a saucepan of boiling water for 1 minute, or until tender. Drain well. Add the sesame oil and 1 tablespoon of the peanut oil and toss well. Place on a baking tray and spread out in a thin layer. Leave in a dry place for at least 1 hour.

**2** Meanwhile, combine the rice wine, 1 tablespoon of the soy sauce and 1 teaspoon of the cornflour in a large non-metallic bowl. Add the chicken and toss well. Cover with plastic wrap and marinate for 10 minutes.

**3** Heat 1 tablespoon of the peanut oil in a small non-stick frying pan over high heat. Add one quarter of the noodles, shaping into a pancake. Reduce the heat to medium and cook for

4 minutes on each side, or until crisp and golden. Drain on crumpled paper towels and keep warm. Repeat with 3 tablespoons of the oil and the remaining noodles to make four noodle cakes in total.

**4** Heat a wok over high heat, add the remaining peanut oil and swirl to coat the side of the wok. Stir-fry the garlic and ginger for 30 seconds. Add the chicken and stir-fry for 3–4 minutes, or until golden and tender. Add the sugar snap peas, shredded wom bok and spring onion and stir-fry for 2 minutes, or until the cabbage has wilted. Stir in the chicken stock, oyster sauce and bean sprouts and bring to the boil.

**5** Combine the remaining cornflour with 1–2 teaspoons cold water. Stir it into the wok with the remaining soy sauce and cook for 1–2 minutes, or until the sauce thickens.

**6** To assemble, place a noodle cake on each serving plate, then spoon the chicken and vegetable mixture on top. Serve immediately, garnished with chilli, if desired.

*BELOW: Chicken chow mein*

CHINESE ROAST DUCK
WITH RICE NOODLES

Using your fingers, remove
the skin and fat from the
duck.

Carefully separate the flesh
from the bones with your
fingers.

## CHINESE ROAST DUCK
## WITH RICE NOODLES

Preparation time: 25 minutes
Total cooking time: 15 minutes
Serves 4

☆ ☆

1.5 kg (3 lb) Chinese roast duck (see Note)
500 g (1 lb) fresh flat rice noodles
  (1 cm/¹/₂ inch) wide)
3¹/₂ tablespoons peanut oil
3 small slender eggplants (aubergines), cut into
  1 cm (¹/₂ inch) thick slices
1 tablespoon thinly sliced fresh ginger
2 small fresh red chillies, finely chopped
4 spring onions, thinly sliced on the diagonal
3 tablespoons torn fresh basil
¹/₄ cup (60 ml/2 fl oz) Chinese barbecue sauce

1 Remove the crispy skin and meat from the
duck, discarding the carcass and fat. Thinly slice
the meat and skin and place it in a bowl—there
should be at least 350 g (11 oz) of meat.

2 Put the noodles in a heatproof bowl, cover
with boiling water and soak briefly. Gently
separate the noodles. Rinse under cold water
and drain well.
3 Heat a wok over high heat, add 2¹/₂ tablespoons
of the peanut oil and swirl to coat the side
of the wok. Add the eggplant and stir-fry for
3–4 minutes, or until softened. Transfer to
a bowl.
4 Heat the remaining oil in the wok over high
heat. Cook the ginger, chilli and spring onion
for 30 seconds, stirring constantly. Return the
eggplant to the wok along with the duck, basil
and barbecue sauce, and gently toss together for
1–2 minutes, or until heated through. Add the
noodles and stir-fry for 1–2 minutes, or until well
combined and heated through, taking care not
to break up the noodles. Serve immediately.
NOTE: Chinese roast duck is a crisp, dark,
glossy-skinned duck that can be bought ready to
eat from Asian barbecue shops or restaurants.
Some Chinese people will only buy Chinese
roast duck if the weather has been fine for at
least 12 hours before purchase—humid weather is
said to prevent the skin from becoming crisp.

*ABOVE: Chinese roast duck
with rice noodles*

# SATAY CHICKEN STIR-FRY

Preparation time: 10 minutes
Total cooking time: 20 minutes
Serves 4

1 1/2 tablespoons peanut oil

6 spring onions, cut into 3 cm (1 1/4 inch) lengths

800 g (1 lb 10 oz) chicken breast fillets, thinly sliced on the diagonal

1–1 1/2 tablespoons Thai red curry paste (see page 56)

1/3 cup (90 g/3 oz) crunchy peanut butter

270 ml (9 fl oz) coconut milk

2 teaspoons soft brown sugar

1 1/2 tablespoons lime juice

1 Heat a wok over high heat, add 1 teaspoon of the peanut oil and swirl to coat. Add the spring onion and stir-fry for 30 seconds, or until softened slightly. Remove from the wok.
2 Add a little extra peanut oil to the wok as needed and stir-fry the chicken in three batches for about 1 minute per batch, or until the meat just changes colour. Remove from the wok.
3 Add a little more oil to the wok, add the curry paste and stir-fry for 1 minute, or until fragrant. Add the peanut butter, coconut milk, sugar and 1 cup (250 ml/8 fl oz) water and stir well. Bring to the boil and boil for 3–4 minutes, or until thickened and the oil starts to separate—reduce the heat slightly if the sauce spits at you. Return the chicken and the spring onion to the wok, stir well and cook for 2 minutes, or until heated through. Stir in the lime juice, season and serve.

## STEAMED RICE

Rinse 1 1/2 cups (300 g/10 oz) jasmine rice in a sieve until the water runs clear. Place in a large saucepan with 1 3/4 cups (440 ml/ 14 fl oz) water. Bring to the boil and boil for 1 minute. Cover tightly, reduce the heat to as low as possible and cook for 10 minutes. Remove from the heat and leave to stand, covered, for 10 minutes. Fluff with a fork before serving. Serve with stir-fries, curries and steamed dishes. Serves 4.

THAI CURRY PASTES
Ready-made curry pastes are available in Asian grocery stores or the Asian section of large supermarkets. Red curry pastes are classified as red because they are made using a high proportion of dried red chillies, which gives them their characteristic colour. In contrast, green curry pastes use fresh green chillies to give the vibrant green colour. Different brands vary in strength, flavour and heat, so experiment until you find your favourite. Alternatively, they are easy to make at home (see page 56), and the taste is far superior. The process of making curry pastes can be quite engaging and rewarding. Many curry paste aficionados swear by the mortar and pestle for making curry pastes, believing that the grinding method garners better results than if a food processor is used.

*LEFT: Satay chicken stir-fry*

## THAI CHICKEN WITH CHILLI JAM AND CASHEWS
(Gai fam prik pao)

Preparation time: 20 minutes +
  20 minutes soaking
Total cooking time: 35 minutes
Serves 4

☆☆

### CHILLI JAM
10 dried long red chillies
$1/3$ cup (80 ml/$2^{3}/4$ fl oz) peanut oil
1 red pepper (capsicum), chopped
1 head (50 g/$1^{3}/4$ oz) garlic, peeled and roughly
  chopped
200 g ($6^{1}/2$ oz) red Asian shallots, chopped
100 g ($3^{1}/2$ oz) grated palm sugar
2 tablespoons tamarind purée

*BELOW: Thai chicken with chilli jam and cashews*

1 tablespoon peanut oil
6 spring onions, cut into 3 cm ($1^{1}/4$ inch)
  lengths
500 g (1 lb) chicken breast fillets, sliced
$1/3$ cup (50 g/$1^{3}/4$ oz) roasted unsalted cashews
1 tablespoon fish sauce
$1/2$ cup (15 g/$1/2$ oz) fresh Thai basil

1 To make the chilli jam, soak the chillies in a heatproof bowl of boiling water for 20 minutes. Drain, remove the seeds and roughly chop the flesh.
2 Transfer the chilli flesh to a food processor, then add the oil, red pepper, garlic and shallots, and blend until a smooth paste forms.
3 Heat a non-stick wok over medium heat and add the chilli mixture. Cook, stirring occasionally, for 15 minutes. Add the sugar and tamarind, and simmer for a further 10 minutes, or until it darkens and reaches a jam-like consistency. Remove the chilli jam from the wok.
4 Wash and dry the wok, then reheat over high heat. Add the oil and swirl to coat the side of the wok. Stir-fry the spring onion for 1 minute. Add the chicken and stir-fry for 3–5 minutes, or until golden brown and tender. Stir in the cashews, fish sauce and $1/3$ cup (60 g/2 oz) of the chilli jam. Stir-fry for a further 2 minutes, then stir in the basil. Serve immediately.
NOTES: It is important to use a non-stick wok or the tamarind purée in the chilli jam might cause the seasoning layer of a carbon-steel wok to be stripped off.
Store any leftover chilli jam in a cleaned glass jar in the fridge for up to 1 month.

## GLAZED HOISIN CHICKEN STIR-FRY

Preparation time: 15 minutes +
  15 minutes marinating
Total cooking time: 15 minutes
Serves 4

☆

$1/2$ teaspoon sesame oil
1 egg white
1 tablespoon cornflour
700 g (1 lb $6^{1}/2$ oz) chicken thigh fillets, cut
  into 1.5 cm ($5/8$ inch) cubes
2 tablespoons peanut oil
2 cloves garlic, chopped

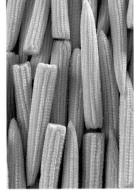

1 tablespoon julienned fresh ginger

1 tablespoon brown bean sauce

1 tablespoon hoisin sauce

1 tablespoon Chinese rice wine

1 teaspoon light soy sauce

4 spring onions, cut into 2 cm (³/₄ inch) lengths
  on the diagonal

1 Combine the sesame oil, egg white and cornflour in a large non-metallic bowl. Add the chicken, toss together, then cover with plastic wrap and marinate in the refrigerator for at least 15 minutes.

2 Heat a wok over high heat, add the peanut oil and swirl to coat the side of the wok. Add the chicken in three batches, stir-frying each batch for 4 minutes, or until cooked through. Remove the chicken from the wok.

3 Reheat the wok over high heat, add a little extra oil if necessary, then add the garlic and ginger and stir-fry for 1 minute. Return the chicken to the wok, then add the bean and hoisin sauces and cook, stirring, for 1 minute. Add the rice wine, soy sauce and spring onion, and cook for 1 minute, or until the sauce is thick and glossy and coats the chicken. Serve with steamed rice.

# SWEET CHILLI CHICKEN STIR-FRY

Preparation time: 10 minutes
Total cooking time: 10 minutes
Serves 4–6

375 g (12 oz) Hokkien noodles

4 chicken thigh fillets, cut into small pieces

1–2 tablespoons sweet chilli sauce

2 teaspoons fish sauce

1 tablespoon vegetable oil

100 g (3¹/₂ oz) baby sweet corn, halved
  lengthways

150 g (5 oz) sugar snap peas, topped and tailed

1 tablespoon lime juice

1 Put the noodles in a large bowl, cover with boiling water for 1 minute, then gently separate. Drain and rinse.

2 Combine the chicken, sweet chilli sauce and fish sauce in a bowl.

3 Heat a wok over high heat, add the oil and swirl to coat the side of the wok. Add the chicken and stir-fry for 3–5 minutes, or until cooked through. Add the corn and peas and stir-fry for 2 minutes. Stir in the noodles and lime juice, then serve.

*ABOVE: Sweet chilli chicken stir-fry*

**2** Reheat the wok over high heat, add the oils and swirl to coat the side. Stir-fry the chicken strips in three batches, tossing constantly, for 3–5 minutes each batch, or until just cooked. Reheat the wok before each addition. Return the chicken to the wok.

**3** Add the julienned leek and the garlic and cook for 1–2 minutes, or until the leek is soft and golden. Check that the chicken is cooked through; if it is not cooked, reduce the heat and cook, covered, for 2 minutes, or until it is completely cooked.

**4** Add the soy sauce, mirin, sugar and toasted sesame seeds to the wok, and toss well to combine. Season, and serve immediately.

## YAKIUDON WITH CHICKEN

Preparation time: 15 minutes +
  20 minutes soaking
Total cooking time: 15 minutes
Serves 4

5 dried shiitake mushrooms

1 clove garlic, crushed

2 teaspoons grated fresh ginger

1/2 cup (125 ml/4 fl oz) Japanese soy sauce

2 tablespoons rice vinegar

2 tablespoons sugar

1 tablespoon lemon juice

500 g (1 lb) fresh udon noodles

2 tablespoons vegetable oil

500 g (1 lb) chicken thigh fillets, thinly sliced

1 clove garlic, extra, finely chopped

1 small red pepper (capsicum), thinly sliced

2 cups (150 g/5 oz) shredded cabbage

4 spring onions, thinly sliced

1 tablespoon sesame oil

white pepper, to taste

2 tablespoons drained shredded pickled ginger

**1** Soak the mushrooms in boiling water for 20 minutes, or until soft. Squeeze dry and reserve 1/4 cup (60 ml/2 fl oz) of the liquid. Discard the stalks, and thinly slice the caps.

**2** Combine the crushed garlic, ginger, Japanese soy sauce, vinegar, sugar, lemon juice and reserved mushroom soaking liquid in a jug.

**3** Cook the noodles in boiling water for 1–2 minutes, or until tender. Drain.

**4** Heat a wok over high heat, add half the oil

## STIR-FRIED SESAME, CHICKEN AND LEEK

Preparation time: 15 minutes
Total cooking time: 20 minutes
Serves 4–6

2 tablespoons sesame seeds

1 tablespoon vegetable oil

2 teaspoons sesame oil

800 g (1 lb 10 oz) chicken tenderloins,
  sliced on the diagonal

1 leek, julienned

2 cloves garlic, crushed

2 tablespoons soy sauce

1 tablespoon mirin

1 teaspoon sugar

*ABOVE: Stir-fried sesame,
chicken and leek*

**1** Heat the wok over high heat, add the sesame seeds and fry until golden. Remove from the wok.

and swirl to coat. Add the chicken in batches and stir-fry for 5 minutes each batch, or until browned. Remove from the wok.

5 Heat the remaining oil in the wok. Add the extra garlic, mushrooms, pepper and cabbage, and stir-fry for 2–3 minutes, or until soft. Add the noodles and stir-fry for 1 minute. Return the chicken to the wok and add the spring onion, sesame oil and the soy sauce mixture, stirring until mixed and heated through. Season with white pepper and scatter with pickled ginger.

## HONEY CHICKEN

Preparation time: 15 minutes
Total cooking time: 25 minutes
Serves 4

500 g (1 lb) chicken thigh fillets, cut into cubes
1 egg white, lightly beaten
1/3 cup (40 g/1 1/4 oz) cornflour
1/3 cup (80 ml/2 3/4 fl oz) vegetable oil
2 onions, thinly sliced
1 green pepper (capsicum), cubed
2 carrots, cut into batons
100 g (3 1/2 oz) snow peas (mangetout), sliced
1/4 cup (90 g/3 oz) honey
2 tablespoons toasted almonds (see Note)

1 Dip the chicken cubes into the egg white, then lightly dust with the cornflour, shaking off any excess.

2 Heat a wok over high heat, add 1 1/2 tablespoons of the oil and swirl it around to coat the side of the wok. Add the chicken in two batches and stir-fry each batch for 4–5 minutes, or until the chicken is golden brown and just cooked. Remove the chicken from the wok and drain on crumpled paper towels.

3 Reheat the wok over high heat, add 1 tablespoon of the oil and stir-fry the sliced onion for 3–4 minutes, or until slightly softened. Add the green pepper and carrot, and cook, tossing constantly, for 3–4 minutes, or until tender. Stir in the sliced snow peas and cook for 2 minutes.

4 Ensure that the wok is still very hot, then pour in the honey and toss with the vegetables until well coated. Return all the chicken to the wok and toss thoroughly until it is heated through and well coated in the honey. Remove the wok from the heat and season well with salt and freshly ground black pepper. Serve immediately, sprinkled with the toasted almonds. Serve with steamed white rice.

NOTE: If you can't find ready-toasted almonds, you can toast blanched almonds at home yourself. Simply dry-fry them in a frying pan or wok over medium heat for 2–3 minutes, tossing occasionally to prevent them from burning on the bottom.

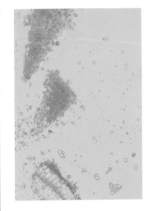

HONEY
There are records of honey being used to season and flavour food in China since ancient times, dating as far back as the 2nd century BC. Honey was the Chinese kitchen's main sweetener for centuries, as sugar-making was not introduced to China until the middle of the 9th century. In China honey is reputed to have medicinal powers and it is used to treat ailments ranging from insomnia and stomach-aches to heart disease and constipation.

*LEFT: Honey chicken*

## CHICKEN WITH WALNUTS AND STRAW MUSHROOMS

Preparation time: 20 minutes
Total cooking time: 15 minutes
Serves 4

☆

375 g (12 oz) chicken breast fillets or
    tenderloins, cut into thin strips
1/2 teaspoon five-spice powder
2 teaspoons cornflour
2 tablespoons soy sauce
2 tablespoons oyster sauce
2 teaspoons soft brown sugar
1 teaspoon sesame oil
oil, for cooking
75 g (2 1/2 oz) walnuts
6 spring onions, sliced
150 g (5 oz) snake beans or green beans,
    chopped
425 g (14 oz) can straw mushrooms, rinsed
227 g (7 oz) can sliced bamboo shoots, drained
    and rinsed

*BELOW: Chicken with walnuts and straw mushrooms*

1 Dry the chicken strips with paper towels and sprinkle with the five-spice powder. Mix the cornflour with the soy sauce in a bowl until smooth. Add 1/2 cup (125 ml/4 fl oz) water along with the oyster sauce, brown sugar and sesame oil.
2 Heat a wok over high heat, add 1 tablespoon of the oil and swirl it around to coat the side. Stir-fry the walnuts for 30 seconds, or until lightly browned. Drain on paper towels.
3 Reheat the wok and add 1 tablespoon of the oil. Stir-fry the chicken in batches over high heat for 2–3 minutes, or until just cooked through. Remove all the chicken from the wok.
4 Add the spring onion, snake beans, straw mushrooms and bamboo shoots to the wok, and stir-fry for 2 minutes. Remove from the wok. Add the soy sauce mixture to the wok and heat for 1 minute, or until slightly thickened. Return the chicken and vegetables to the wok and toss to coat with the sauce. Season well. Serve at once, sprinkled with the walnuts.

## STIR-FRIED CHICKEN AND LEMON GRASS

Preparation time: 15 minutes
Total cooking time: 15 minutes
Serves 4

☆

1 tablespoon fish sauce
3 teaspoons grated palm sugar
1 tablespoon peanut oil
2 teaspoons sesame oil
800 g (1 lb 10 oz) chicken breast fillets, cut
    into strips
2 tablespoons finely chopped lemon grass,
    white part only
1 1/2 tablespoons julienned fresh ginger
2 cloves garlic, finely chopped
2 tablespoons fresh coriander leaves
2 limes, cut into wedges

1 Combine the fish sauce and palm sugar in a small bowl and stir until the sugar dissolves.
2 Heat a large wok over high heat, add half the combined oils and swirl to coat the side of the wok. Stir-fry the chicken in two batches for 4 minutes per batch, adding the remaining oil between batches. Remove from the wok.
3 Add the lemon grass, ginger and garlic to the wok, and stir-fry for 1–2 minutes, then return all

the chicken to the wok and stir-fry for a further 2 minutes. Stir in the combined fish sauce and palm sugar. Scatter with the coriander leaves and serve immediately with noodles or rice and the lime wedges.

# WARM CURRIED CHICKEN SALAD

Preparation time: 15 minutes +
  overnight marinating
Total cooking time: 10 minutes
Serves 4–6

☆ ☆

3 tablespoons mild Indian curry paste
  (see Note)
1/4 cup (60 ml/2 fl oz) coconut milk
750 g (1 1/2 lb) chicken breast fillets, sliced
150 g (5 oz) green beans, halved
2 tablespoons peanut oil
1/3 cup (30 g/1 oz) flaked almonds, toasted
1 red pepper (capsicum), sliced
240 g (7 1/2 oz) rocket (arugula)
100 g (3 1/2 oz) fried egg noodles

LEMON DRESSING
1/3 cup (80 ml/2 3/4 fl oz) olive oil
2 tablespoons lemon juice
2 cloves garlic, crushed
1 teaspoon soft brown sugar

1 Combine the curry paste and coconut milk in a bowl. Add the chicken, toss to coat in the mixture, then cover with plastic wrap and marinate in the fridge overnight.
2 Cook the beans in a saucepan of boiling water for 30 seconds, or until just tender. Refresh under cold running water. Drain thoroughly.
3 Heat a wok over high heat, add half the oil and swirl to coat the side of the wok. Stir-fry the chicken in two batches for 5 minutes per batch, adding the remaining oil in between batches. Remove from the wok. Repeat with the remaining chicken and oil.
4 To make the dressing, place the ingredients in a screw-top jar and shake thoroughly.
5 Place the chicken, beans, almonds, pepper, rocket and dressing in a large bowl, and mix well. Stir in the noodles and serve.
NOTE: You can use any of the home-made curry pastes on pages 58–59, or use a ready-made paste.

## SATAY SAUCE

Place 1 cup (160 g/5 1/2 oz) unsalted roasted peanuts in a food processor and process until finely chopped. Heat 2 tablespoons vegetable oil in a wok. Add 1 chopped onion and cook over medium heat for 5 minutes, or until softened. Add 2 crushed cloves garlic, 2 teaspoons finely chopped fresh ginger, 1/2 teaspoon chilli powder and 1 teaspoon ground cumin, and cook, stirring, for 2 minutes. Add 1 2/3 cups (410 ml/13 fl oz) coconut milk, 1/4 cup (45 g/1 1/2 oz) soft brown sugar and the chopped peanuts. Reduce the heat and cook for 5 minutes, or until the sauce thickens. Add 1 tablespoon lemon juice and season to taste. Makes 1 1/2 cups.
NOTES: If you prefer a smoother sauce, blend the sauce ingredients in a food processor for 30 seconds.
Satay sauce goes well with any meat, but chicken is usually associated with it. Use it for satay sticks, or add to stir-fries or warm Asian chicken salads.

*ABOVE: Warm curried chicken salad*

169

SINGAPORE NOODLES
More commonly known as fried beehoon in the place that gives the dish its name, Singapore noodles is always made with thin dried rice vermicelli, or beehoon. The flavour of Singapore noodles reflects Singapore's cultural diversity—the dried spices or curry powder reflect an Indian influence on what is predominantly a Chinese dish.

*ABOVE: Singapore noodles*

## SINGAPORE NOODLES

Preparation time: 30 minutes +
   30 minutes marinating
Total cooking time: 10 minutes
Serves 4–6

2 cloves garlic, crushed

2 teaspoons grated fresh ginger

1/4 cup (60 ml/2 fl oz) oyster sauce

1/4 cup (60 ml/2 fl oz) soy sauce

250 g (8 oz) chicken breast fillets, thinly sliced

400 g (13 oz) dried rice vermicelli

2 tablespoons vegetable oil

2 celery sticks, julienned

1 large carrot, julienned

3 spring onions, sliced on the diagonal

1 1/2 tablespoons Asian curry powder

1/2 teaspoon sesame oil

65 g (2 1/4 oz) bean sprouts, tailed

1 Combine the garlic, ginger, 1 tablespoon oyster sauce and 2 teaspoons soy sauce in a large non-metallic bowl. Add the chicken, toss well, cover with plastic wrap and marinate in the fridge for 30 minutes.
2 Soak the noodles in boiling water for 6–7 minutes, or until soft. Drain.
3 Heat a wok over high heat, add the oil and swirl to coat. Stir-fry the chicken until browned. Add the celery, carrot and half the spring onion, and stir-fry for 2–3 minutes, or until slightly softened. Add the curry powder and stir-fry for 2 minutes, or until fragrant.
4 Toss in the noodles, stir in the remaining ingredients, then serve.

## CHICKEN IN LETTUCE CUPS

Preparation time: 15 minutes +
   20 minutes soaking
Total cooking time: 10 minutes
Serves 4

4 dried shiitake mushrooms

8 iceberg lettuce leaves

1 tablespoon peanut oil

2 cloves garlic, crushed

2 teaspoons grated fresh ginger

6 spring onions, thinly sliced

400 g (13 oz) chicken mince

1/2 red pepper (capsicum), diced

50 g (1 3/4 oz) bean sprouts, tailed

1/2 cup (70 g/2 1/4 oz) water chestnuts, diced

2 1/2 tablespoons oyster sauce

4 tablespoons fresh coriander leaves

oyster sauce, to serve

1 Soak the dried mushrooms in a bowl of boiling water for 20 minutes. Squeeze the mushrooms dry. Discard the stalks and thinly slice the caps.

2 Sit one lettuce leaf inside another to make a strong lettuce leaf cup. Repeat with the other leaves to make three more lettuce cups. Trim the edges with scissors to neaten, then refrigerate until needed.

3 Heat a wok over high heat, add the oil and swirl to coat the side of the wok. Add the garlic, ginger and spring onion and stir-fry for 30 seconds. Add the chicken mince and cook for 2–3 minutes, or until cooked through, breaking up any lumps with the back of a spoon. Add the mushrooms, red pepper, bean sprouts and water chestnuts and stir-fry for 1 minute. Stir in the oyster sauce and cook, tossing for 1–2 minutes, or until the sauce has reduced slightly. Stir in the fresh coriander and divide the mixture evenly among the lettuce cups. Serve immediately, drizzled with extra oyster sauce, if desired.

and swirl to coat the side of the wok. Add the chicken in batches and stir-fry for 3–5 minutes each batch, or until browned all over, then remove from the wok.

3 Add the spring onion and snow peas to the wok and stir-fry for 2 minutes. Return all the chicken and any juices to the wok and stir-fry for a further 2–3 minutes, or until the chicken is heated through and everything is thoroughly combined. Season to taste with salt and freshly ground black pepper. Serve on a bed of steamed jasmine rice.

NOTES: Serve with wedges of lime—they make an attractive garnish and can be squeezed over the food for extra flavour.

You can either use a home-made curry paste (see page 56) or a ready-made one. If you are using a ready-made paste, you will find that some brands of curry paste are too hot for your taste. Experiment with different brands to find one that you like.

*BELOW: Chicken and snow pea stir-fry*

## CHICKEN AND SNOW PEA (MANGETOUT) STIR-FRY

Preparation time: 15 minutes
Total cooking time: 15 minutes
Serves 4

1 tablespoon red curry paste (see Notes)
2 tablespoons vegetable oil
2 tablespoons fish sauce
2 tablespoons lime juice
3 tablespoons chopped fresh coriander leaves
1 tablespoon grated fresh ginger
1 teaspoon caster sugar
1 teaspoon sesame oil
750 g (1 1/2 lb) chicken thigh fillets, cut into strips
1 tablespoon vegetable oil, extra
10 spring onions, cut into 2 cm (3/4 inch) lengths
100 g (3 1/2 oz) snow peas (mangetout), trimmed

1 Whisk together the red curry paste, oil, fish sauce, lime juice, coriander, ginger, sugar and sesame oil in a large non-metallic bowl. Add the chicken strips and toss until they are evenly coated in the sauce.

2 Heat a wok over high heat, add the extra oil

## LEMON AND GINGER CHICKEN STIR-FRY

Preparation time: 25 minutes +
  20 minutes marinating
Total cooking time: 15 minutes
Serves 4

1 teaspoon grated lemon rind
1/3 cup (80 ml/2³/4 fl oz) lemon juice
1 small fresh red chilli, finely chopped
1 clove garlic, crushed
1 tablespoon grated fresh ginger
2 tablespoons chopped fresh coriander leaves
700 g (1 lb 7 oz) chicken breast fillets, sliced
1 tablespoon sesame seeds
2 tablespoons vegetable oil
150 g (5 oz) snow peas (mangetout), halved
  lengthways
150 g (5 oz) baby corn, quartered
2 tablespoons soy sauce
200 g (6¹/2 oz) bean sprouts, tailed

1 Combine the lemon rind and juice, chilli, garlic, ginger and coriander in a large non-metallic bowl. Add the chicken, toss well, then cover with plastic wrap and marinate in the fridge for 20 minutes.
2 Heat a wok over high heat, add the sesame seeds and stir-fry for 30 seconds, or until light brown. Remove from the wok.
3 Heat 1 tablespoon oil in the wok and swirl to coat. Drain the chicken and stir-fry in batches for 5 minutes, or until lightly browned. Remove from the wok.
4 Heat the remaining oil, then add the snow peas, baby corn and soy sauce, and stir-fry for 2 minutes. Return the chicken to the wok, add the bean sprouts and stir-fry for 1 minute. Sprinkle the sesame seeds over the top and serve with rice or noodles.

## CORIANDER AND LIME CHICKEN

Preparation time: 10 minutes
Total cooking time: 15 minutes
Serves 4

2/3 cup (170 ml/5¹/2 fl oz) coconut cream
1/2 cup (125 ml/4 fl oz) chicken stock
1¹/2 tablespoons lime juice
2 teaspoons grated fresh ginger
4 chicken breast fillets
plain flour, for dusting
2 tablespoons vegetable oil
2 tablespoons chopped fresh coriander leaves
fresh coriander leaves, extra, to garnish

LEMON JUICE
The addition of acidic ingredients, such as lemon juice, to a marinade is not just for flavour, but also to tenderise the meat being marinated, as it helps to break down the connective tissues in the meat. Limes are used for the same purpose in the tropics, where they are native.

*RIGHT: Lemon and ginger chicken stir-fry*

Cook the c
each batch
some extra
Remove th
**4** Reduce t
remaining
together, th
sugar caram
**5** Return a
the coriand
4 minutes,
through an
with steam

## GINGE
## WITH

Preparation
10 minut
Total cook
Serves 4

☆

2¹/₂ tables
¹/₄ cup (60
2 tablespo
600 g (1¹/₄
breast fi
500 g (1 lb
2 tablespo

---

**1** Whisk the coconut cream, stock, lime juice and ginger together in a bowl. Cut the chicken across the grain into 1 cm (¹/₂ inch) slices and lightly coat with flour.

**2** Heat a wok over high heat, add the oil and swirl to coat the side of the wok. Add the chicken and stir-fry over medium heat for 4–5 minutes, or until golden brown. Remove from the wok. Add the coconut cream mixture to the wok and bring to the boil. Cook for 4–5 minutes, or until the sauce is reduced by half and thickened slightly.

**3** Return the chicken strips to the wok, add the coriander and simmer for 1 minute to heat the chicken through. Garnish with the extra coriander leaves. Serve with steamed rice.

## SICHUAN PEPPER CHICKEN STIR-FRY

Preparation time: 25 minutes +
2 hours marinating
Total cooking time: 20 minutes
Serves 4

☆ ☆

3 teaspoons Sichuan peppercorns
2 tablespoons soy sauce
1 clove garlic, crushed
1 teaspoon grated fresh ginger
3 teaspoons cornflour
500 g (1 lb) chicken thigh fillets, cut into strips
100 g (3¹/₂ oz) dried thin egg noodles
oil, for cooking
1 onion, sliced
1 yellow pepper (capsicum), cut into thin strips
1 red pepper (capsicum), cut into thin strips
100 g (3¹/₂ oz) sugar snap peas
¹/₄ cup (60 ml/2 fl oz) chicken stock

**1** Heat a wok over high heat and dry-fry the Sichuan peppercorns for 30 seconds. Remove from the wok and crush with a mortar and pestle or in a spice mill or small food processor.

**2** Combine the soy sauce, garlic, ginger, cornflour and Sichuan pepper in a large non-metallic bowl. Add the chicken and toss to coat in the marinade. Cover with plastic wrap and marinate in the fridge for 2 hours.

**3** Bring a large saucepan of water to the boil, add the egg noodles and cook for 3 minutes, or until tender. Drain, then drizzle with a little oil and toss it through the noodles to prevent them

from sticking together.

**4** Heat the wok over high heat, add 1 tablespoon of the oil and swirl it around to coat the side. Stir-fry the chicken in batches over medium–high heat for 5 minutes, or until golden brown and cooked, adding more oil when necessary. Remove from the wok.

**5** Reheat the wok, add 1 tablespoon of the oil and stir-fry the onion, peppers and sugar snap peas over high heat for 2–3 minutes, or until the vegetables are tender. Add the chicken stock and bring to the boil.

**6** Return the chicken and egg noodles to the wok and toss over high heat until well combined. Serve immediately.

*ABOVE: Sichuan pepper chicken stir-fry*

# GENERAL TSO'S CHICKEN

Preparation time: 10 minutes +
1 hour marinating + 20 minutes soaking
Total cooking time: 10 minutes
Serves 4–6

2 tablespoons Chinese rice wine

1 tablespoon cornflour

1/3 cup (80 ml/2¾ fl oz) dark soy sauce

3 teaspoons sesame oil

900 g (1 lb 13 oz) chicken thigh fillets, cut into
3 cm (1¼ inch) cubes

2 pieces dried citrus peel (2 x 3 cm/
¾ x 1¼ inch)

1/2 cup (125 ml/4 fl oz) peanut oil

1½–2 teaspoons chilli flakes

2 tablespoons finely chopped fresh ginger

1 cup (120 g/4 oz) thinly sliced spring onions

2 teaspoons sugar

thinly sliced spring onion, to garnish

1 Combine the Chinese rice wine, cornflour, 2 tablespoons of the dark soy sauce and 2 teaspoons of the sesame oil in a large non-metallic bowl. Toss the chicken, cover and marinate in the fridge for 1 hour.

2 Meanwhile, soak the dried citrus peel in warm water for 20 minutes. Remove from the water and finely chop—you will need 1½ teaspoons chopped peel.

3 Heat the oil in the wok over high heat. Drain the chicken from the marinade using a slotted spoon and stir-fry the chicken in batches for 2 minutes, or until browned and just cooked through. Remove from the oil with a slotted spoon and leave to drain in a colander or sieve.

4 Drain all the oil except 1 tablespoon from the wok. Reheat the wok over high heat, then add the chilli flakes and ginger. Stir-fry for 10 seconds, then return the chicken to the wok. Add the spring onion, sugar, soaked citrus peel, remaining soy sauce and sesame oil and ½ teaspoon salt and stir-fry for a further 2–3 minutes, or until well combined and warmed through. Garnish with spring onion, then serve with rice.

NOTE: This dish is named after a 19th century Chinese general from Yunnan province.

## THAI MINCED CHICKEN SALAD

(Larb gai)

Preparation time: 25 minutes
Total cooking time: 20 minutes
Serves 6

1 tablespoon jasmine rice

2 teaspoons vegetable oil

400 g (13 oz) chicken mince

2 tablespoons fish sauce

1 stem lemon grass, white part only, chopped

1/3 cup (80 ml/2³/4 fl oz) chicken stock

1/4 cup (60 ml/2 fl oz) lime juice

4 spring onions, thinly sliced on the diagonal

4 red Asian shallots, sliced

1/2 cup (25 g/³/4 oz) finely chopped fresh coriander leaves

1/2 cup (25 g/³/4 oz) shredded fresh mint

200 g (6¹/2 oz) lettuce leaves, shredded

1/4 cup (40 g/1¹/4 oz) chopped roasted unsalted peanuts

1 small fresh red chilli, sliced

lime wedges, to serve

1 Heat a frying pan over low heat. Add the rice and dry-fry for 3 minutes, or until lightly golden. Transfer the rice to a mortar and pestle and then grind to a fine powder.

2 Heat a wok over medium heat. Add the oil and swirl to coat. Add the mince and cook for 4 minutes, or until it changes colour, breaking up any lumps with the back of a wooden spoon. Add the fish sauce, lemon grass and stock and cook for a further 10 minutes. Remove the wok from the heat and allow to cool.

3 Stir in the lime juice, spring onion, shallots, coriander, mint and ground rice and mix together thoroughly.

4 To serve, arrange the lettuce on a serving platter and top with the chicken mixture. Sprinkle with the nuts and chilli, and serve with lime wedges.

LARB
Popular in the north and northeast of Thailand, larb, or dressed salad, originated in neighbouring Laos. The predominant flavours of chilli and lime juice combined with fresh herbs and salad ingredients reflect the emphasis on freshness and raw ingredients that is characterised in Laotian food. In fact, many Laotian larb are entirely raw, using raw fish or meat, such as beef or buffalo. Because Laos is a landlocked country that has historically been quite isolated, Laotian cuisine is based on locally grown ingredients.

*ABOVE: Thai minced chicken salad*

177

# FRIED RICE

To make fried rice, you need cold, cooked rice. Either use leftover rice or cook the rice a day ahead and refrigerate. To calculate the amount of raw rice you need, divide the cooked rice amount by three. For example, 3 cups cooked rice is equivalent to 1 cup raw rice.

## THAI VEGETARIAN FRIED RICE
(Khao pad)
Heat a wok over high heat, add 2 tablespoons vegetable oil and swirl. Stir-fry 3 sliced red Asian shallots, 1 clove finely chopped garlic and 1 finely chopped small fresh red chilli for 2 minutes, or until the shallots start to brown. Add 100 g (3½ oz) sliced snake beans, 1 thinly

sliced small red pepper (capsicum) (cut into 5 cm/2 inch lengths) and 90 g (3 oz) halved button mushrooms. Stir-fry for 3 minutes, or until cooked, then stir in 3 cups (555 g/1 lb 2 oz) cold, cooked jasmine rice until heated through.

Dissolve 1 teaspoon grated palm sugar in ¼ cup (60 ml/2 fl oz) light soy sauce and pour over the rice. Stir in 3 tablespoons shredded fresh Thai basil and 1 tablespoon chopped fresh coriander. Serves 4.

## INDONESIAN FRIED RICE
(Nasi goreng)
Cook 150 g (5 oz) finely chopped snake beans in boiling water for 3 minutes. Drain, rinse and set aside.

Blend 3 roughly chopped cloves garlic, 1 chopped onion and 1 small fresh bird's eye chilli in a food processor into a rough paste. Heat 2 tablespoons vegetable oil in a wok, swirl to coat the side of the wok, and cook the paste for 1 minute, or until fragrant. Add 200 g (6½ oz) peeled and deveined baby prawns and 250 g (8 oz) thinly sliced chicken breast, and stir-fry for 3 minutes, or until the prawns turn pink. Add the beans and 2 tablespoons water and season with salt and pepper. Add 4 cups (740 g/1½ lb) cold, cooked long-grain rice, 4 thinly sliced spring onions, 1 tablespoon kecap manis and 1–2 tablespoons light soy sauce, stirring continuously until heated. Serves 4–6.

NOTE: Nasi goreng is usually served with shredded omelette and prawn crackers (*krupuk udang* in Indonesia and Malaysia) on the top.

## PINEAPPLE BEEF FRIED RICE

Heat a wok over high heat, add 1 tablespoon peanut oil and a few drops of sesame oil and swirl to coat. Add 2 teaspoons finely chopped fresh ginger, 1 finely chopped small fresh red chilli and 2 cloves crushed garlic and stir-fry for a few seconds, then add 250 g (8 oz) beef mince and stir-fry, breaking up any lumps, for 4–5 minutes, or until the beef is cooked through. Add 1/2 cup (80 g/2³/4 oz) cooked frozen peas and 4 finely chopped spring onions and stir-fry for 1 minute, or until the spring onion is soft. Add 4 cups (740 g/1¹/2 lb) cold, cooked long-grain rice, ¹/4 cup (60 g/2 oz) finely diced bamboo shoots,

²/3 cup (175 g/6 oz) very well drained crushed pineapple and toss, then stir-fry for 2–3 minutes, or until the rice is heated through. Add 1¹/2 tablespoons soy sauce, 1¹/2 tablespoons fish sauce and 1 tablespoon rice vinegar and stir-fry for a minute, or until combined. Stir in 2 tablespoons finely chopped fresh coriander leaves and serve. Serves 4–6.

## CHINESE FRIED RICE

Soak 2 tablespoons dried shrimp in boiling water for 20 minutes. Drain and finely chop. Heat a wok over high heat, add 1 tablespoon vegetable oil and swirl to coat the side of the wok. Add 3 lightly beaten eggs and stir until they start to scramble. When almost cooked, cut into small strips, then remove from the wok.

Heat 1 tablespoon vegetable oil in the wok, add 250 g (8 oz) finely diced Chinese barbecued pork and stir-fry for

1 minute, or until heated through. Add 50 g (1³/4 oz) drained, rinsed and finely diced straw mushrooms and the shrimp, and stir-fry for 1–2 minutes. Add 1 tablespoon oil, then gradually add 4 cups (740 g/1¹/2 lb) cold, cooked long-grain rice, tossing for 2 minutes, or until heated through. Reduce the heat to medium, add 2 tablespoons light soy sauce, 3 finely chopped spring onions and 2¹/2 tablespoons finely chopped garlic chives, and stir-fry until mixed and the soy sauce coats the rice. Season with white pepper and a drizzle of sesame oil, and serve topped with the omelette strips. Serves 4.

*FROM LEFT: Thai vegetarian fried rice, Indonesian fried rice, Pineapple beef fried rice, Chinese fried rice.*

SWEET CHILLI PRAWNS

Peel and devein the prawns, keeping the tails intact.

## SWEET CHILLI PRAWNS

Preparation time: 20 minutes
Total cooking time: 10 minutes
Serves 4

☆ ☆

1/3 cup (80 ml/2³/4 fl oz) chilli garlic sauce

2 tablespoons tomato sauce

2 tablespoons Chinese rice wine

1 tablespoon Chinese black vinegar

1 tablespoon soy sauce

1 tablespoon soft brown sugar

1 teaspoon cornflour mixed with 1/2 cup
    (125 ml/4 fl oz) water

2 tablespoons peanut oil

1 x 3 cm (1/2 x 1 1/4 inch) piece fresh ginger,
    cut into julienne strips

2 cloves garlic, finely chopped

5 spring onions, cut into 3 cm (1 1/4 inch) lengths

1 kg (2 lb) raw medium prawns, peeled and
    deveined, with tails intact

finely chopped spring onion, to garnish

1 To make the stir-fry sauce, combine the chilli garlic sauce, tomato sauce, rice wine, vinegar, soy sauce, sugar and cornflour paste in a small jug.

2 Heat a wok over high heat, add the oil and swirl to coat, then add the ginger, garlic and spring onion and stir-fry for 1 minute. Add the prawns and cook for 2 minutes, or until they are pink and starting to curl. Remove from the wok.
3 Pour the stir-fry sauce into the wok and cook, stirring, for 1–2 minutes, or until it thickens slightly. Return the prawns to the wok for 1–2 minutes, or until heated and cooked through. Garnish with the chopped spring onion. Serve with rice or thin egg noodles.

## TAMARIND RICE

Put 2 cups (400 g/13 oz) jasmine rice, 1 cup (250 g/8 oz) coconut cream and 3 tablespoons tamarind purée in a large saucepan. Add enough water to reach 2.5 cm (1 inch) over the rice and cook over high heat until boiling. Reduce the heat to medium, partially cover and allow the rice to absorb the water, then remove from the heat and cover tightly. Stand for 5 minutes, then stir in 1/3 cup (80 ml/2³/4 fl oz) lime juice. Serve with stir-fries. Serves 6.

*ABOVE: Sweet chilli prawns*

# STIR-FRIED SQUID WITH CORIANDER, PEPPER AND CELLOPHANE NOODLES

Preparation time: 30 minutes +
  5 minutes soaking
Total cooking time: 10 minutes
Serves 4

☆ ☆

200 g (6½ oz) cellophane noodles
2 cloves garlic, chopped
2 large fresh red chillies, seeded and chopped
½ cup (25 g/¾ oz) fresh coriander stems and roots, washed well
1 teaspoon black peppercorns, dry roasted and crushed
2 tablespoons peanut oil
300 g (10 oz) cleaned small squid hoods, scored and cut into 3 cm (1¼ inch) pieces
100 g (3½ oz) fresh asparagus, stems thinly sliced, leaving the tips whole
100 g (3½ oz) sugar snap peas, trimmed
2 tablespoons fish sauce
1 tablespoon kecap manis

¼ cup (120 g/4 oz) roasted unsalted peanuts, roughly chopped
½ cup (15 g/½ oz) fresh coriander leaves
1 lime, quartered

1 Place the noodles in a heatproof bowl, cover with boiling water and soak for 3–4 minutes, or until softened. Drain, rinse under cold water, and drain again. Cut into 15 cm (6 inch) lengths.
2 Place the garlic, chilli, coriander, peppercorns and ½ teaspoon salt in a food processor or blender and process to a rough paste, adding a little water if necessary.
3 Heat the peanut oil in a wok over medium–high heat. Add the paste and cook for 3 minutes, or until fragrant, then push to the side of the wok. Add the squid and briefly stir-fry until it curls, stirring in the paste to coat (it should not be in the wok for more than 1 minute). Remove.
4 Add the asparagus, sugar snap peas and 2 tablespoons water to the wok and stir-fry for 3 minutes, or until the greens are tender. Add the squid and noodles and toss well. Stir in the fish sauce, kecap manis and most of the peanuts. Divide among bowls, top with the rest of the peanuts and the coriander and serve with lime.

*LEFT: Stir-fried squid with coriander, pepper and cellophane noodles*

# SWEET AND SOUR FISH WITH HOKKIEN NOODLES

Preparation time: 20 minutes
Total cooking time: 20 minutes
Serves 4

☆☆

425 g (14 oz) Hokkien noodles
1 tablespoon peanut oil
1 clove garlic, crushed
2 teaspoons grated fresh ginger
1 onion, cut into thin wedges
1 carrot, halved lengthways and thinly sliced
1/2 red pepper (capsicum), cut into thin strips
1/2 green pepper (capsicum), cut into thin strips
1 celery stick, thinly sliced
1/2 cup (60 g/2 oz) plain flour
1/4 cup (45 g/1 1/2 oz) rice flour
1 teaspoon caster sugar
1/2 teaspoon ground white pepper
500 g (1 lb) firm white fish fillets, cut into
    3 cm (1 1/4 inch) cubes
1 egg, beaten with 1 tablespoon water
oil, to deep-fry
2 spring onions, sliced on the diagonal

SAUCE
1/4 cup (60 ml/2 fl oz) rice vinegar
1 tablespoon cornflour

1/4 cup (60 ml/2 fl oz) tomato sauce
2 tablespoons sugar
2 teaspoons light soy sauce
1 tablespoon dry sherry
1/4 cup (60 ml/2 fl oz) pineapple juice
2 tablespoons vegetable stock

1 Put the noodles in a heatproof bowl, cover with boiling water and soak for 1 minute. Separate gently, then drain.
2 To make the sauce, combine the vinegar and cornflour in a small jug, then stir in the rest of the ingredients and 3/4 cup (185 ml/6 fl oz) water until combined.
3 Heat a wok over medium heat, add the oil and swirl to coat. Cook the garlic and ginger for 30 seconds. Add the onion, carrot, red and green pepper and celery and stir-fry for 3–4 minutes. Add the sauce to the wok, increase the heat to high and stir-fry for 1–2 minutes, or until thickened. Remove the wok from the heat.
4 Combine the flours, sugar and white pepper in a medium bowl. Dip the fish in the egg, then the flour mix, shaking off any excess. Fill a clean wok one-third full of oil and heat to 180°C (350°F), or until a cube of bread dropped in the oil browns in 15 seconds. Deep-fry the fish in batches for 3 minutes, or until cooked and golden. Drain on paper towels and keep warm.
5 Return the wok with the sauce to medium heat, add the noodles and toss for 3–4 minutes, or until heated through. Gently toss in the fish, top with the spring onion and serve.

*BELOW: Sweet and sour fish with Hokkien noodles*

# THAI LEMON GRASS PRAWNS
(Takrai goong)

Preparation time: 25 minutes
Total cooking time: 10 minutes
Serves 4

6 stems lemon grass, white part only, sliced
2 teaspoons roughly chopped fresh galangal
1 fresh coriander root
2 cloves garlic
2 tablespoons vegetable oil
4 red Asian shallots, sliced
1 kg (2 lb) raw medium prawns, peeled and
    deveined, with tails intact
3 fresh kaffir lime leaves, thinly sliced
2 tablespoons fish sauce
3 teaspoons lime juice
2 tablespoons grated palm sugar
2 spring onions, cut into 2.5 cm (1 inch) lengths
fresh coriander leaves, to garnish (optional)

1 Place the lemon grass, galangal, coriander root
and garlic in a small food processor and process
to form a paste—add 1 teaspoon oil, if needed.
2 Heat a wok over medium heat, add the oil and
swirl to coat. Add the shallots and stir-fry for
2 minutes, or until softened. Add the paste and
stir-fry for 2 minutes, or until fragrant.
3 Add the prawns and cook for 3 minutes, or
until they turn pink. Add the lime leaves, fish
sauce, lime juice, palm sugar and spring onion.
Stir-fry for a further 1 minute. If desired, garnish
with coriander leaves and serve with rice.

# SCALLOPS WITH BLACK BEAN SAUCE

Preparation time: 15 minutes
Total cooking time: 10 minutes
Serves 4–6

600 g (1 1/4 lb) large fresh scallops, without roe
2 tablespoons cornflour
1/3 cup (80 ml/2 3/4 fl oz) peanut oil
3 spring onions, cut into 3 cm (1 1/4 inch) lengths
1 teaspoon finely chopped fresh ginger
2 cloves garlic, crushed
2 tablespoons Chinese rice wine

1/4 cup (55 g/2 oz) black beans, rinsed and
    roughly chopped
1 tablespoon rice vinegar
1 tablespoon soy sauce
1 teaspoon soft brown sugar
1/2 teaspoon sesame oil

1 Remove and discard any veins, membrane or
hard white muscle from the scallops. Toss them
in the cornflour to coat, then shake off any excess.
2 Heat a wok over high heat, add 1 teaspoon
peanut oil and swirl. Add the spring onion and
stir-fry for 30 seconds; remove from the wok.
3 Add 1 tablespoon peanut oil to the hot wok,
then add one-third of the scallops and stir-fry for
1–2 minutes, or until golden and well sealed—no
liquid should be released. Remove from the
wok. Repeat with the rest of the scallops.
4 Add the remaining peanut oil to the wok and
swirl. Add the ginger, garlic, rice wine, black
beans, vinegar, soy sauce and sugar, and stir-fry
for 1 minute, or until the sauce thickens slightly.
5 Return the scallops to the wok and stir-fry for
1 minute, or until heated through and the sauce
has thickened again. Stir in the spring onion and
sesame oil. Serve with steamed rice.

*ABOVE: Thai lemon grass prawns*

SINGAPORE
PEPPER CRAB

Lift the 'apron', the small flap on the underside of the crab, and prise off the top hard shell.

Remove the soft internal organs and pull off the spongy grey fingers (the gills).

Use a sharp, strong knife to cut each crab into four pieces.

# SINGAPORE PEPPER CRAB

Preparation time: 15 minutes + 1 hour freezing
Total cooking time: 20 minutes
Serves 4

☆ ☆

2 kg (4 lb) blue swimmer crabs
2 tablespoons dark soy sauce
2 tablespoons oyster sauce
1 tablespoon grated palm sugar
1–2 tablespoons peanut oil
150 g (5 oz) butter
2 tablespoons finely chopped garlic
1 tablespoon finely chopped fresh ginger
1 small fresh red chilli, seeded and finely
    chopped
1 1/2 tablespoons ground black pepper
1 spring onion, green part only, thinly sliced
    on the diagonal

1 Wash the crabs well with a stiff brush. Pull back the apron and remove the top shell from each crab (it should come off easily and in one piece). Remove the intestine and the grey feathery gills. Using a large sharp knife, cut the crab lengthways through the centre of the body, to form two halves with the legs attached. Cut each half in half again, crossways. Crack the thicker part of the legs with the back of a heavy knife or crab crackers to allow the flavour to get into the meat and make it easier for your guests to break them open to access the crab meat.

2 To make the stir-fry sauce, combine the soy sauce, oyster sauce and palm sugar in a small bowl or jug. Set aside until needed.

3 Heat a wok over high heat, add 1 tablespoon of the oil and swirl to coat the side of the wok. Add the crab pieces in a few batches, stir-frying over very high heat for 4 minutes each batch, or until the shells turn bright orange all over, adding a little more oil if needed. Remove from the wok.

4 Reduce the heat to medium–high, add the butter, garlic, ginger, chilli and pepper and stir-fry for 30 seconds, or until fragrant, then add the stir-fry sauce and simmer for a further minute, or until glossy.

5 Return the crab to the wok, cover with a lid, stirring every minute for 4 minutes, or until the crab is cooked. Sprinkle with the spring onion and serve immediately with rice. Put small bowls of warm water with lemon slices on the table for rinsing sticky fingers.

NOTE: This dish is very rich and best served as part of a banquet. In Singapore, crab is served with paper bibs as it is very messy to eat—a paper towel or serviette will do just as well.

*ABOVE: Singapore pepper crab*

# SALT AND PEPPER SQUID

Preparation time: 15 minutes +
  20 minutes marinating
Total cooking time: 10 minutes
Serves 4

500 g (1 lb) squid hoods, cut in half lengthways
1/3 cup (80 ml/2³/4 fl oz) vegetable oil
4 cloves garlic, finely chopped
1/2 teaspoon sugar
2 teaspoons salt
1 teaspoon ground black pepper
2 tablespoons lime juice
lime wedges, to garnish

1 Rinse the squid in cold water and pat dry with paper towels. Score a diamond pattern on the inside, being careful not to cut all the way through. Cut into 3 x 5 cm (1¹/4 x 2 inch) pieces. Combine the oil, garlic, sugar, and half the salt and pepper, add the squid, toss to coat, cover and refrigerate for 20 minutes.
2 Heat a wok over high heat, add the squid in batches, and stir-fry for 1–2 minutes, or until it is just white and curls. Remove.
3 Return the squid to the wok and add the lime juice and remaining salt and pepper. Heat through. Serve with lime wedges.

# STIR-FRIED FISH WITH GINGER

Preparation time: 20 minutes
Total cooking time: 15 minutes
Serves 4

1 tablespoon peanut oil
1 small onion, thinly sliced
3 teaspoons ground coriander
600 g (1¹/4 lb) boneless white fish fillets
  (e.g. perch), cut into bite-sized strips
1 tablespoon julienned fresh ginger
1 teaspoon finely chopped and seeded fresh
  green chilli
2 tablespoons lime juice
2 tablespoons fresh coriander leaves

1 Heat a wok over high heat, add the oil and swirl to coat the side of the wok. Add the onion and stir-fry for 4 minutes, or until soft and golden. Add the ground coriander and cook for 1–2 minutes, or until fragrant.
2 Add the fish, ginger and chilli, and stir-fry for 5–7 minutes, or until the fish is cooked through, but be careful that the fish doesn't break up. Stir in the lime juice and season to taste with salt and pepper. Garnish with the coriander leaves and serve with steamed rice.

Score a diamond pattern on the inside of the squid hood, then cut into pieces.

*LEFT: Stir-fried fish with ginger*

WATERCRESS
Watercress is an aquatic plant, a type of cress, that is both cultivated and found growing in the wild. Native to Eurasia, watercress now grows in freshwater ponds and streams all over the world. Its dark-green leaves have a peppery, slightly pungent mustardy flavour and are used in salads, sandwiches and as a garnish. It may also be cooked in soups and sauces, although cooking destroys its potency. Buy dark leaves with no yellowing and use soon after purchase. To store, stand stems in a bowl of water, cover with a plastic bag and refrigerate. Quite often a recipe will specify to remove the stems of the watercress and just to use the leaves. The difference between the Western and Eastern uses of watercress is that Westerners are more likely to eat it raw, whereas Asians usually cook it briefly.

## GINGER GARLIC PRAWN SALAD

Preparation time: 35 minutes
Total cooking time: 15 minutes
Serves 4

☆ ☆

2 teaspoons cornflour
1/4 cup (60 ml/2 fl oz) vegetable stock
2 tablespoons soy sauce
2 teaspoons soft brown sugar
oil, for cooking
5 cloves garlic, finely chopped
1 tablespoon grated fresh ginger
1 onion, sliced
500 g (1 lb) raw prawns, peeled and deveined, with tails intact
1 carrot, julienned
2 celery sticks, julienned
100 g (3 1/2 oz) snow peas (mangetout), sliced
100 g (3 1/2 oz) green beans, cut into short lengths
500 g (1 lb) watercress
1/4 cup (40 g/1 1/4 oz) roasted peanuts, roughly chopped

1 Combine the cornflour and a little of the stock in a small bowl and stir until a paste forms. Stir in the soy sauce, sugar and remaining stock.

2 Heat a wok over high heat, add 1 tablespoon of the oil and swirl it around to coat. Stir-fry the garlic, ginger, onion and prawns over high heat for 5 minutes, or until the prawns have turned pink and are cooked. Remove from the wok.
3 Reheat the wok, add 1 tablespoon of the oil and stir-fry the carrot, celery, snow peas and beans over high heat for 3–4 minutes. Pour the stir-fry sauce into the wok and stir until the sauce boils and thickens.
4 Return the prawns to the wok, and stir for 1–2 minutes, or until heated through. Serve on a bed of watercress, and sprinkle the chopped peanuts over the top.

## BLACK FUNGUS WITH PRAWNS AND VEGETABLES

Preparation time: 25 minutes + 20 minutes soaking
Total cooking time: 8 minutes
Serves 4

☆

20 g (3/4 oz) dried black fungus
2 teaspoons cornflour
1/4 cup (60 ml/2 fl oz) mirin
1 tablespoon rice vinegar
1 tablespoon soy sauce
1–2 small fresh red chillies, seeded and finely chopped

*RIGHT: Ginger garlic prawn salad*

1–2 cloves garlic, crushed

2 teaspoons grated fresh ginger

1 tablespoon vegetable oil

500 g (1 lb) raw prawns, peeled and deveined, halved

1/2 red pepper (capsicum), julienned

1 celery stick, julienned

1 carrot, julienned

4 spring onions, cut into short pieces and sliced lengthways

230 g (7 1/2 oz) can water chestnuts, drained

1 Place the black fungus in a bowl and cover with boiling water for 20 minutes, or until it has doubled in volume and softened. Drain, squeeze dry and roughly chop.

2 Mix the cornflour with 1/4 cup (60 ml/2 fl oz) water in a bowl until smooth. Add the mirin, vinegar, soy sauce, chilli, garlic and ginger.

3 Heat the wok over high heat, add the oil and swirl to coat. Stir-fry the prawns briefly until they are just starting to change colour. Add the pepper, celery, carrot, spring onion, water chestnuts and black fungus, and stir-fry over medium–high heat for 2–3 minutes, or until tender. Remove from the wok.

4 Add the sauce to the wok and stir until the mixture boils and thickens. Stir in the prawns and vegetables. Serve at once.

## STIR-FRIED BABY OCTOPUS

Preparation time: 30 minutes +
    overnight marinating
Total cooking time: 10 minutes
Serves 4

☆☆

500 g (1 lb) baby octopus

3 tablespoons chopped fresh coriander

2 cloves garlic, finely chopped

2 fresh red chillies, seeded and chopped

2 teaspoons grated fresh ginger

2 stems lemon grass, white part only, chopped

1 tablespoon vegetable oil

2 tablespoons lime juice

oil, for cooking

550 g (1 lb 2 oz) bok choy, leaves separated

400 g (13 oz) choy sum, leaves separated

2 cloves garlic, crushed, extra

1 teaspoon grated fresh ginger, extra

1 To prepare the baby octopus, remove the head, cut off the eyes, and remove the gut by slitting the head open. Grasp the body firmly and push the beak out with your index finger. Clean the octopus thoroughly under cold running water and pat dry with paper towels. Cut the head into two or three pieces.

2 Combine the coriander, garlic, chilli, ginger, lemon grass, oil and lime juice in a large non-metallic bowl. Add the octopus, cover with plastic wrap and refrigerate for at least 2 hours, or overnight, if time permits.

3 Heat a wok over high heat, add 1 tablespoon of the oil and swirl it around to coat the side of the wok. Stir-fry the vegetables with 1 tablespoon water. Spread on a serving plate.

4 Reheat the wok, add 1 tablespoon of the oil and stir-fry the extra garlic and ginger for 30 seconds, or until fragrant. Add the octopus and stir-fry over high heat for 7–8 minutes, or until cooked through. Serve on a bed of the wilted greens.

*ABOVE: Stir-fried baby octopus*

VIETNAMESE CARAMEL
PRAWNS

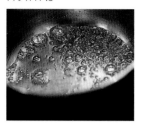

Bring the sugar syrup to the
boil and swirl until it turns a
lovely dark golden colour—
don't stir the liquid.

# VIETNAMESE CARAMEL PRAWNS

Preparation time: 20 minutes
Total cooking time: 10 minutes
Serves 4–6

☆ ☆

1/4 cup (45 g/1 1/2 oz) grated light palm sugar
1.5 kg (3 lb) raw medium prawns, peeled and
　deveined
3 spring onions, finely chopped, white and
　greens separated
1 tablespoon vegetable oil
2 tablespoons fish sauce
1 tablespoon rice vinegar
1 tablespoon grated light palm sugar, extra
2 cloves garlic, finely chopped
large pinch of white pepper
1 tablespoon finely chopped fresh coriander
　leaves (optional)

1 Put the palm sugar and 1 tablespoon water in a
small saucepan over high heat and stir until the
sugar dissolves. Bring to the boil and swirl the
pan occasionally (but don't stir) for 3–4 minutes,
or until it is dark golden and there is the first smell
of toffee. Using a long-handled spoon, gradually
stir in 1/4 cup (60 ml/2 fl oz) water until a thin
caramel sauce forms. Remove from the heat.
2 Combine the prawns and the white part of the

spring onion in a bowl.
3 Heat a wok over high heat, add the oil and
swirl to coat. Add the prawns and stir-fry for
1 minute, or until the prawns turn pink, then add
the caramel sauce, fish sauce, rice vinegar, extra
palm sugar, garlic, spring onion greens and
pepper and stir-fry for 2 minutes, or until the
prawns are curled and glazed. Toss in the
coriander, if using. Serve as part of a banquet.

# SICHUAN PRAWN STIR-FRY

Preparation time: 20 minutes
Total cooking time: 15 minutes
Serves 4

☆

500 g (1 lb) Hokkien noodles
2 tablespoons vegetable oil
2 cloves garlic, sliced
1 onion, cut into thin wedges
1 tablespoon Sichuan peppercorns, crushed
1 stem lemon grass, white part only, finely
　chopped
300 g (10 oz) green beans, sliced
750 g (1 1/2 lb) raw large prawns, peeled,
　deveined and halved lengthways
2 tablespoons fish sauce
1/3 cup (80 ml/2 3/4 fl oz) oyster sauce
1/2 cup (125 ml/4 fl oz) chicken stock

*ABOVE: Vietnamese
caramel prawns*

1 Cover the noodles with boiling water for 1 minute, gently separate, then drain.
2 Heat a wok over high heat, add 1 tablespoon oil and swirl to coat. Add the garlic, onion, peppercorns and lemon grass, and stir-fry for 2 minutes, then add the beans and stir-fry for 2–3 minutes, or until tender. Remove.
3 Reheat the wok, add the remaining oil and swirl to coat. Add the prawns and stir-fry for 3–4 minutes, or until just cooked through. Add the bean mixture and noodles, and stir-fry for 3 minutes, or until the noodles are heated through. Add the sauces and stock, and bring to the boil. Toss well and serve.

## WHEAT NOODLES AND FISH WITH BLACK BEANS

Preparation time: 10 minutes
Total cooking time: 15 minutes
Serves 4

☆

270 g (9 oz) fresh wheat noodles
200 g (6 1/2 oz) gai larn (Chinese broccoli), cut into 5 cm (2 inch) lengths
550 g (1 lb 2 oz) skinless snapper or cod fillets, cut into 4 cm (1 1/2 inch) pieces
2 tablespoons light soy sauce
1 1/2 tablespoons Chinese rice wine
1 teaspoon sugar
1/2 teaspoon sesame oil
2 teaspoons cornflour
1 tablespoon vegetable oil
5 cloves garlic, crushed
2 teaspoons finely chopped fresh ginger
2 spring onions, finely chopped
2 small fresh red chillies, finely chopped
2 tablespoons black beans, rinsed and roughly chopped
150 ml (5 fl oz) fish stock
spring onions, extra, sliced on the diagonal, to garnish

1 Cook the wheat noodles in a large saucepan of boiling water for 2 minutes, or until tender. Drain. Put the gai larn in a steamer and steam for 3–4 minutes, or until slightly wilted. Remove from the heat and keep warm.
2 Put the fish in a bowl. Combine the soy sauce, rice wine, sugar, sesame oil and cornflour. Pour

over the fish and toss to coat well.
3 Heat a wok over high heat, add the vegetable oil and swirl to coat. Add the garlic, ginger, spring onion, chilli and black beans and stir-fry for 1 minute. Add the fish and marinade and cook for a further 2 minutes. Remove the fish with a slotted spoon and keep warm.
4 Add the stock to the wok, reduce the heat to low and bring to a slow simmer. Cook for 5 minutes, or until the sauce has slightly thickened. Return the fish to the wok, cover and continue to simmer gently for 2–3 minutes, or until just cooked.
5 To serve, divide the noodles among the serving dishes, top with the gai larn and spoon the fish and black bean sauce on top. Garnish with the extra spring onion.

*BELOW: Wheat noodles and fish with black beans*

1 Cut the squid hoods in half lengthways. Clean and remove the quills. Score a diamond pattern on the inside of the squid. Cut into 4 cm (1½ inch) square pieces.

2 Put the coriander root, 1 clove garlic and 1 tablespoon oil in a food processor and process to form a smooth paste. Mix together the paste and squid pieces, cover and marinate in the fridge for 30 minutes.

3 Heat a wok over high heat, add the remaining oil and swirl to coat the side. Add the squid pieces and the remaining garlic and stir-fry for 1 minute. Add the peppercorns and stir-fry for a further 2 minutes, or until the calamari is just cooked—it will toughen if overcooked. Add the soy sauce and palm sugar, and stir until the sugar has dissolved. Serve immediately, garnished with Thai basil and green peppercorns.

## SQUID WITH GREEN PEPPERCORNS
(Pla muek kratiem prik Thai)

Preparation time: 10 minutes +
  30 minutes marinating
Total cooking time: 5 minutes
Serves 4

☆ ☆

600 g (1¼ lb) cleaned squid hoods, washed and dried
2 teaspoons chopped fresh coriander root
3 cloves garlic, crushed
⅓ cup (80 ml/2¾ fl oz) vegetable oil
25 g (¾ oz) Thai green peppercorns on the stalk, in brine, or lightly crushed fresh peppercorns
2 tablespoons Thai mushroom soy sauce
½ teaspoon grated palm sugar
⅔ cup (20 g/¾ oz) fresh Thai basil
green peppercorns, extra, to garnish

*ABOVE: Squid with green peppercorns*

## PANCIT CANTON

Preparation time: 30 minutes
Total cooking time: 20 minutes
Serves 4

☆

1½ tablespoons peanut oil
1 large onion, finely chopped
2 cloves garlic, finely chopped
2 x 2 cm (¾ x ¾ inch) piece fresh ginger, shredded
500 g (1 lb) large raw prawns, peeled and deveined
180 g (6 oz) wom bok (Chinese cabbage), thinly sliced
1 carrot, julienned
200 g (6½ oz) Chinese barbecued pork, cut into 5 mm (¼ inch) thick pieces
3 teaspoons Chinese rice wine
2 teaspoons sugar
150 g (5 oz) snow peas (mangetout), trimmed
1⅓ cups (330 ml/11 fl oz) chicken stock
1 tablespoon light soy sauce
225 g (7 oz) pancit canton (Chinese e-fu) noodles
1 lemon, cut into wedges

1 Heat a wok over high heat, add the oil and swirl to coat the side of the wok. Add the onion and cook for 2 minutes, then add the garlic and ginger and cook for a further minute. Add the prawns and cook for 1 minute. Stir in the wom

bok, carrot, pork, rice wine and sugar and cook for a further 3–4 minutes, or until the pork is heated and the vegetables have softened. Add the snow peas and cook for 1 minute, or until tender. Remove the mixture from the wok.
2 Add the stock and soy sauce to the wok and bring to the boil. Add the noodles and cook, stirring, for 3–4 minutes, or until soft and almost cooked through.
3 Return the stir-fry mixture to the wok and toss with the noodles for 1 minute, or until combined. Divide among four warmed serving dishes and garnish with lemon wedges.

# CUCUMBER AND WHITE FISH STIR-FRY

Preparation time: 20 minutes
Total cooking time: 20 minutes
Serves 4

1/2 cup (60 g/2 oz) plain flour
1/2 cup (60 g/2 oz) cornflour
1/2 teaspoon five-spice powder
750 g (1 1/2 lb) firm white boneless fish fillets, such as ling, cut into 3 cm (1 1/4 inch) cubes
2 egg whites, lightly beaten
oil, for deep-frying
1 tablespoon vegetable oil

1 onion, cut into wedges
1 telegraph cucumber, halved, seeded and sliced on the diagonal
1 teaspoon cornflour, extra
3/4 teaspoon sesame oil
1 tablespoon soy sauce
1/3 cup (80 ml/2 3/4 fl oz) rice vinegar
1 1/2 tablespoons soft brown sugar
3 teaspoons fish sauce

1 Combine the plain flour, cornflour and five-spice powder in a shallow bowl, and season with salt and freshly ground black pepper. Dip the fish in the beaten egg white, drain off any excess, then toss gently in the flour mixture, shaking off any excess.
2 Fill a large saucepan one-third full of oil and heat to 180°C (350°F), or until a cube of bread dropped in the oil browns in 15 seconds. Cook the fish in batches for 6 minutes, or until golden brown. Drain on crumpled paper towels.
3 Heat a wok over high heat, add 1 tablespoon oil and swirl to coat the side of the wok. Add the onion and stir-fry for 1 minute, then add the cucumber and stir-fry for 30 seconds.
4 Blend the cornflour with 2 tablespoons water and add to the wok with the sesame oil, soy sauce, vinegar, sugar and fish sauce. Stir-fry for 3 minutes, or until the mixture boils and thickens. Add the fish and toss thoroughly to coat and heat through. Serve hot.

CUCUMBER
One of the oldest cultivated vegetables and, many would say, the most refreshing, the cucumber exists in over 100 varieties— including at least one described as 'burpless'. It can be eaten raw in salads, cooked in a soup or mixed with yoghurt as raita to be used as an accompaniment to curries. In Cantonese cuisine, cucumber is considered a strongly yin food, or one with cooling, soothing and mild properties. The model for this division of food is based on the Taoist concept of opposites in balance, thus yin (cool, water, female) and yang (hot, fire, male). To create balance in a meal, Cantonese chefs will combine the yin of cucumber with the yang of another ingredient, such as chicken.

*LEFT: Cucumber and white fish stir-fry*

## STUFFED PRAWN OMELETTES
(Kai yak sai)

Preparation time: 25 minutes
Total cooking time: 15 minutes
Makes 8

500 g (1 lb) raw prawns

1 1/2 tablespoons vegetable oil

4 eggs, lightly beaten

2 tablespoons fish sauce

8 spring onions, chopped

6 fresh coriander roots, chopped

2 cloves garlic, chopped

1 small fresh red chilli, seeded and chopped,
    plus extra, to garnish

2 teaspoons lime juice

2 teaspoons grated palm sugar

3 tablespoons chopped fresh coriander leaves

fresh coriander sprigs, to garnish

sweet chilli sauce, to serve

*BELOW: Stuffed prawn omelettes*

1 Peel and devein the prawns, then chop the prawn meat.

2 Heat a wok over high heat, add 2 teaspoons of the oil and swirl to coat. Combine the egg with half the fish sauce. Add 2 tablespoons of the mixture to the wok and swirl to a 16 cm (6 1/2 inch) round. Cook for 1 minute, then gently lift out. Repeat with the remaining egg mixture to make 8 omelettes.

3 Heat the remaining oil in the wok. Add the prawns, spring onion, coriander root, garlic and chilli. Stir-fry for 3–4 minutes, or until the prawns are cooked. Stir in the lime juice, palm sugar, coriander and the remaining fish sauce.

4 Divide the prawn mixture among the omelettes and fold each into a small firm parcel. Cut a slit in the top and garnish with the chilli and coriander. Serve with sweet chilli sauce.

## STIR-FRIED SEAFOOD WITH THAI BASIL

Preparation time: 35 minutes
Total cooking time: 15 minutes
Serves 4–6

1 1/2 tablespoons fish sauce

1 1/2 tablespoons lime juice

1 tablespoon light soy sauce

2 teaspoons grated palm sugar

220 g (7 oz) cleaned squid hoods

2 tablespoons peanut oil

1 small carrot, thinly sliced on the diagonal

1 small red pepper (capsicum), cut into thin
    strips

4 spring onions, cut into 5 cm (2 inch) lengths

2 cloves garlic, finely chopped

1 long fresh green chilli, seeded and finely
    chopped

350 g (11 oz) raw medium prawns, peeled and
    deveined, with tails intact

250 g (8 oz) firm white fish fillets (e.g. snapper,
    blue-eye or ling), cut into 3 cm (1 1/4 inch) cubes

150 g (5 oz) scallops, without roe

1/2 cup (25 g/3/4 oz) tightly packed fresh Thai
    basil, plus extra, to garnish (optional)

1 fresh red chilli, sliced (optional)

1 Combine the fish sauce, lime juice, soy sauce and sugar in a small bowl or jug and stir until the sugar has dissolved.

**2** Cut the squid hoods in half lengthways and open them out. Lay the hoods on a work surface with the inside facing uppermost. Score the squid into a diamond pattern, then cut into 4 cm (1¹/₂ inch) pieces.

**3** Heat a wok over high heat, add 1 tablespoon of the oil and swirl to coat the side of the wok. Add the carrot and red pepper and stir-fry for 2–3 minutes, or until just tender, then remove from the wok.

**4** Reheat the wok over high heat, add a little extra oil and swirl to coat the side. Add the spring onion, garlic and chopped green chilli, stir-frying for a minute, or until fragrant. Add the prawns and stir-fry for 2 minutes, or until pink. Add the fish cubes and cook for 2–3 minutes, or until the fish becomes golden. Toss the squid pieces and scallops into the stir-fry, and cook for 2–3 minutes, or until the squid pieces have curled up and the scallops are nearly cooked through.

**5** Return the vegetables to the wok, along with the fish sauce mixture. Toss well, sprinkle with the basil, then toss again gently, being careful not to break up the fish pieces. Serve immediately garnished with extra basil leaves and some chilli, if desired, and accompanied with steamed rice.

## CHILLI SQUID WITH HOKKIEN NOODLES

Preparation time: 25 minutes
Total cooking time: 20 minutes
Serves 4

☆ ☆

500 g (1 lb) Hokkien noodles

750 g (1¹/₂ lb) cleaned small squid hoods

2 tablespoons lime juice

6 red Asian shallots

4 cloves garlic

2 small fresh red chillies, chopped

2 fresh coriander roots

2 stems lemon grass, white part only, chopped

1 tablespoon chopped fresh ginger

2 tablespoons tomato paste (tomato purée)

¹/₃ cup (80 ml/2³/₄ fl oz) peanut oil

300 g (10 oz) baby bok choy, chopped

2¹/₂ tablespoons grated palm sugar

1 tablespoon fish sauce

3 tablespoons fresh coriander leaves

sliced fresh red chilli, extra, to garnish

**1** Cook the noodles in boiling water for 1 minute, then gently separate. Drain.

**2** Cut the squid hoods in half lengthways. Score a shallow diamond pattern over the inside, being careful not to cut all the way through. Cut into 5 cm (2 inch) triangles. Put in a bowl with the lime juice and refrigerate until needed.

**3** Process the shallots, garlic, chilli, coriander roots, lemon grass, ginger and tomato paste in a food processor until a fine paste forms.

**4** Drain the squid. Heat a wok over high heat, add 2 tablespoons oil and swirl to coat the side of the wok. Cook the squid in batches over medium heat for 2–3 minutes each batch, or until tender. Remove from the wok. Cook the bok choy for 2 minutes, or until slightly wilted. Remove from the wok and add to the squid.

**5** Heat the remaining oil in the wok, add the paste and cook, stirring, over medium heat for 5 minutes, or until the oil separates. Return the squid and bok choy to the wok, then add the noodles and combine. Stir in the palm sugar and fish sauce for 1 minute, then stir in the coriander. Garnish with the extra chilli slices and serve immediately.

*BELOW: Chilli squid with Hokkien noodles*

1 Combine the oyster and soy sauces, sesame oil and sugar in a small bowl and stir until the sugar dissolves.
2 Heat a wok over medium heat, add the oil and swirl to coat. Add the garlic and ginger and stir-fry for 30 seconds, or until fragrant. Add the peas and cook for 1 minute, then add the scallops and spring onion and cook for 1 minute, or until the spring onion is wilted. Stir in the sauce and heat for 1 minute, or until heated through and combined. Serve with rice.

## GREEN CURRY PRAWN AND NOODLE STIR-FRY

Preparation time: 20 minutes
Total cooking time: 15 minutes
Serves 4

☆

400 g (13 oz) Hokkien noodles
2 teaspoons grated palm sugar
1 tablespoon fish sauce
2 teaspoons lime juice
1 tablespoon peanut oil
1 onion, cut into thin wedges
1½ tablespoons good-quality green curry paste (see page 56)
150 g (5 oz) baby corn, cut in half on the diagonal
125 g (4 oz) snake beans, cut into 4 cm (1½ inch) lengths
1 cup (250 ml/8 fl oz) coconut milk
½ cup (125 ml/4 fl oz) chicken stock
800 g (1 lb 10 oz) raw king prawns, peeled and deveined, with tails intact
3 tablespoons chopped fresh coriander leaves

1 Put the noodles in a heatproof bowl, cover with boiling water and soak for 1 minute, or until tender and separated. Drain well.
2 Combine the palm sugar, fish sauce and lime juice in a small bowl or jug.
3 Heat a wok over high heat, add the oil and swirl to coat. Stir-fry the onion for 1–2 minutes, or until soft. Add the curry paste and cook for 1 minute, or until fragrant. Add the baby corn, snake beans, coconut milk and stock to the wok and simmer for 3–4 minutes. Add the prawns and cook for 3–4 minutes, or until they are pink and cooked. Stir the sauce into the wok. Add the noodles and chopped coriander and toss well until the noodles are heated through. Serve.

## STIR-FRIED SCALLOPS WITH SUGAR SNAP PEAS

Preparation time: 20 minutes
Total cooking time: 5 minutes
Serves 4

☆

2½ tablespoons oyster sauce
2 teaspoons soy sauce
½ teaspoon sesame oil
2 teaspoons sugar
2 tablespoons vegetable oil
2 large cloves garlic, crushed
3 teaspoons finely chopped fresh ginger
300 g (10 oz) sugar snap peas
500 g (1 lb) scallops, without roe, membrane removed
2 spring onions, cut into 2 cm (¾ inch) lengths

*ABOVE: Stir-fried scallops with sugar snap peas*

# PRAWN SAN CHOY BAU

Preparation time: 20 minutes
Total cooking time: 5 minutes
Serves 4–6

1 iceberg lettuce

2 tablespoons soy sauce

2 tablespoons oyster sauce

2 tablespoons lime juice

1 kg (2 lb) raw medium prawns (see Note)

1 tablespoon vegetable oil

1 teaspoon sesame oil

2 spring onions, finely chopped

2 cloves garlic, crushed

1 x 2 cm (1/2 x 3/4 inch) piece fresh ginger, grated

120 g (4 oz) drained water chestnuts, chopped

1 tablespoon chopped fresh red chilli

1 cup (185 g/6 oz) cold, cooked white rice

1 cup (90 g/3 oz) bean sprouts, tailed

1/2 cup (25 g/3/4 oz) chopped fresh coriander leaves

1/4 cup (60 ml/2 fl oz) hoisin sauce

1 Wash the lettuce and separate the leaves. Shake off any excess water and dry thoroughly on paper towels.

2 Combine the soy sauce, oyster sauce and lime juice in a small bowl or jug. Set aside until needed.

3 Peel and devein the prawns, then, if they are large, cut them into smaller pieces.

4 Heat a wok over high heat, add the vegetable and sesame oils and swirl to coat the side of the wok. Add the spring onion, garlic and ginger and cook for 30 seconds. Add the prawn meat, water chestnuts and chilli, season with salt and freshly ground black pepper and continue stir-frying for 2 minutes. Add the rice, sprouts and coriander and stir until combined.

5 Pour in the stir-fry sauce, toss briefly, then remove the wok from the heat. Transfer the mixture to a serving bowl. Place the dry lettuce cups on a plate. Either fill the lettuce cups with the mixture yourself, or allow your guests to do so at the table. Serve with hoisin sauce, to be drizzled over the top.

NOTE: To save time, you can buy peeled prawns. You will only need 500 g (1 lb)—about half their weight comes from the shells.

WATER CHESTNUTS
Although the dark brown skin and shape of the water chestnut resemble those of the true chestnut, they are, in fact, not nuts at all. The first part of the name is more accurate, as they are actually the edible tuber of a plant grown in water, such as that found in rice paddies. Unlike rice, they are harvested when the paddies are dry. Used in stir-fries, stuffing, dumpling fillings and hotpots, water chestnuts add crispness and textural contrast to many dishes, which is particularly valued in Chinese cuisine.

*LEFT: Prawn san choy bau*

1 Put the prawns in a large non-metallic bowl. Process the egg white, cornflour and 1 tablespoon rice vinegar in a food processor until smooth. Pour over the prawns, season with 1 teaspoon each of salt and pepper, and stir. Marinate for 10 minutes, then drain well.

2 Heat a wok over high heat, add the oil and heat to 190°C (375°F), or until a cube of bread dropped into the oil browns in 10 seconds. Add the noodles and cook for 10 seconds, or until puffed up. Drain on crumpled paper towels.

3 Remove all but 1/4 cup (60 ml/2 fl oz) oil from the wok, add the drained prawns and cook for 2–3 minutes, or until the prawns change colour. Drain on paper towels. Remove all but 1 tablespoon of the oil from the wok.

4 Reheat the wok over medium heat. Add the garlic and ginger and stir-fry for 30 seconds, then add the hoisin sauce, bean sauce, oyster sauce and the remaining vinegar, and stir well for 1 minute. Add the prawns to the sauce and toss to coat, then add the spring onion and cook for 1–2 minutes, or until soft. Arrange the prawns on a bed of crispy noodles, garnish with the coriander and serve with some lemon wedges on the side.

## KING PRAWNS WITH GARLIC BEAN SAUCE

Preparation time: 20 minutes +
    10 minutes marinating
Total cooking time: 10 minutes
Serves 4

1 kg (2 lb) raw medium prawns, peeled and
    deveined, with tails intact
2 egg whites
2 tablespoons cornflour
2 tablespoons rice vinegar
oil, for deep-frying, plus 1 tablespoon extra
125 g (4 oz) cellophane noodles, broken up
    into small pieces
4 cloves garlic, finely chopped
1 teaspoon finely chopped fresh ginger
2 teaspoons hoisin sauce
1 tablespoon bean sauce
1 tablespoon oyster sauce
6 spring onions, cut into 3 cm (1 1/4 inch)
    lengths on the diagonal
1/2 cup (15 g/1/2 oz) fresh coriander leaves
lemon wedges, to serve

*ABOVE: King prawns with garlic bean sauce*

## SWORDFISH WITH BOK CHOY

Preparation time: 20 minutes
Total cooking time: 10 minutes
Serves 4

500 g (1 lb) swordfish steak, cut into bite-sized
    pieces
2 tablespoons freshly cracked black pepper
2 tablespoons hoisin sauce
2 tablespoons rice wine
1 tablespoon oyster sauce
1 tablespoon soy sauce
oil, for cooking
3 cloves garlic, thinly sliced
1 onion, sliced
1 kg (2 lb) baby bok choy, leaves separated
100 g (3 1/2 oz) fresh shiitake mushrooms, sliced
1 tablespoon sesame seeds, toasted
1 teaspoon sesame oil

1 Dip the swordfish in cracked black pepper until coated, then shake off any excess.

2 Combine the hoisin sauce, rice wine, oyster

sauce and soy sauce in a small bowl or jug.

**3** Heat a wok over high heat, add 2 tablespoons of the oil and swirl it around to coat the side of the wok. Stir-fry the swordfish in batches for 1–2 minutes each batch, or until tender. Be careful not to overcook the fish or it will break up. Remove from the wok.

**4** Reheat the wok, add 1 tablespoon of the oil, then stir-fry the garlic for 30 seconds, or until crisp and golden. Add the onion and stir-fry for 1–2 minutes, or until golden. Add the bok choy and mushrooms and cook briefly until the leaves wilt. Pour the sauce into the wok and stir until everything is coated in the sauce.

**5** Return the swordfish to the wok and toss everything together. Serve sprinkled with sesame seeds and drizzled with the sesame oil.

## PRAWNS WITH SPICY TAMARIND SAUCE

Preparation time: 15 minutes
Total cooking time: 25 minutes
Serves 4

1/2 cup (80 g/2³/4 oz) raw cashews
2 cloves garlic, finely chopped
1 1/2 tablespoons fish sauce
1 tablespoon sambal oelek

1 tablespoon peanut oil
1 kg (2 lb) raw medium prawns, peeled and deveined, with tails intact
2 teaspoons tamarind purée
1 1/2 tablespoons grated palm sugar
350 g (11 oz) choy sum, cut into 10 cm (4 inch) lengths

**1** Preheat the oven to moderate 180°C (350°F/Gas 4). Spread the cashews on a baking tray and bake for 5–8 minutes, or until lightly golden—watch carefully, as they will burn easily.

**2** Put the garlic, fish sauce, sambal oelek and toasted cashews in a food processor and blend to a rough paste, adding 2–3 tablespoons of water, if needed, to combine the ingredients.

**3** Heat a non-stick wok over high heat, add the oil and swirl to coat. Add the prawns, toss for 1–2 minutes, or until starting to turn pink. Remove from the wok. Add the cashew paste and stir-fry for 1 minute, or until it starts to brown slightly. Add the tamarind, sugar and about 1/3 cup (80 ml/2³/4 fl oz) water, then bring to the boil, stirring well. Return the prawns to the wok and stir to coat. Cook for 2–3 minutes, or until the prawns are cooked through.

**4** Place the choy sum in a paper-lined bamboo steamer and steam over a wok of simmering water for 3 minutes, or until tender. Serve with the prawns and steamed rice, if desired.

**PRAWNS**
Prawns, known as shrimp in North and South America, are crustaceans found all over the world living in fresh, briny and salt water of varying temperatures. They vary in size from 2.5 cm (1 inch) to 30 cm (12 inches) long, have two long antennae and five pairs of legs. Their flesh is translucent and can be coloured pink, yellow, grey, brown, red, dark red or green, depending on the species. They become opaque and turn pink once cooked. They should not be overcooked or they will become tough and rubbery; 2 to 3 minutes is enough to stir-fry average-sized prawns.

*LEFT: Prawns with spicy tamarind sauce*

### SICHUAN

Located in China's far west, the Sichuan region is famed for its spicy cuisine. Over 2000 years ago, Buddhist traders and missionaries brought Indian spices and cooking techniques to Sichuan, leaving a legacy of imaginative vegetarian cooking. Ginger, garlic, Sichuan peppercorns, dried long red chillies, vinegar, spring onions and black bean sauce are all important, along with red oil and the various hot bean pastes.

*ABOVE: Sichuan prawn and noodle stir-fry*

## SICHUAN PRAWN AND NOODLE STIR-FRY

Preparation time: 20 minutes
Total cooking time: 10 minutes
Serves 4

☆

600 g (1 1/4 lb) thin fresh rice noodles
1/3 cup (80 ml/2 3/4 fl oz) peanut oil
20 raw medium prawns, peeled and deveined, with tails intact
1 tablespoon Chinese rice wine
1 x 2 cm (1/2 x 3/4 inch) piece fresh ginger, julienned
2 cloves garlic, crushed
1–2 small fresh red chillies, seeded and thinly sliced
2 tablespoons chilli bean paste
4 spring onions, thinly sliced on the diagonal
1/2 cup (15 g/1/2 oz) fresh coriander leaves

1 Soak the noodles in boiling water to separate. Drain and refresh under cold running water.
2 Heat a wok over high heat, then add the oil and swirl to coat the side of the wok. Cook the prawns for 1 minute, stirring constantly. Add the wine, ginger, garlic and chilli and cook for a minute. Gently toss in the noodles until mixed

together. Add the chilli bean paste and spring onion. Stir over high heat for a further minute. Sprinkle with coriander and serve.

## SWEET CHILLI SQUID

Preparation time: 20 minutes
Total cooking time: 10 minutes
Serves 4

☆

750 g (1 1/2 lb) cleaned squid hoods
1 tablespoon peanut oil
1 tablespoon finely grated fresh ginger
2 cloves garlic, crushed
8 spring onions, chopped
2 tablespoons sweet chilli sauce
2 tablespoons Chinese barbecue sauce
1 tablespoon soy sauce
550 g (1 lb 2 oz) bok choy, cut into 3 cm (1 1/4 inch) pieces
1 tablespoon chopped fresh coriander leaves

1 Cut the squid hoods open lengthways and score a diagonal pattern across the inside surface, being careful not to cut all the way through. Cut into 2 cm x 9 cm (3/4 inch x 3 1/2 inch) pieces.
2 Heat a wok over high heat, add the oil and swirl to coat. Add the ginger, garlic, spring

onion and squid, and stir-fry for 3 minutes, or
until browned.

**3** Add the sweet chilli, barbecue and soy sauces
and 2 tablespoons water to the wok, and stir-fry
for 2 minutes, or until the squid is just tender.
Add the bok choy and coriander and stir-fry for
1 minute, or until tender.

## PRAWNS IN CHINESE PANCAKES

Preparation time: 20 minutes +
   10 minutes marinating
Total cooking time: 15 minutes
Makes 24

☆☆

1/3 cup (80 ml/2³/4 fl oz) Chinese rice wine

2 tablespoons soy sauce

2 teaspoons sesame oil

24 raw medium prawns, peeled and deveined

2 tablespoons vegetable oil

4 cloves garlic, finely chopped

1 x 4 cm (1/2 x 1¹/2 inch) piece fresh ginger,
   julienned

120–160 ml (4–5¹/2 fl oz) Chinese plum sauce

2 teaspoons chilli sauce

2 spring onions, finely chopped

24 Chinese pancakes (see Note)

1 small Lebanese cucumber, peeled, seeded and
   cut into thin 5 cm (2 inch) long strips

12 garlic chives, cut into 5 cm (2 inch) lengths

**1** Combine the rice wine, soy sauce and sesame
oil in a large non-metallic bowl. Add the prawns
and marinate for 10 minutes.

**2** Heat a wok over high heat, add the vegetable
oil and swirl to coat the side of the wok. Add
the garlic and ginger and stir-fry for 1–2 minutes.
Use a slotted spoon or tongs to remove the
prawns from the marinade and add them to the
wok, reserving the marinade. Stir-fry the prawns
for 2 minutes, or until they start to turn pink,
then add the plum sauce, chilli sauce and the
reserved marinade.

**3** Stir-fry for 2–3 minutes, or until the prawns
are cooked, curled and slightly glazed. Remove
from the heat and stir in the spring onion.

**4** Heat the pancakes in a non-stick frying pan
over medium heat for 1 minute, or until warm.

**5** To assemble, put a prawn, a few slices of
cucumber and a few chive pieces on each
pancake, spoon on some sauce, then fold over.
NOTE: The pancakes are traditionally used for
Peking duck. Buy them in the freezer section
of Asian food stores.

*LEFT: Prawns in Chinese
pancakes*

201

SOY SAUCE
Used in Chinese kitchens for over 3000 years, varieties of soy sauce add depth of flavour and richness to any recipe they are in. The two main types of soy sauce are light and dark. Light and dark soy sauces are used for the different flavours they offer. Contrary to popular belief, light soy sauce is actually saltier than its dark counterpart. Light soy sauce is often used with poultry and seafood, as its light colour and flavour are thought to suit the more delicate nature of white meat. It is the variety most often sold as generic soy sauce. Dark soy sauce is a little sweeter and less salty, and it is often added to provide a rich colour to a dish, as well as extra flavour. Southeast Asia has its own soy sauce—kecap manis—which is sweeter again than Chinese dark soy sauce.

*RIGHT: Prawn and rice noodle salad*

# PRAWN AND RICE NOODLE SALAD

Preparation time: 15 minutes +
    10 minutes soaking
Total cooking time: 15 minutes
Serves 4

☆ ☆

**Dressing**
2 tablespoons dark soy sauce
1 tablespoon fish sauce
2 tablespoons lime juice
1 teaspoon grated lime rind
1 teaspoon caster sugar
1 fresh red chilli, seeded and finely chopped
2 teaspoons finely chopped fresh ginger

150 g (5 oz) dried rice vermicelli
100 g (3 1/2 oz) snow peas (mangetout), trimmed, cut in half widthways
1/4 cup (60 ml/2 fl oz) peanut oil
2/3 cup (100 g/3 1/2 oz) raw cashews, chopped
24 raw medium prawns, peeled and deveined, with tails intact
1/2 cup (10 g/1/4 oz) fresh mint, chopped
1/2 cup (15 g/1/2 oz) fresh coriander leaves, chopped

1 To make the dressing, combine the ingredients in a small bowl.
2 Soak the vermicelli in boiling water for 6–7 minutes. Drain and set aside.
3 Blanch the snow peas in boiling salted water for 10 seconds. Drain and refresh in cold water.
4 Heat a wok over high heat and swirl to coat. Add the cashews and stir-fry for 2–3 minutes, or until golden. Remove with a slotted spoon and drain on paper towels. Add the prawns to the wok and cook over high heat, stirring constantly, for 2–3 minutes, or until just pink. Transfer to a large bowl, pour on the dressing and toss. Chill.
5 Add the noodles, snow peas, mint, coriander and cashews, toss well and serve immediately.

# PRAWN SALAD WITH KAFFIR LIME

Preparation time: 20 minutes
Total cooking time: 8 minutes
Serves 4

☆

3 teaspoons soft brown sugar
2 teaspoons soy sauce
2 tablespoons mirin
2 tablespoons lime juice

1 tablespoon vegetable oil

750 g (1 1/2 lb) raw large prawns, peeled, deveined and cut in half lengthways

4 spring onions, cut into 3 cm (1 1/4 inch) lengths

2 cloves garlic, sliced

1 small fresh red chilli, seeded and finely chopped

2 kaffir lime leaves, finely shredded

3 teaspoons grated fresh ginger

2 cups (70 g/2 1/4 oz) mixed lettuce leaves

1 Combine the sugar, soy sauce, mirin and lime juice in a bowl.

2 Heat a wok over high heat, add the oil and swirl to coat. Add the prawns and stir-fry for 3 minutes, or until nearly cooked.

3 Add the spring onion, garlic, chilli, lime leaves and ginger. Stir-fry for 1–2 minutes, or until fragrant. Pour the sauce into the wok and bring to the boil. Serve on the lettuce leaves.

## SEARED SCALLOPS WITH CHILLI BEAN PASTE

Preparation time: 20 minutes
Total cooking time: 15 minutes
Serves 4

☆

500 g (1 lb) Hokkien noodles

1/4 cup (60 ml/2 fl oz) peanut oil

20 scallops, without roe

1 large onion, cut into thin wedges

3 cloves garlic, crushed

1 tablespoon grated fresh ginger

1 tablespoon chilli bean paste

150 g (5 oz) choy sum, cut into 5 cm (2 inch) lengths

1/4 cup (60 ml/2 fl oz) chicken stock

2 tablespoons light soy sauce

2 tablespoons kecap manis

1/2 cup (15 g/1/2 oz) fresh coriander leaves

1 cup (90 g/3 oz) bean sprouts, washed

1 large fresh red chilli, seeded and thinly sliced

1 teaspoon sesame oil

1 tablespoon Chinese rice wine

1 Put the noodles in a heatproof bowl, cover with boiling water and soak for 1 minute to separate. Drain, rinse, then drain again.

2 Heat a wok over high heat, add 2 tablespoons of the peanut oil and swirl to coat the side of the wok. Add the scallops in batches and sear for 20 seconds on each side, or until sealed. Remove, then wipe the wok clean. Add the remaining peanut oil to the wok and swirl to coat. Stir-fry the onion for 1–2 minutes, or until softened. Add the garlic and ginger and cook for 30 seconds. Stir in the chilli bean paste and cook for 1 minute, or until fragrant.

3 Add the choy sum to the wok with the noodles, stock, soy sauce and kecap manis. Stir-fry for 4 minutes, or until the choy sum has wilted and the noodles have absorbed most of the liquid. Return the scallops to the wok, add the coriander, bean sprouts, chilli, sesame oil and rice wine, tossing gently until combined.

*ABOVE: Seared scallops with chilli bean paste*

**DASHI**
Dashi is a distinctly Japanese-flavoured stock based on fish and seaweed. Other ingredients can be added to make the dashi (literally, stock) but good chefs keep these secret. Dashi takes the place of the widely used chicken, meat or fish stock used in other parts of the world. Used extensively in Japanese cuisine, it is made by steeping konbu, a form of kelp, in hot water, then adding shaved, dried bonito. Instant dashi is sold ready-to-use in powder, liquid and granule forms.

*OPPOSITE PAGE, FROM TOP: Many mushroom noodles; Braised bok choy*

## MANY MUSHROOM NOODLES

Preparation time: 30 minutes +
 20 minutes soaking
Total cooking time: 15 minutes
Serves 4–6

25 g ($^3$/4 oz) dried shiitake mushrooms
500 g (1 lb) thin Hokkien noodles, separated
1 tablespoon vegetable oil
$^1$/2 teaspoon sesame oil
1 tablespoon finely chopped fresh ginger
4 cloves garlic, crushed
100 g (3$^1$/2 oz) fresh shiitake mushrooms, trimmed, sliced
150 g (5 oz) oyster mushrooms, sliced
150 g (5 oz) shimeji mushrooms, trimmed, pulled apart
1$^1$/2 teaspoons dashi granules dissolved in $^3$/4 cup (185 ml/6 fl oz) water
$^1$/4 cup (60 ml/2 fl oz) soy sauce
$^1$/4 cup (60 ml/2 fl oz) mirin
25 g ($^3$/4 oz) butter
2 tablespoons lemon juice
100 g (3$^1$/2 oz) enoki mushrooms, trimmed, pulled apart
1 tablespoon chopped fresh chives

1 Soak the dried mushrooms in 1$^1$/2 cups (375 ml/12 fl oz) boiling water for 20 minutes, or until soft. Drain, reserving the liquid. Discard the woody stalks and slice the caps. Cover the noodles with boiling water for 1 minute, then drain and rinse.
2 Heat a wok over high heat, add the oils and swirl to coat the side of the wok. Add the ginger, garlic, fresh shiitake, oyster and shimeji mushrooms, and stir-fry for 1–2 minutes, or until the mushrooms have wilted. Remove from the wok.
3 Combine the dashi, soy, mirin, $^1$/4 teaspoon white pepper and $^3$/4 cup (185 ml/6 fl oz) reserved liquid, add to the wok and cook for 3 minutes. Add the butter, lemon juice and 1 teaspoon salt and cook for 1 minute, or until the sauce thickens. Return the mushrooms to the wok, cook for 2 minutes, then stir in the enoki and shiitake mushrooms.
4 Add the noodles and stir for 3 minutes, or until heated through. Sprinkle with the chives and serve immediately.

## BRAISED BOK CHOY

Preparation time: 10 minutes
Total cooking time: 5 minutes
Serves 4 (as a side dish)

☆

2 tablespoons peanut oil
1 clove garlic, crushed
1 tablespoon julienned fresh ginger
500 g (1 lb) bok choy, separated, cut into 8 cm (3 inch) lengths
1 teaspoon sugar
1 teaspoon sesame oil
1 tablespoon oyster sauce

1 Heat a wok over high heat, add the oil and swirl to coat. Add the garlic and ginger, and stir-fry for 1–2 minutes, then add the bok choy and stir-fry for 1 minute. Add the sugar, a pinch of salt and pepper and $^1$/4 cup (60 ml/2 fl oz) water. Bring to the boil, then reduce the heat and simmer, covered, for 3 minutes, or until the stems are tender but crisp.
2 Stir in the sesame oil and oyster sauce and serve immediately.

## MARINATED TOFU

Preparation time: 10 minutes +
 overnight marinating
Total cooking time: 15 minutes
Serves 4 (as a side dish)

☆ ☆

$^1$/2 cup (125 ml/4 fl oz) peanut oil
2 cloves garlic, crushed
1 teaspoon grated fresh ginger
2 stems lemon grass, white part only, finely chopped
1 small fresh red chilli, finely chopped
2 tablespoons fish sauce
2 tablespoons lime juice
1 tablespoon soft brown sugar
500 g (1 lb) fried tofu puffs, halved on the diagonal

1 Combine all the ingredients in a flat non-metallic dish. Toss the tofu until coated in the marinade, then cover with plastic wrap and refrigerate overnight.
2 Heat a lightly oiled wok over high heat and stir-fry the tofu in batches for 1–2 minutes, or until browned. Serve hot.

1 cup (90 g/3 oz) bean sprouts, topped and
    tailed
40 g (1 1/4 oz) wom bok (Chinese cabbage),
    finely shredded
1 tablespoon julienned fresh ginger
2 tablespoons vegetarian oyster sauce
1 tablespoon mushroom soy sauce
1 tablespoon light soy sauce
1 tablespoon Chinese rice wine
1 teaspoon sesame oil
ground white pepper, to taste
fresh coriander leaves, to garnish

1 Cover the mushrooms in boiling water and
soak for 20 minutes. Drain. Discard the woody
stalks and thinly slice the caps.
2 Meanwhile, cook the noodles in a large
saucepan of boiling water for 1 minute, stirring
to separate. Drain. Rinse under cold, running
water and drain again.
3 Heat a wok over high heat, add 1 tablespoon
of the peanut oil and swirl to coat the side
of the wok. Stir-fry the carrot and corn for
1–2 minutes, then add the bamboo shoots and
stir-fry for a further 1–2 minutes, or until just
cooked but still crisp. Remove the vegetables
from the wok.
4 Reheat the wok (add 2 teaspoons peanut oil
if necessary) and add the snow peas and red and
green peppers. Stir-fry for 1–2 minutes, or until
just cooked but still crisp. Add to the carrot and
corn mixture. Reheat the wok (add another
2 teaspoons peanut oil if needed), then add
the bean sprouts, wom bok and mushrooms and
stir-fry for 30 seconds, or until wilted. Add the
ginger and stir-fry for a further 1–2 minutes.
Remove from the wok and add to the other
vegetables.
5 Heat the remaining oil in the wok, and
quickly stir-fry the noodles for 1–2 minutes, or
until heated through, taking care not to let them
break up. Stir in the vegetarian oyster sauce,
mushroom soy sauce, light soy sauce and rice
wine and stir thoroughly. Return all the
vegetables to the wok and stir gently for
1–2 minutes, or until well combined with the
noodles. Drizzle with the sesame oil, season with
white pepper and garnish with the coriander
leaves. Serve immediately.
NOTE: Garlic, onions, spring onions and chillies
have been omitted from this recipe because
traditional Chinese vegetarians do not eat them.

## BUDDHIST VEGETARIAN NOODLES

Preparation time: 25 minutes +
    20 minutes soaking
Total cooking time: 15 minutes
Serves 4

☆☆

15 g (1/2 oz) dried shiitake mushrooms
400 g (13 oz) fresh flat egg noodles
2–3 tablespoons peanut or sunflower oil
1 small carrot, julienned
150 g (5 oz) fresh baby corn, quartered
    lengthways
227 g (7 oz) can bamboo shoots, drained and
    julienned
150 g (5 oz) snow peas (mangetout), julienned
1/2 small red pepper (capsicum), julienned
1 small green pepper (capsicum), julienned

*ABOVE: Buddhist vegetarian noodles*

## STIR-FRIED TOFU AND BOK CHOY

Preparation time: 20 minutes +
  10 minutes marinating
Total cooking time: 10 minutes
Serves 4

600 g (1¼ lb) firm tofu, cubed
1 tablespoon finely chopped fresh ginger
2 tablespoons soy sauce
2 tablespoons peanut oil
1 red onion, thinly sliced
4 cloves garlic, crushed
500 g (1 lb) baby bok choy, sliced lengthways
2 teaspoons sesame oil
2 tablespoons kecap manis
¼ cup (60 ml/2 fl oz) sweet chilli sauce
1 tablespoon toasted sesame seeds

1 Put the tofu and ginger in a bowl. Pour in the soy sauce and leave for 10 minutes. Drain.
2 Heat a wok over high heat, add half the oil and swirl to coat. Add the onion and stir-fry for 3 minutes, or until soft. Add the tofu and garlic, and stir-fry for 3 minutes. Remove from the wok.
3 Reheat the wok to very hot, add the remaining oil and the bok choy and stir-fry for 2 minutes, or until wilted. Return the tofu mixture to the wok and toss until heated through.
4 Stir in the sesame oil, kecap manis and chilli sauce. Scatter with the sesame seeds and serve.

## TAMARI ROASTED ALMONDS WITH SPICY GREEN BEANS

Preparation time: 10 minutes
Total cooking time: 5 minutes
Serves 4–6

2 tablespoons sesame oil
1 long fresh red chilli, seeded and finely chopped
2 cm (¾ inch) piece fresh ginger, grated
2 cloves garlic, crushed
375 g (12 oz) green beans, cut into 5 cm (2 inch) lengths
½ cup (125 ml/4 fl oz) hoisin sauce
1 tablespoon soft brown sugar
2 tablespoons mirin
250 g (8 oz) tamari roasted almonds, roughly chopped (see Note)

1 Heat a wok over high heat, add the oil and swirl to coat. Add the chilli, ginger and garlic and stir-fry for 1 minute, or until lightly browned. Add the beans, hoisin sauce and sugar and stir-fry for 2 minutes. Stir in the mirin and cook for 1 minute, or until the beans are tender but still crunchy.
2 Remove from the heat and stir in the almonds just before serving. Serve on a bed of rice.
NOTE: Tamari roasted almonds are available from health-food stores. Tamari is a naturally brewed, thick Japanese soy sauce made with soy beans and rice.

*BELOW: Tamari roasted almonds with spicy green beans*

WOM BOK
Now cultivated year-round, wom bok (Chinese cabbage) is traditionally a winter vegetable, This versatile vegetable is commonly used in stir-fries, braises, soups and hotpots, and even appears in some salads. It is an excellent source of folic acid, vitamin A and potassium. Choose wom bok with tightly packed, green-tipped leaves that show no signs of wilting and that feel firm. To prepare the wom bok, trim the root end from the wom bok and slice it in half lengthways. Cut out the central core and discard.

*ABOVE: Stir-fried vegetables*

## STIR-FRIED VEGETABLES
(Pad pak ruam)

Preparation time: 20 minutes
Total cooking time: 5 minutes
Serves 6

☆

2 tablespoons soy sauce
1 teaspoon fish sauce
1 tablespoon oyster sauce
1/4 cup (60 ml/2 fl oz) stock
1/2 teaspoon grated palm sugar
2 tablespoons vegetable oil
4 spring onions, cut into 3 cm (1 1/4 inch) lengths
3 cloves garlic, crushed
1 fresh red chilli, seeded and sliced
75 g (2 1/2 oz) button mushrooms, quartered
100 g (3 1/2 oz) wom bok (Chinese cabbage), roughly chopped
150 g (5 oz) snow peas (mangetout)
150 g (5 oz) cauliflower, cut into small florets
150 g (5 oz) broccoli, cut into small florets
chopped fresh coriander leaves, to garnish

1 Combine the soy, fish and oyster sauces with the stock and palm sugar in a small bowl.
2 Heat a wok over high heat, add the oil and swirl to coat. Add the spring onion, garlic and chilli. Stir-fry for 20 seconds. Add the mushrooms and wom bok and stir-fry for 1 minute. Stir in the sauce and remaining vegetables. Cook for 2 minutes, or until tender. Garnish with coriander.

## EGGPLANT (AUBERGINE) WITH CHILLI BEAN PASTE

Preparation time: 20 minutes
Total cooking time: 15 minutes
Serves 4–6

☆

1/2 cup (125 ml/4 fl oz) vegetable stock
1/4 cup (60 ml/2 fl oz) Chinese rice wine
2 tablespoons rice vinegar
1 tablespoon tomato paste (tomato purée)
2 teaspoons soft brown sugar
2 tablespoons soy sauce
1/4 cup (60 ml/2 fl oz) peanut oil
800 g (1 lb 10 oz) eggplant (aubergine), cut into 2 cm (3/4 inch) cubes
4 spring onions, chopped
3 cloves garlic, crushed
1 tablespoon finely chopped fresh ginger
1 tablespoon chilli bean paste
1 teaspoon cornflour mixed with 1 tablespoon water into a paste

1 Combine the stock, rice wine, rice vinegar, tomato paste, sugar and soy sauce in a bowl.
2 Heat a wok over high heat, add half the oil and swirl to coat. Stir-fry the eggplant in batches for 3 minutes each batch, or until brown. Remove.
3 Heat the remaining oil in the wok. Stir-fry the spring onion, garlic, ginger and bean paste for 30 seconds. Pour in the sauce and stir-fry for 1 minute. Add the cornflour paste and bring to the boil. Return the eggplant to the wok and stir-fry for 2–3 minutes, or until heated through.

1 Cook the sweet potato in a large saucepan of boiling water for 15 minutes, or until tender. Drain well.
2 Heat a wok over high heat, add the oil and swirl to coat the side of the wok. Stir-fry the garlic and sambal oelek for 1 minute, or until fragrant. Add the sweet potato and water chestnuts and stir-fry over medium–high heat for 2 minutes. Reduce the heat to medium, add the palm sugar and cook for a further 2 minutes, or until the sugar has melted. Add the spinach, soy sauce and stock and toss until the spinach has just wilted. Serve with steamed rice.

## ORANGE SWEET POTATO, SPINACH AND WATER CHESTNUT STIR-FRY

Preparation time: 15 minutes
Total cooking time: 20 minutes
Serves 4

500 g (1 lb) orange sweet potato, peeled and cut into 1.5 cm ($^5$/8 inch) cubes
1 tablespoon vegetable oil
2 cloves garlic, crushed
2 teaspoons sambal oelek
227 g (7 oz) can water chestnuts, sliced
2 teaspoons grated palm sugar
390 g (13 oz) English spinach, stems removed
2 tablespoons soy sauce
2 tablespoons vegetable stock

### STIR-FRIED PEANUTS WITH CHILLI

Heat a wok over high heat, add 2 teaspoons peanut oil and a few drops of sesame oil and swirl to coat the side of the wok. Add 1½ cups (240 g/7½ oz) raw peanuts and stir-fry for 3–4 minutes, or until golden. Add 1 very finely chopped small fresh red chilli, 2 cloves crushed garlic and 1½ teaspoons salt and stir-fry for a further 1–2 minutes, taking care that the nuts don't burn. Sprinkle with 1½ teaspoons caster sugar and toss well. Remove from the wok and cool before serving. Serve as a snack. Makes 1½ cups.

*LEFT: Orange sweet potato, spinach and water chestnut stir-fry*

209

### TEMPEH

Tempeh (or tempe) is a vegetable protein food made by mixing hulled and slightly split cooked soy beans with a vegetarian fermenting agent, then leaving it to ferment. The beans are then bound together to form a firm cake. Unlike tofu, the beans in tempeh are still visible, giving it a nutty aroma and flavour. Tempeh is eaten cooked, sautéed or deep-fried, in stews or a salad. It is sold in blocks in sealed packets, often marinated in spices. Keep sealed and refrigerated to prevent mould forming. Tempeh is particularly popular in Indonesia as an affordable alternative to meat in the diet.

*ABOVE: Eggplant with tempeh*

## EGGPLANT (AUBERGINE) WITH TEMPEH
(Makua pad tempeh)

Preparation time: 20 minutes +
  20 minutes soaking
Total cooking time: 10 minutes
Serves 6

2 small dried red chillies
8 black peppercorns
2 cloves garlic
2 tablespoons chopped fresh coriander stems
  and leaves
1/3 cup (80 ml/2³/4 fl oz) vegetable oil
100 g (3¹/2 oz) tempeh, thinly sliced
250 g (8 oz) slender eggplants (aubergines), cut
  into 2 cm (³/4 inch) chunks
1 tablespoon soy sauce
1 tablespoon fish sauce
1 teaspoon grated palm sugar
1 tablespoon lime juice

1 Soak the chillies in a bowl of boiling water for 20 minutes. Drain, remove the seeds and finely chop the flesh.
2 Put the peppercorns, garlic and coriander in a food processor and process to a smooth paste —add a little water if needed.
3 Heat a wok over high heat, add the oil and swirl to coat. Add the paste and chilli and stir-fry for 10 seconds. Add the tempeh and stir-fry for a further 2 minutes, or until golden brown. Remove the tempeh.
4 Add the eggplant to the wok and stir-fry for 6 minutes, or until golden brown. Add the sauces, palm sugar, lime juice and tempeh and cook, stirring, for a further 30 seconds. Serve immediately with rice.

## TOFU, PEANUT AND NOODLE STIR-FRY

Preparation time: 15 minutes
Total cooking time: 5 minutes
Serves 4

250 g (8 oz) firm tofu, cut into 1.5 cm
  (⁵/8 inch) cubes
2 cloves garlic, crushed
1 teaspoon grated fresh ginger
1/3 cup (80 ml/2³/4 fl oz) kecap manis
1/3 cup (90 g/3 oz) peanut butter
2 tablespoons peanut or vegetable oil

500 g (1 lb) Hokkien noodles
1 onion, chopped
1 red pepper (capsicum), chopped
125 g (4 oz) broccoli, cut into small florets

1 Combine the tofu with the garlic, ginger and half the kecap manis in a small bowl. Put the peanut butter, 1/2 cup (125 ml/4 fl oz) water and remaining kecap manis in another bowl and mix together thoroughly.
2 Heat a wok over high heat, add the oil and swirl to coat the side of the wok. Drain the tofu and reserve the marinade. Cook the tofu in two batches in the hot oil until well browned. Remove from the wok.
3 Put the noodles in a large heatproof bowl. Cover with boiling water and leave for 1 minute. Drain and gently separate the noodles.
4 Add the vegetables to the wok (add a little more oil if necessary), and stir-fry until just tender. Add the tofu, reserved marinade and noodles to the wok. Add the peanut butter mixture and toss until heated through.
NOTE: Kecap manis is an Indonesian sweet soy sauce. If you are unable to find it, use soy sauce sweetened with a little soft brown sugar.

# THAI WATER SPINACH IN FLAMES
(Pahk boong fai daeng)

Preparation time: 10 minutes
Total cooking time: 2 minutes
Serves 4

4 cloves garlic, crushed
2 fresh green chillies, thinly sliced
1 tablespoon black bean sauce
2 tablespoons fish sauce
2 teaspoons sugar
2 tablespoons vegetable oil
500 g (1 lb) water spinach, cut into 3 cm (1 1/4 inch) lengths

1 Combine the garlic, chilli, black bean sauce, fish sauce and sugar in a bowl.
2 Heat a wok over high heat, add the oil and swirl to coat. Add the spinach and stir-fry for 1 minute, or until wilted slightly. Add the sauce and stir-fry for 30 seconds, or until the spinach leaves are well coated. Serve immediately.

WATER SPINACH IN FLAMES
This dish acquired its name after the manner in which it is handled by skilful restaurant chefs. Oil is drizzled into a wok, the heat turned right up and then the water spinach tossed into the oil. The oil splashing over the sides of the wok catches fire and flames usually leap over the edge, adding a smoky flavour to the dish. Best left to the professional, the method in the adjacent recipe lacks some of the drama of the traditional dish, but you have the bonus of keeping your eyebrows.

*LEFT: Thai water spinach in flames*

# NORI OMELETTE WITH STIR-FRIED VEGETABLES

Preparation time: 15 minutes
Total cooking time: 20 minutes
Serves 4

☆

8 eggs
10 cm x 18 cm (4 inch x 7 inch) sheet nori
1/4 cup (60 ml/2 fl oz) vegetable oil
1 clove garlic, crushed
3 teaspoons finely grated fresh ginger
1 carrot, cut into batons
2 zucchini (courgettes), halved lengthways, sliced on the diagonal
200 g (6 1/2 oz) mix of Swiss brown, enoki and oyster mushrooms, larger ones sliced
1 tablespoon Japanese soy sauce
1 tablespoon mirin
2 teaspoons yellow miso paste

1 Lightly beat the eggs. Roll the nori up tightly and snip with scissors into very fine strips. Add to the eggs and season to taste with salt and cracked black pepper.
2 Heat a wok over high heat, add 2 teaspoons of the oil and swirl to coat the side of the wok. Add 1/3 cup (80 ml/2 3/4 fl oz) of the egg mixture and swirl to coat the base of the wok. Cook for

2 minutes, or until set, then turn over and cook the other side for 1 minute. Remove and keep warm. Repeat with the remaining mixture, adding another 2 teaspoons of the oil each time, to make four omelettes.
3 Heat the remaining oil in the wok, add the garlic and ginger and stir-fry for 1 minute. Add the carrot, zucchini and mushrooms in two batches and stir-fry for 3 minutes, or until softened. Return all the vegetables to the wok. Add the soy sauce, mirin and miso paste, and simmer for 1 minute. Divide the vegetables evenly among the omelettes, roll them up and serve immediately with rice.

# UDON NOODLE STIR-FRY

Preparation time: 15 minutes
Total cooking time: 10 minutes
Serves 4

☆

500 g (1 lb) fresh udon noodles
2 tablespoons Japanese soy sauce
2 tablespoons mirin
2 tablespoons kecap manis
1 tablespoon vegetable oil
6 spring onions, cut into 5 cm (2 inch) lengths
3 cloves garlic, crushed
1 tablespoon grated fresh ginger
2 carrots, cut into 5 cm (2 inch) batons

NORI
Made from dried seaweed, nori sheets are generally used in Japanese cuisine for wrapping sushi or onigiri (savoury rice balls). It is rich in vitamins, calcium, protein and iron. Purchased in packets from Asian grocers or the Asian section of large supermarkets, nori comes either untoasted (which then requires toasting over a gas flame before use), or toasted, which is then sometimes labelled 'yakinori'.

RIGHT: Nori omelette with stir-fried vegetables

150 g (5 oz) snow peas (mangetout), cut
   in half on the diagonal
100 g (3¹/2 oz) bean sprouts, tailed
500 g (1 lb) choy sum, cut into 5 cm
   (2 inch) lengths
2 sheets roasted nori, cut into thin strips

**1** Bring a saucepan of water to the boil, add
the noodles and cook for 1–2 minutes, or until
tender and separated. Drain and rinse under
hot water.
**2** Combine the soy sauce, mirin and kecap
manis in a small bowl or jug.
**3** Heat a wok with a lid over high heat, add the
oil and swirl to coat the side of the wok. Add
the spring onion, garlic and ginger. Stir-fry for
1–2 minutes, or until softened. Add the carrot,
snow peas and 1 tablespoon water, toss well,
cover with a lid and cook for 1–2 minutes, or
until the vegetables are just tender. Add the
noodles, bean sprouts and choy sum, then pour
in the sauce. Toss until the choy sum is wilted
and coated with the sauce. Stir in the nori just
before serving.

## TOFU IN BLACK BEAN SAUCE

Preparation time: 20 minutes
Total cooking time: 15 minutes
Serves 4

¹/3 cup (80 ml/2³/4 fl oz) vegetable stock
2 teaspoons cornflour
2 teaspoons Chinese rice wine
1 teaspoon sesame oil
1 tablespoon soy sauce
2 tablespoons peanut oil
450 g (14 oz) firm tofu, cut into 2 cm (³/4 inch)
   cubes
2 cloves garlic, very finely chopped
2 teaspoons finely chopped fresh ginger
3 tablespoons black beans, rinsed and very
   finely chopped
4 spring onions, sliced on the diagonal (white
   and green parts)
1 red pepper (capsicum), cut into 2 cm
   (³/4 inch) chunks
300 g (10 oz) baby bok choy, chopped
   crossways into 2 cm (³/4 inch) pieces

**1** Combine the vegetable stock, cornflour,
Chinese rice wine, sesame oil, soy sauce,
¹/2 teaspoon salt and freshly ground black pepper
in a small bowl.
**2** Heat a wok over medium heat, add the peanut
oil and swirl to coat. Add the tofu and stir-fry in
two batches for 3 minutes each batch, or until
lightly browned. Remove with a slotted spoon
and drain on paper towels. Discard any bits of
tofu stuck to the wok or floating in the oil.
**3** Add the garlic and ginger and stir-fry for
30 seconds. Toss in the black beans and spring
onion and stir-fry for 30 seconds. Add the
pepper and stir-fry for 1 minute. Add the bok
choy and stir-fry for a further 2 minutes. Return
the tofu to the wok and stir gently. Pour in the
sauce and stir gently for 2–3 minutes, or until the
sauce has thickened slightly. Serve immediately
with steamed rice.

*ABOVE: Tofu in black bean sauce*

**SESAME OIL**
Extensively used in Chinese cuisine, sesame oil adds fragrance to a dish. It is usually used in small quantities as it is highly aromatic, and its flavour can overwhelm those of other ingredients if not used with caution. Sesame oil is made by pressing toasted sesame seeds, which give it the characteristic amber colour. A paler version of sesame oil is pressed from raw sesame seeds, but it is not an acceptable substitute as it lacks the nutty fragrance of normal sesame oil.

## TEMPEH STIR-FRY

Preparation time: 15 minutes
Total cooking time: 15 minutes
Serves 4

1 teaspoon sesame oil
1 tablespoon peanut oil
2 cloves garlic, crushed
1 tablespoon grated fresh ginger
1 fresh red chilli, thinly sliced
4 spring onions, sliced on the diagonal
300 g (10 oz) tempeh, cut into 2 cm (³/4 inch) cubes
500 g (1 lb) baby bok choy leaves
800 g (1 lb 10 oz) gai larn (Chinese broccoli), chopped
1/2 cup (125 ml/4 fl oz) vegetarian oyster sauce
2 tablespoons rice vinegar
2 tablespoons fresh coriander leaves
1/4 cup (40 g/1 1/4 oz) toasted cashew nuts

1 Heat a wok over high heat, add the oils and swirl to coat the side of the wok. Add the garlic, ginger, chilli and spring onion and cook for 1–2 minutes, or until the onion is soft. Add the tempeh and cook for 5 minutes, or until golden. Remove from the wok.
2 Add half the greens and 1 tablespoon water to the wok and cook, covered, for 3–4 minutes, or until the greens have wilted. Remove from the wok and repeat with the remaining greens and a little more water.
3 Return the greens and tempeh to the wok, add the sauce and vinegar and warm through. Top with the coriander and nuts. Serve with rice.

## ASIAN MUSHROOM STIR-FRY

Preparation time: 10 minutes
Total cooking time: 5 minutes
Serves 4

1 teaspoon cornflour
1/4 teaspoon five-spice powder
2 1/2 tablespoons Chinese rice wine
1 tablespoon oyster sauce
2 tablespoons peanut oil
1 teaspoon sesame oil
1/3 cup (20 g/3/4 oz) thinly sliced spring onion
2 cloves garlic, finely chopped
1 tablespoon finely julienned fresh ginger
200 g (6 1/2 oz) fresh shiitake mushrooms, halved
100 g (3 1/2 oz) button mushrooms, halved
100 g (3 1/2 oz) oyster mushrooms
100 g (3 1/2 oz) enoki mushrooms, trimmed
1 tablespoon sesame seeds, toasted

*ABOVE: Tempeh stir-fry*

1 Put the cornflour and five-spice powder in a small bowl, and gradually blend in the rice wine and oyster sauce.
2 Heat a wok over medium heat, add the peanut and sesame oils and swirl to coat. Add the spring onion, garlic and ginger and stir-fry over medium heat for 2 minutes. Increase the heat to high, add the shiitake and button mushrooms and stir-fry until the mushrooms become moist and almost tender. Add the oyster and enoki mushrooms and stir-fry until tender.
3 Stir in the five-spice mixture and stir-fry for 30 seconds, or until the mushrooms are glazed, then sprinkle with the sesame seeds.

## BRAISED VEGETABLES WITH CASHEWS

Preparation time: 15 minutes
Total cooking time: 10 minutes
Serves 4

1 tablespoon peanut oil
2 cloves garlic, crushed
2 teaspoons grated fresh ginger
300 g (10 oz) choy sum, cut into 10 cm (4 inch) lengths
150 g (5 oz) baby corn, sliced in half on the diagonal
3/4 cup (185 ml/6 fl oz) chicken or vegetable stock
200 g (6 1/2 oz) sliced bamboo shoots
150 g (5 oz) oyster mushrooms, sliced in half
2 teaspoons cornflour
2 tablespoons oyster sauce
2 teaspoons sesame oil
1 cup (90 g/3 oz) bean sprouts, tailed
75 g (2 1/2 oz) roasted unsalted cashews

1 Heat a wok over medium heat, add the oil and swirl to coat. Add the garlic and ginger and stir-fry for 1 minute. Increase the heat to high, add the choy sum and baby corn and stir-fry for another minute.
2 Add the stock and cook for 3–4 minutes, or until the choy sum stems are just tender. Add the bamboo shoots and mushrooms, and cook for 1 minute.
3 Combine the cornflour and 1 tablespoon water in a small bowl and mix into a paste. Stir into the vegetables, along with the oyster sauce. Cook for 1–2 minutes, or until the sauce is slightly thickened. Stir in the sesame oil and bean sprouts and serve immediately on a bed of steamed rice sprinkled with the roasted cashews.

BABY CORN
Baby corn (also known as miniature corn) are small (up to 10 cm/4 inch), young cobs of corn. Noted for their crunchiness and sweet flavour, baby corn are eaten whole. These edible, miniature, pale yellow corn cobs are often added to stir-fries to add colour and texture to a dish. They are a particular favourite in Chinese and Thai cuisine.

*LEFT: Braised vegetables with cashews*

## CHILLI SNAKE BEANS AND NOODLES

Preparation time: 15 minutes
Total cooking time: 10 minutes
Serves 4

250 g (8 oz) fresh flat egg noodles
5 cloves garlic, peeled
3 red Asian shallots, chopped
1 small fresh red chilli, seeded and chopped
3 fresh coriander roots, chopped
2¹/₂ tablespoons peanut oil
500 g (1 lb) snake beans
2¹/₂ tablespoons fish sauce
1¹/₂ tablespoons grated palm sugar
1 tablespoon kecap manis
1 tablespoon lime juice
1 tablespoon crisp fried onion
1 small fresh red chilli, extra, thinly sliced
lime wedges, for serving

1 Cook the noodles in a saucepan of boiling water for 1 minute, or until tender. Drain well.
2 Put the garlic, red Asian shallots, chilli and coriander roots in a mortar and pestle or small food processor and grind to a smooth paste—add a little water if necessary.
3 Heat a wok over high heat, add the oil and swirl. Stir in the paste and cook for 1 minute, or

until fragrant. Add the beans, stir-fry for 2 minutes, then reduce the heat to low, cover and steam for 2 minutes. Increase the heat to high, add the fish sauce, palm sugar and kecap manis and stir-fry for 1 minute. Toss the noodles through the mixture for 1–2 minutes, or until heated through. Drizzle with the lime juice. Divide among four bowls, garnish with the crisp fried onion and chilli. Serve with lime wedges.

## PUMPKIN WITH CHILLI

Preparation time: 15 minutes
Total cooking time: 15 minutes
Serves 4

800 g (1 lb 10 oz) pumpkin
2 tablespoons vegetable oil
2 cloves garlic, crushed
1 teaspoon grated fresh ginger
2 fresh bird's eye chillies, finely chopped
3/4 cup (185 ml/6 fl oz) chicken or vegetable stock
1¹/₂ tablespoons light soy sauce
1 tablespoon fish sauce
1 teaspoon finely grated lime rind
1 tablespoon lime juice
1 teaspoon shaved palm sugar
3/4 cup (25 g/3/4 oz) fresh coriander leaves, chopped

*BELOW: Chilli snake beans and noodles*

1 Peel the pumpkin and scoop out the seeds to give about 600 g (1 1/4 lb) of flesh, then cut into 1.5 cm (5/8 inch) cubes.

2 Heat a wok over medium–high heat, add the oil and swirl to coat the side of the wok. Add the garlic, ginger and chilli and stir-fry for 1 minute, tossing constantly. Add the pumpkin cubes, stock, soy sauce, fish sauce, lime rind, lime juice and palm sugar, then cover with a lid and cook for 10 minutes, or until the pumpkin is tender.

3 Remove the lid and gently stir for 3–4 minutes, or until any remaining liquid has reduced to just glaze the pumpkin. Gently stir in the coriander and serve immediately.

## MUSHROOM AND WATER CHESTNUT STIR-FRY

Preparation time: 15 minutes
Total cooking time: 10 minutes
Serves 4

1/4 cup (60 ml/2 fl oz) vegetable oil
2 cloves garlic, julienned
1/2 cup (80 g/2 3/4 oz) pine nuts
750 g (1 1/2 lb) mixed fresh mushrooms
    (e.g. Swiss brown, oyster, shiitake), sliced
100 g (3 1/2 oz) snow peas (mangetout), halved
230 g (7 1/2 oz) can sliced water chestnuts,
    drained
150 g (5 oz) bean sprouts, tailed
1/3 cup (80 ml/2 3/4 fl oz) oyster sauce
2 teaspoons sesame oil

1 Heat a wok over high heat, add 2 tablespoons oil and swirl to coat the side of the wok. Add the garlic and pine nuts, and cook, stirring constantly, for 1 minute, or until the pine nuts are light golden brown.

2 Add the mushrooms and stir-fry over high heat for 3 minutes. Add the snow peas and cook for a further 3 minutes, or until the vegetables are just tender, adding the remaining oil, if necessary.

3 Add the water chestnuts, bean sprouts, oyster sauce and sesame oil, and cook for a further 30 seconds. Serve with rice.

## KOREAN PICKLED BEAN SPROUTS (Namul)

Blanch 300 g (10 oz) bean sprouts in boiling water for 1–2 minutes, or until softened but still a little crunchy. Drain, rinse under cold water and drain again. Combine 2 tablespoons soy sauce, 2 tablespoons rice vinegar, 1 1/2 teaspoons sesame oil, 1/2 teaspoon sugar, a pinch of salt, a little finely ground black pepper, 1/3 cup (20 g/3/4 oz) thinly sliced spring onions and 1 tablespoon toasted sesame seeds, then pour over the bean sprouts and mix. Chill for 2 hours before serving as a side salad. You can also mix 1/2 teaspoon chilli flakes in the marinade if you like things a little spicy. Serves 4 as a side dish.

*ABOVE: Mushroom and water chestnut stir-fry*

## SWEET AND SOUR TOFU

Preparation time: 15 minutes
Total cooking time: 20 minutes
Serves 4

☆

$^1/_3$ cup (80 ml/2$^3/_4$ fl oz) rice vinegar

2 tablespoons light soy sauce

1$^1/_2$ tablespoons caster sugar

2 tablespoons tomato sauce

1$^1/_2$ cups (375 ml/12 fl oz) chicken or vegetable
    stock

600 g (1$^1/_4$ lb) firm tofu

3–4 tablespoons vegetable oil

1 large carrot, julienned

2 cups (180 g/6 oz) bean sprouts or soy bean
    sprouts, tailed

1 cup (95 g/3 oz) sliced button mushrooms

6–8 spring onions, sliced on the diagonal

100 g (3$^1/_2$ oz) snow peas (mangetout), cut in
    half on the diagonal

1 tablespoon cornflour dissolved in
    2 tablespoons water

1 Combine the vinegar, soy sauce, sugar, tomato
sauce and stock in a small bowl.
2 Cut the tofu in half horizontally, then cut into
16 triangles in total. Heat a wok over high heat,
add 2 tablespoons of the oil and swirl to coat.
Add the tofu in batches and stir-fry over

medium heat for 2 minutes on each side, or
until crisp and golden. Drain on paper towels
and set aside. Keep warm.
3 Wipe the wok clean, then reheat it over high
heat. Add the remaining oil and swirl to coat.
Add the carrot, bean sprouts, mushrooms, spring
onion and snow peas and stir-fry for 1 minute.
Add the sauce and stir for a further 1 minute.
Add the cornflour paste and cook until the sauce
thickens. Divide the tofu among the serving
bowls and spoon some sauce over the top. Serve
with steamed rice on the side.

## JAPANESE EGGPLANT
(AUBERGINE)

Preparation time: 5 minutes
Total cooking time: 15 minutes
Serves 4

☆ ☆

8 Japanese eggplants (aubergines)

$^1/_3$ cup (80 ml/2$^3/_4$ fl oz) peanut oil

2 teaspoons finely grated fresh ginger

$^1/_2$ teaspoon instant dashi stock powder
    dissolved in $^1/_2$ cup (125 ml/4 fl oz) water

1 tablespoon Japanese soy sauce

1 tablespoon mirin

1 teaspoon sugar

2 teaspoons red miso paste

2 spring onions, thinly sliced

*ABOVE: Sweet and sour tofu*

1 Cut the eggplants into 2.5 cm (1 inch) slices. Heat a wok over high heat, add the oil and swirl it around to coat the wok. Add the eggplant in batches and stir-fry for 3–5 minutes, or until golden. Return all the eggplant to the wok.
2 Add the ginger to the wok and cook for 1 minute. Pour in the dashi, soy sauce, mirin and sugar, and simmer for 2 minutes. Remove the wok from the heat and stir in the miso. Arrange the eggplant on a serving dish and top with the spring onion. Serve with fried fish, rice and Japanese-style pickles.
NOTE: The flavour of the miso is quite mild. For a more robust flavour add 1 tablespoon of paste.

## VEGETARIAN PHAD THAI

Preparation time: 20 minutes +
  20 minutes soaking
Total cooking time: 5 minutes
Serves 4

400 g (13 oz) flat rice stick noodles
1/4 cup (60 ml/2 fl oz) soy sauce
2 tablespoons lime juice
1 tablespoon soft brown sugar
2 teaspoons sambal oelek
2 tablespoons peanut oil
2 eggs, lightly beaten
1 onion, cut into thin wedges

2 cloves garlic, crushed
1 small red pepper (capsicum), cut into thin strips
6 spring onions, thinly sliced on the diagonal
100 g (3 1/2 oz) fried tofu puffs, cut into 5 mm (1/4 inch) wide strips
1/2 cup (25 g/3/4 oz) chopped fresh coriander leaves
1 cup (90 g/3 oz) bean sprouts, tailed
1/4 cup (40 g/1 1/4 oz) chopped roasted unsalted peanuts

1 Soak the noodles in warm water for 15–20 minutes, or until tender. Drain, then set aside.
2 To make the stir-fry sauce, combine the soy sauce, lime juice, sugar and sambal oelek in a small bowl or jug.
3 Heat a wok over high heat and add enough peanut oil to coat the bottom and side. Add the egg and swirl to form a thin omelette. Cook for 30 seconds, or until just set. Remove from the wok, roll up, then thinly slice.
4 Heat the remaining oil in the wok. Add the onion, garlic and pepper and cook over high heat for 2–3 minutes, or until the onion softens. Add the noodles, tossing well. Stir in the slices of omelette, the spring onion, tofu and half of the coriander. Pour in the stir-fry sauce, then toss to coat the noodles. Sprinkle with the bean sprouts and top with roasted peanuts and the remaining coriander. Serve immediately.

*BELOW: Vegetarian phad Thai*

ASIAN MUSHROOMS
Many varieties of
mushroom are grown
throughout Asia, as well as
many types of edible fungi.
Probably the best known
Asian mushroom is the
black mushroom of China
(called shiitake in Japan). It
was discovered a long time
ago that the flavour of this
mushroom improves on
drying, so they are most
commonly available dried.
They must be soaked
before use and the soaking
liquid is often added to
dishes for added flavour.
Oyster mushrooms have a
subtle seafood flavour and
are often used in stir-fries.
Black fungus is valued for its
subtle, delicate flavour and
slightly crunchy 'bite'. It is
also called cloud ear fungus,
because of its resemblance
to clouds.

*ABOVE: Tofu, snow pea and
mushroom stir-fry*

## TOFU, SNOW PEA
(MANGETOUT) **AND**
**MUSHROOM STIR-FRY**

Preparation time: 10 minutes
Total cooking time: 15 minutes
Serves 4

1/4 cup (60 ml/2 fl oz) peanut oil
600 g (1 1/4 lb) firm tofu, drained, cut into
   2 cm (3/4 inch) cubes
2 teaspoons sambal oelek or chilli paste
2 cloves garlic, finely chopped
300 g (10 oz) snow peas (mangetout), trimmed
400 g (13 oz) fresh Asian mushrooms
   (e.g. shiitake, oyster or black fungus), sliced
1/4 cup (60 ml/2 fl oz) kecap manis

**1** Heat a wok over high heat, add 2 tablespoons
of the peanut oil and swirl to coat the side of the
wok. Add the tofu in two batches and stir-fry
each batch for 2–3 minutes, or until lightly
browned on all sides, then transfer to a plate.
**2** Heat the remaining oil in the wok, add the
sambal oelek, garlic, snow peas, mushrooms and
1 tablespoon water and stir-fry for 1–2 minutes,
or until the vegetables are almost cooked but
still crunchy.
**3** Return the tofu to the wok, add the kecap
manis and stir-fry for another minute, or until
heated through. Serve immediately with steamed
jasmine rice.

## STIR-FRIED WOM BOK
(CHINESE CABBAGE) **WITH**
**OYSTER SAUCE**

Preparation time: 10 minutes
Total cooking time: 5 minutes
Serves 4

1 wom bok (Chinese cabbage), finely chopped
1 tablespoon peanut oil
1 teaspoon sesame oil
2 cloves garlic, crushed
2 teaspoons grated fresh ginger
2 small fresh red chillies, seeded and finely
   chopped
4 spring onions, cut into 3 cm (1 1/4 inch)
   lengths on the diagonal

2 tablespoons oyster sauce

1 tablespoon rice vinegar

2 tablespoons sesame seeds, toasted

1 Wash and drain the wom bok, removing as much moisture as possible.

2 Heat a wok over high heat, add the peanut and sesame oils and swirl to coat the side of the wok. Add the garlic, ginger and chilli, and stir-fry for 30 seconds. Add the wom bok and spring onion, and toss for 2 minutes, or until wilted. Pour in the oyster sauce and rice vinegar, stir vigorously and cook for a further minute. Stir the sesame seeds through the wom bok. Season with salt and freshly ground black pepper, then remove from the wok with a slotted spoon. Serve immediately.

## TOFU WITH CHILLI JAM AND CASHEWS

Preparation time: 20 minutes
Total cooking time: 30 minutes
Serves 4

☆☆

1/3 cup (80 ml/2 3/4 fl oz) peanut oil

12 red Asian shallots, chopped

8 cloves garlic, chopped

8 fresh long red chillies, chopped

2 red peppers (capsicums), chopped

1 tablespoon tamarind purée

1 tablespoon soy sauce

100 g (3 1/2 oz) palm sugar, grated

2 tablespoons kecap manis

1 tablespoon peanut oil

6 spring onions, cut into 3 cm (1 1/4 inch) lengths

750 g (1 1/2 lb) silken firm tofu, cut into 3 cm (1 1/4 inch) cubes

3/4 cup (25 g/3/4 oz) fresh Thai basil

2/3 cup (100 g/3 1/2 oz) roasted salted cashews

1 To make the chilli jam, heat half the oil in a frying pan. Add the shallots and garlic and cook over medium heat for 2 minutes. Transfer to a food processor, add the chilli and red pepper and process until smooth. Heat the remaining oil in the pan, add the shallot mixture and cook over medium heat for 2 minutes. Stir in the tamarind, soy sauce and sugar and cook for 20 minutes.

2 To make the stir-fry sauce, combine 2–3 tablespoons of the chilli jam with the kecap manis in a small bowl or jug.

3 Heat the oil in a non-stick wok over high heat and swirl to coat the side of the wok. Add the spring onion and cook for 30 seconds. Remove. Add the tofu, stir-fry for 1 minute, then add the stir-fry sauce. Cook for 3 minutes, or until the tofu is coated and heated through. Return the spring onion to the wok, add the basil and cashews and cook until the basil has wilted.

NOTE: You can keep the rest of the chilli jam in a sterilised jar for up to 6 months. See page 86 for the sterilising method.

*LEFT: Tofu with chilli jam and cashews*

GAI LARN

While available year-round, gai larn (Chinese broccoli) is a winter vegetable, so it is often more readily available and cheaper during the colder months. When purchasing gai larn, look for thin, crisp stalks and green, unblemished leaves. Avoid very thick stalks, yellow leaves or open flowers, as these indicate an older vegetable.

## GAI LARN (CHINESE BROCCOLI) WITH GINGER, LIME AND PEANUTS

Preparation time: 5 minutes
Total cooking time: 5 minutes
Serves 4

☆

40 g (1¼ oz) tamarind pulp
1 tablespoon peanut oil
600 g (1¼ lb) gai larn (Chinese broccoli), trimmed and halved widthways
1 small fresh red chilli, seeded and finely chopped
2 cloves garlic, finely chopped
3 teaspoons finely grated fresh ginger
1 tablespoon sugar
1 tablespoon lime juice
1 teaspoon sesame oil
1 tablespoon roasted unsalted peanuts, finely chopped

1 Put the tamarind in a bowl and pour in ¼ cup (60 ml/2 fl oz) boiling water. Allow to steep for 5 minutes, then strain. Discard the solids.
2 Heat a non-stick wok over high heat, add the peanut oil and swirl to coat. Add the gai larn and stir-fry for 2–3 minutes, or until wilted. Add the

chilli, garlic and ginger and cook for another minute, then add the sugar, lime juice and 1 tablespoon of the tamarind liquid and simmer for 1 minute. Transfer to a plate and drizzle with the sesame oil. Scatter with peanuts, then serve.

## SPICED CAULIFLOWER AND PEAS

Preparation time: 15 minutes
Total cooking time: 10 minutes
Serves 4–6

☆

2 tablespoons vegetable oil
1 small onion, finely chopped
2 teaspoons yellow mustard seeds
3 cloves garlic, crushed
1 tablespoon finely chopped fresh ginger
1 tablespoon ground cumin
2 teaspoons ground coriander
2 teaspoons ground turmeric
1 small head (800 g/1 lb 10 oz) cauliflower, cut into florets
1 cup (155 g/5 oz) frozen peas
3 tablespoons chopped fresh coriander leaves

*ABOVE: Gai larn with ginger, lime and peanuts*

1 Heat a wok over high heat, add the oil and swirl to coat. Add the onion and mustard seeds, and stir-fry for 2 minutes, or until the seeds pop.
2 Add the garlic, ginger, cumin, coriander, turmeric and 1 teaspoon salt, and stir-fry for 1 minute, or until fragrant. Add the cauliflower and stir-fry to coat with the spices.
3 Stir in 1 cup (250 ml/8 fl oz) water, cover and cook for 4 minutes. Add the peas and stir-fry for 2–3 minutes, or until the peas are cooked and the cauliflower is tender but still crisp. Remove from the heat and stir in the coriander.

## ASIAN GREENS WITH TERIYAKI TOFU DRESSING

Preparation time: 15 minutes
Total cooking time: 20 minutes
Serves 6

☆

650 g (1 lb 5 oz) baby bok choy
500 g (1 lb) choy sum
440 g (14 oz) snake beans, topped and tailed
1/4 cup (60 ml/2 fl oz) vegetable oil
1 onion, thinly sliced
1/3 cup (60 g/2 oz) soft brown sugar
1/2 teaspoon chilli powder
2 tablespoons grated fresh ginger
1 cup (250 ml/8 fl oz) teriyaki sauce
1 tablespoon sesame oil
600 g (1 1/4 lb) silken firm tofu, drained

1 Cut the baby bok choy and choy sum widthways into thirds. Cut the snake beans into 10 cm (4 inch) lengths.
2 Heat a wok over high heat, add 1 tablespoon of the oil and swirl to coat the side of the wok. Cook the onion for 3–5 minutes, or until crisp. Remove with a slotted spoon and drain on paper towels.
3 Reheat the wok over high heat and add 1 tablespoon of the oil. Add half the greens and stir-fry for 2–3 minutes, or until wilted. Remove from the wok. Repeat with the remaining oil and greens. Drain any liquid from the wok.
4 Add the combined sugar, chilli, ginger and teriyaki sauce to the wok and bring to the boil. Simmer for 1 minute. Add the sesame oil and tofu and simmer for 2 minutes, turning once—the tofu will break up. Divide the greens among serving plates, then top with the dressing. Sprinkle with the fried onion.

*LEFT: Asian greens with teriyaki tofu dressing*

# DEEP-FRYING

Deep-frying is so much more than doughnuts and french fries. There is a whole world of Asian food that lends itself to brief cooking in very hot oil, which results in a deliciously crisp coating and a moist, tender centre. The Chinese, in particular, have a large selection of dumplings that they typically serve for yum cha. The whole process of deep-frying is evocative, from the sizzle as the first morsels are dropped into the oil to the way the food goes golden and crisp while you watch. Most of the food in this chapter is in the form of small, bite-sized bits or parcels designed for a buffet or a party, or just for eating while standing over the stove in the kitchen.

# HOW TO DEEP-FRY

While not necessarily something you'd do every day, deep-frying is easier than you think, and it's a great way to cook food for yum cha or a party.

Deep-frying is a popular cooking method in Asian cuisines because of the crisp texture and succulent interior it produces. In Western societies, deep-frying has acquired something of a bad reputation in recent years, but really, there's no need to be scared of it. It is true that a lot of oil is used in the cooking process, but when deep-frying is done correctly, little oil is absorbed into the food.

## USING A WOK TO DEEP-FRY

Woks are excellent for deep-frying due to their bowl-shaped sloping sides and wide surface area. Another advantage is that woks are spacious enough to cook large quantities of food without overcrowding.

There is no need for a separate wok for deep-frying: the same all-purpose 30–35 cm (12–14 inch) wok that is suitable for stir-frying, steaming, braises and soups also works perfectly for deep-frying. However, because stability is so important when deep-frying, use a two-handled wok, which is less likely to

overbalance than a one-handled wok. If you are using an electric stove, use a flat-bottomed wok and if a gas stove, use a wok stand to make sure the wok is secure.

## OTHER DEEP-FRYING TOOLS

A mesh ladle (available from Asian food stores) is a popular utensil in Asia. It is a circular steel-mesh strainer attached to a long bamboo handle. Use it to scoop up the cooked food from the oil without bringing too much of the oil with you.

Wooden chopsticks are useful for turning food over so that it cooks evenly on both sides—they are long enough to keep your hands away from splattering oil. Avoid plastic chopsticks because they are harder to manipulate than bamboo.

Some people use a wire rack that sits over the side of the wok, which is useful for keeping cooked food warm while you continue to cook the rest of the food.

Another useful tool is a thermometer to measure the oil temperature. There are thermometers designed especially for deep-frying and confectionery. They

attach to the side of the pan and a probe is immersed in the boiling liquid. They are available from specialist kitchen stores.

## OIL FOR DEEP-FRYING

For deep-frying, even more so than for stir-frying, the choice of oil is crucial. All oils decompose when they reach a certain temperature, called the 'smoke point', but some oils reach this point sooner than others. The tell-tale signs of decomposition are smoky fumes, or the oil becoming darker or flecked with particles. Butter and animal fats have a low smoke point (about 190°C/375°F), which is why they quickly burn when overheated. Vegetable oils have a higher smoke point (about 230°C/450°F). When deep-frying, use an oil with a high smoking point, so that it doesn't smoke and burn the food. Peanut, vegetable or canola oil are all suitable for deep-frying. If using peanut oil, use refined peanut oil rather than cold-pressed. Not only is refined peanut oil cheaper, but it also has an unobtrusive flavour that is perfect for deep-frying.

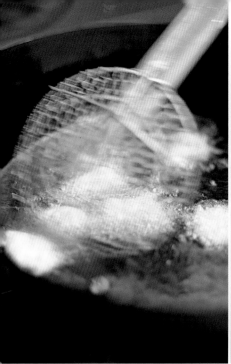

## CAN OIL BE RE-USED?

While it is possible to re-use oil, it is better to use fresh. Not only does oil absorb the flavours of the food that was cooked in it (especially strong flavours, such as seafood), but once oil has been heated, it turns rancid (particularly if there are food particles in it) and its structure alters. Fresh oil ensures that the flavour of the food and not the oil is predominant. If you do re-use oil, strain it before using it and don't overheat it.

## THE RIGHT TEMPERATURE

Along with the choice of oil, the temperature of the oil is also critical. In order to achieve food with a crisp exterior and a tender interior, the oil cannot be too cold (the food will take too long to cook, absorb a lot of oil and be greasy) or too hot (the food will burn on the outside and still be undercooked inside). Our recipes specify the recommended temperature. To be sure that the oil is the required temperature, use a deep-frying thermometer.

If you don't have a thermometer, use the bread test. Heat the oil, then drop a cube of bread into the oil. The length of time it takes for the bread to turn brown indicates the temperature.

| | |
|---|---|
| 5 seconds | 200°C (400°F) |
| 10 seconds | 190°C (375°F) |
| 15 seconds | 180°C (350°F) |
| 20 seconds | 170°C (325°F) |
| 30–35 seconds | 160°C (315°F) |

When food is added to the oil, the oil temperature drops, so you may need to reheat the oil before adding the next batch.

## HINTS AND TIPS

● To avoid being burnt by hot oil when deep-frying in a wok, make sure that the wok is stable. It must be firmly balanced on the stove-top, so either use a flat-bottomed wok, a two-handled wok, or a wok sitting on a wok ring.
● Don't overfill the wok with oil—between one-third and two-thirds full should be sufficient to allow room for splattering and for the oil to bubble up when the food is added.
● To prevent the oil from spitting, the food should be as dry as possible. If it is coated in batter, make sure that any excess is drained off. If food has been marinated, remove it from the marinade with a slotted spoon to allow it to drain.
● When deep-frying individual pieces such as spring rolls or fritters, they can be gently lowered into the wok using a heatproof slotted spoon, slid down the side of the wok, or placed in a long-handled wire-mesh strainer basket and fried. This minimises the oil splattering.
● Bring food to room temperature before adding it to the oil. It will minimise the oil temperature being reduced too much and will also prevent splattering.
● Heat oil to the required temperature and adjust it when cooking (if necessary) to maintain it.

*STEPS TO DEEP-FRYING*
*The first step in deep-frying is to heat the oil to the correct temperature. If you don't have a deep-frying thermometer, use the bread test (see this page).*

*Lower pieces of food one or two at a time into the hot oil, being careful that you don't get splattered. This prevents the oil from overflowing, helps maintain a constant oil temperature and promotes even browing.*

*Cook food in small batches until it is golden, then remove from the oil (a wire-mesh strainer does this job very well).*

*Drain the food on crumpled paper towels while you cook the rest of the food.*

● Add the ingredients in small batches so that the oil doesn't overflow.
● Have a plate lined with crumpled paper towels ready to drain the cooked food.
● If you are cooking a lot of food, heat the oven to warm 160°C (315°F/Gas 2–3) and keep the cooked food warm in the oven while you cook the rest.
● Salting (or sprinkling sweet food with sugar) food after it has been cooked helps minimise oil absorption.
● It doesn't hurt to have a big pot full of water by the side of the stove ready to extinguish any flames if necessary.
● Refamiliarise yourself with the location of your fire extinguisher and fire blanket—you probably won't need them, but it's good to have them on hand just in case.

## SALT AND PEPPER PRAWNS

Preparation time: 20 minutes +
  30 minutes refrigeration
Total cooking time: 5 minutes
Serves 4–6

☆ ☆

1 egg white

2 cloves garlic, crushed

1 kg (2 lb) raw medium prawns, peeled and
  deveined, with tails intact

1 tablespoon peanut oil

1 long fresh red chilli, sliced on the diagonal

1/2 cup (90 g/3 oz) rice flour

1 tablespoon ground Sichuan peppercorns

1 teaspoon ground white pepper

2 teaspoons ground sea salt

1 teaspoon caster sugar

peanut oil, for deep-frying


1 Put the egg white and garlic in a bowl and
mix together before adding the prawns. Stir to
coat the prawns, then cover with plastic wrap
and refrigerate for 30 minutes.
2 Meanwhile, heat the oil in a small frying pan
until hot, add the chilli and cook, stirring, for
1 minute. Remove from the pan and drain on
paper towels. Put the rice flour, Sichuan

peppercorns, white pepper, salt and sugar in a
bowl and combine well.
3 Fill a wok one-third full of oil and heat to
180°C (350°F), or until a cube of bread dropped
into the oil browns in 15 seconds. Coat each
prawn in the flour, shaking off any excess, and
deep-fry in batches for about 1 minute, or until
lightly golden and cooked through. Drain on
crumpled paper towels, season with salt and
pepper and serve.


## SWEET AND SOUR PORK

Preparation time: 20 minutes +
  30 minutes marinating + 30 minutes cooling
Total cooking time: 30 minutes
Serves 4–6

☆ ☆

1 tablespoon light soy sauce

3 teaspoons Chinese rice wine

pinch of white pepper

500 g (1 lb) pork loin, cut into 1.5 cm
  (5/8 inch) cubes

1/2 cup (60 g/2 oz) plain flour

1/2 cup (60 g/2 oz) cornflour

1 teaspoon bicarbonate of soda

oil, for deep-frying

*ABOVE: Salt and
pepper prawns*

## SAUCE

2 teaspoons vegetable oil

1 teaspoon very finely chopped fresh ginger

1 clove garlic, crushed

1 small onion, cut into thin wedges

1 small carrot, thinly sliced on the diagonal

1 small green pepper (capsicum), cut into thin strips about 5 cm (2 inches) long

1/2 cup (100 g/3 1/2 oz) canned pineapple chunks, well drained with 1/3 cup (80 ml/2 3/4 fl oz) juice reserved

1/4 cup (60 g/2 oz) sliced bamboo shoots

1/4 cup (60 ml/2 fl oz) tomato sauce

1 1/2 tablespoons rice vinegar

1 1/2 tablespoons sugar

1 tablespoon light soy sauce

2 teaspoons cornflour combined with 1/2 cup (125 ml/4 fl oz) water

1 Combine the soy sauce, rice wine and white pepper in a non-metallic bowl, add the pork and marinate for 30 minutes.

2 Combine the plain flour, cornflour, bicarbonate of soda and 1 teaspoon salt, then gradually mix in 145 ml (5 fl oz) cold water until you have a thick, sticky batter. Add the pork cubes and mix well with your hands.

3 Fill a wok one-third full of the oils and heat to 180°C (350°F), or until a cube of bread browns in 15 seconds. Using your fingers to separate the pork pieces, drop individual pieces into the oil and cook in small batches for 1 1/2 minutes, or until golden—you may need to carefully loosen the pieces from the bottom of the wok once they have been cooking for about 1 minute, then they should float to the top. Drain well in a single layer on crumpled paper towels and allow to cool to room temperature. Remove the wok from the heat but reserve the oil in the wok.

4 To make the sauce, heat a second wok until very hot, add the oil and swirl to coat. Add the ginger, garlic and onion and stir-fry for 1 minute. Add the carrot and stir-fry for 2 minutes, then add the green pepper and cook for 1 minute, or until the vegetables are tender but still a little crunchy. Add the pineapple chunks and the bamboo shoots, toss well and cook for 1 minute, or until heated through. Remove from the wok. Combine the tomato sauce, rice vinegar, sugar, soy sauce, cornflour mixture and the reserved pineapple juice, and pour it into the wok. Cook over high heat for 2–3 minutes or until the sauce boils and thickens, then return the vegetables to the wok. Stir well, then remove from the heat.

5 Reheat the deep-frying oil to 180°C (350°F). Re-fry the pork in two batches for 1–2 minutes or until crisp, golden and heated through. Drain on paper towels, then quickly combine with the sauce. Serve immediately with rice or as part of a banquet—it will go soggy if it sits for too long.

SWEET AND SOUR PORK
Sweet and sour pork balances the two flavour extremes of sweetness and sourness. It is an adaptation of a classic Cantonese dish that is thought to date back to the Qing Dynasty (1644–1911). The use of pineapple and tomato sauce, however, are more modern, Western additions.

*LEFT: Sweet and sour pork*

THAI FISH CAKES
Thai fish cakes have
become a favourite Thai
restaurant menu staple in
the West, where they are
usually eaten as a starter.
However, in Thailand the
tradition of serving a starter
before the main course has
a very short history, and is
usually only practised in the
larger cities. More usually,
these are eaten as a snack,
or as part of a large
banquet selection.

*ABOVE: Thai fish cakes with
dipping sauce*

## THAI FISH CAKES WITH DIPPING SAUCE
(Tod man pla)

Preparation time: 25 minutes
Total cooking time: 15 minutes
Serves 6

☆ ☆

DIPPING SAUCE
1/2 cup (125 g/4 oz) sugar
1/4 cup (60 ml/2 fl oz) white vinegar
1 tablespoon fish sauce
1 small fresh red chilli, chopped
1/4 small carrot, finely chopped
1/4 cucumber, peeled, seeded and finely chopped
1 tablespoon roasted peanuts, chopped

500 g (1 lb) redfish fillets, skin removed
1 1/2 tablespoons Thai red curry paste (see page 56)
1/4 cup (60 g/2 oz) sugar
1/4 cup (60 ml/2 fl oz) fish sauce
1 egg
200 g (6 1/2 oz) snake beans, sliced
10 fresh kaffir lime leaves, finely chopped
oil, for deep-frying

1 To make the dipping sauce, put the sugar, vinegar, fish sauce, chilli and 1/2 cup (125 ml/

4 fl oz) water in a saucepan. Simmer for 5 minutes, or until thickened slightly. Cool. Stir in the remaining ingredients. Set aside until needed.
2 Put the fish in a food processor and blend until smooth. Add the curry paste, sugar, fish sauce and egg. Process for another 10 seconds, or until combined. Stir in the beans and lime leaves. Shape into golf-ball-size balls, then flatten into patties.
3 Fill a wok one-third full of oil and heat to 180°C (350°F), or until a cube of bread browns in 15 seconds. Cook in batches for 3–5 minutes, turning occasionally. Drain on crumpled paper towels. Serve with the dipping sauce.

## CHICKEN KARAAGE

Preparation time: 15 minutes +
  overnight marinating
Total cooking time: 30 minutes
Makes 20 pieces

☆ ☆ ☆

1.5 kg (3 lb) chicken
1/2 cup (125 ml/4 fl oz) Japanese soy sauce
1/4 cup (60 ml/2 fl oz) mirin
2 tablespoons sake
1 tablespoon finely chopped fresh ginger
4 cloves garlic, crushed
oil, for deep-frying
cornflour, to coat

1 Using a cleaver or a large kitchen knife, remove the wings from the chicken and chop them across the joint. Cut the chicken into 16 even-sized pieces by cutting it in half down the centre, then across each half to form four even pieces. Cut each quarter into four pieces, trying to retain some skin on each piece. You should have 20 pieces in total.

2 Combine the soy sauce, mirin, sake, ginger and garlic in a large, non-metallic bowl. Add the chicken and toss to coat well. Cover and refrigerate overnight, turning occasionally to evenly coat the chicken in the marinade.

3 Preheat the oven to slow 150°C (300°F/ Gas 2). Fill a wok one-third full with oil and heat to 160°C (315°F), or until a cube of bread browns in 30–35 seconds. While the oil is heating, drain the chicken and coat thoroughly in well-seasoned cornflour, shaking lightly to remove any excess. Deep-fry 4–5 pieces at a time for 4–5 minutes, or until crisp and golden and the chicken is just cooked through and tender. Drain well on crumpled paper towels. Keep the cooked pieces warm in the oven while you cook the remainder. Serve hot with lemon wedges.

## DEEP-FRIED WHOLE FISH WITH TAMARIND SAUCE

Preparation time: 25 minutes
Total cooking time: 10 minutes
Serves 4

☆☆☆

2 tablespoons tamarind pulp

2 tablespoons peanut oil

3 cloves garlic, crushed

2 tablespoons grated fresh galangal

2 tablespoons grated palm sugar

2 tablespoons fish sauce

2 tablespoons lime juice

750 g (1 1/2 lb) whole snapper or bream, cleaned and scaled

cornflour, to dust

oil, for deep-frying

1 tablespoon crisp fried shallots

2 small fresh red chillies, seeded and finely shredded

2 tablespoons fresh coriander leaves

1 Put the tamarind pulp and 1/3 cup (80 ml/ 2 3/4 fl oz) boiling water in a bowl and set aside

to cool. Mash the mixture with your fingertips to dissolve the pulp, then strain and reserve the liquid. Discard the pulp.

2 Heat the oil in a saucepan. Add the garlic and galangal and cook for 1 minute. Add the palm sugar, tamarind liquid, fish sauce and lime juice and stir over medium heat until the sugar has dissolved. Boil for 1–2 minutes, or until slightly thickened. Cover and keep hot.

3 Score the fish on both sides in a crisscross pattern 2 cm (3/4 inch) wide and 5 mm (1/4 inch) deep. Pat dry with paper towels. Lightly coat with the cornflour.

4 Fill a wok one-third full of oil and heat to 180°C (350°F), or until a cube of bread dropped in the oil browns in 15 seconds. Deep-fry the fish for 6–7 minutes, or until golden and cooked through—you may need to turn the fish halfway through cooking. Drain on crumpled paper towels and season to taste with salt and freshly ground black pepper.

5 Place the fish on a serving platter and pour the sauce over the top. Serve, sprinkled with the shallot flakes, chilli and coriander leaves.

*BELOW: Deep-fried whole fish with tamarind sauce*

## SON-IN-LAW EGGS
(Kai leuk koey)

Preparation time: 15 minutes
Total cooking time: 15 minutes
Serves 6

☆ ☆

6 eggs

oil, for deep-frying

2 tablespoons vegetable oil, extra

2 cloves garlic, thinly sliced

6 red Asian shallots, thinly sliced lengthways

1/3 cup (80 ml/2³/4 fl oz) fish sauce

150 g (5 oz) palm sugar, grated

1 teaspoon tamarind purée

1 teaspoon sambal oelek

3 tablespoons chopped fresh coriander leaves

1 Put the eggs in a saucepan of cold water and bring to the boil. Cook for 4 minutes. Rinse in cold water and remove the shells.
2 Fill a wok one-third full of oil and heat to 170°C (325°F), or until a cube of bread browns in 20 seconds. Lower the eggs into the oil with a slotted spoon and deep-fry, turning carefully, for 2–3 minutes, or until lightly golden. Keep warm.

3 Heat the extra oil in a small frying pan. Add the garlic and shallots and fry until golden. Drain on crumpled paper towels. Reduce the heat to low, add the fish sauce, palm sugar, tamarind purée, sambal oelek and 1/4 cup (60 ml/2 fl oz) water and cook slowly, stirring, until the sugar dissolves. Cook for 2 minutes, or until the mixture thickens slightly. Stir in the reserved cooked garlic and shallots.
4 Cut the eggs in half and arrange on a plate. Pour on the sauce and garnish with the coriander.
NOTE: This dish is often served at Thai weddings, which may explain its unusual name.

## KOREAN POTATO FRITTERS

Preparation time: 15 minutes +
    10 minutes standing
Total cooking time: 20 minutes
Makes 12

☆ ☆

DIPPING SAUCE
2 spring onions, finely chopped

1 small clove garlic, finely chopped

1 1/2 tablespoons Japanese soy sauce

1 tablespoon mirin

2 teaspoons sesame seeds, toasted and ground

1 teaspoon sugar

drizzle of sesame oil

1/4 teaspoon chilli flakes (optional)

POTATO FRITTERS
500 g (1 lb) all-purpose potatoes (e.g. Desirée)

5 spring onions, shredded

2 eggs, lightly beaten

2 tablespoons cornflour

peanut oil, for deep-frying

1 To make the dipping sauce, combine all the ingredients in a small, non-metallic bowl.
2 Peel and coarsely grate the potatoes into a large non-metallic bowl. Cover with cold water to prevent discolouration and set aside for 10 minutes. Drain and squeeze out any excess moisture with your hands. Put in a clean bowl with the shredded spring onions and mix well. In a separate small bowl, combine the eggs and cornflour and season with pepper. Pour over the potato mixture and mix well.
3 Fill a wok one-third full of oil and heat to 180°C (350°F), or until a cube of bread browns in 15 seconds. Mould handfuls of batter with

*BELOW: Son-in-law eggs*

the palms of your hands, gently flattening them out to about 5 cm (2 inches). Carefully drop four fritters at a time into the oil, using a slotted spoon if desired, and cook, turning once, for 5 minutes, or until golden on both sides, then remove and drain on crumpled paper towels. Serve immediately with the dipping sauce.

# CRISPY NOODLES
(Mee grob)

Preparation time: 30 minutes +
  20 minutes soaking
Total cooking time: 15 minutes
Serves 4–6

☆☆

4 dried shiitake mushrooms
oil, for deep-frying
100 g (3¹/2 oz) dried rice vermicelli
100 g (3¹/2 oz) fried tofu puffs, julienned
4 cloves garlic, crushed
I onion, chopped
I chicken breast fillet, thinly sliced
8 green beans, sliced on the diagonal
6 spring onions, thinly sliced on the diagonal
8 raw medium prawns, peeled and deveined, with tails intact
30 g (I oz) bean sprouts, tailed
fresh coriander leaves, to garnish

SAUCE
¹/4 cup (60 ml/2 fl oz) white vinegar
¹/4 cup (60 ml/2 fl oz) fish sauce
5 tablespoons sugar
I tablespoon soy sauce
I tablespoon sweet chilli sauce

1 Soak the mushrooms in boiling water for 20 minutes. Squeeze dry, discard the stems and thinly slice the caps.
2 Fill a wok one-third full of oil and heat to 180°C (350°F), or until a cube of bread dropped into the oil browns in 15 seconds. Cook the noodles in small batches for 5 seconds, or until puffed and crispy. Drain well on crumpled paper towels.
3 Add the tofu to the wok in batches and deep-fry for 1 minute, or until crisp. Drain. Carefully remove all but 2 tablespoons of oil.
4 Reheat the wok until very hot. Add the garlic and onion, and stir-fry for 1 minute. Add the chicken, mushrooms, beans and half the spring onion. Stir-fry for 2 minutes, or until the chicken has almost cooked through. Add the prawns and stir-fry for a further 2 minutes, or until they just turn pink.
5 Combine all the sauce ingredients in a bowl, then add to the wok. Stir-fry for 2 minutes, or until the chicken and prawns are tender and the sauce is syrupy.
6 Remove from the heat and stir in the noodles, tofu and bean sprouts. Garnish with the coriander and remaining sliced spring onion.

MEE GROB
Mee grob was created by the chef at a restaurant near the royal palace in Bangkok. One day the king returned from a journey and noticed a crowd gathered near the palace. Curious, he enquired why and was informed that the crowds were there to try a new noodle dish called mee grob. The king himself became a big fan of the crispy fried noodle dish. Mee grob is still available from descendants of the creator, but it has spread much further. Throughout Thailand, mee grob is served as a snack or an accompaniment to curry. It is an example of Thailand's fusion cuisine, as it combines traditional Chinese cooking methods with Thai flavours and ingredients.

*ABOVE: Crispy noodles*

## CHILLI SALT AND PEPPER SQUID AND CELLOPHANE NOODLE SALAD

Preparation time: 30 minutes +
   10 minutes soaking + 15 minutes marinating
Total cooking time: 10 minutes
Serves 4

☆☆☆

1 tablespoon dried shrimp

2 tablespoons Chinese rice wine

2 tablespoons light soy sauce

1 tablespoon Chinese black vinegar

2 teaspoons finely chopped fresh ginger

2 spring onions, thinly sliced

1 teaspoon chilli garlic sauce

1 teaspoon sesame oil

*ABOVE: Chilli salt and pepper squid and cellophane noodle salad*

SALAD

600 g (1 1/4 lb) cleaned squid hoods

1/2 cup (125 ml/4 fl oz) lemon juice

250 g (8 oz) cellophane noodles

1 small Lebanese cucumber, seeded and
   cut into batons

1 cup (90 g/3 oz) bean sprouts, tops and
   tails removed

2 tablespoons chopped fresh coriander
   leaves

1 tablespoon Sichuan peppercorns, dry-roasted

2 teaspoons sea salt

1 teaspoon ground white pepper

1 teaspoon freshly ground black pepper

1/4 teaspoon chilli flakes

1/2 cup (60 g/2 oz) plain flour

1/4 cup (45 g/1 1/2 oz) rice flour

peanut oil, for deep-frying

2 egg whites, lightly beaten

fresh coriander leaves, extra, to garnish

1 Put the dried shrimp in a small heatproof bowl, cover with boiling water and soak for 10 minutes. Drain and finely chop. Return the shrimp to the bowl, cover with the rice wine and leave to soak until needed.

2 To make the dressing, put the soy sauce, black vinegar, ginger, spring onion, chilli garlic sauce and sesame oil in a small bowl. Mix together well, then set aside until needed.

3 Open out the squid hoods, then wash and thoroughly pat dry with paper towels. With the soft inside flesh facing upwards, score a shallow diamond pattern in the squid, taking care not to cut all the way through. Cut the squid into 2.5 x 4 cm (1 x 1 1/2 inch) pieces. Put the pieces in a flat, non-metallic dish, then pour the lemon juice on top. Cover with plastic wrap and marinate in the refrigerator for 15 minutes.

4 Meanwhile, put the cellophane noodles in a heatproof bowl, cover with boiling water and soak for 3–4 minutes, or until softened. Drain and rinse under cold running water. Drain again, then transfer to a serving bowl. Add the cucumber, bean sprouts and chopped coriander to the bowl.

5 Combine the dry-roasted Sichuan peppercorns, sea salt, white pepper, black pepper and chilli flakes in a mortar and pestle or spice grinder and grind to a fine powder. Transfer to a bowl with the plain and rice flours and combine thoroughly. Drain the squid and pat dry with paper towels.

**6** Fill a wok one-third full of oil and heat to 180°C (350°F), or until a cube of bread dropped in the oil browns in 15 seconds. Dip the squid pieces in the egg white, then coat well in the seasoned flour. Deep-fry in batches of five or six for about 1 minute each batch, or until lightly golden and cooked through—do not overcrowd the wok. Drain on crumpled paper towels and sprinkle with a little salt—the salt will help to soak up any excess oil.

**7** To serve, add the dressing and shrimp mixture to the bowl with the noodles and gently toss together. Place the salt and pepper squid on top of the noodles, garnish with coriander leaves, then serve immediately.

# THAI STUFFED CHICKEN WINGS
(Peek gai yud sai)

Preparation time: 30 minutes +
    cooling time
Total cooking time: 20 minutes
Makes 12

☆☆☆

12 large chicken wings
20 g (³/4 oz) dried rice vermicelli
1 tablespoon grated palm sugar
2 tablespoons fish sauce
200 g (6¹/2 oz) pork mince
2 spring onions, chopped
3 cloves garlic, chopped
1 small fresh red chilli, chopped
3 tablespoons chopped fresh coriander leaves
peanut oil, for deep-frying
rice flour, well seasoned, to coat
sweet chilli sauce, to serve

**1** Using a small, sharp knife, with each chicken wing, start at the fatter end of the wing and scrape down the bone, pushing the flesh and skin as you go until you reach the connecting joint. Twist and pull the exposed bone from its socket and discard the bone. Take care not to pierce the skin.

**2** Soak the vermicelli in a bowl of boiling water for 6–7 minutes. Drain well. Cut into 2 cm (³/4 inch) pieces with a pair of scissors. Set aside. Put the palm sugar and fish sauce in a small bowl and stir until the sugar has dissolved.

**3** Combine the pork mince, spring onion, garlic, chilli and the fish sauce mixture in a food processor until well mixed. Transfer to a bowl, then stir in the coriander and noodles.

**4** Divide the pork mixture into 12 balls. Stuff each boned-out section of chicken wing with a ball of mixture and firmly secure the opening with a toothpick.

**5** Put the chicken wings in a bamboo or metal steamer over a wok of simmering water—ensure the base of the steamer doesn't touch the water. Cover with a lid and steam for 8 minutes. Remove the wings from the steamer, then set aside to firm and cool.

**6** Fill a dry, clean wok one-third full of oil and heat to 200°C (400°F), or until a cube of bread dropped in the oil browns in 5 seconds. Coat the wings in the seasoned flour. Deep-fry in small batches for 3 minutes each batch, or until the wings are golden brown. Drain on crumpled paper towels. Remove the toothpicks and serve the wings with the sweet chilli sauce.

THAI STUFFED
CHICKEN WINGS

Push the flesh down the bone towards the joint, using a small, sharp knife.

Twist and pull the exposed bone out of the socket.

*BELOW: Thai stuffed chicken wings*

235

INDONESIAN
SPRING ROLLS

Using your fingers, lightly
wet the edges of the
wrapper with the cornflour
paste.

Roll up the spring roll,
tucking in the sides, then
seal with the cornflour
paste.

# INDONESIAN SPRING ROLLS

Preparation time: 30 minutes + 20 minutes soaking
Total cooking time: 25 minutes
Makes 20

☆ ☆

4 dried shiitake mushrooms
80 g (2³/4 oz) dried rice vermicelli
1 tablespoon peanut oil
2 garlic cloves, chopped
2 teaspoons grated fresh ginger
250 g (8 oz) pork mince
250 g (8 oz) raw medium prawns, peeled and
    finely chopped
1 tablespoon light soy sauce, plus extra, to serve
1 tablespoon oyster sauce
1 tablespoon Chinese rice wine
1 carrot, grated
8 water chestnuts, finely chopped
4 spring onions, thinly sliced
200 g (6¹/2 oz) wom bok (Chinese cabbage),
    finely shredded
1 tablespoon sweet chilli sauce
2 teaspoons cornflour
20 large spring roll wrappers
oil, for deep-frying

1 Cover the mushrooms with boiling water and
soak for 20 minutes. Drain and squeeze out the

excess water. Discard the woody stalks and
thinly slice the caps. Meanwhile, soak the
noodles in boiling water for 6–7 minutes, or
until soft and transparent. Drain, then cut into
5 cm (2 inch) lengths.
2 Heat a wok to high heat, add the oil and swirl
to coat. Add the garlic and ginger and cook for
1 minute. Add the pork mince and cook for a
further 3 minutes, stirring to break up any
lumps. Add the prawns and cook for 1 minute,
or until they just turn pink. Stir in the remaining
ingredients except the cornflour and wrappers
and cook for 2 minutes, or until combined.
Season to taste with salt and pepper.
3 Mix together the cornflour and 2 tablespoons
water in a small bowl until a smooth paste forms.
4 Stack the spring roll wrappers under a damp
tea towel. Working with one at a time, place a
wrapper on the work surface with one corner
facing you. Put 2 tablespoons of the filling along
the centre of each spring roll wrapper. Brush the
edges with the cornflour paste and roll up firmly,
tucking in the ends as you go, and sealing with a
little more of the cornflour paste. Continue,
covering the completed rolls with a damp tea
towel to prevent them drying out while you
work with the others.
5 Fill a wok one–third full of oil and heat to
180°C (350°F), or until a cube of bread dropped
in the oil browns in 15 seconds. Cook the spring
rolls in batches of 2–3 rolls, turning gently to
brown evenly for 2 minutes, or until golden.
Drain on crumpled paper towels. Serve with
light soy sauce or your favourite dipping sauce.

*RIGHT: Indonesian spring
rolls*

## SALT AND PEPPER TOFU PUFFS

Preparation time: 15 minutes
Total cooking time: 10 minutes
Serves 4–6

☆ ☆

1/2 cup (125 ml/4 fl oz) sweet chilli sauce

2 tablespoons lemon juice

2 cups (250 g/8 oz) cornflour

2 tablespoons salt

1 tablespoon ground white pepper

2 teaspoons caster sugar

380 g (12 oz) fried tofu puffs, halved and patted dry

4 egg whites, lightly beaten

peanut oil, for deep-frying

lemon wedges, to serve

1 Combine the sweet chilli sauce and lemon juice in a bowl and set aside until needed.
2 Put the cornflour, salt, pepper and caster sugar in a large bowl and mix together well.
3 Dip the tofu into the egg white, then toss in the cornflour mixture, shaking off any excess.
4 Fill a wok one-third full of oil and heat to 180°C (350°F), or until a cube of bread dropped in the oil browns in 15 seconds. Cook the tofu in batches for 1–2 minutes, or until crisp. Drain on crumpled paper towels. Serve immediately with the chilli sauce mixture and lemon wedges.

## JAPANESE CRUMBED PRAWNS WITH PONZU

Preparation time: 15 minutes
Total cooking time: 10 minutes
Makes 18

☆ ☆

18 raw large prawns

2 tablespoons cornflour

3 eggs

2 cups (120 g/4 oz) Japanese breadcrumbs (panko)

peanut oil, for deep-frying

1/3 cup (80 ml/2 3/4 fl oz) ponzu sauce (see Note)

1 Peel and devein the prawns, leaving the tails intact. Cut down the back of each prawn to form a butterfly, then place between two layers of plastic wrap and beat gently to form a cutlet.
2 Put the cornflour, eggs and breadcrumbs in separate bowls. Lightly beat the eggs. Dip each prawn first into the cornflour, then into the egg and finally into the breadcrumbs, ensuring that each cutlet is well covered in crumbs.
3 Fill a wok one-third full of oil, and heat it to 180°C (350°F), or until a cube of bread browns in 15 seconds. Cook six prawn cutlets at a time for about 1 minute each side, or until the crumbs are golden—be careful they don't burn. Serve immediately with ponzu sauce.
NOTE: If ponzu isn't available, mix 1/4 cup (60 ml/ 2 fl oz) soy sauce with 1 tablespoon lemon juice.

*ABOVE: Japanese crumbed prawns with ponzu*

# CURRY PUFFS

Preparation time: 20 minutes +
  30 minutes cooling + 30 minutes refrigeration
Total cooking time: 1 hour 25 minutes
Makes 24

☆ ☆ ☆

1 large dried red chilli, chopped
1 1/2 teaspoons coriander seeds
1/2 teaspoon fennel seeds
250 g (8 oz) potatoes, peeled
1/4 cup (60 ml/2 fl oz) peanut oil
1 carrot, finely diced
3/4 cup (115 g/4 oz) frozen peas, thawed
1 small onion, finely chopped
2 cloves garlic, crushed
2 tablespoons Malaysian curry powder
150 g (5 oz) lean beef mince
1/4 cup (60 ml/2 fl oz) beef stock
6 sheets frozen ready-made puff pastry
2 egg yolks, lightly beaten
peanut oil, for deep-frying
raita, to serve (see page 86)

1 Finely grind the dried chilli, coriander seeds and fennel seeds together, then set aside.
2 Boil the potatoes for 15 minutes, or until just tender but not fully cooked. Cool a little; dice.
3 Heat a wok over high heat, add 1 tablespoon of the oil and swirl to coat. Reduce the heat to medium and stir-fry the carrot for 4–5 minutes, or until it starts to soften. Add the peas and cook for 3 minutes. Transfer to a large, non-metallic, heatproof bowl. Add 1 tablespoon of oil to the wok and stir-fry the potato for 3–4 minutes, or until browned. Transfer to the bowl with the peas.
4 Heat the remaining oil over high heat. Cook the onion and garlic for 1 minute. Stir in the ground spices and curry powder for 30 seconds, or until fragrant. Stir in the mince and cook until browned, breaking up any lumps. Reduce the heat to medium–low, pour in the stock and simmer for 10 minutes. Transfer to the bowl with the vegetables; stir well. Cool for 30 minutes.
5 Meanwhile, separate the pastry sheets with a knife and sit on a wire rack to thaw.
6 Cut out 24 pastry rounds with a 10 cm (4 inch) cutter. Place 1 1/2–2 teaspoons of filling on one side of a round, then fold into a semicircle. Join the edges together, using a little water if necessary. Seal the edges with a fork. Repeat with the remaining pastry rounds and filling. Lightly brush one side of the puffs with egg yolk, place on a tray and refrigerate for 30 minutes.
7 Fill a wok one-third full of oil and heat to 180°C (350°F), or until a cube of bread dropped in the oil browns in 15 seconds. Deep-fry the puffs four at a time for 3–5 minutes, or until browned and the filling is cooked through. Serve with raita or plain yoghurt.

# SAMOSAS

Preparation time: 30 minutes
Total cooking time: 25 minutes
Makes 24

☆ ☆ ☆

1 tablespoon vegetable oil
1 onion, chopped
1 teaspoon grated fresh ginger
1 clove garlic, crushed
2 teaspoons ground coriander
2 teaspoons ground cumin
2 teaspoons garam masala
1 1/2 teaspoons chilli powder
1/4 teaspoon ground turmeric
300 g (10 oz) potatoes, cut into 1 cm (1/2 inch) cubes and boiled
1/4 cup (40 g/1 1/4 oz) frozen peas
2 tablespoons chopped fresh coriander leaves
1 teaspoon lemon juice
6 sheets ready-rolled puff pastry
oil, for deep-frying
raita, to serve (see page 86)

1 Heat a wok over medium heat, add the oil and swirl to coat the side of the wok. Add the onion, ginger and garlic and cook over medium heat for 2 minutes, or until softened. Add the spices, potato, peas and 2 teaspoons water. Cook for 1 minute, or until all the moisture evaporates. Remove from the heat and stir in the coriander leaves and lemon juice.
2 Cut 12 rounds from the pastry sheets with a 12.5 cm (5 inch) cutter, then cut each round in half. Shape 1 semi-circle into a cone, wet the edges and seal the side seam, leaving an opening large enough to spoon in 3 teaspoons of filling, then seal. Repeat to make 23 more samosas.
3 Fill a wok one-third full of oil and heat to 180°C (350°F), or until a cube of bread browns in 15 seconds. Cook in batches for 1–2 minutes, or until golden. Drain on crumpled paper towels and season. Serve with raita or plain yoghurt.

GARAM MASALA
While there are numerous variations of the Indian spice mix, garam (meaning hot) masala (meaning spice mix), they invariably include black pepper, cinnamon, cloves, chilli, cardamom, cumin and coriander seeds, turmeric and nutmeg. To make your own, see page 75.

*OPPOSITE PAGE, FROM TOP: Curry puffs; Samosas*

TEMPURA PRAWNS

Score the underside of the prawns a few times.

Mix the flour into the batter with chopsticks—the batter should be lumpy.

Drizzle the prawns with a little of the remaining batter, but beware of oil spitting up at you.

## TEMPURA PRAWNS

Preparation time: 25 minutes
Total cooking time: 10 minutes
Serves 4

☆ ☆

12 raw large prawns
oil, for deep-frying
1 egg
1 cup (250 ml/8 fl oz) iced water
1 cup (125 g/4 oz) tempura flour, sifted
2 ice cubes
1 sheet roasted nori, shredded

1 Peel and devein the prawns, keeping the tails intact. Using a sharp knife, make three or four diagonal cuts in the underside of each prawn one-third of the way through. Pat the prawns dry with paper towels.
2 Fill a wok one-third full of oil and heat to 180°C (350°F), or until a cube of bread browns in 15 seconds. While the oil is heating, put the egg in a large bowl and, using chopsticks or a fork, break it up. Add the iced water and mix well with chopsticks. Add the sifted flour all at once and mix with chopsticks until just combined, then add the ice cubes—the mixture should be lumpy. Dip the prawns in the batter and deep-fry in batches, four at a time, drizzling with some of the remaining batter to give a spiky effect. Cook for 1 minute, or until crisp.
3 Drain the prawns on crumpled paper towels, sprinkle with the nori and serve immediately.

## AGEDASHI TOFU

Preparation time: 15 minutes + 1 hour soaking
Total cooking time: 15 minutes
Serves 4

☆ ☆

40 g (1 1/4 oz) konbu (kelp)
1–2 tablespoons soy sauce
2–3 teaspoons sugar
2 x 300 g (10 oz) packets silken firm tofu
oil, for deep-frying
potato flour, for dusting
4 spring onions, thinly sliced on the diagonal
20 g (3/4 oz) daikon, grated
1 teaspoon grated fresh ginger

1 Wipe the konbu clean with a damp cloth (do not wash). Put it in a large bowl, cover with 1 litre (32 fl oz) water and leave for 1 hour. Transfer to a saucepan, bring to the boil, but remove from the heat just before boiling point. Discard the konbu. Stir in the soy sauce and sugar, cover and keep hot.

ABOVE: Tempura prawns

**2** Cut the silken firm tofu into 3 cm (1¼ inch) cubes and drain.

**3** Fill a wok one-third full of oil and heat to 190°C (375°F), or until a cube of bread dropped into the oil browns in 10 seconds. Gently dust the flour over the tofu, shaking off any excess. Deep-fry the tofu cubes in three batches for 2–3 minutes each batch, or until lightly golden, turning halfway through if needed. Drain on crumpled paper towels, then sprinkle generously with salt.

**4** Ladle ½ cup (125 ml/4 fl oz) broth into each serving bowl and top with the tofu. Sprinkle with the spring onion, daikon and ginger.

# VEGETABLE TEMPURA PATTIES

Preparation time: 25 minutes
Total cooking time: 15 minutes
Serves 4

☆ ☆

### Wasabi mayonnaise

½ cup (125 g/4 oz) whole-egg mayonnaise

2 teaspoons wasabi paste

1 teaspoon Japanese soy sauce

1 teaspoon sake

1 small zucchini (courgette), grated

1 small potato, julienned

½ carrot, julienned

½ onion, thinly sliced

100 g (3½ oz) orange sweet potato, grated

4 spring onions, green part included, cut into 2 cm (¾ inch) lengths

4 nori sheets, shredded

2 cups (250 g/8 oz) tempura flour, sifted

2 cups (500 ml/16 fl oz) chilled soda water

oil, for deep-frying

2 tablespoons shredded pickled ginger

**1** To make the wasabi mayonnaise, combine all the ingredients in a small bowl. Set aside until ready to serve.

**2** To make the patties, put the zucchini, potato, carrot, onion, orange sweet potato, spring onion and nori in a bowl. Toss together.

**3** Sift the tempura flour into a large bowl and make a well in the centre. Add the soda water and loosely mix together with chopsticks or a fork until just combined—the batter should still be lumpy. Add the vegetables and quickly fold through until just combined.

**4** Fill a wok one-third full of oil and heat to 180°C (350°F), or until a cube of bread dropped into the oil browns in 15 seconds. Gently drop ¼ cup (60 ml/2 fl oz) of the vegetable mixture into the oil, making sure that the patty is not too compact, and cook for 1–2 minutes, or until golden and crisp. Drain on crumpled paper towels and season with sea salt. Repeat with the remaining mixture to make 11 more patties. Serve immediately, topped with the wasabi mayonnaise and the pickled ginger.

WASABI

The edible root of the *wasabia japonica* plant, which grows in Japan, when skinned has a fiery, fierce flavour like horseradish, hence the tag 'Japanese horseradish'. Fresh wasabi is grated or made into a paste, but the dried powder or ready-made paste are more easily available in the West. Beneath the searing heat of wasabi is a refreshing cleansing taste that lifts food.

*LEFT: Vegetable tempura patties*

GINGER
When choosing ginger, choose a piece that feels heavy for its size and that is firm to the touch. It should be quite knobbly with a rough, but not wrinkled, skin. In the summer and spring, young ginger is sometimes available from fruit and vegetable shops. It has a milder flavour and the skin is much more tender than regular ginger, and does not require peeling.

## CHICKEN AND MUSHROOM RICE PAPER PARCELS

Preparation time: 15 minutes +
  2 hours marinating + 20 minutes soaking +
  15 minutes cooling
Total cooking time: 20 minutes
Makes 24

☆ ☆

1–2 tablespoons Chinese barbecue sauce
1 tablespoon Chinese rice wine
2 teaspoons hoisin sauce
2 teaspoons light soy sauce
1/2 teaspoon sesame oil
pinch of five-spice powder
pinch of white pepper
2 teaspoons grated fresh ginger
2 spring onions, finely chopped, white and
  green parts separated
400 g (13 oz) chicken breast fillet, thinly sliced
4 dried shiitake mushrooms
1/4 cup (60 ml/2 fl oz) vegetable oil, plus extra,
  for deep-frying
125 g (4 oz) canned bamboo shoots, rinsed,
  drained and julienned
12 snow peas (mangetout), shredded
2 cloves garlic, finely chopped
24 square Chinese rice paper wrappers
hoisin sauce, for dipping (optional)

1 Combine the Chinese barbecue sauce, rice wine, hoisin sauce, soy sauce, sesame oil, five-spice powder, white pepper, 1 teaspoon of the ginger and the white part of the spring onion in a non-metallic bowl, then add the chicken. Cover and refrigerate for at least 2 hours.
2 Meanwhile, put the shiitake mushrooms in a bowl, cover with boiling water and soak for 20 minutes. Squeeze the mushrooms dry, discard the stalks and thinly slice the caps.
3 Heat a wok over high heat, add 1 tablespoon of the oil and swirl to coat. Add the mushrooms, bamboo shoots and snow peas and stir-fry for 1–2 minutes. Add another tablespoon of oil, the garlic and remaining ginger, and stir-fry for 30 seconds. Transfer to a non-metallic bowl. Heat another tablespoon of the oil in the wok, add the drained chicken and stir-fry for 2–3 minutes, or until the chicken is cooked. Transfer to the bowl with the vegetables. Add the green part of the spring onions to the bowl. Mix well. Cool for 15 minutes.
4 Take a rice paper wrapper and place it diagonally on the work surface, so the bottom corner of a diamond is closest to you. Using 1 tablespoon of the chicken mixture, roll a sausage shape and lay it vertically in the middle of the wrapper. Fold up the wrapper like an envelope, tucking in the edges. Repeat with the remaining wrappers and filling.
5 Fill a wok one-third full of oil and heat to 180°C (350°F), or until a cube of bread browns in 15 seconds. Gently lower 4–6 of the 'envelopes' into the wok at a time, and deep-fry

*RIGHT: Chicken and mushroom rice paper parcels*

Wrap a strip of nori around each mushroom and dampen to seal.

Dip each nori-wrapped mushroom in the tempura batter using chopsticks.

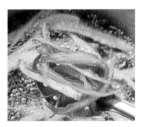

Deep-fry the mushrooms in hot oil until golden and crisp.

for 1–2 minutes, turning halfway through to ensure both sides are evenly browned and crisp, and that the filling is cooked through. Drain well on crumpled paper towels and serve immediately, with some hoisin sauce for dipping, if desired.

## NORI-WRAPPED FRIED MUSHROOMS

Preparation time: 30 minutes
Total cooking time: 15 minutes
Serves 4

☆ ☆

1/3 cup (80 ml/2³/4 fl oz) Japanese soy sauce

100 ml (3¹/2 fl oz) mirin

2 teaspoons grated fresh ginger

2 teaspoons sugar

3 nori sheets, toasted

12 open-cup mushrooms, stalks removed

400 g (13 oz) orange sweet potato

oil, for deep-frying

225 ml (7 fl oz) chilled soda water

1 egg, lightly beaten

1 cup (125 g/4 oz) tempura flour

2 tablespoons wasabi powder

1 To make the sauce, put the soy sauce, mirin, ginger, sugar and 1 tablespoon water in a saucepan and cook, stirring constantly, over medium heat until the sugar has dissolved. Cover and keep warm.

2 Cut the nori sheets into twelve 4 cm (1¹/2 inch) wide strips with scissors. Wrap a strip around each mushroom, dampening the end to help it stick. Cut the orange sweet potato into ribbon strips with a vegetable peeler.

3 Fill a wok one-third full of oil and heat to 190°C (375°F), or until a cube of bread dropped into the oil browns in 10 seconds. Cook the sweet potato in batches for about 30–60 seconds, or until golden and crispy. Drain on crumpled paper towels, season and keep warm.

4 Put the soda water and egg in a large bowl and whisk well. Add the tempura flour and wasabi powder and loosely mix in with chopsticks or a fork until just combined—the batter should still be lumpy. Coat the mushrooms in the batter and cook in batches for 1–2 minutes, or until golden and crisp, turning once. Drain on crumpled paper towels and season with salt. Serve immediately with the sweet potato ribbons and the sauce.

*ABOVE: Nori-wrapped fried mushrooms*

243

**RAITA**

Plain (or natural) yoghurt is used extensively in Indian cooking, less so in other Asian countries. It is rare for an Indian meal to be served without some form of yoghurt and raitas are one of the most widely served accompaniments. Raitas are a mixture of plain yoghurt and another raw or cooked ingredient—cucumber being one of the most popular additions because of its refreshing taste. Other popular additions are white gourd and potatoes. The soothing, cooling quality of yoghurt counter-balances the spiciness and heat of the food. Greek- or European-style unflavoured plain yoghurts are ideal for making raita, as they are slightly sour and thick and creamy. To make your own raita, see page 86.

## VEGETABLE PAKORAS

Preparation time: 30 minutes +
    15 minutes standing
Total cooking time: 20 minutes
Serves 4

☆ ☆

¹/₃ cup (35 g/1¹/₄ oz) besan (chickpea flour)
¹/₃ cup (40 g/1¹/₄ oz) self-raising flour
¹/₃ cup (45 g/1¹/₄ oz) soy flour
¹/₂ teaspoon ground turmeric
1 teaspoon cayenne pepper
¹/₂ teaspoon ground coriander
1 small fresh green chilli, seeded and finely
    chopped
200 g (6¹/₂ oz) cauliflower
140 g (4¹/₂ oz) orange sweet potato
180 g (6 oz) eggplant (aubergine)
180 g (6 oz) fresh asparagus
oil, for deep-frying
raita, to serve (see page 86)

1 Sift the besan, self-raising and soy flours into a bowl, then add the ground turmeric, cayenne pepper, ground coriander, chilli and 1 teaspoon salt. Gradually whisk in 1 cup (250 ml/8 fl oz)

*ABOVE: Vegetable pakoras*

cold water until a batter forms. Set aside for 15 minutes. Preheat the oven to very slow 120°C (250°F/Gas ¹/₂).
2 Meanwhile, cut the cauliflower into small florets. Cut the orange sweet potato and eggplant into 5 mm (¹/₄ inch) slices, and cut the asparagus into 6 cm (2¹/₂ inch) lengths.
3 Fill a wok one-third full with oil and heat to 170°C (325°F), or until a cube of bread dropped in the oil browns in 20 seconds. Dip the vegetables in the batter, then deep-fry them in small batches, for 1–2 minutes, or until pale golden. Remove with a slotted spoon and drain on crumpled paper towels. Keep warm in the oven until all the vegetables are cooked. Serve with the raita or plain yoghurt.

### DEEP-FRIED CORIANDER

Fill a wok one-third full of oil and heat to 180°C (350°F), or until a cube of bread dropped in the oil browns in 15 seconds. Remove the leaves from a bunch of coriander and deep-fry in batches for 30 seconds, or until crisp. Remove with a slotted spoon and drain on crumpled paper towels. Use as a garnish.

# COCONUT PRAWNS WITH CHILLI DRESSING

Preparation time: 35 minutes +
   30 minutes refrigeration
Total cooking time: 30 minutes
Serves 4 as an entrée

24 raw large prawns, peeled and deveined,
   with tails intact

plain flour, to coat

1 egg

1 tablespoon milk

1 cup (60 g/2 oz) shredded coconut

1/2 cup (25 g/3/4 oz) chopped fresh coriander
   leaves

21/2 tablespoons vegetable oil

300 g (10 oz) red Asian shallots, chopped

2 cloves garlic, finely chopped

2 teaspoons finely chopped fresh ginger

1 fresh red chilli, seeded and thinly sliced

1 teaspoon ground turmeric

270 ml (9 fl oz) coconut cream

2 kaffir lime leaves, thinly sliced

2 teaspoons lime juice

2 teaspoons palm sugar

3 teaspoons fish sauce

oil, for deep-frying

1 tablespoon chopped fresh coriander leaves,
   extra

150 g (5 oz) mixed lettuce leaves

1 Holding the prawns by their tails, coat them in
flour, then dip them into the combined egg and
milk and then in the combined coconut and
coriander. Refrigerate for 30 minutes.
2 Heat the oil in a saucepan and cook the
shallots, garlic, ginger, chilli and turmeric over
medium heat for 3–5 minutes, or until fragrant.
Add the coconut cream, lime leaves, lime juice,
sugar and fish sauce. Bring to the boil, then
reduce the heat and simmer for 2–3 minutes,
or until thick. Keep warm.
3 Fill a wok one-third full of oil and heat to
170°C (325°F), or until a cube of bread dropped
in the oil browns in 20 seconds. Gently lower
the prawns into the wok and cook in batches for
3–5 minutes, or until golden. Drain on crumpled
paper towels and season with salt.
4 Add the extra coriander to the dressing.
Divide the lettuce among four bowls, top with
the prawns and drizzle with the dressing.

## CRISP FRIED ONION

Slice 1 onion into paper-thin slices with a
very sharp knife, then drain on paper
towels for 10 minutes. Fill a deep, heavy-
based saucepan one-third full of vegetable
oil and heat to 160°C (315°F), or until a
cube of bread browns in 30–35 seconds.
Cook the onion in batches for about
1 minute, or until brown and crispy. Drain
on paper towels. Cool and store in an
airtight container for up to 2 weeks. Use as
a garnish and flavour enhancer in
Indonesian rice and noodle dishes. Makes
1 cup (serves 12).

*BELOW: Coconut prawns
with chilli dressing*

# YUM CHA

The Chinese tradition of *yum cha*, also known as *dim sum*, has become a leisurely weekend social occasion, not just in southern China where it originated, but also in Chinatowns across the world. Enjoyed for the diversity of small dishes offered, it is a visual and gastronomic feast that is enjoyed without a single menu in sight.

Yum cha literally means 'drink tea' in Cantonese and it brings together two of the great Chinese traditions: drinking tea and eating. The origins of yum cha are that in the Sung Dynasty (960–1279 AD), special tea houses were built where men could gather to do business, relax or catch up on the news. Cooks at the tea houses produced delectable snacks to serve with the tea, and these became known as dim sum. From these beginnings, the Cantonese developed yum cha into an art form. Gradually, specialities from other regions of China, such as Shanghai's soup dumplings (page 276), have been incorporated into the enormous yum cha repertoire.

Tea is the perfect accompaniment to yum cha. Not only does it aid digestion, but it also cleanses the palate and neutralises the oiliness of fried foods. Tea is so important that, in many traditional yum cha restaurants, the first step before even looking at the food is to choose which tea to drink.

## WHAT TO CHOOSE?

Numerous shapes, flavours, colours and textures provide diversity in dim sums. Most yum cha choices consist of some form of dumpling, bun or roll, with a wrapping of dough based on white flour (commonly either wheat, rice or tapioca). Because the array is so great, it is important that yum cha offerings are aesthetically pleasing, simply so that they get noticed among the myriad other offerings. Appearance is important for another reason— the experienced yum cha eye can deduce the filling by looking at the differing wrappers, shapes and sizes of the dumplings. There are four main groups of dishes.

The first and predominant are the steamed dim sum. Recipes for some of the most popular steamed dim sum are included in the Steaming chapter. These include such favourites as Steamed pork buns (page 270), Prawn gow gees (page 290) and Classic steamed pork and prawn dumplings (page 282).

The second group are the deep-fried dishes, with some famous yum cha recipes included in the Deep-frying chapter, such as Chinese spring rolls (page 252) and Gow gees (page 252).

The third group is the variety group, which encompasses anything that doesn't fit neatly into one of the other categories.

The fourth group are the sweet offerings, such as yum cha favourites custard tarts and mango pudding, or steamed sponge cake and coconut jelly. Many of these can be purchased from Chinese-style bakeries.

## YUM CHA AT HOME

The following recipes represent typical yum cha selections. Just like eating yum cha in a restaurant, the choice is yours—based on time and appetite you can decide how few or how many of these dishes to have and whether to round out the menu with some bought items from a Chinese bakery.

### STEAMED
- Vegetable dumplings, page 266
- Sticky rice and pork pockets, page 268
- Steamed pork buns, page 270
- Soup dumplings, page 276
- Chinese steamed chicken and rice parcels, page 277
- Yum cha steamed pork ribs in black bean sauce, page 282
- Classic steamed pork and prawn dumplings, page 282
- Pearl balls, page 288

- Prawn gow gees, page 290
- Pork and chive dumplings, page 287
- Rice noodle rolls filled with prawns, page 292
- Steamed pork and water chestnut dumplings, page 293
- Steamed vegetable rolls, page 294

### DEEP-FRIED
- Chicken and mushroom rice paper parcels, page 242
- Chinese spring rolls, page 252
- Gow gees, page 252
- Crispy vegetables in bean curd sheets, page 254
- Prawn toasts, page 258
- Stuffed pepper (capsicum) pieces, page 259

*CLOCKWISE, FROM TOP LEFT: Steamed gai larn; Stuffed pepper pieces; Steamed pork buns; Classic steamed pork and prawn dumplings; Chinese spring rolls.*

# CORN PANCAKES
(Tod man kaopot)

Preparation time: 15 minutes +
  1 hour refrigeration
Total cooking time: 25 minutes
Makes 12

6 fresh corn cobs or 325 g (11 oz) can corn
  kernels, drained
4 spring onions, finely chopped
1 clove garlic, crushed
1 teaspoon Asian curry powder
2 tablespoons self-raising flour
1 teaspoon soy sauce
1 egg
oil, for deep-frying
sweet chilli sauce, to serve (optional)

1 If using fresh corn, remove the kernels with a sharp knife. Combine the corn, spring onion, garlic, curry powder, flour, soy sauce and egg, mashing lightly with a potato masher. Cover with plastic wrap and chill for 1 hour.

*BELOW: Corn pancakes*

2 Fill a wok one-third full of oil and heat to 180°C (350°F), or until a cube of bread browns in 15 seconds. Drop tablespoons of the corn mixture into the wok—avoid overcrowding. Cook for 2–3 minutes, on each side, or until golden brown—turn carefully to prevent the pancakes breaking. Remove from the wok and drain on crumpled paper towels. Repeat with the remaining mixture. Serve with sweet chilli sauce, if desired.

# RAINBOW BEEF

Preparation time: 25 minutes +
  40 minutes freezing + 2 hours marinating +
  15 minutes resting
Total cooking time: 20 minutes
Serves 4

☆ ☆ ☆

500 g (1 lb) rump steak
1 tablespoon Chinese rice wine
1 teaspoon bicarbonate of soda
1/2 teaspoon sugar
1/8 teaspoon ground Sichuan peppercorns
2 tablespoons cornflour
1 egg white, lightly beaten
peanut oil, for deep-frying
1 carrot, cut into 5 cm (2 inch) lengths and
  finely julienned
2 spring onions, cut into 5 cm (2 inch) lengths
  and finely julienned, plus extra, to garnish

SAUCE
1 tablespoon very finely chopped garlic
2 teaspoons very finely chopped fresh ginger
2 tablespoons Japanese rice vinegar
1 1/2 tablespoons dark soy sauce
1 1/2 tablespoons Chinese rice wine
1–1 1/2 teaspoons chilli bean paste
1/4 cup (60 g/2 oz) sugar
2–3 drops of sesame oil

1 Wrap the meat in plastic wrap and place it in the freezer for about 40 minutes, or until semi-frozen to make it easier to slice. Remove the plastic wrap and cut into very thin, even, 5 cm (2 inch) long slices across the grain. Cut each slice into thin, julienne strips a few millimetres (up to 1/4 inch) wide. Toss the beef with the combined Chinese rice wine, bicarbonate of

soda, sugar, peppercorns and ¼ teaspoon salt, then cover and refrigerate for 2 hours.
**2** Combine the cornflour with the egg white, then combine with the beef and rest for 15 minutes.
**3** Meanwhile, fill a wok one-third full of peanut oil and heat to 190°C (375°F), or until a cube of bread dropped into the oil browns in 10 seconds. Deep-fry the carrot for 1–2 minutes, or until starting to go brown and crispy around the edges, then drain on paper towels. Add the spring onion and cook for 1 minute, or until a little crispy, then drain well and add to the carrot.
**4** Cook the beef in small batches by pulling small handfuls of the strips apart, then adding them to the oil, separating well with long chopsticks so they don't clump together. Cook for 1–2 minutes, or until golden. Drain well on paper towels and cool to room temperature. Deep-fry a second time at the same temperature for 1 minute, or until dark brown and crisp, then drain. This second frying helps to make the beef extra crispy.
**5** To make the sauce, heat a clean wok to very hot, add a drizzle of the deep-frying oil and swirl. Add the garlic and ginger and stir-fry for a few seconds, or until fragrant, then add the vinegar, soy sauce, rice wine, chilli bean paste, sugar, sesame oil and ⅓ cup (80 ml/2¾ fl oz) water and bring to the boil. Cook for 1 minute, or until caramelised and glazed.
**6** Add the beef strips, carrot and spring onion to the wok and toss together well. Sprinkle with spring onion, and serve with rice or as part of an Asian banquet.

## MONEY BAGS
(Toong ngern young)

Preparation time: 30 minutes + cooling
Total cooking time: 15 minutes
Makes 30

☆☆☆

1 tablespoon peanut oil
4 red Asian shallots, finely chopped
2 cloves garlic, crushed
1 tablespoon grated fresh ginger
150 g (5 oz) chicken mince
150 g (5 oz) pork mince
2 teaspoons light soy sauce
¼ cup (40 g/1¼ oz) roasted peanuts, chopped
2 teaspoons grated palm sugar
2 teaspoons lime juice

3 teaspoons fish sauce
3 tablespoons finely chopped fresh coriander leaves
30 won ton wrappers
oil, for deep-frying
garlic chives, for tying

**1** Heat a wok over medium heat, add the oil and swirl to coat. Add the shallots, garlic and ginger and cook for 1–2 minutes, or until the shallots are soft. Add the minces and cook for 4 minutes, or until cooked, breaking up the lumps.
**2** Stir in the soy sauce, peanuts, palm sugar, lime juice, fish sauce and coriander. Cook, stirring, for 1–2 minutes, or until mixed and dry. Cool.
**3** Place 2 teaspoons of the filling in the centre of each won ton wrapper—lightly brush the edges with water. Lift the sides up tightly and pinch around the filling to form a bag. Trim.
**4** Fill a clean wok one-third full of oil and heat to 190°C (375°F), or until a cube of bread dropped in the oil browns in 10 seconds. Cook in batches for 30–60 seconds, or until golden and crisp. Drain. Tie with the chives.

*ABOVE: Money bags*

LEMON CHICKEN
This popular meal of fried chicken glazed with a tart, lemony sauce features on the menus of Cantonese restaurants all around the world. While ready-made lemon sauce is widely available, it often relies on artificial colouring to achieve its sunny yellow colour, and it can be quite gluggy, so it is preferable to make your own.

## LEMON CHICKEN

Preparation time: 15 minutes
Total cooking time: 20 minutes
Serves 4

☆ ☆

800 g (1 lb 10 oz) chicken breast or thigh fillets, trimmed
1 egg, lightly beaten
cornflour, to coat
oil, for deep-frying
1/2 cup (125 ml/4 fl oz) lemon juice
1 tablespoon white vinegar
1/4 cup (60 g/2 oz) sugar
11/2 tablespoons cornflour, extra
sliced spring onions, to garnish
lemon, to garnish

1 Season the chicken with salt and freshly ground black pepper. Coat with the egg, then the cornflour, shaking off any excess.
2 Fill a wok one-third full of oil and heat to 180°C (350°F), or until a cube of bread browns in 15 seconds. Add the chicken in batches and cook for 6 minutes, or until golden brown and cooked through. Drain on paper towels.
3 Combine the lemon juice, vinegar, sugar and 1/4 cup (60 ml/2 fl oz) water in a small saucepan, and stir over low heat until the sugar dissolves. Bring to the boil, then reduce the heat and simmer for 1–2 minutes. Combine the extra cornflour with 1/4 cup (60 ml/2 fl oz) water, add to the pan and mix well. Cook for 1 minute, or until the sauce boils and thickens.
4 To serve, slice the chicken, spoon on the sauce and garnish with the spring onion and lemon. Serve with rice.

## CRISPY LAMB WITH LETTUCE

Preparation time: 15 minutes +
  30 minutes freezing + 3 hours marinating
Total cooking time: 20 minutes
Serves 4

☆ ☆

400 g (13 oz) lamb loin fillets (e.g. backstraps or sirloin)
2 tablespoons light soy sauce
1 tablespoon Chinese rice wine
2 teaspoons fish sauce
1/2 teaspoon sesame oil
2 cloves garlic, crushed
1 teaspoon finely grated fresh ginger
1/3 cup (40 g/11/4 oz) cornflour
1 cup (250 ml/8 fl oz) vegetable oil
12 baby cos lettuce leaves
plum sauce, to serve
4 spring onions, thinly sliced on the diagonal

*ABOVE: Lemon chicken*

1 Wrap the lamb in plastic wrap and put it in the freezer for 30 minutes, or until semi-frozen. Remove the plastic wrap and cut the lamb lengthways into three thin slices, then thinly slice across the grain, so that you have julienne strips. Place the lamb in a bowl with the soy sauce, rice wine, fish sauce, sesame oil, garlic and ginger. Mix well to coat, then cover and refrigerate for 2 hours.
2 Sift the cornflour over the lamb and mix well. Spread the lamb out on a tray, and return to the refrigerator, uncovered, for 1 hour.
3 Preheat the oven to slow 150°C (300°F/ Gas 2). Heat the oil in a wok to 180°C (350°F), or until a cube of bread browns in 15 seconds. Deep-fry the lamb in batches for 5–6 minutes, or until crisp and browned. Lift the pieces of lamb out with a slotted spoon and drain on crumpled paper towels. Keep warm in the oven while waiting for the remainder to cook.
4 To serve, cup a lettuce leaf in your hand. With the other hand, drizzle the inside with a little plum sauce, fill with the lamb mixture and sprinkle with spring onion. Alternatively, arrange the lamb, lettuce, spring onion and plum sauce in separate dishes for your guests to assemble their own 'cups'.

## PORK AND NOODLE BALLS WITH SWEET CHILLI SAUCE

Preparation time: 30 minutes
Total cooking time: 20 minutes
Makes 30

☆☆☆

**Dipping sauce**
1/3 cup (80 ml/2 3/4 fl oz) sweet chilli sauce
2 teaspoons mirin
2 teaspoons finely chopped fresh ginger
1/2 cup (125 ml/4 fl oz) Japanese soy sauce

250 g (8 oz) Hokkien noodles
300 g (10 oz) pork mince
6 spring onions, finely chopped
2 cloves garlic, crushed
4 tablespoons finely chopped fresh coriander leaves
1 tablespoon fish sauce
2 tablespoons oyster sauce
1 1/2 tablespoons lime juice
peanut oil, for deep-frying

1 To make the dipping sauce, combine the sweet chilli sauce, mirin, ginger and Japanese soy sauce in a bowl.
2 Place the noodles in a bowl and cover with boiling water. Soak for 1 minute, or until tender. Drain very well and pat dry with paper towels. Cut the noodles into 5 cm (2 inch) lengths, then transfer to a large bowl. Add the pork mince, spring onion, garlic, coriander leaves, fish sauce, oyster sauce and lime juice and combine the mixture well using your hands, making sure the pork is evenly distributed.
3 Using a tablespoon of mixture at a time, roll each spoonful into a ball to make 30 in total, shaping and pressing each ball firmly with your hands to ensure they remain intact.
4 Fill a wok one-third full of oil and heat to 170°C (325°F), or until a cube of bread browns in 20 seconds. Deep-fry the pork balls in batches for 2–3 minutes, or until golden and cooked through. Drain on crumpled paper towels. Serve hot with the dipping sauce.

*BELOW: Pork and noodle balls with sweet chilli sauce*

## CRISPY VEGETABLES IN BEAN CURD SHEETS

Preparation time: 15 minutes + 30 minutes
    soaking + cooling + 30 minutes refrigeration
Total cooking time: 10 minutes
Makes 6

☆☆

4 large dried shiitake mushrooms
2 tablespoons peanut oil
1 teaspoon grated fresh ginger
2 spring onions, thinly sliced
1 small carrot, julienned
100 g (3½ oz) bamboo shoots, julienned
50 g (1¾ oz) firm tofu, finely chopped
1 tablespoon light soy sauce
½ teaspoon sugar
2 teaspoons cornflour
6 bean curd sheets each 20 x 25 cm
    (8 x 10 inches)
extra peanut oil, for deep-frying

1 Soak the mushrooms in hot water for
20 minutes. Squeeze dry, discard the stalks and finely chop the caps.

2 To make the filling, heat a wok over high heat, add the oil and swirl to coat. Add the mushrooms, ginger, spring onion, carrot, bamboo shoots and tofu, and stir-fry over medium–high heat for 1 minute. Add the soy sauce, sugar and ½ teaspoon salt and cook for a further minute, tossing all the ingredients together. Transfer to a colander sitting over a bowl, and allow to drain and cool.

3 Combine the cornflour with 1 tablespoon water to form a paste. Soak the bean curd sheets in lukewarm water for 10–15 seconds to soften, then drain well and pat dry with paper towels. Lay a sheet on a work surface and brush the edges with the cornflour paste. Place 2 tablespoons of filling at one end of the sheet, then fold the edges over towards the centre and roll up to form a neat rectangular parcel. Repeat with the remaining sheets and filling to make six large rolls. Refrigerate for at least 30 minutes, or until ready to use.

4 Fill a wok one-third full of peanut oil and heat to 180°C (350°F), or until a cube of bread browns in 15 seconds. Deep-fry the rolls in batches for 2–3 minutes each, or until crisp and golden. Drain on crumpled paper towels and serve immediately.

BEAN CURD SHEETS
Dried bean curd sheets are made from drying the thin skin that forms on the surface when soy milk is boiled. Purchased in large bags in Asian grocery stores, bean curd sheets are wrinkled, flat sheets that require brief soaking in warm water before using, to make them pliable. Take care when handling, as they can be quite brittle and break or tear easily. They are a source of protein in the Buddhist vegetarian diet, and are mainly used for wrapping ingredients to be steamed or deep-fried, or used to add texture and protein to soups, braised dishes and some stir-fries.

*RIGHT: Crispy vegetables in bean curd sheets*

# SPICED PRAWN PAKORAS

Preparation time: 20 minutes
Total cooking time: 10 minutes
Makes 16

☆ ☆

<sup></sup>3/4 cup (85 g/3 oz) besan (chickpea flour)
1/2 teaspoon baking powder
1/4 teaspoon ground turmeric
1 teaspoon ground coriander
1/2 teaspoon ground cumin
1/2 teaspoon chilli powder
oil, for deep-frying
1 tablespoon egg white
16 raw medium prawns, peeled and deveined,
   with tails intact

DIPPING SAUCE
1 cup (250 g/8 oz) plain yoghurt
3 tablespoons chopped fresh coriander leaves
1 teaspoon ground cumin
garam masala, to sprinkle

1 Sift the besan, baking powder and spices into a large bowl and season with a little salt. Make a well in the centre, gradually add 1 cup (250 ml/

8 fl oz) water and stir gently until mixed.
2 Fill a wok one-third full of oil and heat to 160°C (315°F), or until a cube of bread dropped in the oil browns in 30–35 seconds. Beat the egg white until firm peaks form, and fold into the batter. Using the tail as a handle, dip the prawns into the batter, then lower gently into the oil.
3 Cook about four prawns at a time, without overcrowding the wok. Cook for 2 minutes, until the batter is lightly golden; it won't become really crisp. Drain on paper towels.
4 To make the dipping sauce, combine the yoghurt, coriander and cumin. Sprinkle with the garam masala. Serve with the prawns.

## MERMAID'S TRESSES

Very finely shred the leaves from 350 g (11 oz) bok choy or choy sum and dry with paper towels. Fill a wok one-third full of peanut oil and heat to 180°C (350°F), or until a cube of bread browns in 15 seconds. Deep-fry the shreds, a handful at a time, for about 20 seconds, or until they stop sizzling and darken—they burn easily, so be careful. Drain on crumpled paper towels. Sprinkle with caster sugar and salt.
NOTE: These are a popular snack in China. Alternatively, they can be used as a garnish.

PAKORAS
Popular in India, pakoras are deep-fried fritters made by coating various ingredients, such as seafood, vegetables and meat, in a batter made from besan flour, which itself is made from finely ground chickpeas. These crispy treats are usually eaten as a snack or appetiser.

*ABOVE: Spiced prawn pakoras*

## SESAME SEEDS

A tropical or subtropical plant that produces seed pods that, when dried, burst open and then are shaken to encourage the release of hundreds of tiny seeds. Sesame seeds are usually cream in colour, but may also be yellow, reddish or black, depending on the variety. The seeds can be used raw, but when toasted, take on a nutty, slightly sweet flavour. The seed consists of about 50 per cent oil and, due to this, the seeds become rancid quickly. Purchase in small amounts or store in the fridge for up to 3 months. Sesame seeds are used around the world, and in China and Japan are further utilised by being toasted and pressed into sesame oil.

*ABOVE: Honey prawns*

## HONEY PRAWNS

Preparation time: 20 minutes
Total cooking time: 15 minutes
Serves 4

☆ ☆

16 raw large prawns
cornflour, for dusting
oil, for deep-frying
3 egg whites, lightly beaten
2 tablespoons cornflour, extra
2 tablespoons vegetable oil, extra
1/4 cup (90 g/3 oz) honey
2 tablespoons sesame seeds, toasted

1 Peel and devein the prawns, leaving the tails intact. Pat them dry and lightly dust with the cornflour, shaking off any excess. Fill a wok one-third full of oil and heat to 180°C (350°F), or until a cube of bread dropped in the oil browns in 15 seconds.
2 Beat the egg whites in a clean dry bowl until soft peaks form. Add the extra cornflour and some salt and gently whisk until combined and smooth. Using the tail as a handle, dip the prawns in the batter, then slowly lower them into the oil. Cook in batches for 3–4 minutes, or until crisp and golden and the prawns are cooked. Remove with a slotted spoon, then drain on crumpled paper towels and keep warm.

3 Heat the extra oil and honey in a saucepan over medium heat for 2–3 minutes, or until bubbling. Place the prawns on a serving plate and pour on the honey sauce. Sprinkle with the sesame seeds and serve immediately with steamed rice.

## CAULIFLOWER KOFTA

Preparation time: 10 minutes
Total cooking time: 15 minutes
Makes 16

☆ ☆

300 g (10 oz) cauliflower florets
100 g (3 1/2 oz) cabbage, shredded
1/3 cup (10 g/1/4 oz) fresh coriander leaves
1 large green chilli, chopped
2 cloves garlic, chopped
1/2 cup (55 g/2 oz) besan (chickpea flour)
1/2 teaspoon ground cumin
1/2 teaspoon ground coriander
1/2 teaspoon garam masala
oil, for deep-frying
raita, to serve (see page 86)

1 Put the cauliflower, cabbage, coriander, chilli and garlic in a food processor, and blend well.
2 Scrape the cauliflower mixture into a bowl

and stir in the besan, cumin, ground coriander, garam masala and 1/2 teaspoon salt. Take 1 tablespoon of the mixture and shape into a ball. Repeat with the remaining mixture.
**3** Fill a wok one-third full of oil and heat to 170°C (325°F), or until a cube of bread browns in 20 seconds. Deep-fry the kofta balls in batches for 3–4 minutes, or until golden and the cauliflower is cooked through. Serve with raita.

## DEEP-FRIED CHICKEN BALLS

Preparation time: 20 minutes +
  30 minutes refrigeration
Total cooking time: 15 minutes
Makes about 30

☆☆

50 g (1 3/4 oz) dried rice vermicelli
500 g (1 lb) chicken mince
3 cloves garlic, finely chopped
1 tablespoon chopped fresh ginger
1 fresh red chilli, seeded and finely chopped
1 egg, lightly beaten
2 spring onions, finely sliced
4 tablespoons chopped fresh coriander leaves
1/3 cup (40 g/1 1/4 oz) plain flour
1/3 cup (60 g/2 oz) finely chopped water chestnuts
oil, for deep-frying

### DIPPING SAUCE
1/2 cup (125 ml/4 fl oz) sweet chilli sauce
1/2 cup (125 ml/4 fl oz) soy sauce
1 tablespoon Chinese rice wine

**1** Put the vermicelli in a heatproof bowl, cover with boiling water and soak for 6–7 minutes. Drain, then cut into short lengths—scissors are the easiest tool for the job.
**2** Combine the mince, garlic, ginger, chilli, egg, spring onion, coriander, flour and water chestnuts in a large bowl. Mix in the chopped lengths of vermicelli, then season with a little salt. Cover with plastic wrap and refrigerate for 30 minutes. Roll heaped tablespoons of the mixture into balls.
**3** Fill a wok or deep saucepan one-third full with oil and heat to 180°C (350°F), or until a cube of bread dropped into the oil browns in 15 seconds. Deep-fry the balls in batches for 2 minutes, or until golden brown and cooked through, then drain on crumpled paper towels.
**4** To make the dipping sauce, combine the sweet chilli sauce, soy sauce and rice wine. Serve with the hot chicken balls. Provide toothpicks or cocktail sticks to pick up the hot balls.

SWEET CHILLI SAUCE
This sticky, sweet condiment is especially popular in Thailand and Malaysia. It is commonly used as a dipping sauce, or in stir-fried noodle dishes. The Malaysian version is less sweet, with a stronger chilli bite.

*LEFT: Deep-fried chicken balls*

# PRAWN TOASTS

Preparation time: 20 minutes
Total cooking time: 15 minutes
Makes 36

☆ ☆

DIPPING SAUCE
1/2 cup (125 ml/4 fl oz) tomato sauce
2 cloves garlic, crushed
2 small fresh red chillies, seeded and finely
    chopped
2 tablespoons hoisin sauce
2 teaspoons Worcestershire sauce

350 g (11 oz) raw medium prawns
1 clove garlic
75 g (2 1/2 oz) canned water chestnuts, drained
1 tablespoon chopped fresh coriander

2 x 2 cm (3/4 x 3/4 inch) piece fresh ginger,
    roughly chopped
2 eggs, separated
1/4 teaspoon white pepper
12 slices white bread, crusts removed
1 cup (155 g/5 oz) sesame seeds
oil, for deep-frying

1 To make the dipping sauce, combine the tomato sauce, garlic, chillies, hoisin sauce and Worcestershire sauce in a small bowl.
2 Peel the prawns and gently pull out the dark vein from each prawn back, starting at the head end. Put the prawns in a food processor with the garlic, water chestnuts, coriander, ginger, egg whites, pepper and 1/4 teaspoon salt and process for 20–30 seconds, or until smooth.
3 Brush the top of each slice of bread with lightly beaten egg yolk, then spread evenly with the prawn mixture. Sprinkle generously with sesame seeds. Cut each slice of bread into three even strips.
4 Fill a large wok one-third full of oil and heat to 180°C (350°F), or until a cube of bread dropped into the oil browns in 15 seconds. Deep-fry the toasts in small batches for 10–15 seconds, or until golden and crisp. Start with the prawn mixture face down, then turn halfway through. Remove the toasts from the oil with tongs or a slotted spoon and drain on crumpled paper towels. Serve with the dipping sauce.

*BELOW: Prawn toasts*

---

# CANDIED WALNUTS

Put 125 g (4 oz) walnuts in a saucepan and cover with water. Bring to the boil, then boil for 2 minutes. Drain, then return to the pan with 1/2 cup (125 g/4 oz) sugar and 1/2 cup (125 ml/4 fl oz) water and cook for 10 minutes. Drain. Coat the nuts in honey. Fill a wok or large saucepan one-third full of oil and heat to 180°C (350°F), or until a cube of bread dropped into the oil browns in 15 seconds. Deep-fry the walnuts for 5–8 minutes, or until golden. Drain on crumpled paper towels, then sprinkle with sesame seeds. Serve as a snack. Makes 1 cup.

# STUFFED PEPPER
## (CAPSICUM) PIECES

Preparation time: 10 minutes +
  30 minutes refrigeration
Total cooking time: 30 minutes
Makes 24

2 green peppers (capsicums)
cornflour, for dusting
400 g (13 oz) pork mince
3 spring onions, chopped
2 cloves garlic, crushed
1 tablespoon light soy sauce
2 teaspoons chopped fresh ginger
2 teaspoons oyster sauce
2 teaspoons Chinese rice wine
1 teaspoon cornflour
1 egg, lightly beaten
1/2 teaspoon caster sugar
oil, for deep-frying
fresh coriander leaves, to garnish

SAUCE
11/2 cups (375 ml/12 fl oz) good-quality
  chicken stock
2 tablespoons black beans, rinsed and mashed
  with a fork
1 tablespoon light soy sauce
3 teaspoons cornflour combined with
  1/3 cup (80 ml/23/4 fl oz) water
2 teaspoons oyster sauce

1 Cut the peppers in half lengthways, then remove and discard the seeds and membrane. Cut each half into three wide strips, then in half crossways to give 24 pieces in total. Dust each capsicum piece with some cornflour.
2 Put the pork mince in a food processor with the spring onion, garlic, soy sauce, ginger, oyster sauce, Chinese wine, cornflour, egg and caster sugar. Season with 1/4 teaspoon salt and process in short bursts until well combined.
3 Place about 2 tablespoons of the mixture on the inside surface of each pepper piece, pressing firmly to help it stick. Cover and refrigerate for 30 minutes.
4 Fill a wok one-third full of oil and heat to 170°C (325°F), or until a cube of bread dropped in the oil browns in 20 seconds. Add the stuffed pepper with the stuffing facing up, and cook four pieces at a time for 3–4 minutes, or until golden and completely cooked through. Remove with a slotted spoon and drain on crumpled paper towels.
5 Remove all but 1 tablespoon oil from the wok. To make the sauce, add the stock, black beans and soy sauce to the wok, and bring to the boil. Slowly pour the cornflour mixture into the boiling stock mixture and stir for 1 minute, or until thickened. Simmer for 1–2 minutes, or until slightly reduced, then remove from the heat and stir in the oyster sauce. Arrange the stuffed peppers on a serving plate, drizzle with the sauce, garnish with coriander and serve immediately.

*ABOVE: Stuffed pepper pieces*

FIVE-SPICE
This is a Chinese mixed spice generally made with star anise, cassia (sometimes cinnamon), Sichuan pepper, fennel seeds and cloves, which gives a balance of sweet, hot and aromatic flavours. Five-spice may also include cardamom, coriander, dried orange peel and ginger. It is used ground together as a powder or as whole spices tied in muslin.

*ABOVE: Crispy-skin chicken with five-spice dipping salt*

# CRISPY-SKIN CHICKEN WITH FIVE-SPICE DIPPING SALT

Preparation time: 10 minutes +
    5 hours 15 minutes standing
Total cooking time: 50 minutes
Serves 4–6

☆ ☆ ☆

1.6 kg (3¼ lb) chicken
3 star anise
2 cinnamon sticks
1 piece dried tangerine or orange peel
1 x 2 cm (½ x ¾ inch) piece fresh ginger,
    lightly smashed
½ cup (125 ml/4 fl oz) dark soy sauce
¼ cup (60 ml/2 fl oz) light soy sauce
⅓ cup (80 ml/2¾ fl oz) Chinese rice wine
¼ cup (60 g/2 oz) sugar
2 litres (64 fl oz) oil, for deep-frying
coriander sprigs, to garnish

GLAZE
¼ cup (90 g/3 oz) honey
2 tablespoons dark soy sauce
2 tablespoons Chinese black vinegar

DIPPING SALT
1 tablespoon fine salt
1 teaspoon five-spice powder
½ teaspoon Sichuan peppercorns
1 teaspoon sugar (optional)

1 Rinse the chicken, pat dry with paper towels and remove any excess fat from the cavity. In a saucepan or pot just large enough to hold the chicken, combine the star anise, cinnamon sticks, tangerine peel, ginger, dark soy sauce, light soy sauce, Chinese rice wine and sugar with 2 litres (64 fl oz) water. Bring to the boil, then reduce to a simmer.
2 Carefully lower the chicken into the simmering liquid and, if necessary, add enough water to just cover the chicken. Simmer for 30 minutes, then remove the pan from the heat and allow the chicken to rest in the liquid for a further 10 minutes. Remove the chicken from the liquid, being careful not to break the skin, and put it on a wire rack over a plate or baking tray for 3 hours in the refrigerator—do not cover the chicken or the skin won't dry properly. After 3 hours, the skin should be very dry and feel like parchment.
3 To make the glaze, put the ingredients in a small wok or saucepan with ¾ cup (185 ml/

6 fl oz) water. Bring to the boil, then brush the mixture over the chicken using a pastry brush, making sure that you coat all of the skin thoroughly. Leave the chicken to dry on the rack in the fridge for another 2 hours.

4 Meanwhile, to make the five-spice salt, heat a small wok or saucepan over low heat and add the salt, five-spice powder, peppercorns and sugar (if desired). Dry-fry for 3–4 minutes, or until the peppercorns turn black and smell fragrant. Sift the peppercorns out of the mixture and discard them. Divide the five-spice salt between two small dishes ready for serving.

5 Just before serving, heat the oil in a large wok over medium heat to 180°C (350°F), or until a piece of bread dropped in the oil browns in 15 seconds. Carefully lower the chicken into the oil and deep-fry on one side until it is a rich, dark brown colour and very crisp. Very carefully turn the chicken over and brown the other side. Extra caution is needed when turning the chicken in the wok as it may be heavy and awkward. When browned all over, carefully remove the chicken with a large sieve and drain well on crumpled paper towels. Sprinkle the skin with a little of the spice salt and allow the chicken to rest for 5 minutes.

6 To serve, use a cleaver or large kitchen knife to chop the chicken in half lengthways, then into pieces small enough that they can be picked up with chopsticks. Place the pieces on a platter, garnish with coriander sprigs and serve immediately with the five-spice salt.

# BONDAS

Preparation time: 30 minutes
Total cooking time: 25 minutes
Makes 24

☆☆

2 teaspoons vegetable oil
1 teaspoon brown mustard seeds
1 onion, finely chopped
2 teaspoons grated fresh ginger
4 curry leaves
3 small green chillies, finely chopped
1.2 kg (2 lb 6¹/2 oz) potatoes, diced and cooked
pinch of ground turmeric
2 tablespoons lemon juice
¹/3 cup (20 g/³/4 oz) chopped fresh coriander
    leaves
oil, for deep-frying

**Batter**
1 cup (110 g/3¹/2 o) besan (chickpea flour)
¹/4 cup (30 g/1 oz) self-raising flour
¹/4 cup (45 g/1¹/2 oz) rice flour
¹/4 teaspoon ground turmeric
1 teaspoon chilli powder

1 Heat a wok over medium heat, add the oil and swirl to coat. Add the mustard seeds and stir for 30 seconds, or until fragrant. Add the onion, ginger, curry leaves and chilli and cook for 2 minutes. Add the potato, turmeric and 2 teaspoons of water and stir for 2 minutes, or until the mixture is dry. Remove from the heat and cool. Stir in the lemon juice and coriander leaves, then season to taste. Using a heaped tablespoon, shape into 24 balls.

2 To make the batter, sift the flours, turmeric, chilli powder and ¹/4 teaspoon salt into a bowl. Make a well in the centre of the dry ingredients. Gradually whisk in 1¹/3 cups (350 ml/11 fl oz) water to make a smooth batter.

3 Fill a clean wok one-third full of oil and heat to 180°C (350°F), or until a cube of bread dropped into the oil browns in 15 seconds. Dip the balls into the batter, then cook in the hot oil, in batches, for 1–2 minutes, or until golden. Drain on crumpled paper towels and season with salt. Serve hot.

*BELOW: Bondas*

# STEAMING

If you're looking for the freshest and cleanest of flavours, steamed food will satisfy. Food is cooked gently in a way that preserves its inherent qualities, making it a joy to eat. Compared with the action of stir-frying, steaming is slow and harmonious, and believed by the Chinese to be healing. There is a wonderful array of steamed foods, from delicately steamed chicken to classic dumplings that will be familiar from yum cha. One of the best aspects of steaming food is that culinary artistry can be brought into use. Those carefully made won tons can be positioned prettily in a bamboo steamer basket and when cooked, taken directly to the table.

# HOW TO STEAM With a

wok and a steamer basket, you're ready to steam food, whether it be whole fish,

tasty dumplings or morsels wrapped in banana leaves.

## THE BENEFITS OF STEAMING
Steaming is one of the gentlest ways to cook food. Steamed food retains its inherent texture, shape and taste. But steaming can also invigorate dried or tough food by adding moisture and tenderness.

There are two methods of steaming. The most common involves cooking food over boiling liquid in a closed pot. The second method is to add a little water to a pot or wok, add the food, then cover with a lid and put over the heat, with the steam from the evaporated liquid cooking the food.

Steaming is a healthy cooking option, as foods are cooked by moist heat rather than being cooked in oil or fat.

## STEAMING ASIAN STYLE
Steaming is a fundamental feature of Asian cookery and occupies a much more important place than in the West. While in the West, steamed food is often considered bland and flavourless, and relegated to the 'dieter's cooking

method', in Asia it is as highly regarded for its restorative qualities as for its ease and aesthetic appeal. In Asian cuisines, steamed foods are often chosen as a delicate and subtle counterpoint to balance the more robust flavours of other dishes served at the same meal, such as curries, deep-fried dishes and stir-fries.

A vast array of Asian dishes take advantage of the attributes of steamed food. Many of the dumplings enjoyed at yum cha are steamed; for example, the yum cha favourite, steamed pork buns (page 270). In addition, many portable foods are steamed in a wrapping of banana, lotus or bamboo leaves, such as Chinese steamed chicken and rice parcels (page 277). A whole steamed fish takes pride of place at many Chinese banquets, particularly during New Year celebrations, as it is a sign of abundance.

## USING A WOK TO STEAM
A wok's broad sides and concave shape allow for a large surface area of water to produce steam, and enough room for the

steam to circulate freely and cook the food. Ensure that the wok is firmly balanced on the stove-top to avoid the hazards of spilled boiling water. The best woks for steaming are a two-handled wok, a flat-bottomed wok, a wok on a wok stand, or an electric wok.

Many Chinese cooks use separate woks for steaming and stir-frying because the hot water used for steaming strips off the seasoning layer that is so valued when stir-frying.

## OTHER STEAMING TOOLS
Apart from a wok (and its lid), the only other piece of equipment you need when steaming is some kind of rack or steamer to sit the food in.

Asian bamboo steamers are great for steaming—they are cheap, effective and can double up as a serving vessel. We have used bamboo steamers in most of our recipes, but there are other options.

You can use stainless steel or aluminium steamers. There are self-contained Chinese steamers of holed

insets that nestle into pots with a heatproof plate on top. Metal steamers are easier to clean and maintain than bamboo, but they are also more expensive and lack the aesthetic appeal of bamboo steamers.

Another option is to use a heatproof dish, such as a glass pie plate, or an Asian soup bowl. If you are using a bowl or plate, you'll need to rest it on a round cake rack that fits inside the wok—the idea is to prevent the plate from touching the water.

## USING A BAMBOO STEAMER

Bamboo steamers come in a range of sizes to fit any wok. For a standard 30–35 cm (12–14 inch) wok, look for steamer baskets about 25–32 cm (10–13 inches) in diameter—buy at least two baskets and a lid so that you can stack them and cook a larger quantity of food at the one time.

When using a bamboo steamer for the first time, immerse it in water for 15 minutes before use to get rid of the strong bamboo smell.

To stop food from sticking to the base of the steamer, the steamer either has to be oiled or lined. The benefit of lining the steamer is that it prevents food from absorbing the bamboo smell. Both baking paper and banana leaves work well— banana leaves have the advantage of being visually appealing.

Once the bamboo basket is lined and the food is in place, fit the lid on the steamer basket (you won't need the wok lid). Place the basket over a wok of simmering water. If you are using layers of baskets and cooking for a long time, swap their positions about halfway through the cooking time so that the food cooks evenly.

Although bamboo steamers are easy to maintain, they do need to be washed after each use and allowed to dry thoroughly before storing, especially after being used to cook strong-smelling food such as fish. If they are stored while still wet, they may mildew.

## TEMPERING

If you are using porcelain or ceramic bowls or dishes for steaming, temper them to prevent them from cracking during steaming. To temper a dish, place a cake rack in the wok, then sit the dish to be tempered on top. Add enough water to completely cover the dish. Cover with a lid, bring the water to the boil and boil for 10 minutes, then turn off the heat and allow the wok to cool to room temperature. The dish is then ready for use when steaming. There is no need to repeat this process—it will remain tempered for its lifetime.

## HINTS AND TIPS

● Fill the wok one-third full of boiling water, or cold water and bring to the boil. Use too much water and it will boil up into the food, spoiling it, or too little and run the risk of it boiling dry.

*STEPS TO STEAMING*

*Bamboo steamers are cheap, attractive and easy to use. Line the base with baking paper to prevent the food sticking to the bottom.*

*Prepare the food to be cooked and place in the steamer, using two layers if necessary.*

*Fill a wok one-third full of water and bring to the boil. Keep a supply of boiling water on hand so that you can add it to the wok if too much water evaporates.*

*Place the steamer in the wok so that it is sitting above the water, but not touching the water. Either cover with the steamer lid or the wok lid.*

*Be careful when you remove the steamer from the wok that the steam doesn't scald you.*

● Ensure the bottom of the steamer dish doesn't touch the water, otherwise the water will taint the food.
● If using a ceramic dish, make sure there is enough room around the side to be able to remove it easily.
● If steaming for longer than 10 minutes, have extra boiling water ready to replenish.
● Maintain the water at a simmer.
● Take care when removing the dish from the steamer—turn off the heat first.
● Be careful when removing the lid— always lift it up so that it forms a shield, preventing the steam from scalding you.
● Even once the steaming dish has been removed from the heat source, the food will continue to cook for some time.

VEGETABLE DUMPLINGS

Use lightly oiled hands to roll the dough into a ball.

Roll out small pieces of dough into flat rounds.

Pinch the edges of the wrapper together so that the filling is enclosed.

# VEGETABLE DUMPLINGS

Preparation time: 40 minutes +
　20 minutes soaking
Total cooking time: 20 minutes
Makes 24

☆ ☆ ☆

8 dried shiitake mushrooms
1 tablespoon vegetable oil
2 teaspoons finely chopped fresh ginger
2 garlic cloves, crushed
pinch of white pepper
100 g (3$^{1}/_{2}$ oz) garlic chives, chopped
100 g (3$^{1}/_{2}$ oz) water spinach, cut into 1 cm
　($^{1}/_{2}$ inch) lengths
$^{1}/_{4}$ cup (60 ml/2 fl oz) chicken stock
2 tablespoons oyster sauce
1 tablespoon cornflour
1 teaspoon soy sauce
1 teaspoon Chinese rice wine
$^{1}/_{4}$ cup (45 g/1$^{1}/_{2}$ oz) water chestnuts, chopped
chilli sauce, to serve

WRAPPERS
200 g (6$^{1}/_{2}$ oz) wheat starch (see Note)
1 teaspoon cornflour
oil, for kneading

1 Soak the mushrooms in hot water for 20 minutes. Squeeze dry, discard the stalks and finely chop the caps.

2 Heat a wok over high heat, add the oil and swirl. Add the ginger, garlic, white pepper and a pinch of salt and cook for 30 seconds. Add the chives and water spinach and cook for 1 minute.
3 Combine the stock, oyster sauce, cornflour, soy sauce and rice wine and add to the spinach mixture along with the water chestnuts and mushrooms. Cook for 1–2 minutes, or until the mixture thickens, them remove from the heat and cool completely.
4 To make the wrappers, combine the wheat starch and cornflour in a bowl. Make a well in the centre and add $^{3}/_{4}$ cup (185 ml/6 fl oz) boiling water, a little at a time, while bringing the mixture together with your hands. When it is combined, immediately knead it, using lightly oiled hands until the dough forms a shiny ball.
5 Keeping the dough covered with a cloth while you work, pick walnut-sized pieces from the dough and, using well-oiled hands, squash them between the palms of your hands. Roll the pieces out as thinly as possible into rounds no larger than 10 cm (4 inches) diameter. Place 1 tablespoon of the filling in the centre of the round. Pinch the edges of the wrapper together to enclose the filling and form a tight ball.
6 Line a bamboo steamer with baking paper. Place the dumplings in a single layer in the steamer, leaving a gap between each one. Cover with a lid and steam each batch over a wok of simmering water for 7–8 minutes. Serve with chilli sauce.
NOTE: Wheat starch is a very fine white powder similar to cornflour in texture. It is available at Asian food stores.

*RIGHT: Vegetable dumplings*

## STEAMED FISH

Preparation time: 15 minutes +
  4 hours marinating
Total cooking time: 25 minutes
Serves 4

☆ ☆

1/4 cup (60 g/2 oz) white miso paste
1 tablespoon vegetable oil
2 cloves garlic, crushed
1 1/2 tablespoons grated fresh ginger
2 tablespoons light soy sauce
2 tablespoons oyster sauce
1.5 kg (3 lb) large whole red snapper, cleaned
  and scaled
4 spring onions, sliced on the diagonal
fresh coriander leaves, to garnish

1 Combine the miso paste, oil, garlic, ginger,
soy and oyster sauces in a food processor until
smooth. If the fish is too big to fit into the
steamer, cut off the head.
2 Make four deep diagonal slashes on both sides
of the fish. Spoon half the paste over one side
of the fish and rub well into the skin and slashes.
Repeat on the other side with the remaining
paste. Place on a plate, cover with plastic wrap
and refrigerate for 2–4 hours.
3 Line a large bamboo steamer with baking
paper. Place the fish in the steamer and sprinkle
with the spring onion. Cover and steam over a

wok of simmering water for 20–25 minutes, or
until the fish is cooked. Replenish the boiling
water, if necessary.
4 Remove the fish from the steamer, pour any
juices collected in the baking paper over the top
and garnish with coriander. Serve with steamed
rice and stir-fried vegetables.

---

### STEAMED GAI LARN
(CHINESE BROCCOLI)

Wash 800 g (1 lb 10 oz) gai larn (Chinese
broccoli), then cut into thirds. Line a
bamboo steamer with baking paper. Place
the gai larn in a single layer on top. Cover,
then steam over a wok of simmering water
for 2–3 minutes, or until the leaves are
wilted and the stems are cooked through.

  Meanwhile, heat 2 teaspoons vegetable
oil in a small saucepan over high heat until
hot but not smoking. Remove from the
heat, then add 2 cloves julienned garlic and
1/2 teaspoon grated fresh ginger and stir for
1–2 minutes, or until fragrant. Return the
pan to the heat, stir in 1/3 cup (80 ml/
2 3/4 fl oz) chicken stock, then add a drizzle
of sesame oil and bring to the boil, stirring,
until the sauce reduces slightly. Remove
from the heat and stir in 2 tablespoons
oyster sauce. Season to taste with white
pepper. Drizzle the gai larn with the sauce
and serve. Serves 4–6.

---

WHITE MISO PASTE
Made from fermented
soy beans and grains, the
flavour, colour and texture
of the various forms of
miso paste depend on the
proportions of soy bean,
salt and kofi (fermenting
mould culture) used, as well
as the length of time it is
aged for. White miso is
younger, and has a more
delicate, less salty flavour
than the more aged and
darker coloured red and
brown varieties.

*ABOVE: Steamed fish*

reserving the soaking liquid. Discard the stalks and slice the caps thinly.

**2** Combine the soy sauce, rice wine, sesame oil and ginger in a non-metallic dish. Add the chicken and turn to coat. Cover and marinate in the refrigerator for 1 hour.

**3** Line a bamboo steamer with baking paper. Place the chicken on top, reserving the marinade. Cover and steam over a wok of simmering water for 6 minutes, then turn the chicken over and steam for a further 6 minutes. Place the bok choy on top of the chicken and steam for a further 2–3 minutes.

**4** Meanwhile, put the reserved marinade, mushrooms and their soaking liquid in a small saucepan and bring to the boil. Add enough stock to the cornflour in a small bowl to make a smooth paste. Add the cornflour paste and remaining stock to the pan and stir for 2 minutes over medium heat, or until the sauce thickens.

**5** Place some bok choy and a chicken fillet on each serving plate, then pour on some sauce. Serve with rice.

## STICKY RICE AND PORK POCKETS

Preparation time: 15 minutes +
  1 hour soaking + 30 minutes marinating
Total cooking time: 45 minutes
Makes 8

☆ ☆ ☆

3 cups (600 g/1 1/4 lb) glutinous white rice
4 large lotus leaves
4 dried shiitake mushrooms
2 tablespoons dried shrimp
350 g (11 oz) pork leg or loin fillet, cut into
  2 cm (3/4 inch) cubes
2 teaspoons thinly sliced fresh ginger
1 1/2 tablespoons soy sauce
1 1/2 tablespoons cornflour
1 tablespoon oyster sauce
2 teaspoons sugar
1 teaspoon sesame oil
2 tablespoons vegetable oil
1 clove garlic, finely chopped
2 lap choong sausages, thinly sliced
2 spring onions, thinly sliced

## STEAMED CHICKEN BREAST WITH ASIAN GREENS AND SOY MUSHROOM SAUCE

Preparation time: 10 minutes +
  20 minutes soaking + 1 hour marinating
Total cooking time: 20 minutes
Serves 4

☆ ☆

10 g (1/4 oz) dried shiitake mushrooms
2 tablespoons light soy sauce
2 tablespoons Chinese rice wine
1/2 teaspoon sesame oil
1 tablespoon thinly sliced fresh ginger
4 x 200 g (6 1/2 oz) chicken breast fillets, trimmed
450 g (14 oz) bok choy, ends removed and cut
  lengthways into quarters
1/2 cup (125 ml/4 fl oz) chicken stock
1 tablespoon cornflour

*ABOVE: Steamed chicken breast with Asian greens and soy mushroom sauce*

**1** Soak the dried mushrooms in 1/4 cup (60 ml/ 2 fl oz) boiling water for 20 minutes. Drain,

**1** Wash the rice in cold water, drain well and put in a saucepan with 2 1/2 cups (600 ml/

20 fl oz) water. Bring to the boil over high heat, then reduce the heat to low, cover with a tightly fitting lid and simmer for 20 minutes. Allow to cool until needed.

**2** Cut the lotus leaves in half. Put the lotus leaves in a large bowl, cover with boiling water and soak for 1 hour. Pat the leaves dry with paper towels. At the same time, put the dried mushrooms and dried shrimp in separate bowls, cover each with boiling water and soak for 20 minutes. Drain well. Remove the stalks from the mushrooms and finely chop the caps.

**3** Meanwhile, put the pork in a food processor and briefly pulse until coarsely ground. Transfer to a bowl with the ginger, 1 tablespoon of the soy sauce and 2 teaspoons of the cornflour, and toss together well. Marinate for 20–30 minutes.

**4** Combine the oyster sauce, sugar, sesame oil and remaining soy sauce in a bowl and stir well.

**5** Heat a wok over high heat. Add the vegetable oil and swirl to coat. When hot, add the pork mixture and stir-fry for 2–3 minutes. Add the chopped mushrooms, soaked shrimp, garlic, sausage and spring onion. Stir-fry for 2 minutes. Add the soy and oyster sauce mixture and toss well. Combine the remaining cornflour with

220 ml (7 fl oz) water, gradually add to the wok and stir for a further minute, or until the pork mixture has thickened.

**6** With wet hands, roll and shape the cooked rice into 16 balls. Fold one end of a lotus leaf piece on the diagonal to form a cone. Hold securely in one hand and spoon in a ball of rice. Make an indent in the centre of the rice, spoon one-eighth of the pork mixture into the middle of the rice, then top with another rice ball. Fold the other end of the lotus leaf over to enclose the filling, then secure with a toothpick. Tie tightly with kitchen string. The parcels should be triangular. Repeat with the remaining lotus leaves, rice balls and filling.

**7** Place the rice parcels in a single layer in a double bamboo steamer. Cover with the steamer lid, and steam over a wok of simmering water for 15 minutes. Reverse the steamers and steam for a further 15 minutes, adding more hot water to the wok as necessary. Serve immediately.

## STICKY RICE AND PORK POCKETS

With the lotus leaf folded to form a cone, add a ball of rice to the middle, then form an indent in the middle of the rice.

Add another ball of rice to the cone, on top of the pork filling.

Fold the other end of the lotus leaf over so that the filling is enclosed.

Once the parcel forms a neat triangle, tie it securely with kitchen string.

*LEFT: Sticky rice and pork pockets*

STEAMED PORK BUNS

Bring the edges of the dough round towards the centre where the baking powder has been sprinkled.

Press each of the twelve dough rounds out into a flat round 12 cm (5 inches) in diameter.

Bring the edge of the dough rounds together to enclose the filling.

# STEAMED PORK BUNS
(Char siu bau)

Preparation time: 40 minutes +
　10 minutes resting + 3 hours rising
Total cooking time: 20 minutes
Makes 12

☆☆☆

### DOUGH
2 tablespoons sugar
1½ teaspoons dry yeast
2½ cups (310 g/10 oz) plain flour
1 tablespoon vegetable oil
½ teaspoon sesame oil
1½ teaspoons baking powder

1 teaspoon vegetable oil
250 g (8 oz) Chinese barbecued pork, finely chopped
2 tablespoons oyster sauce
2 teaspoons sugar
2 teaspoons rice wine
1 teaspoon sesame oil
1 teaspoon soy sauce
12 x 5 cm (2 inch) squares of baking paper

1 To make the dough, pour 1 cup (250 ml/ 8 fl oz) warm water into a small bowl and add the sugar. Stir for a few seconds to dissolve the sugar then add the yeast. Cover the bowl for 10 minutes.

2 Sift the flour into a bowl and make a well in the centre. Pour the yeast mixture and vegetable oil into the well. Quickly stir the ingredients together and turn the mixture out onto a lightly floured surface. Knead for 8 minutes, or until smooth and elastic. Brush a large bowl with the sesame oil and put the dough in the bowl, turning it around in the bowl to coat it all with the oil. Cover the bowl and set aside to rise for at least 3 hours.

3 Lift the dough onto a lightly floured work surface. Punch the dough down and flatten into a large round. Sprinkle the baking powder in the centre of the circle, bringing the edges up towards the centre. Firmly press the edges together, then knead the dough for a further 5 minutes. Divide the dough into 12 equal balls. Cover them with a damp cloth to prevent them from drying out.

4 To make the filling, heat a wok over high heat, add the oil and swirl to coat. Add the pork and cook for 30 seconds, stirring constantly. Add the oyster sauce, sugar, rice wine, sesame oil and soy sauce and stir-fry for 1–2 minutes. Transfer the mixture to a bowl to cool.

5 Take each ball of dough and press it onto a lightly floured surface to form a round 12 cm (5 inches) in diameter. Place a heaped tablespoon of the filling in the centre of each

*RIGHT: Steamed pork buns*

270

dough circle, then bring the edges up to the centre. Press the edges firmly together. Sit each bun on one of the squares of baking paper. Place six pork buns on each layer of a double bamboo steamer. Cover with a lid and simmer over a wok of simmering water for 15 minutes.

# THAI GINGER FISH WITH CORIANDER BUTTER

Preparation time: 15 minutes +
  30 minutes refrigeration
Total cooking time: 10 minutes
Serves 4

60 g (2 oz) butter, at room temperature
1 tablespoon finely chopped fresh coriander
  leaves
2 tablespoons lime juice
1 tablespoon vegetable oil
1 tablespoon grated palm sugar
4 fresh long red chillies, seeded and chopped
2 stems lemon grass, trimmed
4 x 200 g (6¹/2 oz) firm white fish fillets
  (e.g. blue-eye or john dory)
1 lime, thinly sliced
1 tablespoon finely shredded fresh ginger

1 Thoroughly mix the butter and chopped coriander together and roll it into a log. Wrap the log in plastic wrap and chill in the refrigerator for at least 30 minutes, or until required.

2 Combine the lime juice, oil, palm sugar and chilli in a small non-metallic bowl and stir until the sugar has dissolved. Cut the lemon grass into halves.

3 Lay a piece of lemon grass in the centre of a sheet of foil large enough to fully enclose one fish fillet. Place a fish fillet on top and smear the surface with the lime juice mixture. Top with some lime slices and ginger shreds, then wrap into a secure parcel. Repeat with the remaining ingredients to make four parcels.

4 Line a bamboo steamer with baking paper. Lay the fish parcels on top. Cover and steam over a wok of simmering water for 8–10 minutes, or until the fish flakes easily when tested with a fork.

5 To serve, place the parcels on individual serving plates and serve open with slices of coriander butter, steamed rice and some steamed green vegetables.

CORIANDER
Also known as cilantro and Chinese parsley, coriander was introduced to China from Central Asia over 2000 years ago. The prevalence of coriander is such that in some Chinese dialects, the name for parsley translates as 'foreign coriander'. When purchasing, look for coriander with unblemished leaves, which look fresh and show no signs of wilting.

*ABOVE: Thai ginger fish with coriander butter*

## STEAMED MUSSELS WITH LEMON GRASS AND GINGER

Preparation time: 15 minutes
Total cooking time: 10 minutes
Serves 4

2 kg (4 lb) black mussels

1 tablespoon fish sauce

2 cloves garlic, crushed

4 small red Asian shallots, thinly sliced

1 tablespoon finely shredded fresh ginger

2 bird's eye chillies, seeded and thinly sliced

2 stems lemon grass, white part only, bruised
   and cut into 5 cm (2 inch) lengths

4 fresh kaffir lime leaves

1 tablespoon lime juice

1 lime, cut into wedges (optional)

1 Scrub the mussels with a stiff brush and pull out the hairy beards. Discard any broken mussels or open ones that don't close when tapped on the bench. Rinse well.
2 Pour the fish sauce and 1/2 cup (125 ml/ 4 fl oz) water into a wok and bring to the boil. Add half the mussels and scatter with half the garlic, shallots, ginger, chilli, lemon grass and lime leaves. Cover and steam over high heat for 2–3 minutes, shaking the wok frequently, until the mussels have just opened. Remove the mussels with a slotted spoon, discarding any that have not opened. Repeat with the remaining mussels and aromatics (you do not need to add more water or fish stock to the wok at this stage). Transfer the mussels to a large serving bowl, leaving the cooking liquid in the wok.
3 Add the lime juice to the wok and season to taste with salt and pepper. Pour the liquid and all the aromatics over the mussels and serve with the lime wedges, if desired.

## ASIAN OYSTERS

Preparation time: 15 minutes
Total cooking time: 5 minutes
Serves 4

12 oysters in their shells

2 cloves garlic, finely chopped

2 x 2 cm (3/4 x 3/4 inch) piece fresh ginger,
   julienned

2 spring onions, thinly sliced on the diagonal

1/4 cup (60 ml/2 fl oz) Japanese soy sauce

1/4 cup (60 ml/2 fl oz) peanut oil

fresh coriander leaves, to garnish

1 Line a large bamboo steamer with baking paper. Arrange the oysters in a single layer on top.
2 Put the garlic, ginger and spring onion in a bowl, mix together well, then sprinkle over the oysters. Spoon 1 teaspoon soy sauce over each oyster. Cover and steam over a wok of simmering water for 2 minutes.
3 Heat the peanut oil in a small saucepan until smoking and carefully drizzle a little over each oyster. Garnish with the coriander leaves and serve immediately.

## SCALLOPS WITH SOY, GINGER AND SPRING ONION

Preparation time: 5 minutes +
   10 minutes marinating
Total cooking time: 15 minutes
Serves 4–6

24 scallops in their shells

3 teaspoons light soy sauce

3 teaspoons Chinese rice wine

1 tablespoon chicken stock or water

3 spring onions, shredded

1 1/2 tablespoons julienned fresh ginger

1/2–1 tablespoon light soy sauce

1/2 teaspoon sugar (optional)

1 To prepare the scallops, pull off the roe and any vein, membrane or hard white muscle. Remove the scallops from their shells. Rinse and dry the shells and set aside.
2 Combine the soy sauce and rice wine in a non-metallic bowl with the scallop meat, and marinate for 10 minutes.
3 Line a bamboo steamer with baking paper. Arrange six of the shells in a single layer on top, then return a scallop to each shell. Combine the marinade with the chicken stock, then drizzle some over the scallops. Sprinkle with some of the spring onion and ginger. Cover and steam over a wok of simmering water for 2–3 minutes, or until just cooked, being careful not to overcook them. Repeat with the remaining scallops.
4 Serve with some of the soy sauce (dissolve the sugar in the sauce, if using) drizzled over the top and the remainder for dipping, if desired.

STEAMED MUSSELS WITH LEMON GRASS AND GINGER

Scrub all the dirt from the mussels with a stiff brush.

Pull out the hairy beards from the mussels.

*OPPOSITE PAGE, FROM TOP: Steamed mussels with lemon grass and ginger; Scallops with soy, ginger and spring onion*

273

## STUFFED SHIITAKE

Preparation time: 30 minutes
Total cooking time: 20 minutes
Serves 4–6

☆ ☆

300 g (10 oz) raw medium prawns

150 g (5 oz) chicken mince

50 g (1 3/4 oz) pork fat (ask your butcher), very
   finely chopped

30 g (1 oz) ham, finely chopped

1 spring onion, finely chopped

2 large cloves garlic, crushed

1 1/2 tablespoons finely chopped water chestnuts

1 1/2 tablespoons finely chopped bamboo shoots

1 1/2 teaspoons grated fresh ginger

1 tablespoon Chinese rice wine

1 tablespoon oyster sauce, plus extra, to drizzle

1 tablespoon light soy sauce

2–3 drops of sesame oil

1 egg white, beaten until frothy

1/4 teaspoon sugar

pinch of five-spice powder

300 g (10 oz) fresh shiitake mushrooms
   (see Note)

1 litre (32 fl oz) chicken stock

1 star anise

toasted sesame seeds, to garnish (optional)

*ABOVE: Stuffed shiitake*

1 To make the stuffing, peel and devein the prawns. Finely chop the prawn meat and put it in a bowl with the chicken mince, pork fat, ham, spring onion, garlic, water chestnuts, bamboo shoots, ginger, rice wine, oyster sauce, soy sauce, sesame oil, egg white, sugar, five-spice powder and white pepper and mix together thoroughly.

2 Remove the stalks from the shiitake and reserve. Generously fill each mushroom cap with stuffing, rounding the tops slightly. The amount of stuffing you use for each mushroom will differ depending on their size—if the mushrooms are very small you may have some mixture left over.

3 Pour the chicken stock and 2 cups (500 ml/ 16 fl oz) water into a wok and add the star anise and reserved mushroom stalks. Bring to the boil over high heat, then reduce to a simmer.

4 Line a large bamboo steamer with baking paper and place the mushrooms in a single layer on top, filling-side-up. Cover and simmer over the wok for about 15 minutes, or until the filling and the mushrooms are cooked through. Place on a serving platter and pour over a little of the broth. If desired, you can drizzle with a little extra oyster sauce and some toasted sesame seeds. Serve as part of as Asian banquet or as a light entrée to an Asian meal.

NOTE: When purchasing fresh shiitake, choose mushrooms that are plump, with firm caps that curl under. Ignore any with shrivelled, dehydrated caps as they are well past their peak. Choose ones of similar size so they cook evenly.

# PRAWNS STEAMED IN BANANA LEAVES

Preparation time: 25 minutes
  + 2 hours marinating
Total cooking time: 10 minutes
Serves 4

2.5 cm (1 inch) piece fresh ginger, grated

2 small fresh red chillies, finely chopped

4 spring onions, finely chopped

2 stems lemon grass (white part only), finely chopped

2 teaspoons soft brown sugar

1 tablespoon fish sauce

2 tablespoons lime juice

1 tablespoon sesame seeds, toasted

2 tablespoons chopped fresh coriander leaves

1 kg (2 lb) raw prawns, peeled and deveined

8 small banana leaves

1 Put the ginger, chilli, spring onion and lemon grass in a food processor, and process in short bursts until a paste is formed. Transfer the paste to a bowl, then stir in the sugar, fish sauce, lime juice, sesame seeds and coriander and mix well. Add the prawns and toss to coat. Cover and marinate for 2 hours in the fridge.

2 Meanwhile, put the banana leaves in a large heatproof bowl, cover with boiling water and leave them to soak for 3 minutes, or until softened. Drain and pat dry. Cut the banana leaves into 18 cm (7 inches) squares.

3 Divide the prawn mixture into eight portions, and place a portion on each square of banana leaf. Fold the leaf to enclose the mixture, and then secure the parcels with a wooden skewer.

4 Cook the parcels in a bamboo steamer over a wok of simmering water for 8–10 minutes, or until the prawn filling is cooked.

BANANA LEAVES
Banana leaves are used in various Asian countries for wrapping food to be steamed or baked—their pliable nature makes them perfect for this purpose. Before use, the leaves should be rinsed thoroughly, soaked in boiling water until softened and the central spine removed. The leaves are available from Asian food stores and speciality fruit and vegetable shops. Alternatively, you may have a friend with a banana tree.

*LEFT: Prawns steamed in banana leaves*

SOUP DUMPLINGS

With wet fingers, make a deep indentation in the middle of each ball of filling.

Place a cube of jelly in the indentation you have made in the balls of filling.

Place the ball in the centre of a wrapper, moisten the edges and bring two corners together and seal.

Pinch along the seams of the dumplings to seal them completely.

# SOUP DUMPLINGS
(Gun tong gau)

Preparation time: 40 minutes +
　4 hours refrigeration + 1 hour standing
Total cooking time: 10 minutes
Makes 24

☆☆☆

200 g (6¹/₂ oz) pork mince
100 g (3¹/₂ oz) peeled raw prawns, deveined
2 teaspoons grated fresh ginger
2 cloves garlic, crushed
1 spring onion, finely chopped
3 teaspoons Chinese rice wine
2 teaspoons soy sauce
¹/₂ teaspoon sesame oil
pinch of ground white pepper
3 tablespoons beaten egg white
3 teaspoons cornflour
³/₄ cup (185 ml/6 fl oz) chicken stock
1¹/₂ teaspoons gelatine powder
24 won ton wrappers

DIPPING SAUCE
1 tablespoon dark soy sauce
3 teaspoons Chinese black vinegar
1 teaspoon sugar
2¹/₂ tablespoons finely shredded fresh ginger

1 Put the mince, prawn meat, ginger, garlic, spring onion, rice wine, soy sauce, sesame oil and pepper in a food processor and process until combined. Transfer to a small bowl and fold in the egg white and cornflour. Refrigerate for 4 hours, or overnight if time permits.
2 Meanwhile, pour the stock into a small saucepan over high heat, cover and bring to the boil. Remove from the heat, add the gelatine and stir until dissolved. Transfer to an 8 x 25 cm (3 x 10 inch) bar tin and refrigerate for 1–2 hours or until set. Cut it into 1.5 cm (⁵/₈ inch) cubes.
3 To make the dipping sauce, combine the soy sauce, vinegar, sugar and ¹/₂ cup (125 ml/4 fl oz) water and stir until the sugar has dissolved. Add the ginger and allow to stand for 1 hour to allow the flavours to infuse, before serving.
4 Roll 3 teaspoons of filling into a ball with wet fingers and make a deep indentation in the centre of the ball. Place a cube of jelly into the centre and cover completely with the filling. Put in the centre of a won ton wrapper, lightly moisten the edges with water and bring two diagonal corners up to join together and seal. Repeat with the other two corners. Pinch along the seams to seal. Repeat with the remaining ingredients to make 23 more dumplings.
5 Line two bamboo steamers with baking paper. Place a single layer of dumplings in each. Cover and steam over a wok of simmering water for 5–6 minutes, or until cooked through. Serve with the dipping sauce on the side.

*RIGHT: Soup dumplings*

## CHINESE STEAMED CHICKEN AND RICE PARCELS

Preparation time: 20 minutes + 2 hours soaking
  + 10 minutes standing
Total cooking time: 30 minutes
Serves 4

☆ ☆ ☆

2 lotus leaves
6 dried shiitake mushrooms
1¼ cups (275 g/9 oz) short-grain rice
1 tablespoon peanut oil
250 g (8 oz) chicken thigh fillets, cut into
    1.5 cm (⁵/₈ inch) cubes
2 cloves garlic, chopped
3 teaspoons grated fresh ginger
50 g (1³/₄ oz) water chestnuts, chopped
¼ cup (60 ml/2 fl oz) light soy sauce
1 tablespoon Chinese rice wine
1 teaspoon cornflour

1 Soak the lotus leaves in warm water for 2 hours, then cut in half.
2 Soak the shiitake mushrooms in boiling water for 20 minutes. Drain, reserving the soaking liquid, then squeeze the mushrooms dry. Discard the stalks and thinly slice the caps.
3 Rinse the rice, then put it in a saucepan with 1½ cups (375 ml/12 fl oz) water. Bring to the boil, reduce the heat, cover and cook over low heat for 10 minutes. Stand, covered, for a further 10 minutes.
4 Heat a wok over high heat, add the oil and swirl to coat. Add the chicken and cook for 3 minutes, or until browned. Add the garlic, ginger, water chestnuts and mushrooms and cook for a further 30 seconds. Add 2 tablespoons of the soy sauce, the rice wine and ¼ cup (60 ml/2 fl oz) of the mushroom soaking liquid. Mix the cornflour with 1 tablespoon water, add to the wok and cook until the mixture thickens. Add the rice and the remaining soy sauce.
5 Lay each piece of lotus leaf, brown-side-down, on a work surface. Place one-quarter of the rice mixture in the middle of each piece of lotus leaf, making a mound about 6 x 8 cm (2½ x 3 inches). Fold in the short sides, then roll lengthways to create a parcel. Repeat with the remaining mixture. Place the parcels, seam-side-down, in a large bamboo steamer that has been lined with baking paper. Steam over a wok of simmering water for 20 minutes, replenishing the water if necessary. Serve, and unwrap to eat.

LOTUS LEAVES
Lotus leaves are the leaves of a water lily, whose seeds and roots are also used in Asian cooking. Lotus leaves are large, strong and firm so they are suitable for using to wrap ingredients for cooking. While not eaten themselves, they impart a smoky, distinctively earthy flavour to the enclosed ingredients. When using as a wrapping, place the filling on the shiny side, so that the duller-coloured side is external.

*ABOVE: Chinese steamed chicken and rice parcels*

277

WHOLE STEAMED
FISH WITH GINGER

When the fish is cooked, it
will flake apart easily when
tested with a fork.

Put the cooked fish on
serving plates and drizzle
some of the hot oil over
each fish.

## WHOLE STEAMED FISH WITH GINGER

Preparation time: 10 minutes
Total cooking time: 15 minutes
Serves 4

☆

4 x 350 g (11 oz) whole bream, scaled and
   cleaned (see Note)
2 tablespoons julienned fresh ginger
1/4 cup (60 ml/2 fl oz) peanut oil
2–3 tablespoons soy sauce
6 spring onions, sliced on the diagonal
45 g (1 1/2 oz) fresh coriander sprigs

**1** Make two diagonal cuts in the thickest part
of each fish on both sides, then place the fish in
a bamboo steamer lined with baking paper
(depending on the size of your steamer, you will
probably need to use two steamers). Cover and
steam over a wok of simmering water for
10 minutes, or until the flesh flakes easily when
tested with a fork.
**2** Place each fish on a serving plate and scatter
some of the fresh julienned ginger over the top.
**3** Heat the peanut oil in a small saucepan over
medium heat until the oil begins to smoke. Pour
some hot oil over each fish. The oil will sizzle
and splatter, so stand back a little to avoid being
splashed (the oil must be very hot or the fish
won't go crisp and may seem oily). Drizzle the
soy sauce over the fish and garnish with sliced
spring onion and fresh coriander sprigs. Serve
with steamed rice and steamed Asian vegetables.
NOTE: As a variation to the bream, you can also
try whole snapper or flounder.

## CRYSTAL PRAWNS

Preparation time: 15 minutes +
   1 hour marinating
Total cooking time: 10 minutes
Serves 4 (as an entrée)

☆

12 large raw prawns
2 tablespoons Chinese rice wine
2 tablespoons light soy sauce
1/2 teaspoon sugar
2 cloves garlic, crushed
1 tablespoon finely chopped spring onion
2 teaspoons finely chopped fresh ginger
1 spring onion, thinly sliced on the diagonal
1/4 teaspoon sesame oil

*ABOVE: Whole steamed fish
with ginger*

1 Peel and devein the prawns, leaving the tails intact. Put the rice wine, soy sauce, sugar, garlic, chopped spring onion, ginger and $1/4$ teaspoon salt in a large heatproof ceramic pie plate that will fit into a large steamer. Stir to dissolve the sugar and salt. Add the prawns, tossing to coat the prawns with the marinade. Cover and refrigerate for 1 hour.

2 Set the plate with the prawns in the steamer and place over a wok of simmering water. Cover and steam for 8–10 minutes. Serve hot with the extra spring onion scattered over the prawns and drizzled with the sesame oil.

## STEAMED LEMON GRASS AND GINGER CHICKEN WITH ASIAN GREENS

Preparation time: 25 minutes
Total cooking time: 25 minutes
Serves 4

4 x 200 g (6$1/2$ oz) chicken breast fillets
2 stems lemon grass
5 cm (2 inch) piece fresh ginger, cut into
　julienne strips
1 lime, thinly sliced
2 cups (500 ml/16 fl oz) chicken stock
350 g (11 oz) choy sum, cut into 10 cm
　(4 inch) lengths
800 g (1 lb 10 oz) gai larn (Chinese broccoli),
　cut into 10 cm (4 inch) lengths
200 g (6$1/2$ oz) fresh egg noodles
$1/4$ cup (60 ml/2 fl oz) kecap manis
$1/4$ cup (60 ml/2 fl oz) soy sauce
1 teaspoon sesame oil
toasted sesame seeds, to garnish

1 Cut each chicken breast fillet horizontally through the middle so that you are left with eight thin flat chicken fillets.

2 Cut the lemon grass into lengths that are about 5 cm (2 inches) longer than the chicken fillets, then cut in half lengthways. Lay one piece of lemon grass onto one half of each chicken breast fillet, top with some ginger and lime slices, then top with the other half of the fillet.

3 Pour the stock into a wok and bring to a simmer. Line two bamboo steamers with baking paper. Place two of the chicken fillets in each steamer in a single layer. Cover and steam over the simmering stock for 12–15 minutes, or until the chicken is tender, swapping the position of the steamers halfway through cooking.

4 Steam the greens in the same way as the chicken for 3 minutes, or until tender. Bring the stock in the wok to the boil.

5 Cook the noodles in a saucepan of boiling water for 1 minute, then drain and keep warm.

6 Pour the kecap manis, soy sauce and sesame oil into a bowl and whisk together well.

7 Divide the noodles among four serving plates and ladle a little of the boiling stock over them. Top with a neat pile of Asian greens, then add the chicken and generously drizzle each serve with the sauce. Sprinkle with toasted sesame seeds and serve.

NOTE: You can either remove the lemon grass from the chicken before serving, or leave it in. If any of your guests are unfamiliar with lemon grass, inform them that it's not to be eaten.

*BELOW: Steamed lemon grass and ginger chicken with Asian greens*

279

SCALLOP AND
SNOW PEA SPROUT
DUMPLINGS

Place 2 teaspoons of filling
in the centre of each gow
gee wrapper.

Wet the edges of the
wrapper and gather
together to cover the filling,
then squeeze shut.

Place the dumplings, seam-
side-down, in a bamboo
steamer lined with baking
paper.

# SCALLOP AND SNOW PEA
(MANGETOUT) **SPROUT**
**DUMPLINGS**

Preparation time: 30 minutes +
 4 hours refrigeration
Total cooking time: 10 minutes
Makes 24

☆ ☆

1/2 teaspoon baking soda
250 g (8 oz) snow pea (mangetout) sprouts,
 washed, dried and cut into 1 cm (1/2 inch)
 pieces
250 g (8 oz) scallop meat, white part only
1 teaspoon finely grated fresh ginger
1 1/2 tablespoons oyster sauce
1 teaspoon light soy sauce
1 teaspoon Chinese rice wine
1/2 teaspoon sesame oil
1 1/2 teaspoons sugar
1 teaspoon cornflour
1 egg white
24 gow gee wrappers

1 Bring a saucepan of salted water to the boil,
add the baking soda and the snow pea sprouts
and blanch for 10 seconds. Drain and refresh
under cold water. Drain thoroughly until dry.
2 Put the scallops in a food processor with the
ginger, oyster sauce, soy sauce, Chinese rice
wine, sesame oil, sugar, cornflour, egg white and
1/4 teaspoon salt and blend until smooth and
evenly mixed. Transfer to a bowl, cover and
refrigerate for 4 hours. Add the snow pea
sprouts, and mix thoroughly.
3 Place 2 teaspoons of the filling in the centre of
each gow gee wrapper, wet the edges and gather
together to cover the filling, then squeeze shut,
making a round bundle. Break off any surplus
dough. Line a double bamboo steamer with
baking paper. Place the dumplings in the steamer
in a single layer, seam-side-down. Cover and
steam over a wok of simmering water for
8 minutes, or until cooked through.

# STEAMED STUFFED SQUID

Preparation time: 10 minutes +
 1 hour refrigeration + 10 minutes standing
Total cooking time: 10 minutes
Serves 6

☆ ☆

400 g (13 oz) redfish or red snapper fillets,
 cut into chunks
400 g (13 oz) raw medium prawns, peeled,
 deveined and chopped
250 g (8 oz) cooked mussel meat, chopped
1/2 cup (15 g/1/2 oz) coriander leaves and stems,
 chopped
1/3 cup (80 ml/2 3/4 fl oz) coconut cream

*RIGHT: Scallop and snow
pea sprout dumplings*

1/4 cup (60 ml/2 fl oz) fish sauce

6 fresh kaffir lime leaves, finely shredded

2 eggs

2 tablespoons ready-made red curry paste

3 teaspoons chilli sauce

1 teaspoon sugar

10 small squid hoods, 12–14 cm (5 inches) long

Thai chilli fish dipping sauce (Nam pla prik), to serve (page 295)

1 To make the stuffing, put the fish in a food processor and process for 30 seconds or until it forms a ball in the bowl. Transfer to a large non-metallic bowl. Process the prawn and mussel meat for 10 seconds, then add to the bowl with the fish.

2 Place all the remaining ingredients, except the squid hoods and dipping sauce, in the food processor and process for 3 minutes. Add to the fish, then stir with a wooden spoon until thoroughly combined. Cover with plastic wrap and refrigerate for 1 hour.

3 Using a spoon, fill the squid hoods with the stuffing, leaving a 1 cm (1/2 inch) gap at each end—be careful not to overfill. Tightly seal the hoods with toothpicks. Line a bamboo steamer with baking paper. Place the squid in a single layer on top. Cover and steam over a wok of simmering water for 10 minutes. Remove from the heat and leave over the wok for a further 10 minutes. Cut each squid hood into three pieces and serve with the dipping sauce.

## STEAMED TOFU WITH SOY

Preparation time: 15 minutes +
  30 minutes marinating
Total cooking time: 10 minutes
Serves 4

2 tablespoons soy sauce

2 tablespoons kecap manis

1 teaspoon sesame oil

500 g (1 lb) firm tofu, drained

1 1/2 teaspoons julienned fresh ginger

3 spring onions, thinly sliced on the diagonal

1 cup (50 g/1 3/4 oz) chopped fresh coriander leaves

1–2 tablespoons crisp fried shallots

1 Combine the soy sauce, kecap manis and oil in a bowl. Cut the tofu in half widthways, then into triangles. Place on a heatproof plate and pour the sauce over the top. Marinate for 30 minutes, turning the tofu once.

2 Sprinkle the ginger over the tofu. Place the plate on a wire rack over a wok of simmering water. Cover and steam for 3–4 minutes. Sprinkle with the spring onion and coriander, then cover and steam for 3 minutes. Sprinkle with the crisp fried shallots.

CRISP FRIED SHALLOTS Ready-made crisp fried shallots are made from finely sliced red Asian shallots that have been quickly deep-fried until crisp. They are popular in Indonesian cuisine, where they are used to garnish food, adding texture as well as flavour to a finished dish, as well as a deeper, softer onion taste. Crisp fried garlic flakes are also available and used in the same way. They are both available in jars or packets in Asian grocery stores.

*ABOVE: Steamed tofu with soy*

CLASSIC STEAMED PORK
AND PRAWN
DUMPLINGS

Form pleats around the
dumpling to enclose the
filling, leaving the top
exposed.

## CLASSIC STEAMED PORK AND PRAWN DUMPLINGS

(Shu mai)

Preparation time: 25 minutes
Total cooking time: 5 minutes
Makes 24

☆ ☆

300 g (10 oz) pork mince

300 g (10 oz) prawn mince

3 spring onions, thinly sliced

1/3 cup (60 g/2 oz) chopped water chestnuts

1 1/2 teaspoons finely chopped fresh ginger

1 tablespoon light soy sauce, plus extra, to serve

1 teaspoon caster sugar

24 won ton wrappers

chilli sauce, to serve

1 To make the filling, put the pork and prawn
mince, spring onion, water chestnuts, ginger,
soy sauce and sugar in large non-metallic bowl
and combine well.
2 Working with one wrapper at a time, place a
heaped tablespoon of the filling in the centre of
the wrapper. Bring the sides up around the
outside, forming pleats to firmly encase the
filling—the top of the dumpling should be
exposed. Pinch together to enclose the bottom
of the filling, then cover with a damp cloth.

Repeat with the remaining wrappers and filling
to make 24 in total.
3 Line a large double bamboo steamer with
baking paper and arrange the dumplings on the
base so that they don't touch one another.
Cover and steam over a wok of simmering water
for 5 minutes, or until cooked through. Serve
the dumplings with the soy and chilli sauces, for
dipping.
NOTE: If desired, these dumplings can be made
using just pork mince—just double the amount.

## YUM CHA STEAMED PORK RIBS IN BLACK BEAN SAUCE

Preparation time: 15 minutes
Total cooking time: 1 hour 15 minutes
Serves 6–8

☆ ☆

2 1/2 tablespoons black beans (not canned),
  rinsed and crushed well with a fork

2 teaspoons caster sugar

1/4 cup (60 ml/2 fl oz) light soy sauce

2 1/2 tablespoons Chinese rice wine

1 teaspoon sesame oil

1.2 kg (2 lb 6 1/2 oz) pork spare ribs, cut into
  5 cm (2 inch) pieces

1 tablespoon peanut oil

*ABOVE: Classic steamed
pork and prawn dumplings*

1 tablespoon julienned fresh ginger

3 cloves garlic, crushed

1 fresh red chilli, finely chopped

1 cup (250 ml/8 fl oz) chicken stock

2 spring onions, sliced on the diagonal

1 Combine the black beans, sugar, soy sauce, rice wine and sesame oil in a small bowl.

2 Line a large bamboo steamer with baking paper. Put the spare ribs on top in a single layer. Cover and steam over a wok of simmering water for 45 minutes, replenishing the water if needed.

3 Remove the water from the wok and wipe clean. Heat the wok over high heat, add the oil and swirl to coat. Add the ginger, garlic and chilli and stir-fry for 30 seconds. Add the ribs to the wok along with the black bean mixture and stock. Bring to the boil, then reduce the heat to low and cook, stirring occasionally, for about 30 minutes, or until the liquid has reduced and the ribs are crisp and sticky. Sprinkle with spring onion, then serve.

2 Put the pork mince, garlic, ginger, spring onion, cornflour, soy sauce, rice wine and sesame oil in a bowl and mix with your hands.

3 Rinse the wom bok under cold running water. Press dry between layers of paper towels. Add to the pork mixture and combine well.

4 Place a teaspoon of mixture in the centre of a wrapper, brushing the inside edge of the wrapper with a little water. Bring the two edges of the wrapper together to form a semicircle. Using your thumb and index finger, create a pleat, pressing firmly as you do and gently tapping the gyoza on a work surface to form a flat bottom. Repeat with the remaining wrappers and filling.

5 Heat a quarter of the oil in a wok over medium–high heat. Cook ten of the gyozas for 2 minutes, flat-side-down. Reduce the heat and add a quarter of the stock, shaking the wok to unstick the gyoza. Cover and steam for 4 minutes, or until the liquid has evaporated. Remove and keep warm. Repeat with the remaining oil, gyoza and stock. Serve with soy sauce or Chinese black vinegar, if desired.

*BELOW: Gyoza*

## GYOZA

Preparation time: 50 minutes +
  30 minutes standing
Total cooking time: 25 minutes
Makes 40

☆ ☆ ☆

150 g (5 oz) wom bok (Chinese cabbage), very finely shredded

225 g (7 oz) pork mince

2 cloves garlic, finely chopped

2 teaspoons finely chopped fresh ginger

2 spring onions, finely chopped

2 teaspoons cornflour

1 tablespoon light soy sauce

2 teaspoons Chinese rice wine

2 teaspoons sesame oil

40 round Shanghai dumpling wrappers (flour and water)

2 tablespoons vegetable oil

1/2 cup (125 ml/4 fl oz) chicken stock

1 Put the wom bok and 1/2 teaspoon salt in a colander, then sit in a large bowl and toss to combine. Leave for 30 minutes to drain. Stir occasionally. This process will draw the liquid out of the wom bok and prevent the filling from going soggy.

STEAMED FISH IN
BANANA LEAVES

Fold in the cut corners of
the banana leaf squares,
then staple and/or tie
around the edge with
string.

Fill each cup almost to the
top with the fish mixture,
leaving room for the
cabbage.

Sprinkle the shredded
cabbage over each cup with
a little fish sauce.

## STEAMED FISH IN BANANA LEAVES

Preparation time: 45 minutes
Total cooking time: 10 minutes
Makes 10

☆

2 large banana leaves
350 g (11 oz) firm white fish fillets, cut into thin
    strips
1–2 tablespoons red curry paste (see Notes)
1/2 cup (125 ml/4 fl oz) coconut cream
1 cup (75 g/2 1/2 oz) finely shredded cabbage
2 tablespoons fish sauce
2 tablespoons lime juice
1–2 tablespoons sweet chilli sauce
1 fresh red chilli, chopped (optional)

1 Cut the banana leaves into 10 cm (4 inch)
squares and make a 3 cm (1 1/4 inch) cut towards
the centre on each corner. Fold in the corners,
then staple and/or tie around with a piece of
string to form a cup. Trim the corners to neaten,
if necessary.
2 Put the fish in a bowl with the curry paste and
coconut cream and stir gently to mix. Place
spoonfuls of the mixture in each banana leaf cup.
3 Line a large bamboo steamer with extra
banana leaves or cabbage leaves and place the
prepared cups in the basket. Top each piece of

fish with shredded cabbage and a little fish sauce.
Cover and steam over a wok of simmering water
for about 7 minutes. Drizzle lime juice and
sweet chilli sauce over the top and serve
immediately, sprinkled with chilli.
NOTES: You can make your own curry paste
(see page 56) or use a ready-made one.
    The fish can be cooked in foil cups instead of
banana leaves.

## JASMINE TEA STEAMED FISH

Preparation time: 10 minutes
Total cooking time: 15 minutes
Serves 4

☆

200 g (6 1/2 oz) jasmine tea leaves
100 g (3 1/2 oz) fresh ginger, thinly sliced
4 spring onions, cut into 5 cm (2 inch) lengths
4 x 200 g (6 1/2 oz) portions white fish (snapper,
    barramundi, blue-eye)

GINGER SPRING ONION SAUCE
1/2 cup (125 ml/4 fl oz) fish stock
1/4 cup (60 ml/2 fl oz) light soy sauce
3 spring onions, finely sliced
1 tablespoon finely shredded fresh ginger
2 teaspoons sugar
1 large fresh red chilli, sliced

RIGHT: Steamed fish in
banana leaves

1 Line a double bamboo steamer with baking paper. Place the tea, ginger and spring onion in a layer on the bottom steamer basket. Cover and steam over a wok of simmering water for 10 minutes, or until the tea is moist and fragrant.
2 Lay the fish in a single layer in the top steamer basket and steam for 5–10 minutes depending on the thickness of the fish fillet. To test for doneness, insert a skewer into the thickest part of the fillet—there should be no resistance.
3 To make the sauce, combine all the ingredients in a small saucepan with $^1/_2$ cup (125 ml/4 fl oz) water. Heat over low heat for 5 minutes, or until the sugar has dissolved. Drizzle the fish with the Ginger spring onion sauce and serve with steamed choy sum and rice.

## SUGAR CANE PRAWNS

Preparation time: 30 minutes +
   15 minutes refrigeration
Total cooking time: 10 minutes
Makes 10

☆ ☆

1 kg (2 lb) raw medium prawns, peeled, deveined and roughly chopped
2 tablespoons chopped fresh coriander leaves
2 tablespoons chopped fresh mint
1 stem lemon grass, finely chopped
1 small fresh red chilli, seeded and finely chopped
1 clove garlic, crushed
1$^1/_2$ tablespoons fish sauce
2 teaspoons lime juice
$^1/_2$ teaspoon sugar
10 pieces of sugar cane, each 10 cm (4 inches) long, 5 mm ($^1/_4$ inch) wide
lime wedges, to serve

1 Put the prawns and other ingredients (except the sugar cane and lime wedges) and $^1/_4$ teaspoon salt in a food processor and process until smooth.
2 Using wetted hands, roll 2 tablespoons of the mixture into a ball, then mould around the middle of a sugar cane skewer, pressing firmly to secure onto the skewer. Repeat with the remaining mixture and sugar cane. Refrigerate the skewers for 15 minutes.
3 Line a bamboo steamer with baking paper. Place the skewers in a single layer in the steamer. Cover and steam over a wok of simmering water for 7–8 minutes, or until cooked through.

4 Serve the skewers with lime wedges or with a dipping sauce made up of sweet chilli sauce mixed with a little fish sauce.

### CLASSIC VIETNAMESE DIPPING SAUCE
(Nuoc mam cham)

Combine $^3/_4$ cup (185 ml/6 fl oz) fish sauce, $^1/_4$ cup (60 ml/2 fl oz) lime juice, 2 tablespoons grated palm sugar, 2 seeded and finely chopped fresh bird's eye chillies, 1–2 cloves crushed garlic and $^1/_2$ cup (125 ml/4 fl oz) water and stir until the sugar dissolves. Transfer to a small serving dish. Makes 1$^1/_2$ cups.
NOTE: In Vietnam, this sauce is served with every meal. It is particularly good with steamed dumplings.

*ABOVE: Sugar cane prawns*

LIMES IN THAI CUISINE
One of the distinguishing features of Thai cuisine is the prevalence of sour flavours. One of the major sources of sourness in Thai food is lime juice. In addition to the flavour it imparts, lime juice has another important quality as a tenderiser. The Thais have used this quality to their advantage and have devised a simple method to dislodge a fish bone accidentally stuck in the throat. The method is to suck on a piece of lime, swallowing the juice slowly, or to gargle with lime juice. After a short time, the bone will be soft enough to be dislodged with a mouthful of water.

*ABOVE: Steamed whole fish with chilli, garlic and lime*

# STEAMED WHOLE FISH WITH CHILLI, GARLIC AND LIME

(Pla noong mahao)

Preparation time: 20 minutes
Total cooking time: 25 minutes
Serves 4–6

☆☆

1–1.5 kg (2–3 lb) whole snapper, cleaned
1 lime, sliced
finely chopped fresh red chillies, to garnish
fresh coriander leaves, to garnish
lime wedges, to garnish

SAUCE
2 teaspoons tamarind purée
5 long fresh red chillies, seeded and chopped
6 large cloves garlic, roughly chopped
6 fresh coriander roots and stalks
8 red Asian shallots, chopped
1 1/2 tablespoons vegetable oil
2 1/2 tablespoons lime juice
3/4 cup (130 g/4 1/2 oz) shaved palm sugar
1/4 cup (60 ml/2 fl oz) fish sauce

1 Rinse the fish and pat dry with paper towels. Cut two diagonal slashes through the thickest part of the fish on both sides, to ensure even cooking. Place the lime slices in the fish cavity, then cover with plastic wrap and refrigerate until ready to use.
2 To make the sauce, combine the tamarind with 1/4 cup (60 ml/2 fl oz) water. Blend the chilli, garlic, coriander and shallots in a food processor until finely puréed—add a little water, if necessary.
3 Heat the oil in a saucepan. Add the paste and cook over medium heat for 5 minutes, or until fragrant. Stir in the tamarind mixture, lime juice and palm sugar. Reduce the heat and simmer for 10 minutes, or until thick. Stir in the fish sauce.
4 Line a bamboo steamer with baking paper. Place the fish on top. Cover and steam over a wok of simmering water for 6 minutes per 1 kg (2 lb) fish, or until the flesh flakes easily when tested with a fork.
5 Pour the sauce over the fish and garnish with the chilli, coriander and lime wedges. Serve with steamed rice.

# PORK AND CHIVE DUMPLINGS

Preparation time: 45 minutes +
    3 hours marinating
Total cooking time: 15 minutes
Makes 24

 ☆ ☆

1 teaspoon vegetable oil

2 cloves garlic, crushed

2 teaspoons finely grated fresh ginger

250 g (8 oz) garlic chives, cut into 1 cm
    (¹/₂ inch) lengths

200 g (6¹/₂ oz) pork mince

2 tablespoons oyster sauce

3 teaspoons Chinese rice wine

2 teaspoons light soy sauce

¹/₂ teaspoon sesame oil

1 teaspoon cornflour

24 round gow gee wrappers

1 Heat a wok over high heat, add the vegetable oil and swirl to coat the side of the wok. Add the garlic, ginger and garlic chives, then stir-fry for 1 minute, or until fragrant and the chives have wilted slightly. Remove from the heat and allow to cool.

2 Meanwhile, put the pork mince, oyster sauce, rice wine, soy sauce, sesame oil and cornflour in a non-metallic bowl and mix well. Cover and refrigerate for 3 hours. Add the vegetable mixture once it has cooled, mix it into the pork until well combined and return to the fridge for the remainder of the 3 hours.

3 Put 2 teaspoons of the mixture in the centre of a gow gee wrapper. Moisten the edges with water, then fold the sides together to form a semicircle. Pinch the edges together at 5 mm (¹/₄ inch) intervals to form a ruffled edge. Repeat with the remaining filling and wrappers. Line a double bamboo steamer with baking paper. Put half the dumplings in a single layer in each steamer basket. Cover and steam over a wok of simmering water for 12 minutes, or until cooked through.

Place 2 teaspoons of the filling in the centre of a gow gee wrapper.

Fold the wrapper in the middle to form a semicircle.

Pinch the edges of the round side together at intervals to form a ruffled edge.

*LEFT: Pork and chive dumplings*

PEARL BALLS

Roll the pork mixture into balls with your hands.

Roll each ball in the rice until it is evenly covered.

# CAMBODIAN FRAGRANT STEAMED FISH
## (Amok trei)

Preparation time: 15 minutes +
  30 minutes refrigeration + standing
Total cooking time: 30 minutes
Serves 4

☆ ☆

### SPICE PASTE
1 stem lemon grass, white part only, chopped
1 coriander root, washed
2 fresh kaffir lime leaves, finely shredded
3 cloves garlic, crushed
4 red Asian shallots, chopped
2 teaspoons fish sauce

550 g (1 lb 1$^3$/4 oz) boneless white fish fillets
  (e.g. ling or barramundi)
400 ml (13 fl oz) can coconut milk (do not shake)
1$^1$/2–2 tablespoons ready-made red curry paste
3 teaspoons fish sauce
1 teaspoon grated palm sugar
4 fresh kaffir lime leaves, finely shredded
4 large gai larn (Chinese broccoli) or English
  spinach leaves, washed and sliced into
  5 cm (2 inch) strips
1 fresh red chilli, finely shredded

1 To make the spice paste, put the ingredients in a food processor and pulse briefly until a very fine paste forms. Set aside until required.
2 Cut the fish fillets into 2 cm ($^3$/4 inch) strips, then put half in the food processor and pulse briefly until roughly chopped, but not minced.
3 Spoon off the thick coconut cream from the top of the coconut milk—there should be $^1$/2 cup (125 ml/4 fl oz). Combine $^3$/4 cup (185 ml/ 6 fl oz) of the remaining coconut milk, the spice paste, red curry paste, fish sauce, palm sugar and half the kaffir lime leaves in a large non-metallic bowl. Stir in one direction until thoroughly mixed. Add all the fish, then mix with a wooden spoon, stirring in one direction for 1–2 minutes, or until the fish is just incorporated—take care not to overmix, or the mixture will split when cooked. Refrigerate for 30 minutes.
4 Fill a wok one-third full with water, bring to the boil then reduce to a simmer. Line a 1.25 litre (40 fl oz) deep, heatproof soup bowl or pudding basin with gai larn, then spoon the fish mixture into the bowl. Cover the fish with the

reserved coconut cream, then scatter with chilli and the remaining kaffir lime leaves. Put the bowl in a bamboo steamer, then put on the steamer lid and steam over the wok for 30 minutes, or until cooked. To test if the fish is cooked, insert a clean skewer into the centre—it should come out clean. Remove the steamer from the heat and stand for 5–10 minutes, then serve in the bowl, garnished with coriander, if desired.

# PEARL BALLS

Preparation time: 20 minutes +
  20 minutes soaking
Total cooking time: 1 hour 15 minutes
Makes 15–18 balls

☆ ☆

1 small dried shiitake mushroom
300 g (10 oz) pork mince
150 g (5 oz) raw medium prawns, peeled,
  deveined and roughly chopped
1 tablespoon chopped spring onion
2 teaspoons finely chopped fresh ginger
2 teaspoons finely chopped lemon grass, white
  part only
1 kaffir lime leaf, finely shredded
1 clove garlic, finely chopped
1 teaspoon fish sauce
1 egg
1 tablespoon chopped fresh coriander leaves
1 cup (200 g/6$^1$/2 oz) glutinous white rice
sweet chilli sauce, to serve

1 Soak the mushroom in hot water for 20 minutes. Remove the stalk and finely chop the cap.
2 Combine the pork mince, prawn meat, spring onion, ginger, lemon grass, lime leaf, garlic, fish sauce and egg in a food processor. Pulse for 10–15 seconds, or until combined. Transfer to a bowl and stir in the mushroom and coriander.
3 Put the rice in a bowl. With wet hands, roll the pork mixture into balls 2.5–3 cm (1–1$^1$/4 inches) in diameter. Gently roll each ball in the rice until they are evenly covered.
4 Place the balls well apart in a double bamboo steamer lined with baking paper. Steam over a wok of simmering water for 1–1$^1$/4 hours, replenishing the water when necessary. Serve with sweet chilli sauce.

PRAWN GOW GEES

Create pleats in the gow gee wrapper, starting from the centre of the gow gee.

Using your fingers, gently bend the gow gee to form a crescent shape.

# PRAWN GOW GEES
(Har gau)

Preparation time: 40 minutes +
　1 hour refrigeration
Total cooking time: 15 minutes
Makes 24

☆☆

300 g (10 oz) raw medium prawns, peeled, deveined and finely chopped
100 g (3 1/2 oz) pork mince
4 spring onions, white part only, finely chopped
25 g (3/4 oz) bamboo shoots, finely chopped
1 egg white
1 teaspoon finely chopped fresh ginger
1 teaspoon sesame oil
1/4 teaspoon ground white pepper
24 round gow gee wrappers

DIPPING SAUCE
1/4 cup (60 ml/2 fl oz) soy sauce
1 tablespoon Chinese red vinegar
1/4 teaspoon sesame oil

1 To make the filling, mix the prawns, pork mince, spring onion, bamboo shoots, egg white, ginger, sesame oil, white pepper and 1 teaspoon salt in a bowl until well combined. Cover with plastic wrap and refrigerate for 1 hour.

2 Put one gow gee wrapper on a work surface and place 2 level teaspoons of the filling in the centre—position the filling in an oblong shape across the wrapper, rather than a round lump. Lightly moisten the edge of the wrapper with water. Pick up the wrapper and fold the edges together to form a semicircle. Using your thumb and index finger, create a row of pleats along the outside edge of the gow gee, pressing firmly. Twist the corners down to seal and form a crescent shape. Make sure the gow gee is completely sealed or the filling will leak out during steaming. Repeat with the remaining wrappers and filling.

3 Line a 28 cm (11 inch) bamboo steamer with baking paper and arrange the gow gees so that they do not touch—you will need to do this in two batches or use a double bamboo steamer. Cover and steam over a wok of simmering water for 8 minutes, or until cooked through.

4 Meanwhile, to make the dipping sauce, combine the soy sauce, red vinegar and sesame oil. Serve with the gow gees.

RIGHT: Prawn gow gees

SHIITAKE MUSHROOMS
Shiitake was originally the Japanese name for a variety of forest mushroom that grows on rotting wood; the name has spread around the world (although they are called Chinese black mushrooms in China). The origin of the name is very literal: *take* means mushroom and *shii* is the name of one of the rotting trees that acts as a host to these mushrooms (however, they actually prefer other deciduous trees). They have a strong flavour, so are used sparingly. Available fresh and dried, the dried mushrooms have a very concentrated depth of flavour that the fresh ones lack. In their dried form these mushrooms will keep indefinitely in an airtight container. Dried shiitake must be reconstituted in hot water before use.

## CHICKEN WITH MUSHROOMS

Preparation time: 15 minutes +
    30 minutes marinating + 20 minutes soaking +
    10 minutes cooling
Total cooking time: 25 minutes
Serves 4–6

750 g (1 1/2 lb) chicken breast fillets, cut into
    bite-sized pieces

3 spring onions, 1 finely chopped, the others
    cut into 2 cm (3/4 inch) lengths

1 tablespoon very finely chopped fresh ginger

1 tablespoon finely chopped garlic

1 1/2 tablespoons light soy sauce

1 tablespoon oyster sauce

1 tablespoon Chinese rice wine

2 teaspoons cornflour

1/4 teaspoon sugar

2–3 drops of sesame oil

pinch of white pepper

5 dried shiitake mushrooms

1/4 cup (40 g/1 1/4 oz) water chestnuts, thinly
    sliced into discs

spring onion, extra, thinly sliced on the
    diagonal, to garnish

1 Put the chicken, finely chopped spring onion, ginger, garlic, soy sauce, oyster sauce, rice wine, cornflour, sugar, sesame oil and white pepper in a bowl and mix well with your hands until the mixture is evenly combined. Refrigerate for 30 minutes.

2 Meanwhile, soak the dried mushrooms in hot water for 20 minutes, or until soft. Squeeze dry, discard the stalks and cut the caps into quarters.

3 Add the mushrooms, water chestnuts and spring onion lengths to the chicken mixture, mix well, then put in a 1 litre (32 fl oz) ceramic bowl that will fit in a large steamer. Cover with a round of foil or baking paper. Place the bowl in the steamer basket, cover and steam over a wok of simmering water for 20–25 minutes, or until the chicken is just cooked through. If you like, you can stir the chicken halfway through cooking to check that it is cooking evenly.

4 Remove the bowl from the steamer and allow to cool for 10 minutes. Hold a serving platter on top of the bowl and invert the bowl so that the bowl is upside-down. Carefully remove the bowl. Garnish with finely sliced spring onion and serve immediately with boiled rice or as part of an Asian banquet.

*ABOVE: Chicken with mushrooms*

CHINESE SESAME PASTE
Hailing from China's western Sichuan province, Chinese sesame paste is one of the key ingredients in Sichuan's distinctive cuisine. Unlike tahini, its Middle Eastern counterpart, the Chinese version is made from grinding roasted rather than raw sesame seeds, so it has a richer aroma and deeper, more robust flavour. As such, tahini is not really a suitable substitute, although some recipes do advocate its use with the addition of a few drops of Chinese sesame oil, if no other alternative is available.

*ABOVE: Rice noodle rolls filled with prawns*

# RICE NOODLE ROLLS FILLED WITH PRAWNS

Preparation time: 30 minutes + cooling
Total cooking time: 20 minutes
Serves 4

☆

### SAUCE
1/2 cup (140 g/41/2 oz) sesame paste
1/3 cup (80 ml/23/4 fl oz) light soy sauce
1/4 cup (60 ml/2 fl oz) lime juice
1/4 cup (45 g/11/2 oz) grated palm sugar
1 tablespoon sesame oil

2 tablespoons peanut oil
1 teaspoon sesame oil
4 cloves garlic, finely chopped
5 spring onions, thinly sliced
160 g (51/2 oz) garlic chives, cut into 2 cm (3/4 inch) lengths
160 g (51/2 oz) water chestnuts, thinly sliced
1/4 cup (40 g/11/4 oz) sesame seeds, lightly toasted
500 g (1 lb) fresh rice sheet noodles
800 g (1 lb 10 oz) raw small prawns, peeled and deveined
1/3 cup (50 g/13/4 oz) unsalted peanuts, crushed

1 To make the sauce, combine the sesame paste, soy sauce, lime juice, palm sugar and sesame oil in a bowl and stir until the sugar dissolves and the sauce is smooth. Add a tablespoon of water if it appears to be a little too thick.

2 Heat the peanut oil and sesame oil in a frying pan, add the garlic and cook for 1 minute. Add the spring onion and garlic chives and cook for 2 minutes, or until softened. Add the water chestnuts and sesame seeds. Remove from the heat and allow to cool.

3 Unroll the noodle sheets and cut into eight pieces, each 15 x 17 cm (6 x 61/2 inches). Put 1 tablespoon of the chive mixture along one long end. Place four prawns, curled up, side-by-side, on top of the chive mixture and roll up the noodle sheet tightly, then carefully sit it on a plate that will fit in the steamer. Repeat with the remaining rolls and filling ingredients. Lay the rolls side-by-side in two layers, with a layer of baking paper in between the rolls to prevent them sticking together.

4 Place the plate in a steamer, cover and steam over a wok of simmering water for 10 minutes, or until the prawns turn opaque and are cooked.

5 Carefully lift the plate out of the steamer with a tea towel and drizzle some of the sauce over the top, and around the rolls, then sprinkle with the peanuts. Serve extra sauce on the side.

# STEAMED PORK AND WATER CHESTNUT DUMPLINGS

Preparation time: 25 minutes +
  30 minutes resting
Total cooking time: 10 minutes
Makes 24

## DOUGH

1 cup (125 g/4 oz) plain flour
1/2 cup (60 g/2 oz) tapioca flour
30 g (1 oz) lard

250 g (8 oz) pork mince
50 g (1 3/4 oz) water chestnuts, chopped
2 spring onions, chopped
1 teaspoon chopped fresh ginger
2 teaspoons soy sauce
1 teaspoon rice wine
1/2 teaspoon sugar
1/2 teaspoon cornflour
1 egg
1/4 teaspoon sesame oil

1 To make the dough, put the flours and lard in a food processor. Process for several seconds until combined. With the motor running, slowly add 3/4 cup (185 ml/6 fl oz) boiling water to the food processor to form a sticky, thick dough. Place the dough onto a lightly floured surface and knead for a couple of minutes. Roll into a ball, wrap in plastic wrap and set aside for 30 minutes.

2 To make the filling, put the pork mince, water chestnuts, spring onion, ginger, soy sauce, rice wine, sugar, cornflour, egg, sesame oil and 1/2 teaspoon salt in a food processor. Process for several seconds to evenly combine the mixture. Transfer to a bowl.

3 Divide the dough into four equal pieces. Roll each piece into a log about 10 cm (4 inches) long and 2 cm (3/4 inch) in diameter. Cut each log into six pieces, each about 1.5 cm (5/8 inch) wide, then cover with a damp cloth.

4 Place each dough round on a lightly oiled surface and flatten with the oiled flat side of a cleaver to form a very thin, small disc about 10–12 cm (4–5 inches) in diameter.

5 Place 2 teaspoons of the filling into the centre of the dough balls and bring the edges together, pressing firmly and pulling upwards, twisting in one direction, pulling off any excess dough and making sure the dough is not too thick on top.

6 Line a large bamboo steamer with baking paper and place the dumplings in a single layer in the steamer. Cover and steam over a wok of simmering water for 6 minutes, or until cooked through. Serve hot.

Divide the dough into four pieces and roll each piece into a log about 10 cm (4 inches) long.

Flatten each ball with a cleaver to form discs.

Place 2 teaspoons of filling in the centre of each disc and bring the edges together.

Once all the edges are together, press firmly and pull upwards, twisting the excess dough until it comes away from the dumpling.

*LEFT: Steamed pork and water chestnut dumplings*

293

## STEAMED VEGETABLE ROLLS

Preparation time: 20 minutes +
  25 minutes soaking
Total cooking time: 20 minutes
Serves 4–6

DIPPING SAUCE
1/4 cup (60 ml/2 fl oz) hot chilli sauce
2 tablespoons hoisin sauce
1 tablespoon light soy sauce
1 tablespoon crushed, unsalted peanuts

20 g (3/4 oz) dried shiitake mushrooms
250 g (8 oz) wom bok (Chinese cabbage),
  shredded
1 large carrot, grated
4 spring onions, sliced
1/4 cup (60 g/2 oz) bamboo shoots, julienned
2 cloves garlic, crushed
2 tablespoons water chestnuts, finely chopped
2 tablespoons chopped fresh coriander leaves
1 1/2 tablespoons fish sauce
1 tablespoon soy sauce
1 teaspoon grated fresh ginger
2 bean curd sheets

*BELOW: Steamed vegetable rolls*

1 To make the dipping sauce, combine all the ingredients in a bowl. Set aside until ready to serve the vegetable rolls.
2 Soak the mushrooms in hot water for 20 minutes, then drain, remove the stalks and finely shred the caps. Squeeze out any excess moisture. Combine the caps with the rest of the filling ingredients except the bean curd sheets.
3 If the bean curd sheets are large, cut them in half. Soak them in warm water for 30 seconds, then remove from the water one at a time and squeeze out the water.
4 Lay a bean curd sheet on a workbench. Divide the filling into portions for the number of bean curd sheets. Form the filling into logs about 27 cm (11 inches) long. Lay the log along the long side of the sheet and gently but firmly roll the log up, tucking in the sides as you go. Repeat with the remaining sheets and mixture.
5 Line a bamboo steamer with baking paper and place the rolls, seam-side-down, in a single layer in the steamer. Cover and steam over a wok of simmering water for 20 minutes, then remove and set aside to cool. When firm, slice the log into 1.5 cm (5/8 inch) pieces. Serve with the dipping sauce.

## STEAMED FISH CAKES

Preparation time: 15 minutes
Total cooking time: 15 minutes
Makes 24

600 g (1 1/4 lb) firm white fish fillets
  (e.g. ling or bream)
5 spring onions, finely chopped
1 stem lemon grass, white part only, finely
  chopped
3 tablespoons chopped fresh coriander leaves
  and stems
2 cloves garlic, crushed
3 fresh kaffir lime leaves, very finely chopped
2 small fresh red chillies, seeded and finely
  chopped
1/4 cup (60 ml/2 fl oz) coconut milk
1 1/2 tablespoons fish sauce
3 teaspoons lime juice
1 egg, lightly beaten
24 fresh basil leaves
fresh coriander leaves, to garnish
sweet chilli sauce, to serve (optional)

1 Line a bamboo steamer with baking paper. Put the fish, spring onion, lemon grass, coriander, garlic, kaffir lime leaves, chilli, coconut milk, fish sauce, lime juice and egg in a food processor and process until smooth and well combined. Using tablespoons of the mixture, shape into patties about 4 cm (1 1/2 inches) in diameter to make 24 cakes.

2 Sit each cake on a basil leaf and place in the steamer, making sure they are not touching (use a second bamboo steamer if necessary). Cover and steam over a wok of simmering water for 10–12 minutes, or until cooked through. Garnish each fish cake with a coriander leaf and serve immediately on the basil leaves with sweet chilli sauce, if desired.

## STEAMED FISH IN BLACK BEAN SAUCE

Preparation time: 20 minutes
Total cooking time: 10 minutes
Serves 4

☆☆

1 tablespoon black beans

2 tablespoons Chinese rice wine

1 tablespoon oyster sauce

2 teaspoons light soy sauce

1 teaspoon grated fresh ginger

1/2 teaspoon sugar

4 x 120 g (4 oz) snapper fillets

2 spring onions, thinly sliced on the diagonal

1 kg (2 lb) baby bok choy, trimmed and cut into quarters

oyster sauce, extra, to drizzle

1/2 teaspoon sesame oil

1 spring onion, sliced, extra, to garnish

1 Rinse the black beans very well under cold water, drain, put in a small bowl then mash with a fork. Add the rice wine, oyster sauce, soy sauce, ginger and sugar and stir well.

2 Using tweezers, remove any bones from the fish fillets. Dip each fillet in the black bean mix, then place in a single layer on a lightly oiled heatproof dish (a pie dish is ideal). Spoon over any remaining sauce and sprinkle with the spring onion. Place the dish in a bamboo steamer, cover and steam over a wok of simmering water for 5–7 minutes, or until the fish flakes when tested with a fork. Remove the dish, cover and keep warm.

3 Put the bok choy in the base of the steamer, cover and steam over the wok for 2 minutes or until wilted and tender. Place on a serving plate, drizzle with the oyster sauce and sesame oil and top with the fish fillets. Garnish with extra spring onion and serve immediately.

## THAI CHILLI FISH DIPPING SAUCE (Nam pla prik)

Put 1/2 cup (125 g/4 oz) sugar, 1/4 cup (60 ml/2 fl oz) white vinegar, 1 tablespoon fish sauce, 1 chopped small fresh red chilli and 1/2 cup (125 ml/4 fl oz) water in a saucepan. Simmer for 5 minutes, or until thickened slightly. Cool. Stir in 1/4 small finely chopped carrot, 1/4 small peeled, seeded and finely chopped cucumber, and 1 tablespoon chopped roasted peanuts. Use as an accompaniment to Thai meals or snacks as a tasty condiment. Serves 4.

*ABOVE: Steamed fish in black bean sauce*

# INDEX

Page numbers in *italics* refer to photographs. Page numbers in **bold** type refer to margin notes.

# ACKNOWLEDGEMENTS

FOOD PREPARATION: Alison Adams, Michelle Lawton, Valli Little, Ben Masters, Liz Nolan, Kim Passenger, Justine Poole, Christine Sheppard, Angela Tregonning.

PHOTOGRAPHY: Cris Cordeiro, Craig Cranko, Joe Filshie, Roberto Jean Francois, Ian Hofstetter, Andre Martin, Luis Martin, Rob Reichenfeld, Brett Stevens.

STYLISTS: Marie-Hélène Clauzon, Sarah de Nardi, Georgina Dolling, Carolyn Fienberg, Mary Harris, Cherise Koch, Michelle Noerianto.

RECIPE DEVELOPMENT: Alison Adams, Ruth Armstrong, Roslyn Anderson, Rekha Arnott, Julie Ballard, Vanessa Broadfoot, Rebecca Clancy, Judy Clarke, Ross Dobson, Michelle Earl, Sue Forster Wright, Kathleen Gandy, Sonia Greig, Jane Griffiths, Saskia Hay, Katy Holder, Malini Jayaganesh, Caroline Jones, Eva Katz, Kathy Knudsen, Jane Lawson, Valli Little, Barbara

Lowery, Tracey Meharg, Kerrie Mullins, Kate Murdoch, Christine Osmond, Maria Papadopoulos, Sally Parker, Kim Passenger, Sarah Randell, John Skinner, Melita Smilovic, Margot Smithyman, Shauna Stockwell, Barbara Sweeney, Angela Tregonning, Jody Vassallo, Lovoni Welch.

The publisher wishes to thank the following, all in NSW, for their assistance in the photography for this book: AEG Kitchen Appliances; Artiques & Country; Art of Tiles; Bay Swiss; Bertolli Olive Oil; Breville Holdings Pty Ltd; Chief Australia; Country Road; Exclusive Tiles; Global Treasures; Home Utopia; Kitchen Aid; Les Olivades; Liebherr Refrigeration and Wine Cellars; Made in Japan; MEC-Kambrook Pty Ltd; No Chintz; Pacific East India Company; Papaya Studio; Regeneration Tiles; Renditions Tiles; R.M.S. Marble & Granite; Sheldon & Hammond; Southcorp Appliances; Sunbeam Corporation Ltd; Tree of Life.